Sport in the Global

General Editor: J.A. Mangan

THE MAKING OF NEW ZEALAND CRICKET
1832–1914

SPORT IN THE GLOBAL SOCIETY

General Editor: J.A. Mangan

The interest in sports studies around the world is growing and will continue to do so. This unique series combines aspects of the expanding study of *sport in the global society*, providing comprehensiveness and comparison under one editorial umbrella. It is particularly timely, with studies in the political, cultural, anthropological, ethnographic, social, economic, geographical and aesthetic elements of sport proliferating in institutions of higher education.

Eric Hobsbawm once called sport one of the most significant practices of the late nineteenth century. Its significance was even more marked in the late twentieth century and will continue to grow in importance into the new millennium as the world develops into a 'global village' sharing the English language, technology and sport.

Other Titles in the Series

THE MAKING OF
NEW ZEALAND CRICKET
1832–1914

GREG RYAN

Lincoln University, New Zealand

Foreword by

Glenn Turner

FRANK CASS
LONDON • PORTLAND, OR

First published in 2004 in Great Britain by
FRANK CASS PUBLISHERS
Crown House, 47 Chase Side, Southgate,
London, N14 5BP

and in the United States of America by
FRANK CASS PUBLISHERS
c/o ISBS, 920 NE 58th Avenue, Suite 300
Portland, Oregon 97213-3786

Website: www.frankcass.com

British Library Cataloguing in Publication Data

A catalogue record of this book is available
from the British Library.

ISBN 0-7146-5354-3 (cloth)
ISBN 0-7146-8482-1 (paper)
ISSN 1368-9789

Library of Congress Cataloging-in-Publication Data

Ryan, Greg, 1967–
   The making of New Zealand cricket, 1832–1914 / Greg Ryan.
      p.   cm.
   Includes bibliograhical references and index.
   ISBN 0-7146-5354-3 (cloth)
   1. Cricket – New Zealand – History. I. Title.
   GV928.N45R93 2003
   793.358′0993 – dc22

                                          2003017322

Typeset in 10.75/12pt Times New Roman by Frank Cass Publishers
Printed in Great Britain by MPG Books Ltd, Bodmin, Cornwall

For Liz

Contents

Illustrations

Abbreviations

ABCIC	Australian Board of Control for International Cricket
ACA	Auckland Cricket Association
ACB	Australian Cricket Board
ACC	Auckland Cricket Club
ASCA	Auckland Suburban Cricket Association
BCC	Britannia Cricket Club
CCA	Canterbury Cricket Association
CCC	Christchurch Cricket Club
CNZ	Cyclopedia of New Zealand
CSCA	Christchurch Suburban Cricket Association
DCC	Dunedin Cricket Club
D&SCA	Dunedin and Suburban Cricket Association
DNZB	Dictionary of New Zealand Biography
ICC	Imperial Cricket Conference
MCC	Marylebone Cricket Club
MCCC	Midland Canterbury Cricket Club
MHR	Member of House of Representatives
MLC	Member of Legislative Council
MPC	Member of Provincial Council
NSWCA	New South Wales Cricket Association
NZCC	New Zealand Cricket Council
OCA	Otago Cricket Association
UCCC	United Canterbury Cricket Club
UWCC	United Wellington Cricket Club
WCA	Wellington Cricket Association
WCC	Wellington Cricket Club

Tables

Acknowledgements

During the writing of this book and the Ph.D. thesis from which it derives, I have accumulated a multitude of debts, both personal and professional.

The staff of the Macmillan Brown Library, University of Canterbury responded to my numerous and sometimes obscure requests with cheerful efficiency. I am also particularly grateful to: the late David McDonald and the staff of the Hocken Library and Hocken Archives, Dunedin; the New Zealand Room of the Canterbury Public Library; the Nelson Provincial Museum; National Library, Wellington; the New South Wales Cricket Association Library, Sydney, and Stephen Green of the Marylebone Cricket Club Library. Ray Webster, David Studham and the Monday morning team at the Melbourne Cricket Club Library ensured that my visits were both informative and highly entertaining.

For access to official cricket sources I am indebted to Tim Murdoch of New Zealand Cricket Inc.; Tony Murdoch of the Canterbury Cricket Association, and Ali Dunmall and Ron Steiner of the Australian Cricket Board. Stan Cowman at the National Cricket Museum, Wellington, gave me access to the valuable first minute book of the New Zealand Cricket Council and many other useful items. For reproduction of photographs I am grateful to the pictorial archives of Canterbury Museum, Christ's College, Christchurch, Don and Paddianne Neely and Neil Macbeth.

Several people allowed me use of personal research material and manuscripts. My thanks to George Griffiths, Don Hamilton and especially Jim McAloon for access to his history of Nelson – and for other convivial diversions and support as a colleague at Lincoln University. Jeff Carr, Chris Connolly, Jim Gardner, Jean Sharfe, Luke Trainor and Geoff Vincent all supplied useful references and suggestions. Tom Brooking, Richard Cashman, Tony Mason and J.A. Mangan all offered valuable insights that greatly eased the transition from thesis to book.

My family have always provided encouragement, practical assistance and welcome relief from the task at hand. I am also sincerely grateful to a number of people for sustaining me in various ways during this project – especially Belinda Ryan, Brent Giblin, Amber Bianchini, Steve Dunn, Barbara and Trevor Chinn, Colin Hayman, Jeannine Edwards and Liz Martyn.

My greatest debt is to Len Richardson who has guided my work over more than a decade with a perfect combination of academic rigour and good humour. Our discussions have taught me much about sport and much more about its place in the wider scheme of things.

Foreword

My approach to life generally – including cricket – has been to centre largely on matters of the moment and how they might affect what occurs in the future. However, reading Greg Ryan's *The Making of New Zealand Cricket* is an important reminder of just how significant and instructive the past is to any of us planning for the future. As has often been said, those of us who fail to heed the mistakes of the past are doomed to repeat them. In this regard, Ryan's book reminded me of when I was playing for the Worcestershire County Cricket Club from the 1960s to the 1980s. In the early 1970s, the then chairman of the club, Geoffrey Lampard, remarked that 'cricket is not a game, it is a culture' – or words to that effect. Often, in ensuing years, I have pondered that view and affirmed Lampard's opinion. More than any other game I know, cricket reflects the trends and values of the society of the day, which is one reason why some cricket lovers are saddened by what they regard as an erosion of the ethical and moral standards that they saw as underpinning the game and marking it out as something special. Trying to stem the flow and, in some ways, attempting to reverse it will always be much harder than simply giving up and going along with the current impetus. In this regard I think of remarks attributed to Mother Teresa: 'What you spend years building, someone may destroy overnight; build anyway'.

In New Zealand, one could be excused for thinking that cricket has evolved similarly throughout the country, and that differences in organization and attitude have been slight. As Ryan points out, this was not so. Aspects of the class system that characterised life in Britain, from where most of the colonists hailed, emerged in cricket here. So the differences from region to region in New Zealand were quite striking. In Auckland, for instance, the commercial elite who ran cricket were from the lower middle classes and had, therefore, links with a wider community. By contrast, the Canterbury Cricket Association drew on persons with the influence and stature of bishops, baronets, peers, members of parliament and so on. No wonder, then, that Canterbury soon became the spiritual and administrative home of the game in New Zealand and has remained so despite attempts to shift it. And Dunedin, with its Scottish Presbyterian influence, was not going to make it easy for the English and 'their' game to thrive.

Ryan also shows that while colonial women often enjoyed a greater range of opportunities and experiences than their counterparts in Britain, they still operated largely within prescribed roles as wives, mothers and upholders of moral purity. When I read that their presence as spectators lent a civilizing and festive atmosphere to sport, I couldn't help but recall an incident in The Shakespeare, a pub in Worcester, in 1973. I had just married Sukhi, an Indian from the Punjab. She had little knowledge of cricket but wanted to learn. She sat quietly and patiently while a small group of Worcestershire cricketers discussed the game. In an effort to join in she made a couple of brief comments. This drew an immediate response from one of our players, a Yorkshireman, who looked down his nose and, in a broad Yorkshire accent, stated that 'women knew nothing about the game of cricket' and that 'they were at grounds to decorate the place, not talk about the bloody game'. At that time, there were still no-go areas for women at cricket grounds in Britain, but by 1976 my wife had gained sufficiently in confidence to complain to the county cricket club's chairman. She said that she had just come back from a visit to South Africa where she had been discriminated against because of her colour and now, in a so-called more civilised society, she found discrimination on the grounds of her gender. The result of Sukhi's actions was that women at Worcester were allowed into areas previously off-limits – the Member's Enclosure, for instance.

Much of what Ryan reveals bears comparison with what occurs today. I was interested to learn that the importance of sport and physical training was recognised and made an official requirement in New Zealand schools in the years immediately prior to the First World War. The value of actually taking part rather than merely looking on was acknowledged at last and for much of the time since teachers have seen the coaching and supervising of school sport and physical education as part of their job. Unfortunately, for a variety of reasons, this is no longer the case, and to me this is retrograde. Has anyone asked seriously what the results will be? Ryan has interesting things to say about why rugby became more popular than cricket and rightly says it is sometimes hard to come up with facts to dispel myths. He suggests the success of the triumphant 1905 All Blacks team when compared to the failures of our cricket teams of the same period may have had a good deal to do with it. Also, the higher costs of equipment and facilities, the amount of leisure time available and climatic difficulties were very likely major contributing factors, too.

It is apparent that, in the main, the game in New Zealand has been run by those from upper-middle-class backgrounds. However, it was not until I joined Worcester in 1967 that I experienced first-hand the varying social status accorded to cricketers. The first time I set foot in the club's dressing room dispelled any illusions I may have had. I put my cricket case down in a spare space only to have the captain tell me quickly that uncapped players changed in a different dressing room. By then, definitions had changed. For instance, a professional player had a contract and an amateur player did not.

Colin Cowdrey of Kent and M.J.K. Smith of Warwickshire, who both received honorariums as assistant secretaries, were just about the only amateurs remaining. Unsurprisingly, both were batsmen in accordance with the earlier tradition that amateurs were gentlemen and fast bowlers were 'all' labouring professionals in the manner of menial workers. It reminded me of recently reading about how the great amateur C.B. Fry – before he concentrated on becoming a batsman – got away with a suspect bowling action because umpires were former professionals who were unwilling to no-ball a gentleman.

Oddly, perhaps, throwing is still an unresolved issue today even with the benefits of technology. It's often said, and not without accuracy, that old habits die hard. I was thinking of this when reading that while over-arm bowling was legalised worldwide in 1864 various sorts of under- and round-arm bowling were practised in New Zealand at all levels for at least a generation longer. But who would have thought that underarm would have been used against New Zealand by Australia in that infamous one-day match in Melbourne in the 1980–81 season? And when one considers the nature and extent of the concerns and complaints that issue from players today, the word 'inconvenience' takes on a new meaning nowadays compared to what cricketers endured 100 years and more ago. For example, consider the match between Arrowtown and Invercargill played at Lumsden in 1895. The Arrowtown team left home by coach at 4 a.m., set sail by steamer from Queenstown to Kingston at 6.15 a.m. and then took the train to Lumsden, finally arriving at 10.45 a.m.; after the match they left Lumsden at 5.00 p.m. and arrived home at midnight.

As you have seen, reading Ryan's account stimulated me to reminisce a little. To me, Ryan has written a thoughtful, insightful, often fascinating book, and one that will enable many readers to make intriguing comparisons between cricket – and indeed life – then and now, as I have tried to. Comparisons aside, everyone from aspiring academics to the general reader with a serious interest in New Zealand cricket will benefit from reading this book.

GLENN TURNER
June 2003

Series Editor's Foreword

'More English than the English' arguably offers the sharpest insight into the early moments of New Zealand cricket. It could serve, in fact, as a compellingly imaginative title to this Antipodean cricketing story.

Cricket '... is still largely the province of the old imperial realms, which, by the death of Queen Victoria, covered a quarter of the earth's land surface and ... a quarter of the world's population'.[1] There was a common supposition at that time that cricket demonstrated enviable English qualities, especially a sense of 'fair play'. It was a supposition that more than hinted at a crude Lamarckism: 'via acquired characteristics, an aptitude to keep the elbow up was inherited'.[2] In fact, the English confidently proclaimed it!

Of course, the reality, even in the heyday of Victorian imperial self-congratulatory confidence, was somewhat different. Cricket with other games were initially a source of socialisation and considered a means of *transforming* mid-Victorian middle-class hooligans into heroes – of an imperial stamp, supposedly firm of purpose, determined in adversity, calm in crisis and compassionate in conquest.[3]

Eric Midwinter got it right. There was no national gene-bank for the capacity 'to play a straight bat', but there was a powerful set of social imperatives that ensured its public demonstration on and off cricket fields throughout the Empire.[4]

Nurture not nature was the source of a complacent period belief in an English ability to project collective decency on, and beyond, the cricket pitch. Cricket inter alia as a form of social control to ensure the survival of the English public school was the mid-Victorian instrument that the nurturists used to bring about this projected decency.[5]

In short, the cricket field was as much a source of pragmatism as idealism in England and Empire. Strenuous attempts were made in dominions and colonies to clone culturally the inhabitants of these disparate places and produce white, brown and black 'Englishmen', for the supposed benefit of all.[6]

As has been remarked elsewhere, 'there *was* more than wishful jocularity in these lines by Norman Gale:

> There will be a perfect planet
> Only when the Game shall enter

Every country, teaching millions
How to ask for Leg or Centre.
Closely heed a level-headed
Sportsman far too grave to banter:
When the cricket bags are opened
Doves of Peace fly forth instanter!'[7]

Many now mock this period Utopianism but it was well meaning; it had some merit; it did some good.[8] Is cricket more decent in ambition in the twenty-first century?

The Making of New Zealand Cricket tells the story of this Utopianism, and much else, in a distant nation, almost as far from 'Mother England' as it is possible to get. The story adds yet another narrative piece to the colourful literary jigsaw of an imperial ambition that placed sport at the centre of political socialisation with the clear intention of creating 'manly' character through cricket above all else, and thus creating in turn imperial cultures that were to be tranquil, decent and healthy. Fanciful? Undoubtedly. Yet not an ignoble ambition.

J. A. MANGAN
Director, International Research Centre for Sport, Socialization and Society
De Montfort University (Bedford)
July 2003

NOTES

1. Eric Midwinter, *Quill on Willow: Cricket in Literature* (Chichester, 2001), p. 73.
2. Ibid., p. 74.
3. See J.A. Mangan, *Athleticism in the Victorian and Edwardian Public School: The Emergence and Consolidation of an Educational Ideology* (London, 2000), passim.
4. Midwinter, *Quill on Willow*, p. 74.
5. See Mangan, *Athleticism*, passim.
6. The most colourful of decent moralists – recorded in literature, albeit of unshakeable ethnocentric certainty – was probably Cecil Tyndale-Biscoe. See J.A. Mangan, *The Games Ethic and Imperialism: Aspects of the Diffusion of an Ideal* (London, 1998), Ch. 7. For details of another well-intentioned imperial sporting moralist, see J.A. Mangan's Chapters One and Two entitled 'Imperial Origins: Christian Manliness, Moral Imperatives and Pre-Sri Lankan Playing Fields – Beginnings' (pp.11–34), and 'Imperial Origins: Christian Manliness, Moral Imperatives and Pre-Sri Lankan Playing Fields – Consolidation' (pp. 35–66) respectively in J.A. Mangan and Fan Hong (eds), *Sport in Asian Society: Past and Present* (London, 2003). For wider discussion of the whole socialisation in imperial contexts, see J.A. Mangan (ed.), *Making Imperial Mentalities: Socialisation and British Imperialism* (Manchester, 1990) and J.A. Mangan (ed.), *The Imperial Curriculum: Racial Images and Education in the British Colonial Experience* (London, 1993).
7. See J.A. Mangan, Prologue 'Britain's Chief Spiritual Export: Imperial Sport and Moral Metaphor, Political Symbol and Cultural Bond', in J.A. Mangan (ed.), *The Cultural Bond: Sport, Empire, Society* (London, 1992), p. 6.
8. See especially Mangan, *The Games Ethic*, Ch. 7.

FIGURE 1a

MAP OF NEW ZEALAND

FIGURE 1b

MAP OF NEW ZEALAND

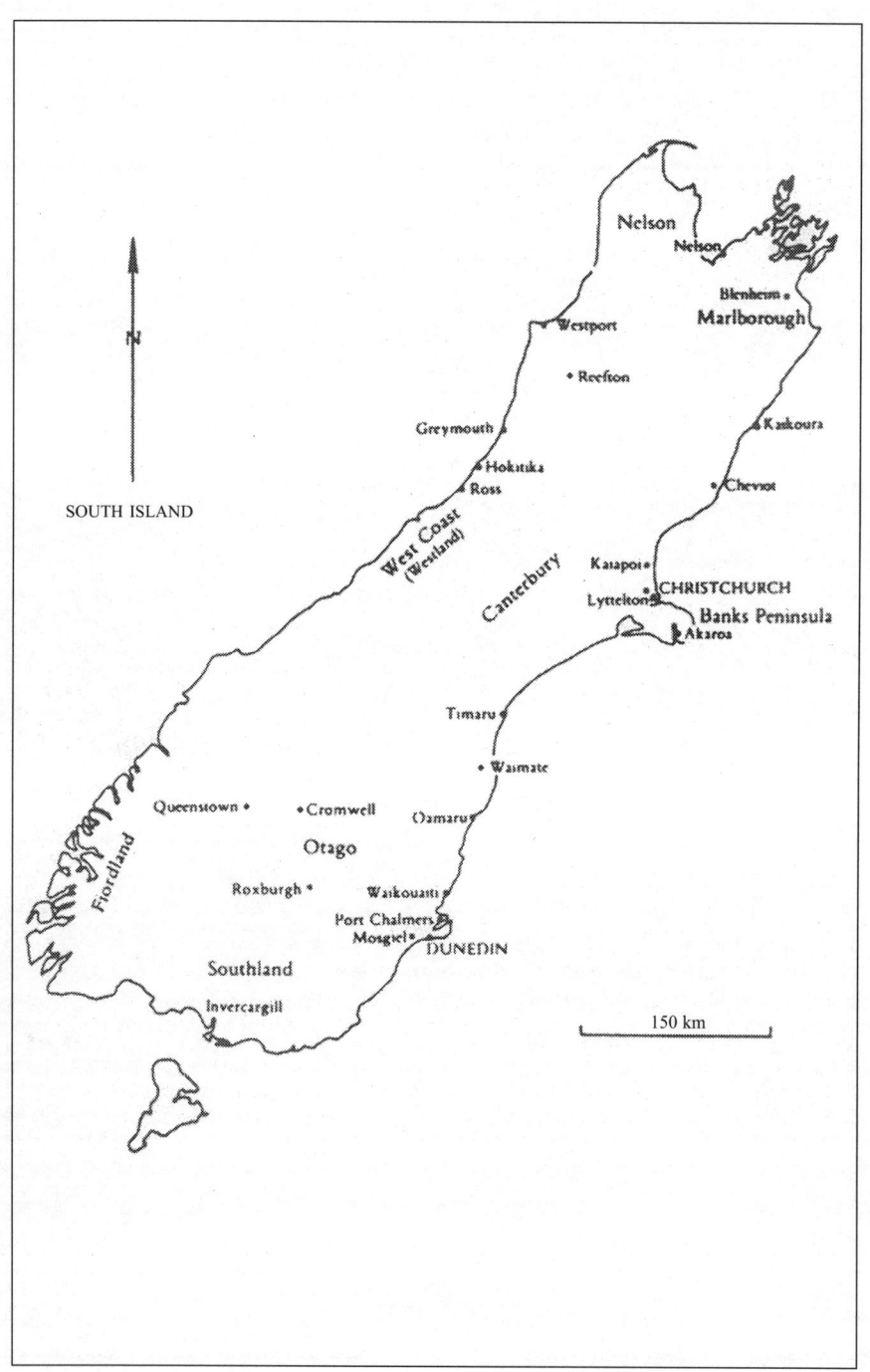

Introduction

It is no coincidence that the growth of a 'new' British Empire during the second half of the nineteenth century was accompanied by an even greater expansion of sport. By 1900 Britain had witnessed the reinvention and formal codification of a multitude of existing games and pastimes, the invention of many others and the consolidation of sport as an integral part of life for all classes. A century later, long after Britain ceded her imperial prerogative, and in the three-quarters of the inhabited world where no such formal mechanism ever existed, it is impossible to avoid the pervasive influence of sport and all that it entails. Sport has been, and forever will be, inextricably bound to the workings of economies, political ideologies and cultural systems.

Nowhere is this phenomenon more apparent than in New Zealand, the most distant component of the British Empire. From the earliest years of major European settlement during the first third of the nineteenth century, sport was nurtured by the highest echelon of public officials, military commanders, clerics, educators and journalists. Moreover, contemporary observers were never content to rest in the knowledge that games were merely being played. For them, the 'form' and etiquette of sport, attention to the correct techniques of play and their embellishment with prevailing ideals of discipline and personal morality were concepts that transcended the sports field and seemingly revealed much about the quality of life in the emerging colony. And of all sports, this rhetoric was most frequently expressed through cricket, as Keith Sandiford reminds us:

> Cricket was much more than just another game to the Victorians. Indeed, they glorified it as a perfect system of ethics and morals which embodied all that was most noble in the Anglo-Saxon character. They prized it as a national symbol, perhaps because – so far as they could tell – it was an exclusively English creation unsullied by oriental or European influences. In an extremely xenophobic age, the Victorians came to regard cricket as further proof of their moral and cultural supremacy.[1]

Irrespective of the achievements of an increasing number of New Zealand sportsmen from the late nineteenth century onwards, especially on the rugby field, devotion to the nexus between cricket and Englishness – and an equal amount of frustration at the perceived failure of the game to match expectations – remained strong in New Zealand.

Among countries subject to the greatest British settlement, only the United States and Canada failed to adopt cricket as a leading sport. Cricket was established early in the United States and enjoyed considerable popularity during the antebellum period. But it failed for a variety of reasons to establish an 'American character' in harmony with the distinctive cultural divergence, sporting and otherwise, of the United States from Britain. As the nineteenth century progressed and direct British influence declined, the game was superseded in importance by baseball. In turn, the failure of Canadian cricket can be explained in large part by its proximity to the cultural power and influence of the United States.[2]

In Australia, India and the Caribbean cricket is undoubtedly the 'national' game. In New Zealand, and among white South Africans, that mantle is occupied by rugby, with cricket a distinct second. The dominance of rugby over cricket among white South Africans must, for want of more thorough research, be explained in terms of the unique colonisation of that country and the marked bifurcation of interests and tastes between those of British and Dutch origin. It is revealing that a clear demarcation has existed: cricket as a predominantly Anglo game with rugby in Afrikaner hands.[3]

New Zealand is therefore the oddity within the fabric of international cricket. Although cricket could claim to be the leading game in the colony until at least the early 1890s, it was gradually superseded by rugby which established a stronger infrastructure and secured a clear monopoly on the title of 'national game' during the first decade of the twentieth century. Yet unlike the decline of cricket relative to baseball in the United States, the New Zealand game showed no such failure to translate to the dominant culture. On the contrary, cricket developed in an environment in which the preservation of British social and cultural values was pursued with considerable determination. Indeed, the reference in the title of this work to the 'making' of New Zealand cricket is an embodiment of the active and deliberate process by which the game was established and developed in the new colony. At the heart of what follows is both a corrective to those who emphasise the historical and cultural primacy of New Zealand rugby to the detriment of a broader sporting landscape and, at the same time, an explanation of why cricket was *relatively* unable to secure the prominent position it achieved in other parts of the world.

The first task, in chapters 1 and 2, is to consider the major elements contributing to the establishment of European New Zealand during the nineteenth century and the processes that shaped its sporting life. Broadly speaking, the key contexts for the different patterns of regional development within New Zealand cricket are to be found in the implementation and failure of Edward Gibbon Wakefield's theory of systematic colonisation during the 1840s, the British military presence 1840–70, the expansion of pastoralism from the 1850s and discoveries of gold during the 1860s.

From such diverse and sometimes hesitant beginnings, the three decades after 1870 were marked by great changes throughout New Zealand. With rapid population growth, dramatic improvements to coastal and internal transport networks, and significant advances in postal and cable communication, the once-isolated regions of New Zealand began to forge a basic uniformity. In sporting terms, these changes contributed to regulated local competitions, the formation of provincial administrative bodies and a growing number of interprovincial and international fixtures. By the time the New Zealand Cricket Council (NZCC) held its inaugural meeting in Christchurch on 27 December 1894 it was possible to talk of 'New Zealand cricket' and less of a distinct version for each locality.

Yet the process of change was far from smooth. As the population of the main cities increased, and economic depression gripped New Zealand during the 1880s, clear divisions emerged based on social class. Diversity in working hours and disposable income and in the amenities available in different residential areas translated into equally diverse experiences for cricketers from working-class and middle-class backgrounds. The way in which these different groups interacted both on the field and in the administration of the game is especially important. For it is popularly held that sport, especially Australian cricket and New Zealand rugby, has been a vital force in cutting across class barriers and removing all social distinctions, with participants apparently judged not on origin but on ability. The reality, as Chapter 3 will demonstrate, is a more complicated mirror of broader social divisions.

It is, therefore, essential to consider the predominance of middle-class cricket as being to the detriment of its working-class counterpart. Were the hierarchies embodied in the New Zealand provincial cricket associations deliberately exclusive? Or is the low level and somewhat peripheral nature of working-class participation better understood as the inevitable adjunct of a wider social structure in which income and working conditions placed a premium on leisure opportunities? Implicit in these questions is a discussion of the social and structural origins of the formal institutions of New Zealand cricket. The provincial cricket associations formed in the main centres between 1875 and 1883 and the NZCC formed in 1894. While the careers of many leading players were relatively short, those of administrators frequently ranged over three or more decades and involved networks linking a wide range of sports, business and political interests. Certainly, they brought continuity to New Zealand cricket during crucial years of development. But it is equally apparent that their ideals and objectives were not always in accordance with those of many players.

As much as a passion for cricket shaped many lives, it is more the case that the diverse experiences of the nineteenth-century New Zealand social pattern shaped cricket. Unravelling the class dynamics of the game therefore requires much more than trawling the contents of the New Zealand sporting press – exhaustive though it was by the end of the nineteenth century. This study traces the social context of its subjects through business and trade directories, electoral information, local and central government records, local and regional histories, school publications, memoirs and other bio-graphical details. However, in the interests of brevity, many of the specific details are not included in this work. They, along with an explanation of the methodology used to obtain them, can be found in my doctoral thesis.[4]

The emergence of a relatively coherent structure within New Zealand society is also evident in the ideological framework that grew around cricket. Those whose primary concern had initially been the mere fact that the game should be played as a reassuring confirmation of the supposed Englishness of the new colony were now able to devote their energies to the manner in which cricket ought to be played and its utility in a wider social context. As Chapter 4 explains, observers of New Zealand cricket reiterated many of the familiar Victorian maxims regarding manliness and morality. They also endorsed standard proscriptions against women's cricket as representing an encroachment on the masculine domain and a threat to ideals of femininity and domesticity.

Unlike many other parts of the British Empire, there was never a racial component to the rhetoric of New Zealand cricket. Although the earliest reports of cricket in New Zealand included Maori players under missionary tutelage, the number of Maori players who appeared in formal games during the later nineteenth century was miniscule. Given the relative vigour with which Maori adopted rugby and aspects of its attendant Victorian morality, an explanation is required in terms of the nature of Maori society and the diffusion of cricket in relation to the location of the Maori population.

The role of school sport in general and cricket in particular was also essential in creating and perpetuating the moral ideology. Among those schools committed to an English public school model, and among the primary schools beyond which the majority of the population did not proceed, there was a quite deliberate use of sport to promote broader educational ideals such as discipline and conformity. The likes of C.C. Corfe at Christ's College and Joseph Firth at Wellington College not only propounded the direct moral and physical qualities of cricket to the personal development of their pupils, but placed much stress on its wider social context – and especially its role within the Empire. These themes will be examined in Chapter 5.

This account of structural and ideological growth must be balanced with a growing contemporary perception of failure. Put bluntly, many observers felt that cricket did not capitalise on the start that it was given. The first cricket clubs were formed at least 20 years before the first football club – Christchurch in 1863 – and the first interprovincial cricket match in 1860 was played 15 years before the equivalent rugby match. But the initiative had seemingly been lost by the early twentieth century. The first representative New Zealand rugby team toured Australia in 1884, 15 years before its cricketing counterpart, and Britain in 1905, 22 years before the NZCC finally dispatched a team to England.[5] Moreover, the formation of the New Zealand Rugby Football Union in 1892 preceded the Cricket Council by two years. Contemporary explanations – highlighting everything from the rise of tennis to the constrictions of the climate – suggest that the shift in sporting emphasis can be traced to certain factors specific to cricket, and many others inevitable within the broader social fabric of New Zealand.

At one level there was expansion and increasing continuity in which previously isolated cricketing provinces came more regularly into contact from the 1860s. It was frequently held that the example set by cricket was a critical stimulus to the search for unity within New Zealand society as a whole. But the reality, outlined in Chapters 6 and 7, was that provincial cricket and the ambitions of the NZCC were not economically viable. A combination of government policy, demography and sub-standard play ensured that the survival of cricket depended in part on charity and fundraising activities totally unrelated to the game itself. The period of cricket's greatest expansion was also the period of its greatest decline relative to other sports – and to rugby in particular. That it survived at all is testimony to a powerful Victorian world view, which constantly idealised the social and cultural values of the game.

These structural difficulties are inevitably reflected in the rhetoric that accompanied efforts to bring an international dimension to the game. 'Imperial cricket' and 'muscular Christianity' were as much phenomena in New Zealand as anywhere. But as rugby, and especially the 1905 All Blacks, carved a vital niche in conceptions of national identity, reactions to cricket in 1914 were in many respects little different from those of 50 years earlier. While Keith Sinclair and others have traced the growth of 'a destiny apart' in elements of New Zealand's emergent nationalism, cricket encompasses the other end of a spectrum that lingered well into the twentieth century. For every rugby success that could be turned to to demonstrate the vitality of New Zealand life and the right to an important function within the Empire, there was a cricket tour to highlight limitations, insecurities and the reality that New Zealand was one of the smallest components of a much larger scheme.

The last three chapters show that, with the exception of brief moments of confidence on the part of Canterbury, the earliest English and Australian tours of New Zealand during the period 1864–88 encapsulate a glorification of the power and endurance of a British Empire in which New Zealand was but a humble and imperfect part. Similarly, cricketing contacts with Australia during the period 1890–1914, after some initial successes, juxtapose the increasingly separate identities of New Zealand and Australia and the decline of a previously significant 'Australasian' identity. Important to this discussion are elements of provincialism and provincial rivalries that hindered efforts to create a sense of national unity within New Zealand cricket. As a contrast to Australian competitiveness, New Zealand pursued an English cricketing idyll that placed a premium on 'form' rather than the attainment of victory. The tone of the first three New Zealand tours of England (1927, 1931, 1937), emanating from a land where many still called England 'home', suggest that New Zealand cricket was finally approaching the objective that it had set itself a century earlier – to play the game in a manner more English than the English.

Notes

1. K. Sandiford, *Cricket and the Victorians* (Aldershot, 1994), p. 1.
2. T. Melville, *The Tented Field: A History of Cricket in America* (Bowling Green, 1998). See also M.L. Adelman, *A Sporting Time: New York City, and the Rise of Modern Athletics, 1820–70* (Urbana, 1986), pp. 91–184; G.B. Kirsch, *The Creation of American Team Sports: Baseball & Cricket, 1838–72* (Urbana, 1989).
3. See C. Merrett and J. Nauright, 'South Africa' in B. Stoddart and K.A.P. Sandiford (eds), *The Imperial Game: Cricket, Culture and Society* (Manchester, 1998).
4. G.J. Ryan, 'Where the Game was Played by Decent Chaps: The Making of New Zealand Cricket 1832–1914' (Ph.D. thesis, University of Canterbury, 1996). See, in particular, pp. 15–21.
5. A predominantly Maori 'New Zealand Native Football Team' also toured Britain in 1888–89. However, this team was not fully representative of New Zealand rugby. See G.J. Ryan, *Forerunners of the All Blacks: The 1888–89 New Zealand Native Football Team in Britain, Australia and New Zealand* (Christchurch, 1993).

1

Colonisation and the Export of Sport

The timing of European exploration and subsequent colonisation of New Zealand ran parallel to the dramatic transformation of the British sporting world from the mid eighteenth century onwards. Indeed, many of the factors that contributed to sporting change – the transformation of the rural economy, industrialisation, urbanisation, the expansion of the middle class and its quest for respectability – were the same factors that shaped a growing sense of unease and triggered mass emigration from Britain amid the search for new opportunities, which – in turn – contributed to the emergence of a global economy. Therefore, the development of New Zealand cricket can only be understood in relation to the intersection between the changing sporting world and the varied colonisation patterns affecting different regions of New Zealand.

The Changing Sporting World

There were numerous games and contests played and supported throughout Britain during the pre-Victorian period. Many were linked to seasonal festivals and parish holidays but nevertheless possessed complex rules and strict customs. A select few sports – boxing, cricket, racing and rowing – attracted enough aristocratic patronage to enable significant levels of organisation and something of a 'national' following by the late eighteenth century. Yet it was only during the nineteenth century that these initial excursions into organised sport were consolidated as an important component of British society, embraced by a broad spectatorship and cemented by powerful national and international governing bodies.[1]

There is an obvious correlation between the emergence of modern society and modern sport. In explaining the evolution from the ascribed status of individuals in traditional society to their achieved status in modern society, Allen Guttmann highlights the emergence in the seventeenth century of secularism, equality, specialisation, rationalism, bureaucratic organisation and quantification. These coalesced to a more 'scientific' world view characterised by the eighteenth century Enlightenment emphasis on empiricism above folk tradition. As Guttmann summarises the sporting context,

'The mathematical discoveries of the seventeenth century were popularised in the eighteenth century, at which time we can observe the beginnings of our modern obsession with quantification in sport'.[2]

But the most profound changes were located in the shifting social structure of Britain from the early eighteenth century as the rural, quasi-feudal 'moral economy', characterised by long leases and common rights to land, was eroded by enclosure and the shift to a market economy. The development of water and steam power, moreover, triggered industrial growth and with it a dramatic increase in urbanisation. In 1760 the population was only 21 per cent urban, 53 per cent of it was engaged in agriculture and 24 per cent in industry, but by 1849 it was 48 per cent urban, 29 per cent was engaged in agriculture and 47 per cent in industry. Underpinning all of this was an increase in the population of England from 5.5 to 8.6 million during the eighteenth century and to 16.7 million by 1850.[3]

In terms of sport, urbanisation removed easily accessible playing spaces and broke down the 'folk' traditions of rural culture. Industrialisation, with its emphasis on time and work discipline, constricted the working week and established leisure time in more clearly defined proportions – especially the curbing of 'Saint Monday' observance in return for a more regulated Saturday half-holiday. Regular working hours, a higher disposable income, the expansion of rail and other transport networks during the 1840s, and the growth of the popular press in response to improving educational standards by the 1870s all assisted the emergence of a much wider following for sport than had been previously possible.[4]

The question of how best to use new-found leisure time was coupled with what Norbert Elias has termed 'the civilising process'. Gradual demilitarisation and the growing central power of the state, assisted by the main tenets of Puritanism from the sixteenth century onwards, produced a much higher threshold against disorder, idleness and excess; the new evangelical spirit stressed sobriety, discipline and the Protestant work ethic. From the first years of the nineteenth century, blood sports such as animal-baiting and cock-fighting were being suppressed, as were the violent extremes of folk football and similar village activities. The emphasis shifted to 'rational' and 'improving' recreations, which displayed control and conformity rather than traditional individualism.[5]

The Formalisation of Cricket

While many sports encompassed the new objectives and values to a greater or lesser degree, cricket stood – and, indeed, stands – supreme. No other game has attracted such a large and diverse body of literature or has had its virtues eulogised and editorialised to anything like the extent of cricket. It has always been the pre-eminent vehicle by which the perceived higher values of sport have been conveyed to a wider audience.

The exalted position of cricket during the nineteenth century was largely due to its formal structures and institutions having been set in place long before the wider impact of the leisure revolution. County matches were being played as early as 1709, a formal set of laws was published in 1744 and both royal and aristocratic patronage ensured a wide following and respectability for the game by the late eighteenth century.[6]

At the end of the eighteenth century cricket was further boosted by its adoption at the universities of Oxford and Cambridge and within the burgeoning network of public schools. Eton and Harrow were playing each other before 1791 and established a regular fixture at Lord's by 1822. Oxford and Cambridge began their annual fixture five years later.[7] Graduates of these institutions inevitably made the transition to patronage of the game at a local, national and ultimately imperial level.

While football and other team games remained traditional and localised until at least the 1860s, cricket was able to seize the initiative with its single standardised form. Certainly the Victorians purged cricket of its gambling excesses and greatly increased its scale and infrastructure, but they made little substantive alteration to the game itself. Nonetheless, by the time round-arm bowling was legalised in 1835, cricket had progressed a long way from the earlier game of rolled balls and heavy curved bats. The final shift to over-arm bowling in 1864 was inevitable rather than innovative. Eighteenth-century bowlers had begun to experiment with the subtleties of length and spin, and batsmen responded with a similar analysis of the range of appropriate shots. It remained for the Victorians to gradually lengthen the over from four to six deliveries, to refine the equipment used by batsmen and to improve the quality of playing surfaces.[8]

Such a pedigree gave cricket a definite advantage during the nineteenth century. Amid massive social and technological change, industrialisation and urbanisation, cricket remained a stable and respectable force. In an increasingly xenophobic Victorian age it was also an exclusively English creation that conveyed tones of cultural and moral superiority. In the words of Keith Sandiford, 'It was a ritual as well as a recreation, a spiritual as well as a sporting experience. Its values and its language came to be freely used by politicians, philosophers, preachers and poets.'[9]

From the 1840s there was an explosion of interest in cricket at all levels – village, club, league, school, university, county and, finally, international cricket. Beginning with William Clarke's All England Eleven in 1845, and its various imitators through to the early 1870s, professional touring teams did a great deal to generate popular support for the game. There were 15 County clubs in 1840; by 1870 only five counties did not have clubs. Between 1836 and 1863 the number of County fixtures approximately trebled, and the County Championship was formalised in 1873. Numerous festivals were also inaugurated, such as Canterbury Week in 1842. The Victorian cricketing mania even extended to the playing of regular ice cricket during the severe winters of the late 1870s.[10] The game, then, took many forms and catered to all tastes.

While cricket may have dramatically broadened its player and spectator appeal during the nineteenth century, it remained strictly delineated along class or amateur and professional lines. As David Lemmon observes, 'The social divisions that existed in cricket were ... simply a mirror of the way in which society itself was structured'.[11] The eighteenth century gambling imperative was gradually eroded, but its legacy was a precedent whereby cricket continued to embrace professionalism as a necessary means of securing the services of its best players. Indeed, the professionals were in the ascendant from the mid 1840s and did most to sustain the dramatic expansion of the game. When amateurism reasserted control through the County clubs during the early 1870s, there was never any of the soul searching over professionalism that marked soccer and rugby during the late nineteenth century.[12]

The amateur/professional relationship was, however, dependant on a series of carefully observed distinctions. Amateurs and professionals in English county cricket used different facilities – dressing rooms, gates and dining rooms, travelled in different train compartments and stayed at different hotels. On the field there was also something of a demarcation between the amateur gentleman as batsman and the labouring professional as bowler. Spectator facilities were also designed with the objective of separating the elite from the multitude. Most grounds developed separate, and higher priced, members' stands, pavilions and balconies.[13] The extent to which these distinct patterns of tradition and etiquette were translated to New Zealand is the focus of what follows.

Britain and New Zealand before 1840

Broadly speaking, the processes that transformed the sporting world also contributed to the dramatic expansion of British interest in the Pacific, and ultimately New Zealand, from the late eighteenth century. The plundering activities of British privateers against the Spanish in the Pacific from the late seventeenth century and the intensity of Anglo-French rivalries during the eighteenth prompted more concerted British exploration of the area from the 1760s. In the context of an Enlightenment ethos which sought to redirect the forces of nature to the benefit of humankind, British mercantile interests and the emerging scientific community embodied in the Royal Society viewed the Pacific as an abundant source of raw materials to satisfy the demands of an expanding and industrialising economy. Extensive exploration by James Cook during the decade from 1769 and the establishment of a British penal colony at Botany Bay, New South Wales, in 1788 resulted in a small European foothold in New Zealand from the early 1790s. Although not under formal British jurisdiction, the area was a major component of the burgeoning New South Wales commercial frontier. Seals, whales, flax and timber were exploited for purposes as diverse as the vogue for felt hats, the use of whale oil for lighting London and the need for timber and rope in order to maintain British maritime supremacy.[14]

As the European presence in northern New Zealand became more secure after 1810, the area began to attract interest from Christian missionaries seeking to convey the gospels and the material advantages of European 'civilisation' to the indigenous Maori. From 1814, but more effectively from the mid 1820s, Anglican, Weslyan and, later, Catholic missionaries sought converts in the north. With growing acceptance from Maori, they were able to extend their operations further south during the late 1830s. By 1845 there were perhaps fifty mission stations operating in New Zealand.[15]

The growing European population in New Zealand – with more than a sprinkling of escaped and emancipated New South Wales convicts, Britain's expanding missionary and mercantile interests, and its sometimes fraught relations with Maori escalated formal British intervention in New Zealand from the mid 1830s. The numerical strength and bellicosity of Maori, combined with strong humanitarian influences in London, initially dictated a policy of minimum intervention. Indeed, the signing of the Treaty of Waitangi on 6 February 1840 between the Crown and various Maori leaders was viewed by its proponents as constituting a just basis for controlled settlement and harmonious race relations as it set out the extension of formal British sovereignty in conjunction with the maintenance of Maori authority over their land and resources. But within five years, and especially with the return to office of a Whig government in 1845, the terms of the Treaty were subverted in favour of policies encouraging rapid British settlement and the large scale purchase of Maori land. It is in the context of this shift in emphasis that the transplant of British sporting values to New Zealand began to occur.[16]

Britain's Economic Crisis and Systematic Colonisation

The wave of British immigration to New Zealand from the early 1840s must be understood in terms of both push and pull factors. While the new colony possessed abundant resources and obvious potential for investors, the willingness to take up such opportunities so far from home represented a growing disillusionment within Britain. The main demographic, economic and social causes of the transformation of British society after *c.*1750 have been noted already. But in terms of emigration to New Zealand it is the perception of their impact, whether real or imagined, that is immediately important. For there is no doubt that many in Britain perceived a society in crisis – if not on the verge of wholesale collapse. Equally, there is no doubt that others played on such fears to boost their own maverick schemes and commercial interests.

The relative peace of the post-Napoleonic period also witnessed increased competition for employment at all levels – as much for the middle-

class who had constituted the officer corps of the services as for the demo-
bilised working-class rank and file. Moreover, Britain's population
increased by 15 per cent in the decade after 1821, accentuating widespread
unemployment and pauperism. Expenditure on poor relief increased from
four million pounds in 1801 to nearly seven million in 1831. While hard
economic data indicates that the mass of the people were better off in
'absolute' terms in 1850 than they had been a century earlier, it is clear that
they were worse off in relative terms and that they were acutely aware of the
growing disparity between rich and poor. Moreover, urban poverty and
dependency on wage labour was an altogether more daunting prospect than
earlier rural scarcity.[17]

The resultant wave of political unrest from the 1790s – with the Luddites
and later Chartist campaigns as its most visible manifestation – and the pronounced Malthusian sense of an economy unable to sustain a growing population contributed to a new preoccupation with 'emigration theory' as the
best solution. Exporting people and capital would not only create new
opportunities for Britain overseas, it would reduce pressure at home. To this
end, various relatively successful, but small-scale, schemes were set in place
during the 1820s to send paupers to Canada.[18] But the most significant of the
schemes – systematic colonisation – emerged during the early 1830s under
the guidance of Edward Gibbon Wakefield.

Systematic colonisation remains one of the most influential ideas of the
nineteenth century – and Wakefield its most determined and capable publi-
cist. Like Karl Marx, he saw the inevitability of a class war as the rapid
social change and tensions of the post-Napoleonic world came to a head. But
Wakefield's solution to the problem, unlike that of Marx, lay not in a wholesale changing of the social order, but in the creation of a safety valve for the
existing one. He expounded 'an art of colonisation' – a set of almost scientific principles that would relieve social pressure by exporting population.
Wakefield's idyll was not to remove paupers but to create something akin to
eighteenth-century rural England, described by Keith Sinclair as 'a vertical
section of English society excluding the lowest stratum. It would form not a
new people, but an extension of an old, retaining its virtues, but eliminating
its poverty and overcrowding.'[19]

The motives for Wakefield's scheme are a moot point. Conventionally he
is portrayed as a Tory reactionary determined to counter the twin threats of
industrial chaos and creeping European democracy. More recently his vision
has been presented as a bold post-Enlightenment experiment in which
reason and moral sentiment were used to diagnose the ills of society and to
remedy them by the application of rigid social and political principles in the
new colonies. Alternatively, Wakefield is conceived as the deeply
flawed centrepiece of his own fantasy world who produced most of his
writing on systematic colonisation as a psychological escape from the mis-
eries of Newgate Prison, where he was serving three years for the abduction
of an heiress.[20]

Wakefield's essential mechanism was a 'sufficient price' on land – set at such a level as to both limit the number of landowners and guarantee a regular workforce for those who did secure land. Labourers, unable to afford land, would be obliged to seek employment in the vicinity of landholding employers. With population distribution confined in this way, Wakefield saw a means of preventing the perceived chaos and dislocation of 'frontier' settlements in Australia and North America. In short, his ideal was a close-knit, agricultural settlement where land policy regulated class relationships – a society with room for both 'mechanics' and a leisured landowning class.[21] In New Zealand these principles, implemented initially by the New Zealand Company and later by the separate Otago and Canterbury associations, guided the establishment of Wellington in 1840, Nelson and New Plymouth in 1842, Otago in 1848 and Canterbury in 1850. Only Auckland, of the major settlements, was not inspired by Wakefield's idealism.

Recent historiography has significantly scaled down the overall impact of systematic colonisation. In total it brought only 15,600 people to New Zealand – perhaps 4 per cent of what might be regarded as the pioneering population of 1830 to 1880. It is also clear that the quality of immigrants, both in terms of skills and social class, was nothing like the Company image-makers would have us believe. Indeed, as we will see later in this chapter, the Company's greatest legacy was perhaps its ability to create myths of Britishness and respectability in New Zealand.[22] But the guiding principle of the theory and the nature of its initial application still have important implications for the emergence of New Zealand cricket. With the exception of Scottish Otago, the first colonial leaders of New Zealand's other 'systematic' settlements represented Wakefield's intention to emulate and replicate social delineation. Hence sport, an essential institution of England in general and its leisured class in particular, emerged early and naturally along with literary and dramatic societies and gentlemen's clubs at a time when one might normally expect other basic amenities and causes to have taken priority. Indeed, Wakefield wrote in 1850, 'I tell the boys in Summer time to play at cricket and play well, that those who are the best cricketers most likely will be the best readers and writers'.[23] To this end, as the next chapter will demonstrate, there were ample signs of a Wakefieldian impetus in the sporting cultures of Wellington, New Plymouth, Nelson and Canterbury during the 1840s and 1850s.[24]

Yet Wakefield's plans foundered on several key points. Initially sluggish sales of land allotments, accentuated by increasing economic depression in Britain from 1842, led to a shortage of development capital and funds for the assisted passage of labourers. In Nelson, for example, fewer than half of the available sections had been sold by the beginning of 1843. Among those who did invest there were also a significant number of absentee owners. Hence there were insufficient employers of the labour force. Those who did arrive quickly discovered that Company propaganda vastly underestimated the work required to bring land to cultivation. But the most significant obstacle of all was investigations by William Spain, under the direction of the Crown, that invalidated a large proportion of New Zealand Company land purchases and returned substantial quantities to the original Maori owners by 1844.[25]

For those who were able to secure legitimate title to land, it soon became evident that agricultural settlement was not economically viable. Aside from the lack of close markets to sustain an agricultural economy of perishable goods, most of the available land was in fact pre-eminently suitable for sheep – entailing exactly the kind of dispersed larger landholdings and iso-lated populations that Wakefield had striven to avoid. Furthermore, with the collapse of the 'sufficient price' workmen themselves had greater opportu-nities to become landowners, and there were consequently few 'gentlemen' employers and no prospect of maintaining the idealised class relationship. The failure of the New Zealand Company to deliver on its basic promises of land and labour inevitably led to departures, with perhaps only 85 of the original 436 colonists remaining in Wellington by 1848.[26]

What emerged instead were settlements more akin to the Australian and American experience. While there was always a gap between rich and poor and a small clique tended to monopolise all public institutions, relatively speaking there was a general reaction against the more extreme delineations of the English class system. Newly empowered landowners of more humble origin saw no reason to accept an inferior status. Those vestiges of the Wakefield ideal that remained were also swamped during the early 1850s by a stream of random, unselected migrants who easily assumed the 'levelling' social attitudes implicit in the new, unrestricted opportunities open to them. Indeed, the transformation of Wellington by 1848 was such as to draw from John Robert Godley, leader of the Canterbury Association colonists and first president of the Christchurch Cricket Club, a damning critique: 'bitter, abusive, disloyal, democratic, in short, colonial'.[27]

As we will see, these struggles reveal a pattern in which the vicissitudes of systematic colonisation travelled side by side with those of sport in gen-eral, and cricket in particular, in the various New Zealand settlements. Canterbury, relatively speaking, was the most successful and prosperous of the settlements and enjoyed a similar status for its sport. Wellington sport, like its surroundings, was hamstrung by unyielding geography and rapidly departing settlers. The precarious hold of sporting organisations in Auckland and, more dramatically, in Otago is equally instructive. The former owed nothing to a systematic tradition and its attendant transplanting of institu-tions. The later, although systematic, was Scottish rather than English and therefore lacking a coherent emphasis on sport.

Settling New Zealand, 1850–1880

William Fox, sometime Premier of New Zealand, aptly titled his 1851 book *The Six Colonies of New Zealand* as a testimony to the isolated and disparate nature of the main settlements. Equally useful is Alan Grey's summary of the colonisation of New Zealand:

> After a decade of settlement, the six main settlements, each having a different origin, physical geography and cultural and economic character, were united only by an external and unreliable saltwater highway ... There was little complementarity between the settlements and each faced outwards towards the world and its trade.[28]

Travel and communication between the settlements was difficult and time-consuming. Irregular coastal shipping services meant that the journey between Dunedin and Auckland took as long as two weeks in 1859 and news and commercial information between the settlements frequently travelled more rapidly via Sydney than directly between them. These barriers were gradually eroded from the early 1860s with the development of more regular steam shipping and the establishment of telegraph services.[29] But New Zealand, while possessing a central government that moved from Auckland to Wellington in 1865, was primarily administered by separate provincial councils between 1853 and 1876.

The real impetus for growth and unity came from a diversity of sources. Despite the apparent loss of impetus in the various Wakefield settlements by the early 1850s, incentives for emigration to New Zealand remained strong. Indeed, the escalation of the Highland clearances during the 1840s and the severity of the Irish famine at the same time were abundant proof to many of both a society in turmoil and the desirability of pursuing opportunities elsewhere. General patterns of migration doubled the European population of New Zealand from 26,707 to 59,413 between 1851 and 1858. But far more rapid growth came after 1861 as pastoralism, gold discoveries and military campaigns against Maori opened up the country and brought relative continuity to its previously isolated settlements. These factors were augmented in the 1870s by a new wave of assisted emigration schemes from Britain. The European population reached 254,928 in 1871, 487,889 in 1881 and 624,471 in 1891.[30] We will see in Chapter 10, however, that such expansion was only relative. Aside from the four relatively small major cities, there were few provincial towns of substance and the extent of road and rail communications within the rural hinterland remained difficult until at least the 1920s.

Expansion beyond the coastal settlements during the 1850s initially revolved around pastoralism. The failure of the Wakefield ideal of close agricultural settlement dictated that the future of much of the South Island at least lay in large-scale sheep farming. By 1865 all Canterbury land worth stocking, and some that was not, was part of one of the more than 200 sheep runs. A similar pattern was also unfolding in Otago and parts of Southland.[31] While the pastoralists were not numerically significant, they did come to exert a marked influence on New Zealand's emerging sporting culture – and not least on the character of country cricket. Even allowing for the fact that we must cast aside the standard portrayal of a New Zealand pastoral world dominated by a leisured 'southern gentry' of English aristocratic origin, there is ample evidence of a conscious determination to replicate many of the sporting and cultural customs of 'home' in the rural areas of the new colony.[32]

Gold, as it had done in California and eastern Australia, transformed New Zealand's population, infrastructure and culture on a much greater scale. While there were small gold discoveries on the Coromandel in 1852 and at the Buller and Collingwood in 1857, the first great 'rush' was to Otago in 1861. The population of Central Otago soared from perhaps 300 in May 1861 to 24,000 by the end of 1863. Although it had plummeted to 7,000 by April 1865 as a result of new gold discoveries in Nelson and on the West Coast, the legacy was a network of new towns, roads, railways and other amenities. Gold made Otago the most prosperous province in New Zealand. By 1870 it contained one-quarter of the entire European population and provided one-third of all exports.[33]

Gold also transformed the cultural landscape. During the 1850s the Scottish Presbyterian Free Church founders of the Otago settlement did their best to discourage English sports and their attendant elements of gambling and socialising. After 1861 such idealism was swamped by an influx of athletically inclined gold seekers, entertainers and entrepreneurs. As we will see in subsequent chapters, this confluence of people and gold capital, and especially its financing of a visit by George Parr's All England XI in 1864, was vital to the growth of cricket in the South Island.

But the North Island during the mid nineteenth century was an altogether more complex terrain. After the initial Crown policy of minimum intervention and humanitarianism was replaced by Whig expansionism and acquiescence to the growing demand for land during the mid 1840s and a broader desire to exert British sovereignty over Maori, northern New Zealand witnessed increasing racial tensions. Fighting broke out in the mid 1840s, unfolded in extensive military campaigns from 1860 to 1864 and continued with sporadic brutality until 1872. Much of the central North Island was still considered 'off limits' to European expansion until at least the 1890s.[34] The British military presence in New Zealand fluctuated accordingly. While Governor William Hobson's Auckland-based colonial administration of 1841 has been characterised as '39 genteel officials and their assistants, and [an] army of eleven alcoholic New South Wales police troopers',[35] troop numbers and quality increased after 1845. There were *c*.8,000 troops by July 1863 and *c*.12,000 by May 1864 – at which point there were more Imperial troops in New Zealand than in Britain.[36]

Aside from their rather inconclusive attempts to pacify Maori, the military contributed a great deal to the opening up of the North Island in terms of land clearance, road-making and the establishment of garrison settlements – many of which would eventually blossom into established towns. Inevitably, they also laid the foundations of sporting growth. Especially in those areas such as Auckland that did not experience even an initial burst of Wakefieldian idealism, a structured military presence, and the encouragement of cricket in particular, were essential for both recreation and discipline.

The final elements that are important in setting the context of this study are the ambitious programmes of expansion and immigration during the 1870s. With the relative decline of gold revenue during the late 1860s, the Colonial Treasurer, Julius Vogel, initiated an extensive programme of overseas borrowing by central government – £20 million during the 1870s – to finance new settlement and extensive public works such as roads, bridges, railways and telegraphs. These schemes were also critical to completing the process of Europeanisation and centralisation. The structure of separate provinces that had dominated since the foundation of the various Wakefield settlements during the 1840s was replaced in 1876 by central government administration reinforced by a network of transport and communications that made it much easier for European New Zealand to begin to conceive of itself as a single entity.[37] At the same time, further upheaval in the British agricultural economy during the early 1870s – and especially the 'Revolt of the Field' – culminated in an alliance between the National Agricultural Labourers Union and the New Zealand government whereby assisted passages were provided to bring in excess of 100,000 new settlers to New Zealand. The European population, which had exceeded that of Maori in 1858, constituted 92.7 per cent of the total by 1891.[38]

The distribution of this growing population was largely rural and engaged in primary occupations. By 1911 only 31.5 per cent of Europeans lived in the four main cities – the largest of which was Auckland at 102,000 – and the European population of the twenty largest urban areas comprised only 42 per cent of the total; the majority lived on farms or in towns of less than 1,000. The Maori population was almost entirely rural, isolated and based in the North Island. Indeed, Maori urbanisation stood at only 11 per cent in 1936.[39] This population distribution reflected the occupational dominance of the farming sector and New Zealand's growing prominence from the 1880s – due to new refrigeration technology – as an exporter of wool, meat and dairy products. Those engaged on the land comprised around 40 per cent of the adult male population in the three decades before 1914. While the industrial and commercial sectors expanded rapidly after 1900, the professional workforce constituted little more than 5 per cent.[40] Naturally, these structures had a significant bearing on who was able to participate in the growth of New Zealand cricket.

Ties with Britain

The specific origins of New Zealand's broadly 'European' population are also important to what follows. Despite the manifest failings of the various

Wakefield schemes, a strong mythology has endured wherein New Zealand was settled and shaped by the best type of carefully selected, loyal British 'stock'. Indeed, New Zealanders increasingly came to regard themselves as 'better Britons' – inhabiting a land combining the best of the 'Old Country' with liberating and progressive strains of colonial egalitarianism, ingenuity and self-reliance.[41] In a more specific focus, it was claimed that New Zealand was not just a British paradise but an English one. Of the 266,529 born overseas, who constituted 49.7 per cent of the New Zealand population in 1881, 44.7 per cent came from England, 19.8 per cent from Scotland, 18.5 per cent from Ireland and 6.5 per cent from Australia. In 1901 the 33.2 per cent of the population born overseas contained 43.6 per cent from England, 18.6 per cent from Scotland, 16.9 per cent from Ireland and 10.5 per cent from Australia. Of the native born, excluding Maori, the vast majority were of British origin – although not of the magnitude of the 98.5 per cent claimed by one zealous anglophile during the 1920s.[42]

These ties to Britain were magnified by efforts to maintain a clear distinction between 'wholesome' New Zealand and 'convict' Australia. Amid competition for migrants during the nineteenth century, propagandists in the service of the Wakefield and, later, Vogel schemes sought to overcome the impediments to New Zealand settlement – distance, cost and the bellicose reputation of Maori – by denigrating the nearby Australian colonies as sordid bastions of convictism. Even at the end of the nineteenth century the debate preceding New Zealand's failure to federate as part of the Commonwealth of Australia reveals a strong sense of moral superiority and a determination to avoid being tainted by the 'convict stain'. It did not matter that transportation to New South Wales had ended in 1840 and that most of Australia had no direct experience of convict transportation. Nor did it matter that Australia and New Zealand shared a multitude of trans-Tasman cultural, economic, political and social exchanges that sometimes coalesced as a formal 'Australasian' identity.[43]

Beyond myths of Britishness, it is possible that the lack of a convict origin or such a dominant Irish population, with its attendant level of social and economic grievance against England, did mean that New Zealand lacked the same base from which to ferment the sort of anti-English feeling that characterised some elements of the Australian working class during the late nineteenth century. Irish immigrants constituted *c*.13 per cent of the New Zealand total during the nineteenth century, as opposed to *c*.25 per cent in Australia.[44] It may also be the case that the slightly later colonisation and growth of New Zealand compared to eastern Australia meant that an immigrant rather than native-born population predominated for longer – with the result that ties to Britain remained stronger.

These connections were cemented by a substantial economic relationship with distant Britain rather than closer Australia. Between 1885 and 1935 exports to Britain, largely comprising wool, meat and dairy products, increased from 72.9 per cent to 85.2 per cent of the total. Britain also provided at least 60 per cent of imports up to the First World War.[45] Motivated by a desire to secure these commercial networks of Empire, leading pastoralists, merchants, bankers, shipping company owners and the like were also at the forefront of a strong pro-British militarism that gripped New Zealand from the 1890s onwards. They were especially visible in New Zealand branches of the Navy League and other similarly patriotic organisations. Perhaps the height of devotion to Britain and the Empire was reached in March 1909 when the New Zealand Premier Joseph Ward, without evident consultation, committed the country to the purchase of a Dreadnought-class battleship for the British navy. *HMS New Zealand*, at a cost of £1,706,000 plus interest on loans, was launched on 1 July 1911.[46]

Agitation for various Imperial Federation schemes and for much closer social and political ties with Britain continued for much longer than many Australians deemed necessary or desirable. Every New Zealand Premier from 1883 to 1912 can be quoted as favouring Imperial Federation and, at the various Colonial and Imperial conferences between 1897 and 1911, the most distant colony was the only one to consistently advocate closer union.[47] Rapid responses to the outbreak of the South African War and the Great War also reveal both an unyielding loyalty to the mother country and a preoccupation with portraying the best qualities of New Zealand manhood. Political dissenters, conscientious objectors and transgressors of military discipline were prosecuted with rather more severity than was the case in Australia.[48]

In this environment, concepts of colonial assertiveness and later national identity – sporting or otherwise – were never expressed as forcefully in New Zealand as in Australia. We will see in the last three chapters that this entrenched Anglophilia had a profound impact on both the structure of New Zealand cricket and the attitudes and objectives of its administrators.

Sport and Community in New Zealand, 1840–*c*.1870

What role did sport play in the emergence of nineteenth-century New Zealand society? Much as the following chapters will reveal cricket as the 'national game' during the nineteenth century – that is to say the most publicly visible sport and that possessed of the most influential patrons – it is important to remember that it existed as only one part of a broader sporting fabric and that this fabric was, in turn, shaped by the prevailing social structure.

Those who migrated from Britain after 1840 were far more likely to carry a predilection for the moral and social values of organised sport in their 'cultural baggage' than those who had departed for North America a century earlier. Not only did the eighteenth century colonist come from a less developed sporting culture, but in the New England colonies especially there was a determined Puritan opposition to sports that retarded their growth and contributed to an enduring cleavage between English and American

traditions.[49] Unencumbered by such obstacles, New Zealand revealed a pronounced enthusiasm for sport, voluntary societies and clubs very early in the
founding of the new settlements where one might normally expect other
requirements of colonial life to have taken priority. Leisure in general and
organised sport in particular embodied familiar and reassuring elements of
'home' that were necessary to ease the transition to a new colonial setting.
It also served as a means of social harmony, a common ground upon which
settlers from various points of origin could be integrated into the fabric and
values of the emerging community. It was also well understood that progress
in a new land required the sort of cooperation and desire for self-improvement characteristic of sporting endeavour.

Sport emerged as a regular feature of the earliest anniversary days and
public holidays in all of the settlements. Typical are the Canterbury anniversary days of 1851 and 1852 which featured a cricket match as well as foot
and horse races, a sack race, hurdle race, shooting match, quoits match,
greased pig and soaped pole – hence a mixture of serious sport and village
fete.[50] Water sports also flourished. The first rowing regatta was apparently
staged shortly after the signing of the Treaty of Waitangi in February 1840.
Regular regattas took place in Auckland from 1842 with contests between
whaleboats and Maori canoes compensating for the lack of specialist racing
craft. Yachting also became a regular part of these regattas. The first rowing
club was established in Christchurch in 1861.[51]

Aside from cricket, horse racing was the most organised sport in mid-
nineteenth-century New Zealand. The first formal race meeting occurred in
Wellington in January 1841 and such events were quickly initiated in all of
the settlements. New Zealand trainers were importing bloodstock from
Australia by the early 1850s and sending their own horses for competition
in New South Wales by the end of the decade.[52] Indeed, the devotion to horse
racing quickly caught the attention of John Robert Godley when he first
visited Wellington in the late 1840s:

> It is quite curious by the bye to see the exaggeration of British sporting
> propensities in these colonies. Everybody in this place (Wellington)
> has been 'in training' and is known and valued primarily for his racing
> qualifications; and I understand that during the races, all shops are shut,
> and you won't even get a labourer to do a job for you.[53]

Racing clubs were established in Wellington in 1848, Auckland in 1849 and
Christchurch in 1854. By 1864 the Canterbury Jockey Club had erected a
stone grandstand with seating for 400, and its premier event, the Canterbury
Cup, carried a very substantial stake of 1,000 sovereigns by 1866.[54]

Hunting and shooting were also popular among wealthier settlers.
With little thought to future environmental consequences, acclimatisation
societies were established from the early 1860s to introduce game
birds, deer and sporting fish. By the 1890s the Tourism Department

was actively promoting New Zealand as an angler's and deerstalker's paradise.[55]

The desire to encourage a sporting culture in New Zealand is also evident in a reaction against the extent of privilege and patronage in Britain that severely restricted access to playing spaces and recreational amenities. An early example is the 1854 Canterbury Reserves Ordinance which stated that 'The land commonly known as Hagley Park ... shall be reserved for ever as a public park, and shall be open for the recreation and enjoyment of the public'.[56] One can see a similar pattern in New Zealand game laws that were always far more liberal than their British antecedents.[57] George Thomson described the new colonial approach in these terms:

> They recalled the sport that was forbidden to all but a favoured few, but which they had often longed to share in – the game preserves, the deer on the mountains or in the parks, the grouse on the heather-clad hills, the pheasants in the copses and plantations, the hares and partridges in the stubbles and turnip fields, the rabbits in the hedgerows and sandy warrens, and the salmon of forbidden price in their rivers – and there rose up before their vision a land where all these desirable things might be found and enjoyed.[58]

This is not to suggest that New Zealand was an egalitarian sporting paradise. The following chapters will reveal abundant evidence of social hierarchies, class consciousness and an uneven distribution of opportunity. But it is certainly the case that a relative degree of liberality existed in the colony.

All of these sporting developments were sustained by the patronage of local social and administrative elites. As subsequent chapters will show, the administration of New Zealand's leading cricket clubs and later provincial associations, and similarly the dominant figures in racing, rowing and rugby, were inextricably bound to both landed wealth and political influence. In many cases a sound public school or Oxbridge pedigree also dictated that this patronage was sustained by an active presence on the field as the manifestation of a genuine interest rather than a social necessity. Consequently, there was little opposition to the burgeoning sporting culture and nothing comparable with the earlier Puritan opposition that lingered in the United States during the nineteenth century. Aside from the lofty ideals of the Scottish Presbyterian leadership in Otago during the early 1850s, the influence of which was eroded by the gold seeking population of the following decade, there are no signs of a coherent opposition to sport. Certainly there was an entrenched Sabbatarianism well into the twentieth century and a strong moral objection to the culture of gambling and bookmaking which attached itself to sport generally and horse racing in particular, but these concerns both represented a desire to control the conduct of the activity rather than an objection to sport per se.[59]

The Parameters of Sporting Participation, *c.*1870–*c.*1914

Despite the initial determination to establish a sporting culture in New Zealand's first European settlements there were several factors that shaped subsequent patterns of growth and participation and, therefore, circumscribed certain popularly held notions of colonial egalitarianism. The most significant factors were the nature of colonial working conditions and the nature of colonial geography. While there is ample evidence of adherence to pre-industrial work and leisure patterns during the early years of settlement, the expansion of the colonial economy heralded a more regulated relationship between work and leisure. Hence, as we will see in Chapter 3, a game such as cricket that took longer than others to play was particularly vulnerable to variations in working hours and conditions between occupational sectors. In both country and town the Saturday half-holiday, or any half-holiday for that matter, was still not standardised, even after the turn of the century. In terms of the selection of representative provincial and national teams in a number of sports, the period before 1914 was dominated by the inability of many of the best players to secure work leave. And even if they could secure unpaid leave from a sympathetic employer, the small and financially vulnerable sporting organisations in colonial New Zealand had no resources to provide the necessary compensation for lost earnings.[60] Thus, by necessity, and generally by inclination, New Zealand sport was primarily amateur and was without even a small cadre of professional sportsmen like those who began to appear in Australia during the last third of the nineteenth century.[61]

There was also an impediment in the predominantly rural character of nineteenth-century New Zealand society and in the difficulties of inter-provincial communication. The dominant interpretation of New Zealand sport, derived from the work of Jock Phillips, links the emergence of rugby in particular and New Zealand's sustained success in the international arena to a set of rural, pioneering virtues. Frontier egalitarianism and the physicality of outdoor life required to tame the land and secure a livelihood were supposed to have produced a New Zealand male 'type' superior to its apparently sedentary urban counterpart in Britain. This theme was particularly relevant to the 1905 All Blacks whose extraordinary success in Britain was used to assuage contemporary concerns about urban physical deterioration and declining racial virility in the British Empire during the crucial years between the South African War and the Great War.[62]

Yet as I have argued elsewhere with regard to New Zealand rugby, and subsequent chapters will reveal that cricket is no different, the relative concentrations of population, resources and finance even in the small New Zealand cities allowed opportunities that were not accessible to the rural community. While there was no shortage of initial sporting enthusiasm to be found in the early years of many settlements, the subsequent history of their sports clubs, and especially attempts to expand from intra- to inter-community competition, fell victim to the constraints of population and isolation. In short, the majority of New Zealand sporting representatives were drawn from the relatively small proportion of the population resident in the four main cities and from those groups who could most easily secure the time and resources to participate.[63]

As Table 1 reveals, almost all of the national administrative bodies for men's sport were formed during the two decades after 1885 when the standard of coastal, and to a lesser extent rail, communication between the four main cities had significantly advanced from the levels that had hindered inter-provincial competition during the 1860s and 70s. All of these bodies, with the brief exception of the Lawn Tennis Association that started life in Napier before moving to Christchurch, were based in the main cities. A perusal of the foundation dates of the various provincial associations within these national bodies also reveals that those in the main cities generally came first.

Given this strong urban influence, it is also easy to see why Maori did not figure prominently in the nineteenth century sporting culture. We will see in Chapter 4 that those who made a contribution to cricket – and it is equally true of nineteenth century rugby – had generally been exposed to the European school system and the social values it espoused. It is also probable, although much more research is required on this point, that they were drawn from those tribes who had displayed greatest cooperation with or loyalty to the Crown during the conflicts of earlier decades. For many other Maori, especially in the central and northern North Island, contact with Europeans in general, let alone European sport, was at a premium until the twentieth century.

For rather different and more deliberate reasons, women were also marginal to the developing sporting culture. It is true that colonial women, by

TABLE 1

FORMATION OF NEW ZEALAND SPORTING BODIES

1860	New Zealand Rifle Association
1885	New Zealand Bowls Association
1886	New Zealand Lawn Tennis Association
1887	New Zealand Amateur Athletics Association
	New Zealand Amateur Rowing Association
	New Zealand Racing Conference
1889	New Zealand Golf Association
1890	New Zealand Amateur Swimming Association
1891	New Zealand Football Association
	New Zealand Polo Association
1892	New Zealand Rugby Football Union
1894	New Zealand Cricket Council
1896	New Zealand Trotting Conference
1902	New Zealand Boxing Association
	New Zealand Hockey Association
1908	New Zealand Women's Hockey Association
1910	New Zealand Rugby League
1924	New Zealand Basketball Association (Netball)
1930	New Zealand Women's Bowling Association
1934	New Zealand Women's Cricket Council

the necessity of pioneering circumstances, generally enjoyed a wider range of opportunities and experiences than their counterparts in Britain, but these were still largely within their prescribed roles as wives, mothers, home-makers and upholders of moral purity.[64] In this light, the dominant Victorian attitudes to the participation of women in sport were just as firmly entrenched in New Zealand as they were in Britain.

Unsurprisingly, then, for most of the nineteenth century women maintained a purely supporting role within the male sporting community, being called upon to launch boats, donate trophies and provide victuals for participants. There was also a view that their presence as spectators lent a civilising and fes-tive atmosphere to sport. Broadly speaking, opposition to women's sport was couched as a quasi-medical concern for the preservation of their maternal func-tion. Vigorous sport posed a grave threat to reproductive capability. Prevailing notions of modesty and decorum also painted sport as both ungraceful and unfeminine. Here, there was a more practical impediment in that accepted norms of dress – voluminous skirts and tight sleeves in particular – posed immediate difficulties to all but the most sedate forms of exercise.[65]

As in Britain, the development of higher education for New Zealand girls and women during the last two decades of the nineteenth century, combined with a growing recognition of the incompatibility between older ideas of weak female bodies and the new imperative of producing a virile generation of imperial defenders, contributed to increasing acceptance of some physical activity as a necessary component of female development. But the sanc-tioned sports tended to be those such as tennis, croquet and golf that were either individual or less traditionally associated with overt masculinity. These were sports commonly pursued as social rather than competitive activities within a private sphere such as one's family or school. Swimming, because it took place in an enclosed setting, away from the public gaze, also became an acceptable and popular activity for women during the early years of the twentieth century. When women did begin to play team sports in greater numbers, they generally opted for those such as hockey that pos-sessed a less pronounced masculine heritage.[66] Conversely, as we will see in Chapter 4, opposition to serious participation in cricket remained strong and little formal progress was made in the women's game until the interwar period. In this respect, as in many others, New Zealand cricket clung tenaciously to important English social mores despite the quite different environment in which the game developed.

Notes

1. D. Underdown, *Start of Play: Cricket and Culture in Eighteenth-Century England* (London, 2000), pp. 22–45; R. Holt, *Sport and the British: A Modern History* (Oxford, 1989), pp. 12–73. Holt also points out that many of the 'traditional' sports, and cock-fighting in particular, remained popular well into the twentieth century despite official efforts to outlaw them.
2. A. Guttmann, *From Ritual to Record: The Nature of Modern Sports* (New York, 1978), pp. 81–5.
3. M.J. Daunton, *Progress and Poverty: An Economic and Social History of Britain 1700–1850* (Oxford, 1995), pp. 45, 574.

4. E.P. Thompson, 'Time, Work-Discipline and Industrial Capitalism', *Past and Present*, 38 (1967); K. Sandiford, 'The Victorians at Play: Problems in Historiographical Methodology', *Journal of Social History*, 15, 2 (1981), pp. 271–8; W.F. Mandle, 'W.G. Grace as a Victorian Hero', *Historical Studies,* 19, 76 (1981), pp. 355–6.
5. Holt, *Sport and the British*, pp. 28–44; Sandiford, 'Victorians at Play', pp. 275–8.
6. Underdown, pp. 1–21; A. Hignell, *Rain Stops Play: Cricketing Climates* (London, 2002), pp.13–37; E.W. Swanton (ed.), *Barclay's World of Cricket* (London, 1986), pp. 1–12.
7. Sandiford, *Cricket and the Victorians*, pp. 22–3.
8. Ibid., pp. 19–33; J. Hill, 'First-Class Cricket and the Leagues: Some Notes on the Development of English Cricket, 1900–40', *International Journal of the History of Sport*, 4, 1 (1987), p. 69.
9. K. Sandiford, 'Cricket and the Victorian Society', *Journal of Social History*, 17, 2 (1983), p. 303.
10. Sandiford, *Cricket and the Victorians*, pp. 53–63.
11. D. Lemmon, *The Crisis of Captaincy: Servant and Master in English Cricket* (London, 1988), p. 12.
12. Sandiford, *Cricket and the Victorians*, pp. 80–3.
13. Ibid., pp. 25–9, 80–1.
14. A. Salmond, *Two Worlds: First Meetings Between Maori and Europeans 1642–1772* (Auckland, 1991), pp. 63–119; A. Salmond, *Between Worlds: Early Exchanges Between Maori and Europeans 1773–1815* (Auckland, 1997), pp. 175–314; J. Belich, *Making Peoples: A History of the New Zealanders from Polynesian Settlement to the end of the Nineteenth Century* (Auckland, 1996), pp. 117–55.
15. J.M.R. Owens, 'Christianity and the Maoris to 1840', *New Zealand Journal of History*, 2, 1 (1968); J. Binney, 'Christianity and the Maoris to 1840, a comment', *New Zealand Journal of History*, 3, 2 (1969).
16. P. Adams, *Fatal Necessity: British Intervention in New Zealand, 1830–47* (Auckland, 1977); C. Orange, *The Treaty of Waitangi* (Auckland, 1987), pp. 6–136.
17. Daunton, *Progress and Poverty*, pp. 420–76; E.P. Thompson, 'The Moral Economy Reviewed', *Customs in Common* (Harmondsworth, 1991), pp. 259–351.
18. P. Burns, *Fatal Success: A History of the New Zealand Company* (Wellington, 1989), pp. 30–5; J. McAloon, *Nelson: A Regional History* (Nelson, 1997), pp. 10–11.
19. K. Sinclair, *A History of New Zealand* (Auckland, 1991), pp. 60–1; J.A. Daly, *Elysian Fields: Sport, Class and Community in Colonial South Australia, 1836–90* (Adelaide, 1982), pp. 6–7; Burns, *Fatal Success*, pp. 11–42.
20. E. Olssen, 'Mr Wakefield and New Zealand as an Experiment in Post-Enlightenment Experimental Practice', *New Zealand Journal of History*, 31, 2 (1997); G. Martin, 'Wakefield's Past and Futures' in Friends of the Turnbull Library, *Edward Gibbon Wakefield and the Colonial Dream: A Reconsideration* (Wellington, 1997).
21. Sinclair, *History of New Zealand*, pp. 57–61; W.D. McIntyre (ed.), 'Introduction' to *The Journal of Henry Sewell: 1853–7*, vol.1 (Christchurch, 1980), pp. 31–2.
22. Belich, *Making Peoples*, p.279; McAloon, *Nelson*, pp. 15–17.
23. E.G. Wakefield to Justice Chapman, 1 April 1850, quoted in C. Lansbury, 'A Straight Bat and a Modest Mind', *Victorian Newsletter*, 49 (1976), p.13.
24. The province of New Plymouth changed its name to Taranaki in 1853.
25. McAloon, *Nelson*, pp. 25–48.
26. Sinclair, *History of New Zealand*, pp. 93–6; McIntyre, *Journal of Henry Sewell*, pp. 32–5.
27. Sinclair, *History of New Zealand*, p.96.
28. A.H. Grey, *Aotearoa and New Zealand: A Historical Geography* (Christchurch, 1994), pp. 166–8.
29. E. Pawson and N.C. Quigley, 'The Circulation of Information and Frontier Development: Canterbury 1850–90', *New Zealand Geographer*, 38, 2 (1982).
30. Belich, *Making Peoples*, pp. 278–375; D. Thorns and C. Sedgwick, *Understanding Aotearoa / New Zealand: Historical Statistics* (Palmerston North, 1997), p. 32.
31. L.G.D. Acland, *The Early Canterbury Runs*, 4th ed. (Christchurch, 1975), pp. 22–6.
32. See S. Eldred-Grigg, *A Southern Gentry* (Wellington, 1980). A substantial revision of these claims is provided by J. McAloon in an article entitled 'The Colonial Wealthy in Canterbury and Otago: No Idle Rich' (*New Zealand Journal of History*, 30, 1 (1996)).
33. E. Olssen, *A History of Otago* (Dunedin, 1984), pp. 51–70. See also J.H.M. Salmon, *A History of Gold Mining in New Zealand* (Wellington, 1963).
34. J. Belich, *The New Zealand Wars and the Victorian Interpretation of Racial Conflict* (Auckland, 1986); A. Ward, *A Show of Justice: Racial 'Amalgamation' in Nineteenth Century New Zealand*, rev. ed. (Auckland, 1995), pp. 92–167.
35. Belich, *Making Peoples*, p. 191.

36. Ibid., pp. 181, 191, 236.
37. R. Arnold, *The Farthest Promised Land: English Villagers, New Zealand Immigrants of the 1870s* (Wellington, 1981); R. Dalziel, *Julius Vogel: Business Politician* (Auckland, 1986), pp. 80–115; Thorns and Sedgwick, *Understanding Aotearoa*, p. 55.
38. R. Arnold, 'English Rural Unionism and Taranaki Immigration 1871–76', *New Zealand Journal of History*, 6, 1 (1972).
39. E. Olssen, 'Towards a New Society' in G.W. Rice (ed.), *The Oxford History of New Zealand*, 2nd ed. (Auckland, 1992), p. 256; S.H. Franklin, 'New Zealand's Population in the Welfare Era, 1901–61' in R.F. Watters (ed.), *Land and Society in New Zealand: Essays in Historical Geography* (Wellington, 1965), pp. 162–4. In 1911 the population threshold for the 20 largest towns was 4,058 – the number living in Lyttelton, the smallest of the 20.
40. Figures derived from *New Zealand Census of Population and Dwellings* [variable title] (Wellington, 1871–1911).
41. J. Belich, *Paradise Reforged: A History of the New Zealanders from the 1880s to the Year 2000* (Auckland, 2001), pp. 76–87.
42. *New Zealand Census of Population and Dwellings* (1881), p.191; (1901), p. 123; Sinclair, *History of New Zealand*, pp. 335–8.
43. Belich, *Making Peoples*, p.285; *Paradise Reforged*, pp. 46–52.
44. K. Sinclair, *A Destiny Apart: New Zealand's Search for National Identity* (Auckland, 1986), p. 96.
45. Grey, *Aotearoa and New Zealand*, p. 345.
46. J. McAloon, *No Idle Rich: The Wealthy in Canterbury and Otago 1840–1914* (Dunedin, 2002), pp. 119–23; Belich, *Paradise Reforged*, pp. 76–81.
47. Sinclair, *A Destiny Apart*, p.99.
48. See, for example, P. Baker, *King and Country Call: New Zealanders, Conscription and the Great War* (Auckland, 1988); C. Pugsley, *On the Fringes of Hell: New Zealanders and Military Discipline in the First World War* (Auckland, 1991).
49. For a brief summary of the debate on this point, see A. Guttmann, *A Whole New Ballgame: An Interpretation of American Sport* (Chapel Hill, 1988), pp. 23–34.
50. *Lyttelton Times*, 31 May 1851, p. 5; 20 Dec. 1851, p. 1; 11 Dec. 1852, p. 2.
51. J.R. Barclay, 'An Analysis of Trends in New Zealand Sport from 1840 to 1900' (BA Hons research essay, Massey University, 1978), p.15.
52. Ibid., pp. 13–15.
53. Quoted in ibid., p. 14.
54. J. Costello and P. Finnegan, *Tapestry of Turf: The History of New Zealand Racing 1840–1987* (Auckland, 1988), pp. 26–44.
55. R. Galbraith, *Working for Wildlife: A History of the New Zealand Wildlife Service* (Wellington, 1993), pp. 1–16.
56. D.F. Robilliard, 'Hagley Park: Some Aspects of its History and Landscape Since 1850' (MA Thesis, University of Canterbury, 1971), pp. 11, 16; *The Ordinances of the Province of Canterbury*, Reserves Ordinance, Session V, 2 (23 Sept. 1855).
57. R.M. McDowall, *Gamekeepers of the Nation: The Story of New Zealand's Acclimatisation Societies 1861–1990* (Christchurch, 1994), pp. 1–10.
58. Quoted in ibid., p. 7.
59. P. Lineham and C. Collins, 'Religion and Sport' in C. Collins (ed.), *Sport in New Zealand Society* (Palmerston North, 2000); D. Grant, *On a Roll: A History of Gambling and Lotteries in New Zealand* (Wellington, 1994), pp. 15–98.
60. For example, G.J. Ryan, 'Rural Myth and Urban Actuality: The Anatomy of All Black and New Zealand Rugby 1884–1938', *New Zealand Journal of History*, 35, 1 (2001), pp. 55–6.
61. R. Cashman, *Paradise of Sport: The Rise of Organised Sport in Australia* (Melbourne, 1995), pp. 54–71.
62. See in particular, J.O.C. Phillips, *A Man's Country? The Image of the Pakeha Male – A History* (Auckland, 1987).
63. Ryan, 'Rural Myth and Urban Actuality', pp. 46–62.
64. For example, B. Brookes, C. Macdonald and M. Tennant (eds), *Women in History: Essays on European Women in New Zealand* (Wellington, 1986).
65. A. Else (ed.), *Women Together: A History of Women's Organisations in New Zealand* (Wellington, 1993), pp. 406–8; S. Coney, *Standing in the Sunshine: A History of New Zealand Women Since they Won the Vote* (Auckland 1993), pp. 238–9.
66. Coney, *Standing in the Sunshine*, pp. 242–9.

2

Diverse Growth, 1840–1870

New Zealand cricket followed closely the contours of early European set-tlement patterns. Those who left Britain just as the cricket revolution was unfolding were anxious to see the game flourish in the new colony. But the burst of cricketing enthusiasm that accompanied settlement in the 1840s was not sustained during the 1850s as Wakefieldian idealism foundered to be replaced by a more pragmatic need to tame the new environment and secure economic prosperity. Thus, while the cultural baggage of systematic coloni-sation ensured that cricket made a start in New Zealand's main settlements, there were other equally important elements that sustained the game and enabled its growth during the crucial decades after 1860. Broadly speaking these elements were the British military presence, gold discoveries and wealthy pastoralists. Individually, they touched different parts of New Zealand at different times; collectively, they ensured that cricket was in a relatively solid position to benefit from the stronger colonial infrastructure – communication, transportation and urbanisation – which developed from the 1870s.

At the same time we need to consider what sort of game emerged in New Zealand. To what extent, cosmetically and in its various social mores, did New Zealand cricket during the third quarter of the nineteenth century resemble the game of England? More to the point, to what extent was it obliged to make concessions to its new colonial setting? These questions become crucial to later discussions of the relationships between different cricketing groups within the burgeoning cities and to the place of New Zealand cricket within the sporting fabric of the British Empire.

Cricket in Wellington

It is possible that cricket was played in a 'scratch' form soon after the arrival of missionaries in northern New Zealand in 1814. But the first definite ref-erence to the game comes from the journal of Henry Williams – leader of the Anglican Church Missionary Society mission. After conducting school examinations for the English children of settlers at the Bay of Islands, Williams supervised a cricket match at Pihea on 20 December 1832 – noting

'Very expert, good bowlers' in his diary for that date. By the end of the fol-
lowing year Williams had apparently imported cricket equipment from
England and arranged further matches, almost certainly including local
Maori who were associated with the mission station.[1]

On 21 December 1835, during the historic voyage of *HMS Beagle*,
Charles Darwin noted young Maori men playing cricket with the son of a
missionary at Waimate, Bay of Islands: 'These young men and boys
appeared very merry and good-humoured; in the evening I saw a party of
them playing cricket; when I thought of the austerity of which the
Missionaries have been accused, I was amused at seeing one of their sons
taking an active part in the game'.[2]

Undoubtedly, there was other cricket during the late 1830s, perhaps even
organised matches involving both Maori and European players. Mention is
certainly made of another game at the Bay of Islands during 1841.[3]

The activities of Williams and his colleagues in involving Maori in these
games were surely no coincidence. Under the banner of 'muscular
Christianity', organisations such as the London Missionary Society and the
Church Missionary Society contributed a great deal by the end of the nineteenth century to the development of cricket in areas as diverse as Barbados,
Ceylon and Srinigar. In the finest public school and Oxbridge tradition, from
whence the majority of the leading missionaries were recruited, healthy
sport and the discipline it embodied was seen as an ideal complement to the
civilising properties of Christianity.[4]

But the beginning of New Zealand cricket proper – with a formal club and
some attempt to play on a consistent basis – is to be found in Wellington. By
February 1841, thirteen months after the arrival of the first body of New
Zealand Company colonists, there seems to have been a quite active cricket fraternity in the settlement. Ensign Best, in his journal for 15 to 17 February 1841,
mentions a match – presumably including military players, while the possibility
of another between 'All Wellington' and the 'Bachelors Club' was most enthu-
siastically anticipated by the *New Zealand Gazette & Wellington Spectator*:

> Cricket: We have great pleasure in recording that a cricket club has
> been established at Wellington, by a number of young men, who are
> anxious that so manly an exercise should not be forgotten in the
> Antipodes. Several games have been played during the last fortnight on
> Thorndon Flat, for the purpose of practice: and some excellent science
> displayed. We hope to see this club prosper. New Zealand is admirably
> adapted for the game, as the climate will permit its being played
> throughout the year.[5]

Such a charitable attitude to Wellington weather would be questioned by
many cricketers in later years.

There appears to have been no cricket during the 1841–42 season. But in
November 1842 a Wellington Cricket Club (WCC) was formed with the

patronage of many leading colonists. In December the Albion club was formed by tradesmen.[6] Wellington played its first internal match in late December, attracting an encouraging review from the *Spectator*:

HOLIDAY SPORTS

> We notice with pleasure that the members of the Wellington club played a match between themselves, and one in which all may be said to have been winners, as after the sports of the day, they adjourned to the Ship's Hotel, where they partook of a true Christmas dinner of roast beef and plum pudding, and so equally were the parties matched that it was difficult to say who first bowled out his neighbour.[7]

Amidst the festivities, the 'Blues' defeated the 'Reds' by 67 and 59 notches to 60 and 64. But in its first encounter with Albion in late January 1843 the WCC was defeated by an innings.[8]

An air of earnest Wakefieldian endeavour is certainly evident in reports of the formation of the WCC. On 3 November 1842 the newly elected committee was instructed to draft formal rules and procedures to be adopted at a subsequent meeting. The committee was possessed of education, capital, respectability and initiative in public affairs and the overall composition of the club is unmistakably elite. It included John Dorset, principal surgeon to the New Zealand Company, George Moore, one of Wellington's wealthiest merchants, John Howard Wallace, a successful auctioneer and general merchant, and several others who later served in local and colonial politics.[9]

This is in sharp contrast to Albion. Among others, this club contained two labourers, a butcher and a rope maker, and none of its members figured in public affairs.[10] While there is no evidence of how the two clubs regulated their membership, the division between them is clearly deliberate – especially as Albion's innings victory over Wellington suggests that they possessed the better players.

But just as the early appearance of Wellington cricket was consistent with Wakefield's objective of a society regulated by strict class relationships, so its subsequent struggle reflects the failure of this ideal. The Crown's repudiation of New Zealand Company claims to Maori land, the departure of many of the original settlers from Wellington and their gradual replacement with a more socially disparate group of colonists served to undermine the sort of earnest, moral purpose that had been evident in the WCC players of 1842. Indeed, this club and Albion were probably defunct by the end of 1843, and there was little organised play until early 1846 when a Britannia Cricket Club was formed to play matches against the military garrison. With the exception of George Moore, John Howard Wallace and Henry St Hill, magistrate and sheriff of Wellington, the new club had few pretensions to status – its membership covered the entire occupational spectrum.[11]

The few extant descriptions of club activities convey a tone of both festivity and laxity. Nowhere is this more apparent than in the verdict of the
Wellington Independent on the very one-sided intra-club match on 21
November 1846: 'We had at first anticipated a more equal contest, and are yet
of opinion that if a certain member of the losing side had partaken less of the
donations of Bacchus, the game might have had a different result'. A reporter
of the match played a week later was evidently more transfixed by spectators
than cricketers: 'Every one seemed pleased with their day's amusement, and
we only regret that the day was not more congenial so that the fairer portion
of creation might have enlivened the scene with their presence'. But any
inclination towards a genteel environment for cricket was more than offset by
rumours of heavy betting on the outcome of all matches.[12]

The fortunes of the club remind us that despite initial enthusiasm and a
determination to replicate the familiar institutions of 'home', cricket was a
fairly peripheral aspect of life – fluctuating according to various other commitments of Wellington settlers. There was little, if any, play in the summer
of 1847–48 or in the following year, and the Britannia Cricket Club was
finally laid to rest in February 1849, an event recorded in the *Wellington
Independent* as follows:

> Died – at Barrett's Hotel, after a lingering illness of upwards of two
> years, the highly respected Britannia Cricket Club. Deceased suffered
> from the poverty fever, and in the absence of pecuniary aid, has met
> death in silence, deeply regretted by those who knew its indisposition,
> without being able to furnish the necessary assistance to prolong its
> existence.[13]

The club simply did not have the necessary capital or influence to establish
a regular ground, let alone one that could be developed to encourage a reasonable standard of play. Added to this was the constriction imposed by
Wellington geography. Nestled along a small stretch of coastline bounded by
hills, there was very little flat land – and even less for recreational purposes.
Throughout the 1840s games were played on rough surfaces at Thorndon, Te
Aro Flat and the Mt. Cook parade ground. The Basin Reserve, the home of
Wellington cricket after 1867, was not formed until a major earthquake in
1855 transformed the Basin lake into a drainable swamp.[14]

Village Cricket in Nelson

Cricket in Nelson, the second of the Wakefield settlements, offered little
indication of the struggle that was to follow. In comparative terms the
Nelson cricket fraternity acted even more rapidly than their counterparts in
Wellington to organise an inaugural game. On New Year's Day 1842, a
month before the arrival of the first settlers, the New Zealand Company

survey cadets played a game using gear brought from England. On 26 November 1842 the *Nelson Examiner* called 'existing' members of the Nelson Cricket Club to a meeting, and advertised a 'field day' for 10 December. That Nelson's first anniversary sports were held on land designated as the 'Cricket ground' suggests a degree of permanence.[15]

The *Examiner* did not report any matches during 1843, and it seems that the Club lapsed for a time – almost inevitable in the aftermath of the Wairau affray when 22 colonists, including the leader, Arthur Wakefield, were killed in a dispute with Maori over land surveying and purchase.[16] In March 1844 a match was played between the New Zealand Company surveyors and 'All Nelson' for a dinner given by Mr Harley of the Carpenters Arms. Nelson scored 72 and 48 against 20 and 58 by the surveyors. On the following day various single wicket matches were staged. Enthusiasm was such that a challenge was sent to Wellington suggesting that a match should be played in each settlement. There was no reply and the two teams did not finally meet until December 1862.[17]

When cricket resumed in January 1846 it was apparently in the form of 'scratch' matches rather than an organised club. But these were also short-lived and there was only one other report of a cricket match (29 April 1848) before March 1850 when 'Hampshire Men' played 'All England' and a 'Married XI' played a 'Single XXII'.[18]

Nelson's topography was more yielding than that in Wellington. Its climate was certainly superior and it was not without its share of economic successes. But again the New Zealand Company fell well short of its objectives. It failed to secure a site with sufficient agricultural land, was incompetent in applying the selection principles necessary for a workable balance between capital and labour and allowed too much absentee land ownership. The severe shortage of capital in the settlement during the early 1840s contributed to an oversupply of labour, prompting a number of artisans to leave. In 1843 only 39 of 884 male immigrants were listed as having professional occupations.[19]

The lack of a numerically strong and centralised elite does much to explain the subsequent struggle of Nelson cricket – there were simply not enough 'gentlemen' to provide patronage. Only George Duppa and the Tytler brothers, all wealthy runholders, were cricketers of any social prominence during the early 1840s.[20] The numerous cricket clubs that existed in the town of Nelson and its surrounding villages from 1842 to 1870 were dominated by artisans and farmers. In as much as there was a devoted sporting elite, it was directed largely towards the jockey club rather than the cricket club. Nelson held its first race meeting on 1 February 1843 and the annual race meeting and race ball were a feature thereafter.[21] In contrast, the one incarnation of the Nelson Cricket Club that did show signs of social exclusiveness during the early 1860s was neither enduring nor particularly rigorous in its insularity. Moreover, in sharp contrast to other centres, only four cricketers can be found among Nelson provincial politicians from 1853 to 1876.[22]

Nelson, however, was the only province where country cricket was consistently stronger, in both playing and organisational terms, than the urban areas. The rise of country cricket went hand-in-hand with the developing pattern of the provincial economy. Except in the Wairau and Awatere districts, the short supply and variable quality of land precluded the dispersed population commonly associated with large-scale pastoralism. Instead, Nelson developed a core of small agricultural farms, the average size being 80 acres, on the best suburban land around the town of Nelson, on the Waimea Plains and at Moutere. All of the outlying townships, such as Richmond, Spring Grove and Wakefield, emerged as small service centres in agricultural areas where the population was in relatively close proximity. All had cricket teams and were able to arrange games between themselves with relative ease.[23]

Auckland Cricket and the Military Tradition

As cricket struggled to take hold in the Wakefield settlements of Wellington and Nelson during the early 1840s, Auckland embraced a different pattern of growth. The game was probably being played there during 1841, and definitely by October 1842 when matches were arranged between 'Garrison' and 'Civilians' at Epsom. There were two clubs during the following season – a socially exclusive Albion, and Union, a club for 'mechanics'.[24] Yet, after the end of 1845 there appears to have been only the Auckland Cricket Club (ACC) in existence, which had in excess of sixty members and was apparently in a very healthy financial position.

The ACC was, moreover, an organisation that served more than a purely recreational role. Amid increasing tension caused by conflict with Maori in the north during 1845, the club was portrayed as a bulwark of calm and orderly Englishness:

> Cricket – it is with much pleasure we announce that this truly British healthful recreation is again being practiced at Auckland. While our friends in England may be excited and alarmed beyond measure by the receipt of the news of the warlike rebellious events occurring in the colony, it is rather anamolous [sic], but not less amusing, that the settlers are quietly yet earnestly making arrangements for the enjoyment of English sports. The Auckland Cricket Club have [sic] again taken the field under renewed and most favourable auspices … We would suggest to our fellow townsmen to follow this example and during the summer months to renew their English practises and in honourable competition attain the honour so ardently contended for on the merry greens of old England.[25]

As Auckland was not a Wakefield settlement, it is unlikely that its cricket club was rigorously exclusive. In so far as there was an elite in Auckland, it revolved around a small group of government servants and staff whose claims to respectability were not taken entirely seriously by the majority of the population. When Governor Hobson selected Auckland as the capital in 1841 he attempted to create an 'aristocracy' based on the administrative function of colonial officials. But, as S.M.D. Martin pointed out in 1845, most questioned both the competence of this group and the substance of their pretension. 'The government officers assume to themselves the highest place, simply, I suppose, because they live upon the rest. Both Captain Hobson and Mr Shortland endeavoured to establish what they called an "official aristocracy" – a class of exclusives consisting of the refuse of cast-off officers of the Botany Bay government.'[26] Gradually, the officials were absorbed into the merchant/professional elite.

If there was any systematic aspect to settlement in Auckland, it consisted of 500 distressed weavers from Paisley and 92 boys from the Parkhurst Reformatory, who arrived in 1842, and 1,700 military pensioners, who arrived in 1847. A starker contrast could not be found to Wakefield's ideal of a class-based society excluding the lowest stratum. Instead, Auckland grew haphazardly from commercial and trading interests, attracting land speculators and labourers from the Bay of Islands and Australia. In the period 1845–51 there were 2,155 arrivals from New South Wales and per- haps only 1,500 direct from Britain. By 1853 it was estimated that half of the population had come from New South Wales, including many poor and a not inconsiderable number of ex-convicts. Further eroding prospects for a leisured English tradition, the population was 31 per cent Irish, and mostly poor Irish, compared with only 2 per cent in Wellington. The Auckland 'gentry' remained a very small group. The census of 1844 reveals only 98 men classified as professionals or merchants in a population of 2,754 and in 1853 only about 200 invitations were issued for the 'principal gentry of Auckland' to attend the Queen's Birthday Ball.[27]

Consequently, while officials and staff are fairly well represented in all of Auckland's cricket clubs, the majority of players were drawn from an artisan or labouring background. The leading figures were Percival Berry, the Sheriff of Auckland, Frederick Merriman, a prominent barrister, and Frederick Whitaker, future Premier and Attorney General, whose career as a top order batsman seems to have included only one double figure score between 1845 and 1851.[28]

The sustenance, though, for Auckland cricket until the 1870s, and indeed for the game throughout much of the North Island, was undoubtedly military patronage. The military played a critical role in the diffusion of the game throughout the British Empire. Long before the systematic formalisation of sport in Britain, it had begun to assume an essential function in military life – especially among the officer corps in India where as much as a third of the British army was stationed by the late nineteenth century. In part, sport served a practical function. Polo, hunting and horse racing were ideal for maintaining the fitness and efficiency of the cavalry, and sport in general was a way of keeping up morale, encouraging social contact and staving off boredom in isolated garrisons and outposts. To this end, it was decreed in 1841 that all barracks were to be accompanied by a cricket ground.[29]

Much of the impetus for cricket in India came from garrison teams, and it is no coincidence that the maidans, where most cricket is still played in Calcutta and Mumbai, were in front of Fort William and Fort George respectively.[30] Similarly, early West Indian cricket arose from the activities of Caribbean garrisons during the post-Napoleonic period and South African cricket from the British soldiers stationed at the Cape after 1795, expanding into Natal under the influence of the 45th Regiment of Foot during the early 1850s.[31] Meanwhile, Australian cricket had flourished under military patronage. The first game in Sydney in 1803 was probably between free settlers and army officers. The first club in the city was the Military Cricket Club formed in 1826. Similarly, the first game played by the Melbourne Cricket Club following its formation in 1838 was against a military team.[32]

Auckland is thus unexceptional. Almost all of the cricket played from 1845 to 1855 involved garrison teams drawn from the 58th (Rutlandshire) and 65th (Yorkshire North Riding) regiments.[33] The few intra-club fixtures played by the ACC, such as the usual 'Married' against 'Single', always incorporated a high proportion of military players.[34] The garrison also controlled the only cricket ground in Auckland for most of the 1850s.[35]

The matches played by the regiments were not without community support and elite patronage. Reports of the match between the ACC and the garrison in March 1848 were quick to point out the presence of leading members of the community, and an account of a similar match at the end of the year reveals festivities on a grand scale. 'The day proved a delightful one. The ground was in beautiful order. The rival competitors in high spirits. And the friends of both parties in a state of anxious expectation. Add the presence of beauty and the charms of music, and we think we have enumerated ample materials for general enjoyment.'[36] The emphasis on 'general enjoyment' also points to evidence that the cricket played by regiments in New Zealand was more integrated than was apparently the case in other parts of the Empire. With the exception of some specifically designated matches such as those between 'Officers' and 'NCOs', it appears that officers and other ranks were combined in most military teams. Given that the encouragement of sport for other ranks, to say nothing of its integration with the activities of the officer corps, was not evident in Britain until much later in the century, it is perhaps the case that the limited number of participants in the colonial setting dictated a pragmatic response.[37]

In the longer term, though, support for cricket in Auckland was limited. The departure of many of the regimental players on active service during the mid 1840s or the reduction of the garrison during a period of peace throughout the 1850s removed the focal point of the game. There was probably no organised cricket in Auckland from February 1853 until late 1857, when a series of matches were resumed between the garrison and civilians – the latter not designated as a particular club. Cricket declined again after the departure of troops to the large-scale punitive campaign against Waikato Maori in mid 1863. There were only occasional matches between the Auckland Militia and Rifle Volunteers, the 40th (Somersetshire) Regiment and 65th Regiment, and the Garrison and Navy. The military maintained their Albert barracks ground, but the Auckland Domain, which had apparently been secured as a cricket ground in the late 1850s, was allowed to revert to weeds.[38]

In a similar vein, the few matches reported in Wellington during the 1850s involved military and general civilian teams, none of which were designated as particular clubs. For three seasons – 1850/51 to 1852/53 – the focus of all Wellington cricket was an annual three-match series between the 65th Regiment and 'Staff and Civilians'; the majority were won by the Regiment. A three-match series was also played in January 1853 between 'Officers' and 'NCOs and Men' – the latter winning 2–1.[39] The departure of the 65th Regiment signalled the virtual extinction of Wellington cricket until the early 1860s.

With such a significant role for garrisons in Auckland and Wellington, it is no coincidence that much of the central and north of the North Island traces its earliest cricket to the presence of imperial troops and local militia at the height of Anglo-Maori conflict during the 1860s. In the Wairarapa such early games as Greytown Volunteers against Featherston Volunteers in early 1864 and Greytown against Masterton five years later were dominated by military players, as was the Rangitikei XI which defeated Wanganui in February 1867 and a Hutt XI the following year.[40] Military influence on cricket was at its peak in the Waikato after a large force under Governor George Grey invaded from Auckland in July 1863. A Zingari club was formed in the Hamilton area in about 1864, followed by others at Taupiri and Ngaruawahia. Further north, there was an active club at Opotiki by February 1867 with at least 35 members, many of them military. In the far north a Whangarei team dominated by military players journeyed down to play Onehunga at least twice during 1867.[41] But most of these clubs had sporadic lives determined by the movements of troops and the Armed Constabulary that succeeded the imperial forces after 1870.

The determination of soldiers to play cricket whilst on active service may be judged from the lengthy account by 'Colonel' George Hamilton-Browne of a match played during Easter 1866 at Pungarehu, South Taranaki. Played between troopers and forest rangers during the most heated period of the Hauhau conflict, the match was notable as much for the state of military preparedness as for the cricket:

Naturally the players were all out of practice, their dress far from accurate and the pitch – well damnable! But we turned to with glee, though to bat, bowl, or even field, belted as each man was with his revolver and 50 rounds of ammunition, was very trying. Moreover, the fieldsmen had to pick up their carbines when they changed places at the call of 'Over', and the umpires held the batsmen's guns. Now the main bush in which the gay and festive Hau Haus [sic] lived and gambolled was about 1000 yards away from the fort, but there were big patches of bush up to within 400 yards of it. Well, the game commenced, and of course attracted the attention of the gentle savage. Word was passed into the recesses of the bush that the white man was up to some new and inexplicable devilment, so that before long we had a highly interested if not appreciative gallery who, emerging from the bush, squatted down, and for a time behaved itself with decorum. Now we could have made allowances for their ignorance or their want of appreciation, though they were self-invited, and had paid no gate money, even should they have gone so far as to hiss, but I maintain that when it comes to expressing dissatisfaction with tuparas (two-barrelled guns) and Enfield rifles, it is high time for the performers to skip or clear the ground.

Despite the need to repel several Hauhau attacks, Hamilton-Browne records that the game was played to a conclusion.[42]

As it transpired, Hamilton-Browne was an impostor who did not arrive in New Zealand until 1872, at least six years after the events outlined above. He apparently did not see active service, and investigations by the New Zealand Government in 1908 and 1909 rejected his claims for a military pension.[43] Yet Hamilton-Browne's account of the military campaign is an accurate one that very closely resembles the career of Christopher Louis Maling, a member of the corps of guides and former Nelson surveyor who was a regular member of the Nelson Cricket Club in 1859–60. There is also at least one surviving photograph of members of the No.9 Taranaki Company playing cricket during the mid 1860s whilst wearing pistol holsters.[44] In short, there is ample room to question the accuracy of the Hamilton-Browne legend but much less to question the determination of the military to perpetuate their well-established cricket traditions in New Zealand.

The strong military presence had a considerable bearing on Taranaki cricket in general. Undoubtedly, there were games played after the establishment of New Plymouth – the least prosperous or significant of the Wakefield settlements – in 1841. But the first recorded cricket in Taranaki was an encounter between 'Bush' and 'Fern' in February 1855, followed by a meeting between 'Bush' and the 65th Regiment a year later.[45] Over the next decade, and especially at the height of Anglo-Maori conflict during 1862–63, there were regular matches involving members of the garrison stationed at New Plymouth and later between the garrison and the Taranaki Cricket Club, which appears to have been formed in 1861.[46]

Canterbury Cricket and Pastoralism

Turning to the South Island, and a world quite removed from the bellicose firmament of the north, the progress of cricket was altogether more secure. The structure of Canterbury cricket during its first three decades, and the consolidation of Christchurch as the 'spiritual' and administrative home of the New Zealand game by the turn of the century, is a direct reflection of the founding Canterbury Association. It is perhaps significant that the Association was formed in 1848 – the year of European revolution; its members readily embraced Wakefield's gloomy preoccupation with a breakdown of democracy and a threatening industrial proletariat. To this they added more personal and deeply religious perceptions of a declining moral standard and excessive politicisation within the Church of England. While the Wakefield principle provided the basic mechanism of social order in the new colony, Canterbury was also to be a diocesan settlement complete with bishop, cathedral chapter and clergy and denominational schools.[47]

The Canterbury Association possessed considerable status and influence from the outset. Its initial list of 59 members included 2 archbishops, 7 bishops, 4 baronets, 14 other peers and 16 members of parliament. Canterbury was also the best organised and planned of the Wakefield settlements. Emigration selection criteria were somewhat strictly geared to the objective of providing a sober and industrious labouring class to serve the cultivated elite who could afford Wakefield's 'sufficient price'. If Canterbury could not quite obtain a noble family to place at the top of its colonial hierarchy, it is still safe enough to say that it attracted a disproportionate number of English public school and Oxbridge graduates who arrived in New Zealand in the years 1850–80.[48]

Ultimately, though, the Canterbury ideal collapsed as it did everywhere else. Initially slow land sales created a deterrent for later investors, and it was soon found that – even more than in the north – the land of the Canterbury plains was suited to pastoralism rather than close agricultural settlement. Thus pragmatism contributed to a broadening of social attitudes among even the most dedicated Canterbury Association colonists. Nevertheless, L.C. Webb's verdict on Canterbury is a reminder of how relatively successful the settlement was: 'Wakefield's aspiration to found a colony which would reproduce the social gradations of an English county was more nearly realised in Canterbury than in any of the other settlements in Australia or New Zealand, chiefly because upper middle class colonists were attracted to Canterbury and flourished there'.[49] It is also worth noting that even when estrangement developed between the Canterbury Association and its colonists during the early 1850s, a majority of

Association supporters were returned in the first Provincial Council election in 1853.[50] Their ideals may have been eroded, but they set a lasting social and administrative tone.

The inauguration of cricket in Canterbury was signalled by an advertisement for the Christchurch Cricket Club (CCC) in the *Lyttelton Times* on 21 June 1851, seven months after the arrival of the first settlers. The club had apparently secured a designated ground in Hagley Park and the subscription and initial entrance fees were a relatively preclusive 10s.6d.[51]

The membership of the club during its first two years could not have provided a more deliberate embodiment of the Canterbury hierarchy, and the first match left no doubt as to the proposed social order. On the first anniversary of the settlement, 16 December 1851, the club played a 'Working Men's XI'. When play ended owing to darkness, the club required 34 to win – having scored 131 and dismissed their opponents for 72 and 93, high scores for the period in New Zealand. John Robert Godley, Harrow-educated High Church Tory and leader of the settlement, contributed 24 – the second highest score. But, more importantly, the occasion exhibited many familiar characteristics of 'home':

> It was difficult to believe that [the] occasion was not much more remote than a mere twelve month, so English was the appearance of that part of the great grassy plain in which the revellers assembled themselves: the scene bore no unapt resemblance to the open air holiday-making in the neighbourhood of some country town at home.

The only major differences were the wide open spaces and the much more orderly conduct of spectators compared to England.[52]

Despite the egalitarian strains of this inaugural contest, the majority of early matches were internal 'Married' against 'Single' members-only affairs, and the 'Working Men's XI' of 1851 reappeared only once more, in early 1852.[53] Without exception, the members of the club were 'gentleman' of status who did a great deal to shape the future of the province and the colony as a whole. Of the 41 players who appeared consistently during a season or seasons in the first five years (1851–56), 15 were at some time members of the Canterbury Provincial Council and 9 served in the New Zealand General Assembly, either in the House of Representatives or Legislative Council. While many assumed these positions after their active playing days, it is clear enough that the club was inextricably bound to both landed wealth and political influence – what might be termed the 'elite of the Canterbury elite'. This patronage was also sustained rather than sporadic, indicative of a genuine interest rather than a social necessity.

Breaking into this circle entailed having the time and resources to play cricket. Working men encountered difficulty gaining leave from employers and it was unlikely that they could easily afford an annual subscription that climbed as high as £2 in 1867.[54] The greatest barrier, though, was that entry to the club was by nomination, and this process was certainly operated with discretion. When a new incarnation of the Christchurch Cricket Club sought to secure the lease for a new Hagley Park ground at the end of 1860, revised provincial government regulations dictated that it could only do so if it abandoned existing membership restrictions and became 'quite public'. The constitution was accordingly revised and the name of the club changed to the Canterbury Cricket Club.[55] However, the change was cosmetic rather than actual.

Implicit in the club membership system is some explanation as to why Canterbury cricketers, and sporting enthusiasts generally, had much less difficulty than those in other centres in securing funds and, above all, permanent or semi-permanent playing fields. By the time the second major match, 'Married Gentlemen' against 'Single', was played in April 1852 a £30 subscription had been raised for improvements to the Hagley Park ground. By September 1854, further generous subscriptions had enabled more improvements and the erection of a pavilion, possibly the first in New Zealand. The *Lyttelton Times* reported that every arrangement had been made for the comfort of members and visitors, and hinted that a groundsman had been employed to maintain facilities during the winter.[56]

It is equally apparent that the Christchurch club had the resources and leisure to travel further afield reasonably regularly. Matches were being played against Kaiapoi by late 1853, Lincoln by late 1854 and Rangiora by February 1855. While these areas are virtually within the confines of modern Christchurch, they constituted a long and arduous journey during the early 1850s. Indeed, the efforts of the Club at Rangiora did not go unnoticed by the *Lyttelton Times*. 'Their energy in getting up cricket so far up the country, will give a spirit to this thoroughly English game, which it is to be hoped will not flag'.[57]

Such initiatives from Christchurch were the basis for a strong cricketing tradition among Canterbury pastoralists. Mid-Canterbury cricket reveals a close relationship between country players and the elite United Canterbury Cricket Club. During the 1860s there were a number of games at Rakaia involving 'Hills' and 'Plains' XIs, Ashburton, Ellesmere and visitors from Christchurch.[58] At least a third of the 31 players who represented 'Hills', 'Plains' or Ashburton in 1866–67 were pastoral runholders, 4 others were run managers and many of the remainder were almost certainly their employees. While a number of so-called runholders in the South Island were more realistically managers financed by sleeping partners, several of those identified in a cricketing context display prosperity on their own account.[59] Among them were William Campbell Walker, an Oxford MA who served as Minister of Education and Immigration in the Seddon Ministry during the 1890s, and Alfred Cox, an Australian-born runholder and land speculator who accumulated a solid fortune and served both the Provincial Council and the House of Representatives.[60]

The earliest cricket in South Canterbury rests on an equally prominent foundation. A club was formed in Timaru in 1862 and played its first game against Arowhenua on 14 January 1863. Clubs existed at Burkes Pass and Winchester by the early 1870s and at Geraldine, Temuka and Waimate by 1884. The leading Burkes Pass player was C.G. Hawdon, a runholder and Rugbean. Cricket in Waimate owed most to the patronage of Robert Heaton Rhodes Jr. and the Studholme brothers – all of whom followed an Oxford education with the accumulation of vast landholdings in South Canterbury.[61] The public school influence was such that an annual match between Christ's College, Christchurch, and English public school old boys was still being played at Geraldine in the early 1950s.[62]

Later in the century North Canterbury cricket was initiated by Duncan Rutherford of the Amuri who had been captain of the Christ's College XI during the 1860s. With his brothers he established the Amuri Cricket Club in October 1875, which provided the stimulus for frequent matches between Rotherham and Waiau and with Kaikoura. As most of the leading players were prominent runholders or their employees, there were also regular matches between stations.[63] Moreover, there is some suggestion that this enthusiasm for the game also embodied more complex relationships of social status and attempted social control between employers and employees in rural districts. Certainly, the Revd W.R. Campbell's response to R.A. Chaffey's efforts to foster North Canterbury cricket among farm workers is revealing: 'Go ahead with your scheme; the men are better playing cricket than two-up, or drinking whisky'.[64] At the same time, one suspects that W.J. Gardner's verdict on station cricket is equally applicable: 'The pitches were rough, and the bowling ragged; the batsmen had one aim: to send the ball soaring over woolshed or plantation'.[65]

Cricket in Scottish Otago

If Canterbury and its cricket was the relative success story of the Wakefield settlements, Otago embraced an entirely different contour. The beginning of Otago cricket was swift, if not highly presumptuous. On 13 December 1848, nine months after the beginning of the settlement, but three weeks before any match was played in Dunedin, an intriguing notice appeared in the *Otago News*:

> Challenge – the cricket players of Dunedin hereby publicly challenge the Cricket Club at Wellington to a trial of skill, at any point equidistant between the port of Otago and Port Nicholson: due notice of the acceptance of the challenge to appear in the 'Wellington Independent', or by letter, addressed to Mr Watson, the Commercial Inn, Dunedin, Otago – High Street, Dunedin, Dec. 9, 1848.[66]

Although the challenge produced no response, this did not hinder enthusiasm for the game in the south. An *Otago News* leading article on 27

December 1848 listed a cricket club among the active institutions of the growing Dunedin settlement, and it played its first match – 'Married' against 'Single' – on 1 January 1849 on the site of the present Octagon, an area with a slope more pronounced than the famed Lord's ridge. Another match was almost certainly played on Dunedin's anniversary day in late March, and an advertisement for the sale of cricket gear in mid April 1849 suggests the game was not entirely primitive.[67]

But cricket faded quickly – or the press stopped reporting it. Whichever is the case, the basic reason is the same. Dunedin was in essence a Scottish Presbyterian Free Church settlement. This is not to suggest that the Scots did not play cricket, but that these were the wrong sort of Scots. There was a strong cricketing tradition among the middle class and educated of Edinburgh and in the South of Scotland generally but those who joined this particular incarnation of the Wakefield colonising zeal were predominantly working class, small farmers and villagers from remote parts of Scotland that had not been penetrated by Sassenach diversions.[68]

In common with Wakefield, Thomas Burns and William Cargill in Scotland harboured a profound sense of regret at the passing of pre-industrial, agrarian society and at ominous democratic rumblings moving across Europe. At the same time they were dealing with a major schism in the Presbyterian Church of Scotland. In 1843 one third of the Church membership broke with the establishment in a reaction against what they saw as excessive moderation, permissiveness and interference in church affairs from both the state and landowning gentry. The new Free Church adopted a much stronger evangelical position emphasising predestination and a strong godly enthusiasm in conjunction with self-help and self-discipline.[69]

Plans for a theocratic community in the new world faltered until the Otago Block was transferred to the New Zealand Company in 1847 and the scheme came more directly under Wakefield's influence. But rather than a carefully planned society governed by strong Evangelical principles and the mechanism of the 'sufficient price', the response to the Free Church scheme produced a preponderance of artisans and an elite consisting of farmers' sons, self-employed shopkeepers and tradesmen. Without capital, these Scots acquired only 85 of the first land selections, while the few wealthier English in the settlement were able to acquire 95. Indeed, the presence of an English faction, or 'Little Enemy' as they became known, posed no small threat to Scottish idealism. That many of the English were Crown officials did not sit easily with democratic Free Church objections to unwieldy and 'despotic' Crown Colony government. Moreover, there was an inevitable unease at any sign of a Church of England influence permeating Dunedin. To the intense relief of Cargill in particular, some 12,000 immigrants, mostly Scottish Presbyterians, reached Otago by the late 1850s to ease fears of English social domination. In due course, intermarriage also eroded what were essentially trivial squabbles and national–religious divisions between the English and Scottish elites.[70]

Yet it is important to keep the 'Little Enemy' firmly in mind when considering the first forays of Otago cricketers, for there were few, if any, Scots. A number of players had links with Charles Kettle's Crown survey in the two years before formal settlement, while even among the colonists the cricketers are drawn from the *John Wickliffe* that sailed from Gravesend, London, rather than the *Philip Laing* that sailed from Glasgow. Perhaps the most notable figure among this group is Samuel Shaw. A painter by trade, Shaw's advocacy of an eight-hour working day, instead of ten, created enemies. Cargill labelled him a 'cockney spouter', and Shaw, as much as anyone, came to epitomise the position of the 'Little Enemy' in Scottish Otago.[71]

The organisation of social activities, cricket matches, anniversary sports days and race meetings by the English faction did not impress Cargill and Burns, who feared for their determinedly civilised and hard-working ideals. As the first anniversary approached, Burns left the settlement in no doubt as to how he felt it ought to be celebrated: 'I would not press you with so much as one argument for keeping this anniversary as a day for religious duties – for I feel that I would, in so doing, be offering an insult to your religious feelings and convictions of duty'.[72] In subsequent years Burns did not apparently see the need to comment on anniversary days. Recreation, and cricket especially, receded into the background as settlers turned their attention to more practical matters of survival.

The Scottish-dominated press, as much as a genuine lack of cricketers, also had a part to play in the decline of the 1850s. Under the editorship of W.H. Cutten, the like-minded son-in-law of Cargill, the *Otago Witness* maintained a diet of political and governmental information, studiously avoiding the activities of the English faction. Coverage only improved, albeit marginally, after a falling-out between Cutten and Cargill in 1855.[73] By Christmas 1858 Cutten was strongly advocating the importance of recreation to the community.

> The early closing movement and half-holiday system in the shops and factories of the old country may with equal advantage be adopted here, and the introduction of its manly and time-honoured games such as cricket, football … and other healthful exercises would, we are convinced, be hailed with delight by young and old as a happy release from the cares of business, as a means towards the preservation of health and towards the furtherance of good feeling and harmony in the community.[74]

To this end efforts had been made to establish sports grounds in north Dunedin.

Finally, in February 1860 plans were announced for the formation of a new cricket club, and application was made to the Superintendent for lease of a section of the town belt near the 'swamp road'. The club secured its ground, and made preparations, but played little, if any, cricket. It remained, according to the *Colonist*, 'a splendid introduction to nothing'.[75]

Cricket and Gold

The growth of cricket, as with all things in the province, was triggered by the discovery of gold in Central Otago early in 1861. In January 1862, in response to numerous enquiries from recently arrived Australian miners – mostly from the Victorian goldfields, *The Colonist* renewed calls for the establishment of a cricket club in Dunedin. Within two weeks, a meeting had been held and practices arranged: 'The meeting, though not as large as we could have wished, was hopeful, and indicative of an interest having been evoked well calculated to give confidence to a belief that the manly and beneficial exercise of cricketing will speedily become generally appreciated and established as the favourite game of the people'.[76] Despite a very wet and swampy ground, where it was apparently necessary for players to roll up their trousers, the new Dunedin Cricket Club played its first match in late February 1862 – losing to the 70th (Surrey) Regiment by one wicket.[77]

With support from an Otago Provincial Council confident and rejuvenated by gold prosperity, cricket began to flourish in Dunedin and its surrounds. With labour provided by the Provincial Superintendent, detailed plans were developed to drain the swampy ground with trenches and water channels. By February 1864 it was fully fenced and a grandstand had been erected. The ambition of the club is also quite apparent from the *Rules and Regulations of the Dunedin Cricket Club* it published in 1863 and 1864. Membership was by nomination only, with such nomination requiring a seconder and approval by the committee. The subscription was a relatively high one guinea in 1863/64, but was doubled for the following season. No person could be admitted to the club ground or facilities unless introduced by a member, and no Dunedin resident, other than a member, was allowed on the club ground on practice days, although members could invite a non-resident friend. The club stipulated a uniform of white flannel trousers, sky-blue shirt and scarlet cap – compulsory in all club matches. Smoking was prohibited on the field during play. Upon receiving a copy of the *Rules* the *Otago Witness* expressed the hope that all clubs in Otago would adhere to the authority of the new club in the manner of the Marylebone Cricket Club (MCC).[78]

In large part, it was this Dunedin club that assisted a local entrepreneur, Shadrach Jones, in bringing George Parr's All England XI from Australia to New Zealand in February 1864 (the tour will be discussed in Chapter 8). The club controlled and developed the ground and selected the Otago team for the All England games and, indeed, the first interprovincial fixture against Canterbury. Yet, for all this, the Dunedin-based club did not necessarily embody the playing strength of Otago cricket. For that the net had to be cast much wider to include miners and others on the goldfields.

Cricket outside Dunedin had been played at East Taieri as early as 1858 and two teams of Waikouaiti squatters played a match for a full set of cricket gear and a champagne dinner in November 1863. A club was functioning at Port Chalmers by the end of 1863, and others appeared rapidly following gold discoveries. A club existed at Dunstan by November 1862, which played a match at Alexandra in September 1863; Arrowtown played Queenstown in December; Oamaru had a strong club by the beginning of 1864; and Cromwell almost certainly played Clyde at the end of the same year.[79]

These developments are clearly reflected in the Otago teams that opposed All England. Six of the team came from the Wakatipu/Queenstown goldfields area, and of the eight recently arrived from Australia it is likely that all were, at some stage, miners. Among them were the Mace brothers, from a strong cricketing tradition in Bedale, Yorkshire, who worked as miners throughout the 1860s before turning to small farming.[80] Another, William Gilbert Rees, was a first cousin of the Grace and Pocock cricketing dynasties. Educated at the Royal Naval School, Rees worked on the gold-fields and as a station manager in Australia before becoming the first run-holder at Lake Wakatipu. After losing his land to gold prospectors, he became a run manager and government stock inspector. He never tired of highlighting his cricketing relations and displayed certain of the other W.G.'s renowned idiosyncrasies and gamesmanship. On one occasion, when bowled in a country match, he claimed to have been distracted by a flock of sheep on a distant hill. 'Sheep in the eye' became legendary in the district, if not a mode of dismissal recognised by MCC.[81]

Ultimately, the long-term prospects for Otago cricket were as tenuous as anything related to gold-seeking. Gold brought much needed capital and an influx of quality players, yet much of the gold population was transitory – always willing to move in search of the next great opportunity. The depar-ture of miners to the West Coast, the Thames and overseas goldfields reduced the base of players and caused stagnation – temporary or permanent – among many of the early goldfields' clubs.

Gold, moreover, did little to alter the limited cricketing component of the permanent population of Dunedin and its surrounds. The ambitious Dunedin Cricket Club of 1862 was struggling by the end of 1865 when the intra-club match between 'North' and 'South' Dunedin mustered only nine players on each side. Another match a month later also failed to draw a full comple-ment, or an umpire, and there were complaints when the *Otago Witness* declined to publish the score.[82] Lack of opposition undoubtedly contributed to the declining interest. The club frequently played 1st XI against next XVIII or 'Married' against 'Single', and in February 1869 it was proposed to play '1st XI with pick handles' against '2nd XI with bats'.[83]

The Otago provincial team also experienced declining fortunes. From 1864 to 1870 they won five of their first seven interprovincial matches against Canterbury, with one drawn. But with the retirement of the core of leading players from the gold period there was nothing to sustain this success. During the 1870s Otago lost 10 of the next 11 matches against Canterbury – 5 by an innings.[84]

Gold may have provided a much-needed tonic, but the cure for the ills of Otago cricket under the Scots was a much more gradual process, one dependant as much as anywhere on the pattern of urban growth (discussed in Chapter 3).

As gold declined in Otago, discoveries on the West Coast of the South Island during the mid 1860s contributed to the development of cricket in that area. The Hokitika Cricket Club was established in September 1867 under the Presidency of James Bonar, a prosperous merchant, shipping agent, sometime Goldfields' Secretary and the first Mayor of Hokitika. The Vice President was George Samuel Sale, formerly of Rugby school, Cambridge, and the Canterbury XXII against All England and now Westland Goldfields' Commissioner. Such was the determination of cricketers that a game between Hokitika and Ross was reportedly played on a pitch consisting of planks placed over old gold tailings.[85]

Nelson's position as a transit point to the Marlborough and West Coast goldfields during the mid 1860s did much to assist the fortunes of cricket in that province – and especially in Nelson city, which had always languished in the shadow of the surrounding village teams. 'Diggers' defeated 'Publicans' of Nelson in December 1864, and there were enough visitors for the Nelson Cricket Club to play 'Outsiders' a week later. The steady increase in population and commerce that accompanied the peak gold rush period in 1866–67 manifested itself in new clubs and a wide variety of 'scratch' teams: 'Nelson City Butchers', 'Cabmen', 'Draymen', 'Bankers' and 'Butchers and Blacksmiths' all played in the period 1867–69. In Nelson province teams also took the field at the gold mining towns of Collingwood and Takaka as early as 1860, and the two continued to play regular matches throughout the decade.[86]

The Nature of the Colonial Game

It is evident that the beginnings of New Zealand cricket were as varied as the settings in which it emerged and that it prospered or struggled in unison with its environment. Given these variations, something must be said of the nature of the game as it was played during these formative years. For, as subsequent chapters will demonstrate, New Zealand was to become almost obsessed with pursuing the correct 'form' of the game – even to the point of eschewing opportunities for growth and success.

Determining the extent to which early New Zealand cricket conducted itself in accordance with the manners and mores of the game in England is complicated by both a paucity of press accounts for anything other than the most important matches and the fact that the English game itself was still in relative flux during the mid nineteenth century. Within the span of a generation – 1835–65 – legal bowling styles evolved from underarm to overarm, there were numerous technical innovations in batting, equipment and ground preparation, and the professional touring teams triggered a huge broadening of interest in the game. It is clear that the fledgling colonial press reported these developments with some dedication, but it is equally apparent that the rudimentary nature of the New Zealand colonial setting often made proper emulation of them impossible.

The most immediate problem during the early years of settlement was the shortage of flat playing areas of a sufficient size and the very rough state of those that did exist. As we shall see in Chapter 6, many cricket clubs and provincial bodies lacked the resources, financial or technical, to develop grounds. Densely grassed outfields were a common feature. One group of cricketers north of Auckland are depicted playing in the midst of a burnt-out forest with large tree stumps and other obstacles close at hand.[87] Even on the flat land of Christchurch it was necessary to clear native tussock and flax. Improvements, and especially pitch quality, also depended on the importation and sewing of English grasses. Rollers and mowers did not appear in New Zealand until late in the century.[88] The Wellington *Spectator* observed of a match at the end of 1846 that 'The ground is in a very rough state, though every pain was taken to make it level, and from its hardness the round handed bowlers were not so effective as they otherwise would have been, the balls almost invariably rising over the wicket'.[89] Conditions were no better for the interprovincial fixture between Wellington and Auckland in December 1862, when Rayner of Auckland was dismissed by 'a "sneaker" from Brewer disarranging his perpendiculars'.[90] On such rough surfaces, batting was generally a lottery. Few reached double figures and extras were frequently the highest score by some distance. In the 'Married' vs. 'Single' match at Christchurch on 17 December 1853, the 'Single' innings of 167 included 37 byes and 15 wides; 'Married' replied with 102 – including 6 byes and 29 wides.[91] Not surprisingly, games frequently finished in one day – although some, such as Civilians vs. Military at Wellington in 1846, lasted two days.[92]

Difficult ground conditions were accentuated by scarce and sub-standard equipment. Although colonial merchants were importing cricket gear from the 1840s to supplement that brought by individual settlers, numerous photographs survive of batsmen and wicket-keepers without pads or with only one pad. Batting gloves were a rare luxury.[93] Furthermore, although leading clubs such as the Dunedin Cricket Club specified shirts and sashes of a particular colour, as was still the custom in England, standard attire, let alone white, was more conspicuous by its absence.[94]

As with most nineteenth-century cricket, the New Zealand version was overwhelmingly a bowler's game – and one that embraced the full range of styles and innovations. In December 1845 the *New Zealander* reminded

Auckland cricketers that the rules relating to round-arm bowling, which had been legalised in 1835, stipulated that the ball must be bowled and not thrown.[95] In an Auckland Cricket Club match in 1859, 'Mr Muttit employed his "underhand twist" which, judging from the score, produced the desired effect. This style of bowling might be advantageous for a few overs or so, but we doubt if its continuance throughout a match is desirous or advantageous.'[96] As in England, various degrees of underarm and round-arm bowling continued in New Zealand cricket at all levels for at least a generation after overarm bowling was legalised in 1864. It was apparently agreed that overarm would not be used in the interprovincial fixture between Wellington and Nelson in 1864 because a formal copy of the new rules had not yet arrived from England.[97]

Irrespective of the match conditions, it seems that dedication to practice and play sometimes left much to be desired – at least in the eyes of the press. In January 1846 the Wellington *Spectator* 'recommend[ed] some of the respective parties to exercise themselves frequently, as many runs were scored from bad fielding'.[98] In 1862 the Auckland press offered even sharper criticism of the Wellington provincial team:

> [W]e would strongly recommend the Wellington cricketers to engage the services of a man who has made cricket his profession, for such services cannot be too highly appreciated by those who aspire to eminence in the game. We recommend this course because most of our Wellington friends appear to be unacquainted with the first principles of batting, both as regards position, style and execution.[99]

Similarly, the visit of the All England XI to Christchurch in 1864 prompted *The Press* to defend its often acerbic criticisms of local cricketers:

> We have ridiculed the attempt to display the cricket players of Canterbury in the eyes of mankind without taking the usual measures for placing our play in its best light. There is a very good team to be got in Canterbury. But the best players cannot take up a bat and play without practice. We believe that the public attention called to the subject in this journal has been the means of stirring up the cricketers to the necessity for exertion.[100]

As we will see later, this outburst did not have the desired impact.

Regardless of the apparent or imagined limitations of the participants, many cricket matches were well-patronised social spectacles. As T.W. Reese observed in his monumental *History of New Zealand Cricket*, 'The standard of play in those early days left much to be desired; not so the pleasure and enjoyment which the pioneers derived from the games and the subsequent socials and dinners'.[101] Considerable effort was made to cater to the comforts of players and spectators alike. Military bands were a regular part of the entertainment – even in the most primitive settings, such as the match between members of the 57th (West Middlesex) Regiment at Poverty Flat, New Plymouth, in November 1862.[102] Marquees and 'refreshment booths' were also commonplace, providing local publicans and victuallers with a healthy trade. Nathaniel Valentine, a regular player himself during the 1850s, provided good service to Wellington cricket in this respect – the hotels that he owned, variously in Wellington and the Hutt Valley, were regularly used for cricket meetings and match dinners.[103] Another group who appear to have derived a prosperous trade from cricket were bookmakers and other gamblers. Gambling on everything from individual scores to the exact result of the game was common until at least the 1880s when the government moved to curb such behaviour – in public at least.[104]

As most of the settlements tended in their early years to subscribe to pre-industrial work rhythms – working more according to the demands of the task than the discipline of the clock – cricket was often played on weekdays.[105] Moreover, it was not uncommon for a half-holiday to be declared on the occasion of a 'big' match, especially an interprovincial fixture.[106] Only in the late 1870s are there signs of an effort to standardise the Saturday half-holiday – and this for moral as much as practical reasons, if the *Lyttelton Times*' report of the movement in Christchurch is any indication. 'It has been found that by a methodical arrangement of the work in hand, this can be done so as to be a benefit both to the workmen and their employers. It is more than probable that the institution in the trade of this movement will effectually stamp out the evils attendant upon the too frequent worship of saints Monday and Tuesday.'[107]

Although it is clear that many cricket matches in the early years were well-supported, there is no way of determining even approximate spectator numbers during this formative period. Aside from a few very general references to 'good' and 'large' crowds, the press is surprisingly silent on the matter. Perhaps, given the sometimes rigorous critique of the players, attendances were one aspect of proceedings generally considered to be satisfactory. In so far as the early colonial press did comment on the spectators, it was to encourage the presence of women at games. A report of a match between the Britannia CC and the garrison of Wellington in November 1846 expressed 'regret that the day was not more congenial so that the fairer portion of creation might have enlivened the scene with their presence'.[108] A similar fixture in Auckland at the end of 1859 was prefaced by a direct plea to female supporters: 'The playing members of the Auckland club are exceedingly anxious in particular for the presence of the ladies when they thus meet solemn tourney, conscious no doubt, as were the knights of old, that there is nothing so inspiring as to have their deeds witnessed and approved by the eyes of their fair friends'.[109] However, another encounter a month later left the local press 'gratified to see so many ladies on the ground'.[110] No doubt the presence of women was seen as providing a civilising counterpoise to a male gathering that was not infrequently marked by gambling and the consumption of alcohol.

There can be no doubt, then, that cricket was firmly entrenched throughout New Zealand as part of the European cultural fabric by the late 1860s. Certainly, the game only had a tenuous hold in some areas, fluctuated in others, and was seldom played in a manner familiar to observers of increasingly formal club and county cricket in England. But above all else, the most distant component of the British Empire possessed an abundance of cricketing intent – sporting settlers determined to persist with the game despite its own constraints and the numerous practical demands of their new world. This determination was to be even more pronounced after 1870 amid a new phase of rapid immigration, economic boom and urban growth.

Notes

1. L.M. Rogers (ed.), *The Early Journals of Henry Williams* (Christchurch, 1961), p. 268. See also: K.J. Nobbs, 'History of the First Recorded Cricket Match in New Zealand', unknown source (Te Kauwhata, 1990); T.W. Reese, *New Zealand Cricket: 1914–1933* (Christchurch, 1936), p. 13.
2. R. Darwin Keenes (ed.), *Charles Darwin's Beagle Diary* (Cambridge, 1988), p. 390.
3. Reese, *New Zealand Cricket 1914–33*, p. 15. Nobbs refers to the German explorer Ernest Dieffenbach witnessing a game at Kaitaia in 1841 (See Nobbs, 'History of the First Recorded Cricket Match in New Zealand'); I have been unable to locate further details in Dieffenbach's journal.
4. J.A. Mangan, 'Christ and the Imperial Games Fields: Evangelical Athletes of the Empire', *British Journal of Sports History*, 1, 2 (1984), pp. 184–8; B. Stoddart, 'Sport, Cultural Imperialism and Colonial Response in the British Empire', *Comparative Studies in Society and History*, 30, 4 (1988), p. 655.
5. N.M. Taylor (ed.), *The Journal of Ensign Best: 1837–43* (Wellington, 1966), p. 275; *Spectator*, 20 Feb. 1841, p. 2. As one Wellington newspaper altered its name frequently during the 1840s (*New Zealand Gazette, New Zealand Gazette & Britannia Spectator, New Zealand Gazette & Wellington Spectator, New Zealand Spectator & Cook Strait Guardian*), the abbreviated title *Spectator* is used in these notes.
6. *New Zealand Colonist & Port Nicholson Advertiser*, 4 Nov. 1842, p. 3; 8 Nov. 1842, p. 2.
7. *Spectator*, 28 Dec. 1842, p. 2.
8. *New Zealand Colonist & Port Nicholson Advertiser*, 27 Jan. 1843, p. 2. Scoring by the traditional method of notching all runs on a stick apparently remained in vogue for some years in New Zealand.
9. *New Zealand Colonist & Port Nicholson Advertiser*, 4 Nov. 1842, p. 3; *Spectator*, 9 Nov. 1842, p. 2; D. Hamer and R. Nicholls (eds), *The Making of Wellington 1800–1914* (Wellington, 1990), pp. 134, 156, 175–8.
10. Derived from Wellington Burgess's Rolls for 1842 and 1843, in A.H. Carman, *The Birth of a City: Wellington 1840–1843* (Wellington, 1970), pp. 128–38, 173–6.
11. Derived from jury list published in the *Wellington Independent*, 11 Feb. 1845.
12. *Wellington Independent*, 28 Nov. 1846, p. 3; *Spectator*, 5 Dec. 1846, p. 3; 26 Dec. 1846, p. 3.
13. *Wellington Independent*, 7 Feb. 1849, p. 3.
14. D. Neely, *100 Summers: The History of Wellington Cricket* (Wellington, 1975), pp. 11–16.
15. L. Broad, *Jubilee History of Nelson* (Nelson, 1892), p. 14; *Nelson Examiner*, 26 Nov. 1842, p. 1; R. Allan, *Nelson: A History of Early Settlement* (Wellington, 1965), pp. 181–2.
16. McAloon, *Nelson*, pp. 29–37.
17. *Nelson Examiner*, 9 March 1844, p. 2; 16 March 1844, p. 6.
18. Ibid., 16 March 1850, p. 2.
19. McAloon, *Nelson*, pp. 25–9, 37–41.
20. M.D. Lash (ed.), *Nelson Notables 1840–1940* (Nelson, 1992), p. 52; E. Bohan, *Edward Stafford: New Zealand's First Statesman* (Christchurch, 1994), pp. 25, 35, 44.

21. By the 1850s Nelson had established itself as a centre of New Zealand horse breeding. Allan, *Nelson*, p. 182; Bohan, *Edward Stafford*, pp. 61–2, 75–6.
22. Derived from jury lists published in the *Nelson Examiner*, 18 Feb. 1860; 16 Feb. 1861. See also: 7 Jan. 1863, p. 2; 10 Jan. 1863, p. 2.
23. McAloon, *Nelson*, pp. 20–25, 49–56.
24. Taylor, *Journal of Ensign Best*, pp. 376, 378; *Southern Cross*, 25 Nov. 1843, p. 1.
25. *New Zealander*, 6 Dec. 1845, p. 2.
26. Quoted in J.R. Phillips, 'A Social History of Auckland 1840–53' (MA thesis, University of Auckland, 1966), pp. 75–7.
27. Ibid., p. 68–73, 81; Sinclair, *History of New Zealand*, pp. 49, 100.
28. Derived from jury lists published in the *New Zealand Government Gazette*, 26 Jan. 1842; 3 Feb. 1844; 1851–52.
29. G.D. West, *The Elevens of England* (London, 1988), p. 1.
30. M. Bose, *A History of Indian Cricket* (London, 1990), p. 20.
31. M. Manley, *A History of West Indies Cricket* (London, 1988), pp. 20f.; Swanton, *Barclay's World of Cricket*, pp. 113–21.
32. J. Pollard, *The Formative Years of Australian Cricket, 1803–93* (North Ryde, NSW, 1987), pp. 6–21, 40–2.
33. For example, *New Zealander*, 11 March 1848, p. 3; 9 Dec. 1848, p. 2; 27 Jan. 1849, p. 3; 21 Jan. 1852, p. 3.
34. For example, ibid., 13 Dec. 1851, p. 3.
35. T.W. Reese, *New Zealand Cricket 1841–1914* (Christchurch, 1927), p. 22.
36. *New Zealander*, 9 Dec. 1848, p. 2.
37. See J.D. Campbell, '"Training for Sport is Training for War": Sport and the Transformation of the British Army, 1860–1914', *International Journal of the History of Sport*, 17, 4 (2000), pp. 22–9, 47.
38. *New Zealander*, 28 Feb. 1860, p. 2; 3 Jan. 1858, p. 2; 30 Jan. 1858, p. 2; *New Zealand Herald*, 19 Dec. 1863; 29 Dec. 1863; 11 Nov. 1864; 15 Nov. 1864; Reese, *New Zealand Cricket 1841–1914*, pp. 22–3.
39. *Wellington Independent*, 14 Dec. 1850, p. 3; 4 Jan. 1851, p. 2; 17 Jan. 1852, p. 3; 22 Jan. 1853, p. 3; 26 Jan. 1853, p. 2.
40. A.G. Bagnall, *Wairarapa: An Historical Excursion* (Masterton, 1976), pp. 507–8; *Wellington Independent*, 14 Feb. 1867, p. 5.
41. Reese, *New Zealand Cricket 1914–33*, p. 584; *New Zealand Herald*, 11 March 1867, p. 5; 7 Nov. 1867, p. 4.
42. Quoted in D. and P. Neely, *The Summer Game: The Illustrated History of New Zealand Cricket* (Auckland, 1994), p. 19.
43. B. Gilling, 'George Hamilton-Browne' in C. Orange (ed.), *The Dictionary of New Zealand Biography: Vol.2 1870–1900* (Wellington, 1993), pp. 191–2 (hereafter *DNZB*).
44. Neely and Neely, *The Summer Game*, p. 19.
45. *Taranaki Herald*, 28 Feb. 1855, p. 2; C. Richmond to J. Atkinson, 13 Feb. 1856, in G. Scholefield (ed.), *The Richmond–Atkinson Papers: Vol. 1* (Wellington, 1960), p. 195.
46. *Taranaki Herald*, 7 Feb. 1857, p. 2; 22 Feb. 1862, p. 2; 24 Jan. 1863, p. 3; 19 Dec. 1863, p. 3; 13 Feb. 1864, p. 2.
47. L.C. Webb in J. Hight and C.R. Straubel (eds), *A History of Canterbury: Vol.1 to 1854* (Christchurch, 1957), pp. 135–51.
48. Ibid., pp. 150, 157, 163, 178; McIntyre, *Journal of Henry Sewell*, pp. 34–5.
49. Webb in *A History of Canterbury*, p. 233.
50. Ibid., pp. 213–14.
51. *Lyttelton Times*, 21 June 1851, p. 1.
52. Ibid., 20 Dec. 1851, p. 1.
53. An attempt to form a Mechanics cricket club apparently amounted to nothing.
54. Ibid., 2 Oct. 1852, p. 1; *The Press*, 20 May 1867, p. 2; 20 August 1867, p. 2.
55. *Lyttelton Times*, 27 Oct. 1860, p. 4.
56. Ibid., 3 April 1852, p. 3; 7 Jan. 1854, p. 7; 29 April 1854, p. 7; 30 Sept. 1854, p. 4.
57. Ibid., 20 Dec. 1851, p. 1; 7 Jan. 1854, p. 7; 20 Jan. 1855, p. 5; 7 March 1855, p. 4.
58. *The Press*, 4 April 1866, p. 2; 22 Oct. 1866, p. 2; 2 Nov. 1867, p. 2; 7 Nov. 1867, p. 2.
59. Ibid., 22 Oct. 1866, p. 2; Acland, *The Early Canterbury Runs,* passim.
60. G. Scholefield (ed.), *Dictionary of New Zealand Biography, Vols 1 and 2* (Wellington, 1940), vol.1, pp. 179–80; vol.2, p. 453.

61. Ibid., vol.2, pp. 347–8.
62. O.A. Gillespie, *South Canterbury: A Record of Settlement* (Timaru, 1958), pp. 430–1; K. Ogilvie, *100 Years of Cricket in Temuka* (Temuka, 1984), p. 4; R. Pinney, *The Early South Canterbury Runs* (Wellington, 1971), pp. 33, 39, 139.
63. J. Holm, *Nothing But Grass and Wind: The Rutherfords of Canterbury* (Christchurch, 1992), pp. 101–5.
64. Campbell quoted in W.J. Gardner, *The Amuri, A County History* (Culverden, 1956), pp. 242–5.
65. Ibid., p. 242. In the North Island, Wairarapa cricket, aside from its military origins, also owed much to the energies of wealthy local farmers and runholders. They were involved with the formation of clubs in Carterton, Featherston, Greytown and Masterton during the late 1860s, and initiated frequent games between stations from the mid 1870s. See: Bagnall, *Wairarapa*, pp. 507–8; *Seventy Five Years of Cricket: A History of the Wairarapa Cricket Association (Inc) 1894–1969* (Masterton, 1969), pp. 5–6.
66. *Otago News*, 13 Dec. 1848, p. 1.
67. Ibid., 27 Dec., 1848, p. 2; 21 March 1849, p. 2; 16 April 1849, p. 1; G. Griffiths, *Sale, Bradshaw, Manning, Wills and the 'Little Enemy': notes on some early arrivals in Otago, No.4* (Dunedin, 1971), p. 11.
68. Griffiths, *Sale, Bradshaw, Manning, Wills and the 'Little Enemy'*, p. 13.
69. Olssen, *A History of Otago*, pp. 31–5.
70. Ibid., pp. 38–44. See also D.M.J. Richmond, 'Dunedin in the 1860s: Some Aspects of Settlement' (MA thesis, University of Otago, 1972), pp. 7–15.
71. Griffiths, *Sale, Bradshaw, Manning, Wills and the 'Little Enemy'*, pp. 13–15; E. Olssen, 'Samuel Shaw' in W.H. Oliver (gen. ed.), *DNZB: Vol. 1, 1769–1869* (Wellington, 1990), p. 393.
72. *Otago News*, 21 March 1849, p. 2.
73. Griffiths, *Sale, Bradshaw, Manning, Wills and the 'Little Enemy'*, p. 15.
74. *Otago Witness*, 25 Dec. 1858, p. 2.
75. *The Colonist*, 24 Feb. 1860, p. 5; 10 Jan. 1862, p. 4.
76. Ibid., 24 Jan. 1862, p. 7.
77. *Otago Witness*, 25 Jan. 1862, p. 5; 22 Feb. 1862, p. 5.
78. Ibid., 8 Nov. 1862, p. 5; 15 Nov. 1862, p. 5; 12 Dec. 1863, p. 4; *Rules and Regulations of the Dunedin Cricket Club 1863–4 & 1864–5* (Dunedin, 1863/1864).
79. *Otago Witness*, 21 Nov. 1863, p. 5; Otago Cricket Association, *Centennial Souvenir Programme 1876–1976* (Dunedin, 1976), p. 14.
80. G. Griffiths, *The Maces of Macetown, notes on some early arrivals in Otago, No.2* (Dunedin, 1969).
81. G. Griffiths, *W.G. Rees and his Cricketing Cousins, notes on some early arrivals in Otago, No.3* (Dunedin, 1971); *King Wakatip* (Dunedin, 1971).
82. *Otago Witness*, 25 Nov. 1865, p. 12; 16 Dec. 1865, p. 12.
83. For example, *Otago Daily Times*, 27 Nov. 1868, p. 2; 25 Jan. 1869, p. 3; 30 Jan. 1869, p. 2; 27 Feb. 1869, p. 2.
84. Reese, *New Zealand Cricket 1841–1914*, pp. 149–209.
85. P. R. May, *The West Coast Gold Rushes* (Christchurch, 1965), p. 336; Reese, *New Zealand Cricket 1914–33*, p. 587.
86. *Nelson Examiner*, 14 April 1860, p. 3; 8 Dec. 1864, p. 2; 15 Dec. 1864, p. 2; 12 Jan. 1867, p. 3; 1 Feb. 1868, p. 3; 27 March 1869, p. 3; 28 April 1868, p. 2; 6 Nov. 1869, p. 3.
87. Neely and Neely, *The Summer Game*, pp. 25, 27.
88. Reese, *New Zealand Cricket 1841–1914*, p. 28.
89. *Spectator*, 5 Dec. 1846, p. 3.
90. *New Zealander*, 20 Dec. 1862, p. 5.
91. *Lyttelton Times*, 17 Dec. 1853, p. 10.
92. *Spectator*, 31 Jan. 1846, p. 7.
93. See, for example, Neely and Neely, *The Summer Game*, pp. 16, 23.
94. See, for example, ibid., p. 35.
95. *New Zealander*, 13 Dec. 1845, p. 2.
96. Ibid., 14 Dec. 1859, p. 3.
97. Neely and Neely, *The Summer Game*, p. 17.
98. *Spectator*, 31 Jan. 1846, p. 7.
99. *New Zealander*, 20 Dec. 1862, p. 5.

100. *The Press*, 5 Jan. 1864, p. 2.
101. Reese, *New Zealand Cricket 1841–1914*, p. 21.
102. *Taranaki Herald*, 22 Nov. 1862, p. 3.
103. *Wellington Independent*, 10 Jan. 1860, p. 3; 14 Jan. 1862, p. 3; 4 Dec. 1869, p. 3.
104. Grant, *On a Roll*, pp. 39–43.
105. McAloon, *Nelson*, p. 53.
106. For example, Neely and Neely, *The Summer Game*, p. 23.
107. *Lyttelton Times*, 9 March 1878, p. 2.
108. *Spectator*, 5 Dec. 1846, p. 3.
109. *New Zealander*, 10 Dec. 1859, p. 3.
110. Ibid., 7 Jan. 1860, p. 3.

3

Fashioning a Middle-Class Game: Cricket and Class, 1870–1914

Despite the varied contributions of systematic colonisation, the military, gold discoveries and pastoralism to the formative years of New Zealand cricket, the game functioned within fairly narrow parameters. The only real continuity throughout the nineteenth century, and arguably well into the twentieth, was to be found in the four main cities – Auckland, Wellington, Christchurch and Dunedin. As we will see later in this – and subsequent – chapters, idealism and dedication in the smaller provincial towns and rural districts was no match for isolation and limited human, physical and financial resources.

The growth and dynamics of cricket in the cities was inextricably bound to the dramatic social and economic transformation of New Zealand society from the 1870s to 1914. By world standards, and even those of neighbouring Australia, the scale of urbanisation in New Zealand was minute. But as Table 2 demonstrates, the combined population of the four cities increased more than fivefold during the four decades after 1870.

At the same time, the urban industrial workforce increased more than six-fold.[1] In this environment, notions of colonial egalitarianism that had gained sustenance relative to the more entrenched class delineations of Britain were revealed to be rather less than absolute. Erik Olssen explains the changes that were taking place as follows: 'Residential differentiation, rooted in different life-chances and opportunities, intensified class distinctions. Institutions such as lodges, churches and sports clubs, which mediated between social strata in small communities, compounded class differences in the cities and provided a necessary but not sufficient condition for the

TABLE 2

POPULATION OF THE FOUR MAIN CITIES, 1871–1911

	1871	1881	1891	1901	1911
Auckland	22,370	27,686	39,177	67,226	102,676
Wellington	7,908	20,563	37,135	49,344	70,729
Christchurch	11,075	25,070	37,336	57,041	80,193
Dunedin	21,517	40,950	45,869	52,390	64,237

growth of class consciousness.'[2] These disparities were compounded by economic depression for most of the period 1879–96.

In cricketing terms, urbanisation produced much greater scope in terms of who would play with whom. Where small colonial settlements sustained one or two struggling clubs in 1860, the developing cities of 1900 each boasted perhaps 40 teams in a variety of different competitions with their own customs and priorities. It is therefore important to examine patterns of club formation, class representation, the nature of local administration and interaction between players from diverse social backgrounds. New clubs and competitions certainly blossomed and there is ample evidence of growth in working-class cricket from the early 1880s, but there are clear limits to this participation. At senior club, provincial and national level,[3] that is to say the publicly visible face of the game upon which the rhetoric associated with New Zealand cricket was based, the dominance of many established middle-class clubs lingered well into the twentieth century. Working-class cricket tended to be confined to a narrow grouping of skilled and semi-skilled workers – unskilled workers were largely neglected – or confined to mid-week suburban and league competitions that operated largely beyond the influence of the major cricket associations.

Yet caution is essential in assessing the role of social class in New Zealand cricket. As we will see, open class conflict certainly did occur, most notably in Dunedin during the 1880s. But the extent to which the stratification of the game was deliberately constructed and maintained by an influential middle-class element is debatable. Rather, the opportunities for cricketers need to be set firmly within an understanding of issues such as population distribution, occupational structure and educational attainment – factors that shaped the broader social structure.

Creating an Urban Game, 1860–1880

As the four main cities began to grow from the early 1870s, the standard pattern of one or two dominant clubs was replaced by an expanded pool of cricketers and a proliferation of new clubs. After the struggles of the 1860s and the almost total dominance of the game by military teams, there were no less than 12 cricket clubs in the Auckland district by the time the provincial team embarked on a landmark tour of New Zealand at the end of 1873.[4] Similarly, although Wellington cricket had all but disappeared following the departure of the military during the early 1850s, real progress was made after 1865. To what extent this can be linked to the transfer of New Zealand's capital from Auckland to Wellington in that year is a moot point, but there were surely advantages to be gained from the presence of a group of influential politicians and public figures – of whom a good proportion were educated in the public school and Oxbridge sporting tradition. A new United Wellington Cricket Club emerged in January 1868 under the presidency of the Provincial Superintendent, Isaac Featherston, and dominated the Wellington game for most of the 1870s.[5]

Patterns of growth were even more dramatic in the South Island. Christchurch cricket, because it had been established with much greater Wakefieldian deliberation, was considerably more advanced than that in any other part of New Zealand. In addition to the elite United Canterbury CC, which was a direct descendant of the founding club of 1851, there were also numerous local, trade and business clubs in Christchurch from the late 1860s. Regular matches were played between butchers and bakers, painters and plasterers, carpenters and joiners, companies of the Canterbury Rifle Volunteers, the *Press* and *Lyttelton Times* newspaper offices and between Christchurch clubs and the surrounding districts – Heathcote Valley, Kaiapoi, Lincoln, Lyttelton, Mt. Herbert and Rangiora. A range of intra-club and scratch matches also took place, for example 'Public Schools and Christ's College XI' against 'The World', 'Tall' against 'Short' (5 ft 9 in. was the threshold between the two), and a fixture in 1869 between those learning their cricket in England and those learning in the colonies – won easily by the latter. A number of these games were played during early evening after work.[6]

Cricket in Dunedin was initially slow to take advantage of the impetus offered by either gold or the visit of the All England XI in 1864. There were probably only four active clubs in 1868, and the strength of the Otago game remained as much with the various goldfields teams. But as Dunedin rapidly industrialised during the 1870s and 80s, leading the colony in population growth, commerce and wealth,[7] a plethora of new clubs and single teams emerged. In addition to the 4 or 5 dominant clubs that played in the senior competition at various times before 1914, there were as many as 60 teams in Dunedin during the early 1880s – although this number had declined by as much as half by the early 1890s. Some were schoolboy teams, many were fairly informal groupings, and most survived for only one or two seasons. Among the more active were Naval Brigade, St Matthew's Choir, Hillside Workshops, New Zealand Clothing Factory, City Guards Band, Headquarters Band, Saddlers Union, Coomb's Tannery, Combined Ironmongers, and Watchmakers and Jewellers. The Hillside railway workshops were especially dominant within the fabric of South Dunedin. They employed more than 400 staff by 1900 and maintained a strong involvement in numerous local sporting institutions.[8]

Such growth in the cities posed significant problems in terms of both the coordination of fixtures and the allocation of scarce playing spaces. For these reasons as much as a desire to arrange competition at an interprovincial and intercolonial level, the four main provincial cricket associations were formed between 1875 and 1883.

The earliest proposals to form associations stemmed from plans to send teams to Australia during the late 1860s. After the Canterbury/Otago match in Christchurch in February 1867 the two teams discussed the possibility of bringing a Victorian team to New Zealand. The outcome was a motion 'That no further steps be taken towards establishing the match with Victoria until a cricketing association be formed in each of the provinces of Otago and Canterbury'. Only four people attended another meeting on the subject held a month later, and nothing more was heard on the matter.[9] Instead, the first successful steps were taken in Wellington.

Under the chairmanship of C.A. Knapp, a solicitor and product of Lancing College, Sussex, seven clubs attended the inaugural meeting of the Wellington Cricket Association (WCA) on 22 October 1875. The Governor, the Marques of Normanby, accepted the position of Patron, and the Provincial Superintendent, William Fitzherbert, was elected President. Each club paid a £3.3s subscription and 11s for each match played on the Basin Reserve. These funds contributed to the employment of a full-time groundsman.[10] But the overriding concern was the need to present a united front to the public and to such bodies as the Wellington City Council with regard to developing the Basin Reserve and other grounds. The disjointed efforts of individual clubs had failed to raise sufficient funds from public subscriptions or to gain Council support for various deputations concerning future development.[11]

In different ways, both the Otago and Canterbury associations were founded in response to the visit of James Lillywhite's All England XI in February 1877. The Otago Cricket Association (OCA), 'Having for its objective the management of inter-provincial matches and the general advancement of the game' was formed at a meeting on 16 July 1876. Under the Presidency of W.D. Murison, editor of the *Otago Daily Times*, the original OCA was more of an elite 'super-club' designed to coordinate a strong Otago team to oppose the All England XI. To this end, a determination was also expressed to involve country cricketers in order to make the OCA truly provincial rather than just a Dunedin entity.[12] Conversely, the Canterbury Cricket Association (CCA) emerged to counter perceived apathy, disorganisation and jealousies between the leading Christchurch clubs that had marked arrangements for the game against the All England XI. E.C.J. Stevens, a provincial player and prosperous estate agent, initiated several meetings that led to the formation of a cricket association in June 1877.[13] After false starts in 1873, 1879 and 1881, the Auckland Cricket Association (ACA) was finally established on 20 October 1883.[14] As we will see in Chapter 7, other 'minor' associations followed from the early 1890s onwards.

For the most part, the four associations possessed influential leadership. This was especially the case in Wellington where the WCA had only two presidents from 1880 to 1936. The first, William Hort Levin, was an extremely prosperous businessman, philanthropist and Member of the House of Representatives (MHR).[15] His successor from 1893 was Francis Henry Dillon Bell, a New Zealand-born graduate of St John's College, Cambridge. Regarded as the leader of the New Zealand Bar from the early 1890s, he became one of the country's first King's Counsel in 1907. Several times Mayor of Wellington and an MHR, Bell held various ministerial port-folios, the attorney generalship and was acting prime minister for various periods during the early 1920s. Following W.F. Massey's death in 1925, he briefly held office as the first New Zealand-born prime minister.[16] Among the vice presidents and committee members of the WCA were various doc-tors, wealthy merchants and lawyers.[17]

The OCA committees during the late nineteenth century included the Commissioner of Crown Lands, leading Dunedin merchants, solicitors and a prosperous shipping agent. In Christchurch, the first four presidents of the CCA, H.P. Lance, 1877–78, E.C.J. Stevens, 1878–84, W.H. Wynn Williams, 1884–1902, and A.E.G. Rhodes, 1902–07, were all notable Canterbury public figures and MHRs. They were followed by Frederick Wilding, 1907–23, a solicitor, sporting patron extraordinaire and father of Anthony Wilding, four times Wimbledon tennis champion. Among the secretaries were T.D. Harman, a prominent solicitor, and F.C. Raphael, a successful estate agent. Both were to have a leading role in the formation of the New Zealand Cricket Council (NZCC) in 1894.[18] Similarly, although the ACA generally embraced a broader social spectrum, it began under the Presidency of James McCosh Clark, prominent businessman and former Mayor of Auckland, and featured numerous solicitors, company managers and a pro-fessor of classics among its committee members. The presidency was occu-pied from 1903–45 by Frederick Earl KC, a distinguished figure in the legal and public affairs of Auckland.

The Growth of the Minor Cricket Associations

Beyond the four main cities, patterns of cricketing growth and patronage were also evident in the few more populous provincial towns that were emerging by the late 1870s. By 1877 there were at least five clubs in the vicinity of Napier – including a Tradesman's CC and a Press CC.[19] Further clubs appeared in the wake of the visit of the first Australian team in 1878, including many in the surrounding country districts such as Parongahau, Wainui, Waipawa and Wairoa.[20] By 1879 Hamilton and Cambridge were combining for annual matches against Waipa County and there were suffi-cient clubs around Hamilton to establish a regular cup competition in 1888 – although this had fragmented by the late 1890s.[21] Six clubs were func-tioning in the vicinity of Palmerston North by the early 1890s, and in Taranaki both Hawera and New Plymouth provided strong focal points for local club cricket.[22] Support for cricket in the Wairarapa was particularly widespread. Aside from numerous short-lived clubs, there were more stable tradesmen's teams in Carterton and Masterton during the early 1890s, and the Wairarapa Farmers Co-Operative Association also boasted a club. At various times between 1895 and 1910 there were also enough teams to justify a Thursday Cricket Association, dominated by tradesmen and workingmen and separate from the more middle-class Wairarapa Cricket Association.[23]

The proliferation of clubs and the need to secure and control facilities naturally prompted the formation of local cricket associations. Waikato was first in 1881,[24] followed by Hawke's Bay in 1882 and regular inaugurations during the early 1890s: Southland was formed in 1891; North Canterbury (soon to become the Ashley County Cricket Association) in 1892; Manawatu, Marlborough, South Canterbury and Taranaki in 1893; and Wairarapa in 1894; by 1898 Westland also had an association.[25]

As with the main cities, control of these bodies was largely the preserve of local elites. The first president of the Hawke's Bay Cricket Association, William Russell was a soldier who became a wealthy runholder. An MHR 1875–81 and 1884–1905, he was Colonial Secretary, Minister of Defence and Minister of Justice 1889–91 and acknowledged leader of the opposition 1894–1905. Founding President of the New Zealand Racing Conference in 1887, he was created a Knight Batchelor in 1902.[26] His successor as Hawke's Bay president was E.H. Williams, a wealthy solicitor and runholder and the energetic first president of the NZCC. The Wairarapa CA benefited by similar influential patronage. The first president was W.C. Buchanan, a runholder with an extensive list of achievements in local affairs. He was MHR for all but six years from 1881 to 1914, MLC 1915–24, and knighted in 1913.[27] Among the thirteen presidents of the South Canterbury Cricket Association from 1893 to 1914 were five doctors, the son of an English peer and two of the region's wealthiest runholders – A.E.G. Rhodes and E.C. Studholme. Rhodes, educated at Christ's College, Christchurch, and Jesus College, Cambridge, was a solicitor who served as MHR 1887–93 and Mayor of Christchurch in 1901. Aside from numerous company directorships and other public posts, he was President of the Canterbury CA, the Canterbury Rugby Union and twice president of both the NZCC and the New Zealand Rugby Football Union.[28] Among the doctors, J.S. Hayes was educated at Trinity College, Dublin, and ran a private hospital in Temuka. C.E. Thomas, President of the NZCC in 1905–06, was resident surgeon at Timaru Hospital, and Norman Cox was a very prosperous dental surgeon who applied his administrative skills to a wide variety of athletic activities.[29]

Yet, as we will see shortly, these levels of patronage were not enough to overcome numerous demographic, economic and geographic obstacles that greatly restricted significant growth and participation until well after the turn of the twentieth century. Indeed, the plethora of minor associations was not to assume a significant role in New Zealand cricket until at least the 1950s.

Class Differentiation and Participation

The impetus for the provincial cricket associations lay very much with the dominant figures of the already-established clubs of the early 1870s who sought to bring a degree of continuity to an expanding network of clubs. But the urban growth of the last quarter of the nineteenth century presented them with new challenges in terms of reconciling the relative scarcity of grounds and resources with an increase of playing numbers and a diversity of competitive and social cricketing tastes.

An occupational analysis of club formation and composition in the senior competitions of the four main cities – based on 397 players traced for the seasons 1879/80, 1889/90 and 1899/1900 – reveals that social class provided the strongest defining element between the membership of different clubs, if not as explicitly stated as it had been during the early years of settlement.[30] To varying degrees, the four cities reveal correlations linking club membership with either broad occupational types or residential differentiation. It is common, for example, for a club composed largely of manual workers to emanate from a residential area of similar composition.

It is also apparent from the occupational analysis that working-class players are significantly under-represented in the upper echelons of New Zealand cricket – the senior club competitions and especially interprovincial teams – in relation to their proportion of the population. While those variously described as manual or blue-collar workers comprised a fairly static 60 per cent of the New Zealand adult male workforce during the period 1896 to 1926 it is doubtful whether they constituted much more than a third of senior players in the four cities.[31] Furthermore, and this can be said with some certainty despite the perils of occupational classification, the vast majority of this group appear to belong to the skilled, and – to a lesser extent – the semi-skilled, working-class (for example, carpenters, saddlers, compositors, printers and plumbers); labourers and other unskilled workers are entirely absent. We will see later in this chapter that necessity and a degree of inclination attracted more working-class cricketers to a variety of competitions below the publicly visible senior grades of the four main cities.

The manner in which the provincial associations integrated the various clubs is not a subject for generalisation. Much as the trend of recent New Zealand historiography has been to eschew the regional in favour of the general,[32] cricket reminds us that the varied origins of the settlements and their quite distinct geographical settings produced equally diverse and enduring legacies. Whereas Auckland and Wellington administrators appear to have been willing and able to accommodate an increase in numbers and a broadening of the social fabric, those in Dunedin and Christchurch became embroiled in decidedly acrimonious exchanges. It is necessary, then, to briefly consider each of the cities in turn.

Relative Tranquillity in the North

The lack of hierarchy and elite patronage during the formative decades of Auckland cricket appears to have continued throughout the nineteenth century. As Russell Stone points out, the vast majority of the Auckland com-mercial elite were derived from the English lower-middle class who, typi-cally, were comparatively young men when they began to establish their careers in New Zealand. Establishing a career – and with it success and status – in Auckland society came to depend less on professional standing than on judicious investment.[33]

For those members of the Auckland elite who were involved with cricket, it is not unreasonable to apply the argument used by Eric Dunning and Kenneth Sheard when describing the more diverse class composition of rugby in the North of England. They suggest that although many men were accumulating sufficient fortunes to be considered part of the upper-middle class from which sports administrators were commonly drawn, they initially lacked the traditional respectability, public school and Oxbridge traditions of 'gentlemen'. Thus, they were more easily able to maintain links with the wider community and their class of origin and to incorporate working people within their clubs.[34] In a similar vein, it seems that the class origins of many among the Auckland cricketing elite more readily disposed them towards clubs and competitions which involved players from a wider social spectrum than that encouraged by the vestiges of Wakefieldian idealism in other parts of New Zealand. Consequently, while it is evident that a greater proportion of Auckland's senior cricketers were engaged in professional, clerical and administrative rather than manual occupations, correlations between occu-pation, residential differentiation and the composition of specific cricket clubs are not necessarily obvious.[35]

Auckland generally had 5 or 6 stronger clubs engaged in a regular senior competition throughout the 1880s and the ACA expanded from 9 clubs with 12 teams in 1895/96 to 18 clubs and 39 teams by 1902/03.[36] Critical to such expansion was the development of several good-quality grounds. The Auckland City Council took control of the two-hundred-acre Auckland Domain in 1884 and, despite a constant shortage of funds, carried out major development of the area during the 1890s. By 1899 the Domain was able to cater for as many as sixteen matches on a Saturday afternoon and by 1908 grounds had also been established at Albert Park, at Victoria Park – on reclaimed land in Freeman's Bay, at Eden Park and at the Devonport Domain on the North Shore.[37]

Perhaps the clearest indication of the inclusive approach of the ACA can be seen in its adoption of a district cricket scheme during the 1903/04 season. Drawing on developments in Sydney and Melbourne club cricket during the 1890s, the scheme created a competition in which club member-ship was determined by residence within local body electoral boundaries rather than by player preference. The objective was to increase the com-petitiveness of local competitions by equalising the strength of the clubs, but, as much as anything, the scheme reflected the suburban expansion of Auckland's population during the early years of the twentieth century. District cricket did not automatically lead to the dismantling of established clubs. Rather, this tended to happen by default as the ACA no longer made any provision for them to play in its competitions. Nonetheless, the 1904 ACA Annual Report referred to the new competition as 'an unqualified success', with 498 registered players in six clubs.[38]

Similar patterns of growth are evident in Wellington. From the early 1880s the WCA presided over a senior competition that always contained at least four relatively strong clubs. By the 1890s there were also second and third grades composed of club, trade and school teams.[39] By 1905 the WCA had 33 teams in 4 Saturday grades, and the Wellington Wednesday Cricket Association boasted a further 14 teams.[40]

Nigel Beckford's analysis of Wellington club cricket certainly reveals some obvious differences in class participation. Those clubs with the greatest percentage of working-class participants were all from the newly industrialised areas of outer Wellington and none achieved senior status within the WCA competitions until the twentieth century. Of the clubs with the least percentage of working-class participants, all were from older and wealthier inner city areas and four of the six held senior status.[41] These patterns, though, were probably more a matter of pragmatism than deliberate policy by the WCA. Many of the newer suburban clubs obviously took time to develop a standard of play worthy of senior status.

The constant obstacle to clubs in Wellington was a lack of grounds. During the 1880s the Basin Reserve was the only ground that could be used for club cricket. In 1884 it staged one senior and two junior games each Saturday, with the other two senior teams obliged to sit out.[42] In 1892 the WCA announced that any junior team losing three games would be retired from competition at the end of January as the No.2 wicket was required for final senior matches.[43] This constraint was not satisfactorily resolved until 1904–05 when the WCA acquired suburban grounds at Days Bay, Johnsonville, Waiwhetu and Miramar.[44]

The willingness of the WCA to suspend senior matches in order that junior teams could participate perhaps served to dilute any potential objection to middle-class domination of senior cricket. Moreover, once a larger number of grounds became available, the WCA embraced a district cricket format in 1909/10. This was greeted with considerable optimism, although some complaint was directed at the Wellington Junior Cricket Association for not adopting district cricket as it was suggested that many players who remained with their old clubs in the lower grades should have been playing for senior district teams.[45] Whether their motives in not making the transition were purely social, or a reaction against the varied social origins of those whom they may have been obliged to play with in district clubs, is pure speculation. The Wellington press did not dwell on the matter and there is no sign of any further conflict over it.

Animosity in Dunedin

In the two South Island cities, similar problems to those faced by the WCA were rather less happily resolved. The single greatest difficulty facing the OCA and the diverse body of clubs that had emerged in Dunedin by the early 1880s was a lack of suitable grounds or the finance to develop appropriate sites if they could be found. As Dunedin's population and industry expanded rapidly within a limited area of flat land, its supply of even the most basic cricket grounds was constantly being eroded. As a result, many matches were played on rough paddocks and teams shared facilities that were seldom adequate for one of them.[46]

As concerns access to cricket, by 1882 the OCA's response to the issue was producing open hostility. The first salvo in the dispute came from a supporter of the working-class Albion club who bitterly attacked the failure to include any of its players among the 27 to practise for the match against Alfred Shaw's All England XI. The omission, according to the correspondent, was undoubtedly a reflection of the domination of the OCA by the elite Carisbrook club to the detriment of working-class cricketers.[47] Precisely what happened during the next few months is uncertain. Sometime during early June 1882 a meeting was held to form a predominantly working-class Dunedin and Suburban Cricket Association (D&SCA).[48] In a long letter to the *Evening Star*, 'Progress' reiterated the widespread lack of faith in the OCA:

> That the old Association have failed to carry out their fundamental principles must be generally conceded. Formed for the ostensible support and encouragement of the game, they have, from the exclusiveness of their proceedings, forfeited the confidence of the great majority of our cricketers. Their proceedings have long ceased to carry influence beyond their own magic circle, and for many years past the feeling of dissatisfaction has been generally expressed. The causes for such opinions are not difficult to arrive at. A cricketing Association, to be successful in its operations, should, in the onerous duty of selecting our representative cricketers, be represented by gentlemen in whom the general body of cricketers have every confidence. I am quite aware that it is a very difficult matter to give satisfaction to all, especially in selecting a team; but I have always considered that for representative teams to be selected by a Carisbrook-*cum*-Phoenix coalition as heretofore savours too much of exclusive representation to ever be acceptable to the cricketers generally.[49]

The D&SCA intended to overcome the perceived elitism of the OCA by electing a selection committee based on the votes of all of its member clubs. Nevertheless, it had every intention of working alongside the OCA to develop a more egalitarian approach to cricket in Dunedin:

Slowly but surely the feeling is gaining ground that the cricket field should be a platform on which all ranks should meet untrammeled [sic] by nice social distinctions, and I cannot but think the new project will be successful, if only from its endeavours to bring about this much needed reform.[50]

In similar tone, W.H. Skitch of the working-class Excelsior CC condemned the high subscription demanded by the OCA and concluded that 'it is not an association of cricketers, but of one particular class, who would not humble themselves to mix with the like of me and many others'. Members of the working-class could not afford to pay such a high subscription for 'the mere chance of playing in the interprovincial match'.[51]

Not all observers felt that a new cricket association was the answer. Addressing the problem of the limited number of playing areas in Dunedin, 'Free Ground' suggested that progress would only be made when cricketers combined together and petitioned parliament for control of grounds. As for the D&SCA, it constituted an unnecessarily divisive element in the efforts of Otago cricketers to reach an agreement with the Caledonian Society to use their ground:

The recently formed Association are [sic] the outcome of a movement in the wrong direction, which emanates from brains of a refreshing greenness in Otago cricket. It simply throws into the hands of the Caledonian Society the means of acquiring a continued revenue from cricket, when such should be devoted to cricket alone; and instead of bridging the gulf that I am sorry to say exists here amongst a few, it widens it irreparably. The exclusiveness that was somewhat admitted is now distinct and pronounced, and in this respect I fear the new Association will be ... a failure.[52]

In retort, 'Progress' insisted that the new Association would not be necessary if the old one had performed properly.[53]

Early in July 1882 meetings attended by both OCA and D&SCA delegates failed to reach agreement on an amalgamation, but it was suggested that the OCA should alter its rules in order to work in harmony with the new body.[54] Accordingly, a special meeting of the OCA in mid July initiated several amendments to the rules. Most importantly, the fee for individual members was reduced from 10s.6d to 2s.6d and the club subscription from two guineas to one. Each club would be entitled to 1 delegate on the management committee for each 30 members, with a maximum of 3 delegates. Later, a Challenge Cup competition was introduced in an effort to expand cricket among junior teams. Following these changes, the 1882 OCA Annual Report insisted that all possible measures had been taken to remove inequalities.[55]

However, progress toward unification or harmonious coexistence was halted by the politics of personality. In the first of several letters to the press,

Henry Hamer of the Carisbrook CC attacked the motives of the D&SCA and suggested that any reform to the OCA constitution should be pursued in legitimate fashion by a majority decision of the annual general meeting. The dominance of Carisbrook men was entirely the fault of other clubs who had made no attempt to curb their influence. A week later, Hamer was more forthright in his accusation. 'I insist upon saying that the D and SCA is composed of gentlemen banded together for malicious motives, and that their attitude is an affront to Otago cricketers'.[56] There were further bitter exchanges when the D&SCA met to formalise its rules on 23 July. When Henry Rose, a Repton- and Cambridge-educated businessman and committee member of the OCA, attempted to address the meeting, the chairmen refused to depart from the set agenda to allow him to speak. Rose and at least 20 others then left the meeting.[57] Thereafter the two associations went their separate ways.

By October 1882 the D&SCA claimed the support of 6 senior and 11 junior clubs with a combined membership of over 500; it had also negotiated terms for the use of the Caledonian Society ground and hired a groundsman. The OCA was now composed largely of members from the middle-class Carisbrook and Phoenix clubs, some from Albion who had declined to secede and the semi-rural Taieri and Kaikorai clubs which were elevated to a senior status that they would not otherwise have obtained.[58] In November the D&SCA, rather than the OCA, secured a match against the touring Auckland team. When the visitors arrived the OCA informed them that the home team was in no sense representative of Otago. Indeed, it was styled 'Dunedin and Suburban Cricket Association XI' rather than 'Otago', and the match has never been deemed first-class. Few spectators were willing to bet anything in favour of the local team, their judgement being confirmed as Auckland won by an innings and 45 runs. Three weeks later, Carisbrook defeated the same D&SCA XI by an innings and 110 runs.[59]

After these setbacks the D&SCA disintegrated. There is no mention of it beyond the end of 1882, and its members soon moved back within the fold of the OCA. Players formerly aligned with each association appeared in the Otago team that played Canterbury in February 1883.[60] Under its revised rules the OCA reported a considerable increase in membership, with 220 players being registered in October 1883. But the committee also warned of problems ahead unless more grounds could be found to accommodate the increase in numbers. If clubs, it entreated, would only combine into numerically and financially stronger bodies there would be more chance of securing facilities.[61]

The warning was not heeded and controversy resurfaced again in September 1884 with familiar protagonists. Under the auspices of the Carisbrook CC, a meeting of those clubs in possession of grounds was held to discuss the growing disparity between the number of clubs and the number of available grounds in Dunedin. To initiate proceedings, Henry Rose moved a motion to restrict the club programme of the OCA to competition between nine senior clubs and their 2nd XIs. Trusting that all clubs would accept the spirit of the meeting, he argued that Otago cricket would best be served by a small number of strong teams on few grounds, rather than a large number of scattered, weak teams. The motion was carried unanimously and a programme formalised for the season.[62]

The reaction from those clubs not invited to the meeting was immediate and predictable. In two letters to the *Otago Daily Times* 'Junior' outlined a widely held view that Rose's motion was a thinly disguised attempt to revive Carisbrook's domination of the OCA after the voting power of all clubs had rejected its delegates for committee positions at the previous annual general meeting. Furthermore, the unilateral decision to award senior status to such working-class clubs as Albion, Kaikorai and Roslyn, who were no better than many junior clubs and had inferior facilities, was nothing more than an attempt to buy their support for future OCA motions. Paramount among these motions, according to 'Junior', was a plan to raise OCA subscriptions to such a level that the association would soon revert back to the elite body of 1882. Finally, it was unfortunate that there were so few grounds in Dunedin, but this was not the fault of the juniors and they resented any plan that would force many of them to give up cricket. With or without Rose's scheme, there would still be the same number of willing cricketers in Dunedin.[63]

In an effort to reduce tensions and establish a compromise, a meeting of junior cricketers on 4 November 1884 suggested that the OCA should be invited to provide a trophy for competition among those teams excluded from its new nine-team competition. Amid complaints that such a trophy would produce nothing tangible for junior cricket, the motion was passed by a narrow majority.[64]

During the next ten months several junior teams seceded from the OCA, leading to a state of affairs in which only nine teams from seven clubs participated in the Junior Cup competition – a situation that once again left that body in a precarious financial position. By 1885 subscriptions from individual members had declined from 263 to 154 and club subscriptions amounted to only the £16.16s.0d derived from the nine senior clubs. Overall, the OCA paid a heavy price for its increasing alienation of working-class cricketers. The bank balance declined from £66 in 1880 to £1.6s in 1883 and an overdraft of £23 in 1885.[65] This left little finance for such important activities as the staging of interprovincial fixtures.

The need to secure paying members made the OCA far more cautious and diplomatic during the late 1880s. Although it could not overcome the shortage of grounds in Dunedin, the association endeavoured to make sure that all cricketers had a say in the use of those that were available. There was potential for controversy at the annual general meeting in October 1887 when a resolution was passed restricting the Senior Cup to only those teams that could provide a ground. At the same time, though, the constitution was entirely revised to make it more equitable. Monopoly by larger clubs was averted when it was resolved that only nominated club delegates and committee members, and not the financial members of all clubs, were entitled to vote at OCA meetings.[66] By October 1891 an OCA subcommittee was also making strenuous efforts to find and develop grounds, especially in North Dunedin. Although largely unsuccessful, this represented a significant advance on the rather insular standpoint of the early 1880s.[67]

After a decade of disharmony, the OCA was finally able to preside over an effective competition and a relatively democratic administrative structure from the 1890s onwards. Unlike its provincial counterparts, the OCA never felt the need to adopt a district cricket scheme, and there are no signs of agitation for one. But the transformation from the 1880s was achieved at some considerable cost to all but the best cricketers: a comparison between the 1882/83 and 1888/89 seasons reveals that a large number of the smaller clubs and trade teams had disappeared. During the 1882/83 season the *Otago Daily Times* reported the activities of 59 non-senior teams, of whom 35 played more than 5 games. Even allowing that the criteria for reporting cricket and other sports may have changed, only 14 non-senior teams were reported in 1888/89, of whom 11 played more than 5 games. Albion was described during 1888 as a 'mere wreck of its former self' and even the powerful Carisbrook CC fell on hard times, its membership declining from 137 in 1882 to 52 in 1889.[68]

The compromises reached in Wellington cricket suggest that the conflict in Otago was not inevitable. While there was not enough land or finance to accommodate the large numbers wishing to play cricket during the early 1880s, the arbitrary manner in which the OCA initially handled the crisis, and the broader class-based tensions that underpinned the respective positions, ensured that the dispute was more acrimonious and drawn out than it needed to be. The outcome can only be described as a qualified victory for egalitarianism.

The Changing Order in Christchurch

Christchurch cricket, because it did not suffer the problems of playing space endemic to Dunedin and Wellington, produced nothing during the nineteenth century to match the animosity of its southern neighbour. There were established and secure facilities at Hagley Park, Lancaster Park and, later, Sydenham Park, and a general abundance of flat land. The collective influence of Canterbury cricketers from 1850 onwards ensured that the prevailing concern was less a matter of finding suitable grounds as improving those they had. This, though, is not to suggest that Christchurch was entirely immune from controversy. Disputes between the United Canterbury and Albion clubs during the late 1860s, and between the successors of the same clubs and the CCA in 1905 and 1907, demonstrate that class consciousness was never far removed from the game.

The United Canterbury Cricket Club (UCCC) was the most enduring club in New Zealand, maintaining continuity from 1860 until at least 1907. It was generally debt-free, had an excellent ground and its matches were usually well patronised. The only thing it lacked in Christchurch was strong opposition. Moreover, Canterbury had not experienced the influx of new players seen in Otago during the peak gold era. While the revival of the working-class Albion club at the end of 1867 went some way to broadening the strength of Christchurch cricket, relations between the two clubs were variable. The first point of tension came over the matter of selecting provincial teams. An innings loss to Otago in February 1867 prompted the UCCC to announce that henceforth the provincial selection committee should be determined at a public meeting, but such damage control came too late. A letter to *The Press* from 'stumps' implied that the loss to Otago was in large part due to petty jealousy. The UCCC selectors had invited Albion players to attend practices for the interprovincial match, but they had not done so. Further, they were guilty of cricketing 'martyrdom' for their failure to assist with preparing Hagley Park for the match. In reply, 'Bat' insisted that Albion players had never been asked to attend practices and had not been considered for selection.[69]

That this dispute was perceived as a conflict of class is evident in the tone of 'stumps' first letter:

> Cricket is one of those games which ought to generate a sort of freemasonry among all those who take part in the game, no matter be they rich or poor, professional men or mechanics, as long as they conduct themselves in a respectable manner all differences of position should be thrown off with the ordinary everyday costume, and when the flannels are put on everyone should be equal, all striving to excel each other in the game.[70]

But 'stumps' determination to portray the UCCC as anything but exclusive did not sit easily alongside the decision of the club in 1868 to charge Albion £25 rent for practice and matches on its Hagley Park ground as against £5 paid by Christ's College – a body with a much sounder financial base. Although the rent was reduced to £20 during the 1869/70 season, the UCCC reserved for themselves all use of the pavilion.[71] It is also revealing that Albion, despite its meagre resources, arranged a wide variety of matches against clubs and surrounding districts while almost all of the UCCC fixtures were internal or scratch matches involving Christ's College players.[72]

The UCCC altered little over subsequent decades. The XI of 1884/85 contained at least 9 Christ's College old boys, and the 15 players who appeared in the senior team during the 1899/1900 season comprised 5 solicitors and a law clerk, 4 bank officers, an estate agent, a journalist, a secretary, a schoolmaster and a clerk. The last named was Arthur Sims, soon to become one of the wealthiest and most significant benefactors of New

FIGURE 2

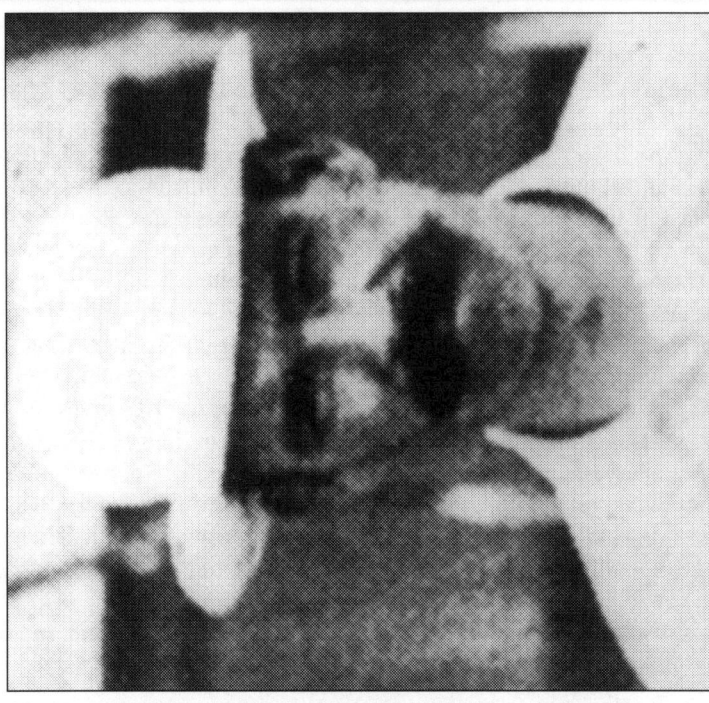

Alec Downes (1868–1950). Undoubtedly the best spin bowler in New Zealand prior to 1914, Downes' career was limited by the inability to gain regular leave from employment as a brass finisher; he played only two games in the North Island. (Weekly Press photo, Canterbury Museum: Ref. 14802)

FIGURE 3

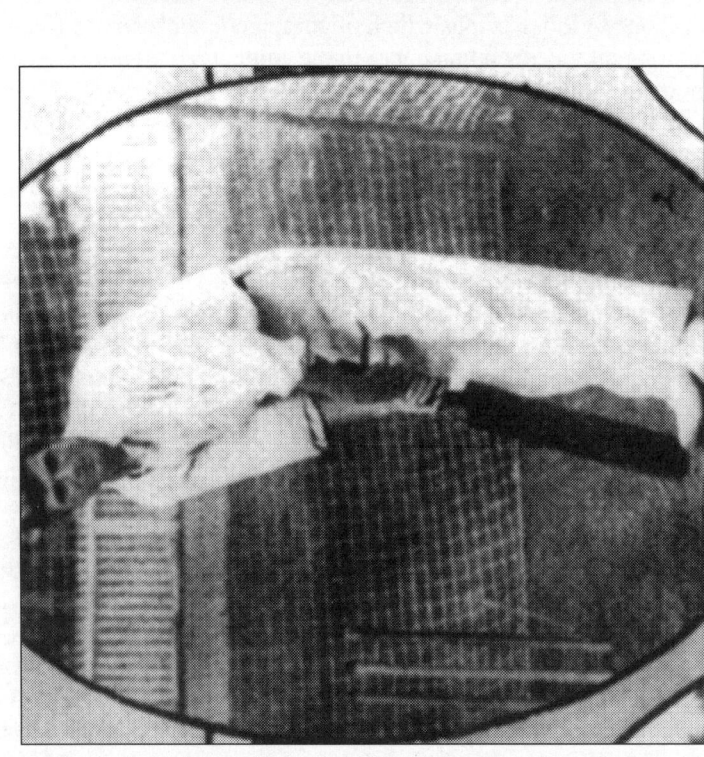

Arthur Sims (1877–1969). As a batsman Sims was good enough to play for, and captain, New Zealand. As a philanthropist, he financed the 1914 Australian team to New Zealand, and served for a long period as a New Zealand representative to the Imperial Cricket Conference. (Weekly Press photo, Canterbury Museum: Ref. 14801)

Zealand cricket during the twentieth century. The other increasingly dominant club, the Midland Canterbury Cricket Club (MCCC), which had
evolved from the former Albion CC around 1870, was always a more 'open'
body. The leading players of the 1880s and 90s included a bricklayer, a car-
penter, a draper, a salesman, a boot-maker, a compositor, a miller, a
telegraphist, various clerks and a schoolmaster – all of whom had played for
the Canterbury provincial team. By the turn of the century, though, the membership had become more middle class in character. It included L.T.
Cobcroft, a solicitor and the New Zealand captain on the 1899 tour to
Australia, and Daniel Reese, an engineer and – at the age of 20 – already
regarded as New Zealand's most talented player. From the 1883/84 season
these two clubs were joined in a formal senior competition by the Lancaster
Park CC, composed almost exclusively of clerks, and by various and more
sporadic Addington and Sydenham teams drawn from the new industrial
areas of the city. By 1905 there were at least 4 grades and in excess of 25
teams under the auspices of the CCA.

In March 1905, probably under the influence of Charles Bannerman – the
former Australian Test batsman who spent three years coaching at Christ's
College, the CCA established a subcommittee to initiate district cricket. At
further meetings in early June, Frederick Wilding stated that such a scheme
would increase the number of senior cricketers, promote rivalry between
them and increase public interest in the local competition. Obed Caygill
added that there were certainly sentimental difficulties regarding the long-
established clubs but the district cricket scheme was a progressive one and
opposition to it was selfish and unworthy of cricket. By a margin of 15 to 5
the CCA formally adopted district cricket in late July.[73] The working-class
Addington and Sydenham clubs quickly endorsed the scheme by majority
vote and Lancaster Park, under Wilding's influence, did so unanimously. But
the MCCC rejected the scheme outright, and the UCCC only adopted it on
the votes of its junior members. A later motion to have this decision reversed
was rejected. The general consensus was that district cricket would be given
a two-year trial.[74]

After the first season, the CCA had no doubt that it had made the right
move. As the 1906 Annual Report stated, 'The inception of District Cricket
has produced the greatest change that has yet taken place in connection with
our local cricket'.[75] Yet as the third season approached, the UCCC began to
agitate for change. At a club meeting on 6 July 1907 it was claimed that district cricket had been given a fair trial, but there was little interest in the
scheme and all clubs were now happy to revert to the old order. Keith
Ollivier, soon to represent New Zealand, suggested that district cricket had
been introduced 20 years too soon and that there were many incompetent
players in the senior grade. Eric Harper, a leading solicitor, added that there
had been far more sociability among the old clubs than now existed. Despite
some objections from junior members and accusations of disloyalty to the
CCA, a motion to revert to club cricket was carried 15 to 7.[76]

Critics of the UCCC had no doubt that the central issue was class rather than cricket. Writing to *The Press* on 9 July Obed Caygill criticised former players for trying to make decisions for younger club members. With six senior teams rather than four, district cricket ultimately exposed more players to a higher standard of cricket, and the social side was a small sacrifice against the improvements that were becoming evident.[77] D.H. Thomson, sometime Otago delegate to the NZCC, stressed that the social aspect of district teams would evolve in time: 'It is a question really for the members themselves, and if class distinction will only be set aside there is no fear for the social element'.[78] Ironically, though, the strongest criticism of the UCCC appeared under the pseudonym 'Old Christ's College Boy':

> There are a lot of good fellows in the UCCC, and first-rate sports who always play the game, come what may: but yet one finds also 'a heap of rotters' who deem it infra dig [sic] to play cricket nightly with men who earn their bread by honest toil ... Men of the calibre mentioned are not sports in the true sense of the word, but would be better termed social cricketers. If they would accept a hint from me, I would suggest that they quickly acquire part of the Exhibition buildings in North Park and get the front lawns and form a 'Rounders club' where their tribe might disport themselves and drink tea ad lib. Let us improve our cricket and sink the motives so apparent among the few.

The writer also accused UCCC members of disrupting the St Albans district club and failing to attend practices.[79]

Class was also the primary concern of a rather less sarcastic criticism of the UCCC by 'sporting Patriot'. He suggested that the old club system had produced strong cliques among Christchurch cricketers and certain feelings of 'caste', and 'unless one could claim possession of a distinct social status, a member of such a club would feel as much out of place as a salmon on a sidewalk'. Sporting Patriot went on to add that the advantage of district cricket was that it gave an opportunity to any player of suitable ability regardless of his background and that it would be unfair to abandon the new club system after two seasons in which it had not been possible to give it a fair trial, especially as one of the seasons had been very wet and the other was disrupted by the Christchurch International Exhibition of 1906–07.[80]

In reply to accusations of exclusivity, a member of the UCCC coupled the introduction of the district scheme – and the accompanying loss of club traditions – with the spectre of radical industrial unionism which was beginning to appear in New Zealand:

> Now ... a socialistic feeling ... a feeling akin to trade-unionism has even crept on to the cricket field, and cricketers are subject to dictation and can no longer follow their own inclinations. If cricket is to be a business, and nothing more than a business, then preserve your district

scheme and curtail the liberty of the cricketer. If it is to be a combination of cricket, good-fellowship and sportsmanship, then preserve the old club.[81]

Certainly, as long-established bodies, the UCCC and MCCC stood to lose more through district cricket than many younger, less secure clubs.

The MCCC presented more pragmatic objections to the district scheme, claiming that it was subject to abuse in that players were deliberately moving between districts in search of better clubs. Not even a plea from Daniel Reese, the New Zealand captain and a strong advocate of district cricket, could prevent a motion being carried 14 to 4 to revert to the club system.[82]

Finally, the CCA decided to resolve the matter once and for all by holding a plebiscite on the future of the district scheme, with voting to be restricted to current players from the competing clubs. A combined meeting of the MCCC and UCCC then insisted that voting should be open to school players and recent players. Furthermore, they threatened to withdraw Hagley Park from use by district clubs unless the CCA arranged a conference to discuss voting procedures. The CCA stood firm, insisting that it had its dignity to maintain and would not meet the two disgruntled clubs until their threat was withdrawn. The CCA position was overwhelmingly vindicated when the plebiscite endorsed district cricket by 262 votes to 40. At this point the two clubs conceded defeat, and faded quietly into obscurity.[83]

Feelings, however, did not die completely. In October 1911 the CCA found it necessary to alter the district boundaries to assist the East Christchurch and West Christchurch clubs, which were both struggling for members. Shades of the old debate resurfaced as critics claimed that district cricket had done little to increase the popularity of the game or satisfy players. Before the dispute could escalate, the CCA made East Christchurch an 'open' club and pointed out that the real obstacle to district cricket was a lack of suburban grounds for each club. As long as all cricket was concentrated on Hagley Park, Lancaster Park and Sydenham Park, boundaries between the clubs appeared a little arbitrary,[84] but the CCA did not have the necessary finance to develop more suburban grounds in order to resolve the dispute by such means.

Impediments to Working-Class Participation

There is, then, ample evidence that the administration of cricket in the four main cities and the limited resources available were dominated by middle-class interests. In some instances this was clearly by design, but this is offset by an evident determination on the part of many administrators and players to expand the basis of participation – especially through the district cricket schemes. Hence, explanations for the limited participation of working-class cricketers in the city club competitions should be phrased less in terms of deliberate exclusion and more in terms of aspects of the social structure that conspired against working-class cricket. Most important in this respect are the extent of urbanisation, regional and national infrastructure, occupational structure and working hours, and educational opportunities. Only when these elements of the social structure began to change during the early twentieth century did the composition of cricket follow suit.

First and foremost, representative cricket and a reasonable standard of senior-grade cricket could only function in an urban context, and New Zealand was not a highly urbanised society. A clear indication of this is the slow rise of the percentage of the total European population living in the four main cities – from 19.8 per cent in 1871 to 22.95 per cent in 1891 and 31.52 per cent in 1911.[85] Moreover, the total European population in towns of more than 8,000 people – other than the four main cities – increased from only 2.64 per cent in 1896 to 7.35 per cent in 1911. Compounding population issues was the fact that the distribution of this population was not conducive to organised sport. By 1891 there were still only 36 boroughs and town districts outside the four main cities with a population in excess of 1,000, a figure that increased to 52 by 1906.[86] In short, most regions lacked a potential pool of cricketers large enough to sustain strong local competition. As Chapter 6 will explain in more detail, the establishment and maintenance of good quality grounds and facilities – an issue far more pronounced in cricket than the various football codes – entailed expenses and effort beyond the reach of small groups and clubs in isolated rural areas. Even the four main provincial cricket associations were encumbered with huge debts for their troubles – not least in Wellington, where an estimated £2,590 was spent on the Basin Reserve. With the exception of Hawke's Bay and Nelson, the fortunes of the cricket associations outside the main cities were rather haphazard.[87]

Secondly, most of New Zealand's hinterland did not possess transport and communication networks favourable to country cricket. While the main towns on the East Coast of the South Island were well connected by rail from the late 1870s, coverage in the eastern and central North Island was limited. Following the Anglo-Maori conflicts of the 1860s, European penetration of the King Country and parts of Waikato was restricted until the late 1890s. Additionally, the main trunk railway linking Wellington and Auckland was not completed until 1908. Only after the turn of the century did rail networks, especially in the North Island, progress substantially beyond links between the main coastal centres. Dairying areas such as the Taranaki plains and Southland were relatively well served during the late nineteenth century by a growing road network of variable quality, while the generally drier climate and greater wealth of Canterbury and Otago ensured that they too made internal progress. Conversely, areas such as Northland and the central regions of both islands posed considerable difficulties for road travel until at least the late 1920s.[88]

The difficulty in arranging cricket matches under these conditions is typified by Arrowtown's journey to Lumsden to play Invercargill at the end of 1895. Despite the match being played at a mid-point between the two towns, the itinerary for the Arrowtown team was exhausting to say the least:

4.00 a.m.	coach left Arrowtown
6.15 a.m.	steamer left Queenstown
8.45 a.m.	train left Kingston
10.45 a.m.	team arrived at Lumsden
5.00 p.m.	train left Lumsden
12.00 a.m.	team arrived at Arrowtown

For their efforts, Arrowtown were beaten by 80 runs.[89]

The third major determinant of participation was the occupational structure. During the late nineteenth century New Zealand's four main cities contained the wealthiest and most influential stratum of businessmen and professionals, along with the vast majority of managerial, semi-professional, clerical and administrative occupations. Until the expansion of the industrial sector during the late 1890s semi-skilled and unskilled workers were predominantly rural,[90] hence these groups would always be under-represented in the stronger cricket competitions of the four main cities.

The considerable occupational transience of semi-skilled and unskilled workers, and the pre-industrial work patterns of many of the occupations, also posed problems for their cricket. Analysis of the 1891 Census reveals that seasonal workers – who were largely rural – constituted perhaps one third of the adult male European labour force and that more than half were transient for some part of the year. Indeed, two quite different means of measuring transience of European workers, taken over a 10- or 15-year period, have concluded that the New Zealand rate ranged from 50 per cent to as high as 75 per cent during the late nineteenth century. As one example, it is estimated that between 1900 and 1922 only half of all miners and watersiders were resident in one locality long enough to be included in street directories. Of the stable half, perhaps 70 per cent remained for less than five years and 50 per cent less than two.[91] Transience was a strong characteristic of young, single males – always the largest group of sporting participants, with obvious implications for regular and effective participation and for attempts to establish and administer clubs. For although sports clubs and other voluntary associations undoubtedly played a role in providing community cohesion and in incorporating some new arrivals into the local fabric, the best evidence available suggests that they catered for only a minority of the population and that this minority tended to be the settled core of long-term residents.[92]

Working hours also presented a barrier to playing regular cricket. The Saturday half-holiday – or any half-holiday for that matter – was still not standard for rural labourers after the turn of the century.[93] Indeed, the desire for such a holiday was one of the first points delivered in evidence by the Canterbury Agricultural and Pastoral Labourers Union in their unsuccessful attempt to gain an award in 1907–08. One of the few concessions made by the Arbitration Court when it finally rejected their claim was that 'whenever it is reasonably practicable each farm-worker shall be allowed a half-holiday on one day of the week, if he desires it'. Even then, it seems that the half-holiday was viewed by many workers not as an opportunity for recreation, but as a time for doing washing and other chores in order to keep Sunday free for rest and recreation.[94] This is an important distinction in that prevailing sabbitarianism ensured that organised, competitive cricket was not played on Sunday until at least the late 1960s.[95]

Nor were urban workers necessarily in a better position to participate in cricket. There is clear evidence of transience among the urban population as well as long working hours and limited application of the half-holiday. Moreover, low wages and periods of economic depression, especially during the 1880s, reduced disposable income and severely restricted opportunities for leisure. Significant change occurred only after 1890 when a wave of Liberal reform legislation, and particularly the Shops and Shop Assistants Act 1894 and the Shops and Offices Act Amendment Act 1905, formalised opportunities for leisure. They allowed for a weekly half-holiday beginning at 1 p.m. and stipulated that all commercial offices were to close no later than 5 p.m. on weekdays and 1 p.m. on Saturday.[96] Yet many workers remained outside the scope of this legislation, and others were still denied access to representative cricket in that their half-holiday was on Wednesday or Thursday, rather than Saturday – when all senior-grade cricket was played.

The problem was even more pronounced for those selected in provincial representative teams. With work leave required for days or weeks at a time in order to play and tour, interprovincial cricket became the domain of those with independent means or the most flexible working arrangements. Unsurprisingly, numerous provincial and national teams were dogged by the inability of original selections to tour. The most extreme case was undoubtedly Alec Downes of Otago. Unchallenged as the best spin bowler in New Zealand before 1914, Downes' inability to obtain leave from employment as a brass-finisher meant that he missed numerous Otago matches and played only twice in the North Island during a 26-year first-class career.[97] Moreover, as we will see in Chapters 6 and 7, there was little prospect of the financially strapped cricket associations or the NZCC adequately compensating anyone for loss of earnings. Indeed, an attempt to do so by the Council in 1914 almost triggered its demise.

Finally, educational opportunities were another significant impediment. In 1901 less than 3 per cent of the European population attended public secondary schools, with another 5 per cent in district high schools or Standard Seven classes. Despite the availability of free secondary education from 1902 and the increasing educational emphasis demanded by a changing occupational structure, the overall attendance figure had risen to only 13 per cent in 1921 and perhaps 20 per cent in 1939.[98] Yet as Chapter 6 will demonstrate, the secondary schools, and especially the elite institutions which followed the English public school model, were crucial training grounds for a disproportionate number of senior and representative cricketers as they provided good facilities and equipment and, most importantly, expert coaching. Even after 1900, primary schools were slow to shift from quasi-military physical drill to the codified sports of their secondary counterparts. The majority of the population therefore went without the benefits of easy access to formal instruction.

On a more speculative level, it is probable that many players simply had no interest in playing formal grade cricket – irrespective of whether they could afford it. Then, as now, some undoubtedly preferred a social game with workmates rather than the demands of competition. To cater for the social cricketer, and for those with a mid-week half-holiday, all of the main cities had developed separate competitions by the mid 1890s. Exactly how these were formed or operated is less easily understood. Press coverage of their proceedings is minimal, and coverage of their play makes it difficult to reliably identify individuals.

The Auckland Cricket Association inaugurated a Wednesday competition for the 1903/04 season, but it was not until 1913 that Auckland's various mid-week and workplace competitions came together under the Auckland Suburban Cricket Association (ASCA). At a series of meetings in September and October 1913, the new body stated that its objectives were to loosen the 'prevailing conservatism' of Auckland cricket by providing cheaper and more accessible facilities for the many young people wishing to play in the city and suburbs. But having said this, the new association remained firmly affiliated to the ACA. Its first president was Frederick Earl KC and its patron W.F. Massey, New Zealand Prime Minister 1912–25.[99]

Among the earliest teams to join the ASCA were Auckland Gas Company, Brotherhood, Carlton, Druids, Herald (newspaper staff), Maritime, Newmarket, Onehunga, Papatoetoe, Plasterers Union, Railway Workshops, Remuera and Tramways – all of which were geographically specific or workplace-based teams. By April 1914 an ASCA team had played three matches on a tour of the far north, and matches were arranged against junior representative teams from the ACA.[100]

A Wednesday Cricket Association was active in Wellington from at least 1892 and a Wellington Junior Cricket Association was formed during the same year.[101] Although little can be determined of developments during the next two decades, the Wednesday Cricket Association was strong enough to promote a tour by the South Melbourne CC in 1912/13.[102] In July 1921 the Wellington Mercantile Cricket League was established, and from an initial entry of 16 teams it expanded to 38 by 1930 and 60 by 1937.[103]

Such competitions were even more active in Christchurch. From the early 1860s there were regular games between workplaces and trades, with the butchers and bakers in particular having active clubs. By 1898 a Thursday Cup competition was well established and the Thursday Cricket Association was affiliated to the CCA. With an increasing number of fixtures between suburban and workplace teams, the Christchurch Suburban Cricket Association (CSCA) was formed in late 1905. Under the guidance of the Rev. R.J. Gray of the Oxford Tce Baptist Church, the original membership consisted of eight clubs: Addington Railway Workshops, A.J. White's (furniture manufacturers), Lyttelton, Oxford Tce Baptist Church, Spreydon, St Matthew's Guild, Sumner and Templeton.[104] By 1908 their were 17 teams and a total of 354 registered players, who each paid a 6d fee; in 1914 there were 40 teams and 500 registered players, with clubs like Islington-Hornby, Sydenham Hockey Club, Druids and Waimairi now becoming involved.[105] By 1910 teams from the CSCA were regularly visiting country areas and Banks Peninsula, and at Christmas 1914 a representative team visited Dunedin to play in the recently formed Otago Cricket League; a team from the Wellington Boys' Cricket League visited Christchurch soon after. As ever, the major problem facing the CSCA was a lack of grounds. Numerous negotiations with the Christchurch City Council resulted in access to a ground in South Hagley Park, and another was obtained from the Canterbury Football Association, but facilities were never adequate.[106]

The Otago Cricket League, formed at the beginning of the 1913/14 season, is the most difficult to trace. It included two teams from the Hillside Railway Workshops, one each from the YMCA, Railways and Tramways, two from Reid and Grey's (engineers/ironfounders), one from Hayward's (furniture manufacturers) and one from Standard. There are no reports of either meetings or administrators for this League.[107]

Without a more detailed analysis of the membership of these organisations it is unwise to characterise them as a purely working-class response to the established order. In part they were an expedient based on work patterns and personal preference. Yet their increased formalisation and expansion during the first decade of the twentieth century may be as much a reflection of urban growth and changing occupational structure. While many clubs were based on workplaces and trades, many others were geographically based – encompassing cricketers who lived in new suburbs at some distance from the old inner city clubs that revolved around grounds such as Hagley Park in Christchurch or the Basin Reserve in Wellington. Even among the older cricket associations, the shift to district cricket schemes is a clear acknowledgment of the changed distribution of the population.

One can also speculate as to whether these new suburban clubs were necessarily a bastion for working-class cricket. Urbanisation, industrialisation and specialisation altered the occupational structure considerably from 1890 to 1914. While the percentage of employers and professionals in the workforce remained fairly constant, that of semi-professionals and white-collar workers in general expanded rapidly – especially in secretarial, clerical and sales positions. Conversely, the percentage of skilled and semi-skilled workers expanded more slowly and the unskilled shrank dramatically.[108] There is no reason to doubt that cricket clubs also embodied such change.

Without detailed press coverage and extant club records, it is impossible to pursue this line of enquiry much further. Moreover, without an analytical framework that avoids the pitfalls of occupational classification and imprecise identification, it is stretching credibility to theorise about developments too far beyond the publicly visible domain of cricket associations and their constituent senior clubs. The participation rate in representative cricket for semi-skilled and unskilled workers in 1890 was kept to a minimum by a lack of urbanisation as much as by inflexible working conditions. Provincial and national teams were drawn almost exclusively from competitions played on Saturdays in the four main cities. But in 1914, when many of the earlier impediments had been removed, the lower participation rate of semi-skilled and unskilled workers may reflect nothing more than their diminishing percentage of the population – and the urban population in particular. This, then, says more about demography than it does about cricket.

At best it can be said that the cricket associations maintained a passive rather than active attitude to expansion in that their senior competitions and representative teams remained firmly geared to the Saturday half-holiday and to the preferences of the middle-class cricketer. Certainly, the leading administrators were generally drawn from a privileged background, but this is no basis for a sustainable theory of class exclusiveness. Indeed, the relative lack of dispute and antagonism within the cricketing fabric of the four main cities suggests that most cricketers found their niche.

Notes

1. E. Olssen, 'Social Class in Nineteenth Century New Zealand' in D. Pitt (ed.), *Social Class in New Zealand* (Auckland, 1977), p. 34.
2. Ibid., p. 35.
3. In New Zealand the term 'senior' is commonly used to denote competition between the first XIs of leading clubs within a city or district. First-class provincial teams, equivalent to English county or Australian state teams, are selected from participants within the senior competitions.
4. *New Zealand Herald*, 10 Oct. 1873, p. 3; 17 Nov. 1873, p. 3.
5. Reese, *New Zealand Cricket 1841-1914*, p. 24; *Wellington Independent*, 25 Jan. 1868, p. 4; 1 Feb. 1868, p. 5.
6. See, for example, *Lyttelton Times*, 2 March 1861, p. 5; *The Press*, 3 Jan. 1863, p. 6; 11 Dec. 1863, p. 4; 10 Oct. 1865, p. 2; 2 Dec. 1867, p. 2; P. Norris, 'A Social Portrait of Canterbury in 1870' (MA thesis, University of Canterbury, 1963), pp. 77–8.
7. Olssen, 'Social Class', p. 35.
8. G. Tait, 'The History of the Otago Cricket Association in the Nineteenth Century' (MA thesis, University of Otago, 1974), p. 55; E. Olssen, *Building the New World: Work, Politics and Society in Caversham 1880s–1920s* (Auckland, 1995), pp. 27–8, 42; *Centennial Souvenir Programme*, p. 35.
9. *The Press*, 14 Feb. 1867, p. 2; R.T. Brittenden, *100 Years of Cricket: The History of the Canterbury Cricket Association 1877–1977* (Christchurch, 1977), p. 7.

10. *Evening Post*, 23 Oct. 1875, p. 2; 28 Oct. 1875, p. 2.
11. Neely, *100 Summers*, p. 21.
12. *Otago Daily Times*, 17 July 1876, p. 3.
13. *The Press*, 11 May 1877, p. 3; 8 Aug. 1877, p. 3.
14. *100 Not Out: A Centennial History of the Auckland Cricket Association* (Auckland, 1983), p. 13; *New Zealand Herald*, 22 Oct. 1883, p. 6; ACA, Annual Report, 1885.
15. Scholefield, *Dictionary*, *Vol.1*, p. 495.
16. W.J. Gardner, 'Francis Henry Dillon Bell' in Orange (ed.), *DNZB: Vol.2*, pp. 34–6.
17. N. Beckford, 'Working Class Participation in Wellington Club Cricket 1878–1940' (BA Hons research essay, Victoria University of Wellington, 1981), p. 53.
18. G.R. Macdonald, Canterbury Biographical Dictionary, Canterbury Museum Library, Christchurch, passim.
19. F.F. Cane, *Cricket Centenary: The Story of Cricket in Hawke's Bay 1855–1955* (Napier, 1955), p. 15.
20. Ibid., pp. 17, 21; M.D.N. Campbell, *Story of Napier 1874–1974* (Napier, 1974), p. 276.
21. Reese, *New Zealand Cricket 1914–33*, pp. 584–5.
22. Ibid., pp. 585–6.
23. *Seventy Five Years of Cricket*, pp. 9, 13, 15.
24. Reese, *New Zealand Cricket 1914–33*, p. 585.
25. NZCC Annual Report, 1898.
26. S.W. Grant, 'William Russell Russell' in Orange (ed.), *DNZB, Vol. 2*, pp. 436–7.
27. Scholefield, *Dictionary*, *Vol.1*, p. 124.
28. Ibid., *Vol.2*, p. 229.
29. *The Cyclopedia of New Zealand: Industrial, Descriptive, Historical, Biographical*, Vols. 1–6 (Wellington and Christchurch, 1897–1905), Vol. 3, pp. 143–4, 991; hereafter referred to as *CNZ*.
30. These details are derived from Chapters 6 and 7 of my Ph.D. thesis, 'Where the Game was Played by Decent Chaps'.
31. P. M. Meuli, 'Occupational Change and Bourgeois Proliferation: A Study of New Middle Class Expansion in New Zealand 1896–1926' (MA thesis, Victoria University of Wellington, 1978), pp. 28–38.
32. See in particular M. Fairburn, *The Ideal Society and its Enemies: The Foundations of Modern New Zealand Society 1850–1900* (Auckland, 1989).
33. R.C.J. Stone, *Makers of Fortune: A Colonial Business Community and its Fall* (Auckland, 1973), pp. 41–2.
34. E. Dunning and K. Sheard, *Barbarians, Gentlemen and Players: A Sociological Study of the Development of Rugby Football* (Canberra, 1979), pp. 141–2.
35. Olssen, 'Towards a New Society', p. 256; R.W. Armstrong, 'Auckland by Gaslight: An Urban Geography of 1896', *New Zealand Geographer*, 15, 2 (1959), p. 182.
36. *100 Not Out*, p. 111.
37. Ibid.; G.W.A. Bush, *Decently and in Order: The Government of the City of Auckland, 1840–1971* (Auckland, 1971), pp. 168–70.
38. ACA, Annual Report, 1904.
39. Beckford, 'Wellington Club Cricket', p. 29; Neely, *100 Summers*, p. 45.
40. Beckford, 'Wellington Club Cricket', p. 29; Neely, *100 Summers*, p. 67.
41. Beckford, 'Wellington Club Cricket', p. 30.
42. Neely, *100 Summers*, p. 29.
43. Ibid., p. 45.
44. Ibid., pp. 66–7.
45. *The New Zealand Free Lance*, 2 Oct. 1909, p. 19; 19 March 1910, p. 18; 26 March 1910, p. 18.
46. Tait, 'History', p. 55.
47. *Otago Daily Times*, 10 Jan. 1882, p. 3.
48. *Evening Star*, 16 June 1882, p. 2.
49. Ibid., 21 June 1882, p. 2.
50. Ibid.
51. S.A.G.M. Crawford, 'A History of Recreation and Sport in Nineteenth Century Colonial Otago' (Ph.D. thesis, University of Queensland, 1984), p. 240.
52. *Evening Star*, 22 June 1882, p. 4.
53. Ibid., 24 June 1882, p. 4.
54. *Otago Daily Times*, 3 July 1882, p. 2; 5 July 1882, p. 2; 8 July 1882, p. 2.

55. *Otago Witness*, 22 July 1882, p. 21; OCA, Annual Report, 1882.
56. *Otago Daily Times*, 31 July 1882, p. 2.
57. Ibid., 24 July 1882, p. 3.
58. G. Griffiths, 'A History of Otago Cricket', *c.*1976. Dunedin, unpub. MS.
59. *Otago Witness*, 2 Dec. 1882, p. 21.
60. Reese, *New Zealand Cricket 1841–1914*, p. 231.
61. OCA, Annual Report, 1883; *Otago Daily Times*, 1 Oct. 1883, p. 3.
62. *Otago Daily Times*, 29 Sept. 1884, p. 2.
63. Ibid., 9 Oct. 1884, p. 3; 13 Oct. 1884, p. 3.
64. Ibid., 5 Nov. 1884, p. 4.
65. Ibid., 14 Nov. 1885, p. 3; OCA, Annual Report, 1880, 1883, 1885.
66. OCA, Annual Report, 1887; *Otago Daily Times*, 3 Oct. 1887, p. 3; 10 Oct. 1887, p. 3.
67. OCA, Committee Minutes, 7 Nov. 1891, 30 Sept. 1892.
68. Griffiths, 'History of Otago Cricket', n.p.
69. *The Press*, 20 May 1867, p. 2; 20 Aug. 1867, p. 2; 23 Aug. 1867, p. 2; 26 Aug. 1867, p. 2.
70. Ibid., 20 Aug. 1867, p. 2.
71. Ibid., 24 Sept. 1867, p. 2; 15 Sept. 1868, p. 3; 7 Sept. 1869, p. 2; UCCC, Annual Report, 1869.
72. *The Press.*, 13 Dec. 1866, p. 2; 21 Nov. 1867, p. 2; 29 Nov. 1867, p. 2; 9 Dec. 1868, p. 2.
73. CCA, Committee Minutes, 10 June 1905; 20 June 1905; *New Zealand Referee*, 5 April 1905, p. 55; 26 July 1905, p. 50.
74. *New Zealand Referee*, 5 July 1905, p. 53; 12 July 1905, p. 55; 19 July 1905, p. 55; 30 Sept. 1905, p. 49.
75. CCA, Annual Report, 1906.
76. *The Press*, 8 July 1907, p. 7.
77. Ibid., 9 July 1907, p. 8.
78. Ibid.
79. Ibid., 10 July 1907, p. 8.
80. Ibid., 17 July 1907, p. 12.
81. Ibid., 12 July 1907, p. 7.
82. Ibid., 15 July 1907, p. 8.
83. Ibid., 24 July 1907, p. 6; 5 Aug. 1907, p. 9; 21 Aug. 1907, p. 7; CCA, Committee Minutes, 23 July 1907; 20 Aug. 1907; CCA, Annual Report, 1907.
84. *Lyttelton Times*, 3 Oct. 1911, p. 6; 11 Oct. 1911, p. 6.
85. Figures derived from Olssen, 'Towards a New Society', p. 256; Olssen, 'Social Class', p. 35.
86. Olssen, 'Towards a New Society', p. 256; *New Zealand Census*, 1891: Pt.1, pp. 24–7; 1906, pt.1. pp. 29–31.
87. Reese, *New Zealand Cricket 1914–33,* p. 135f.
88. Grey, *Aotearoa and New Zealand*, pp. 333–7.
89. Reese, *New Zealand Cricket 1841–1914*, p. 110.
90. Olssen, 'Towards a New Society', pp. 272–3; Olssen, 'Social Class', pp. 34–5.
91. Olssen, 'Towards a New Society', p. 275; J.E. Martin, *The Forgotten Worker: The Rural Wage Earner in Nineteenth Century New Zealand* (Wellington, 1990), pp. 14–15; Belich, *Making Peoples*, pp. 413–15.
92. Belich, *Making Peoples*, p. 416; Fairburn, *Ideal Society*, pp. 158–87.
93. Fairburn, *Ideal Society*, pp. 185–7.
94. B.J.G. Thompson, 'The Canterbury Farm Labourers' Dispute, 1907–8: a study of the first attempt by a union of farm labourers to come under the New Zealand arbitration system' (MA thesis, University of Canterbury, 1967), pp. 40–60, 220–3.
95. Lineham and Collins, 'Religion and Sport', pp. 298–9.
96. Fairburn, *Ideal Society*, pp. 125–34, 185–7; *New Zealand Statutes*, 1894, No.32; 1905, No.43.
97. D. Richmond, 'Alexander Dalziel Downes' in Orange, *DNZB: Vol.2*, pp. 123–4.
98. Olssen, 'Towards a New Society', pp. 276–7.
99. ACA, Annual Report, 1904; T. Hyland, *Golden Jubilee of Domain Cricket* (Auckland, 1964), p. 11.
100. Hyland, *Domain Cricket*, p. 12.
101. Beckford, 'Wellington Club Cricket', pp. 24–8; Neely, *100 Summers*, p. 45.
102. W. Wilhelm, typescript notes on South Melbourne CC tour of New Zealand 1912–13, in possession of author.

103. Reese, *New Zealand Cricket 1841–1914*, p. 99; *50 Years of Cricket, 1921–71: The History of the Wellington Mercantile Cricket League (Inc.)* (Wellington, 1971), pp. 7–9.
104. W.E. Skelton, *Not Out … 75: The Official History of the Christchurch Suburban Cricket Association* (Christchurch, 1980), pp. 15–17.
105. Ibid., p. 17.
106. Ibid., pp. 19–24.
107. *Otago Witness*, 29 Oct. 1913, p. 54; 5 Nov. 1913, p. 55.
108. Olssen, 'Towards a New Society', pp. 272–3.

4

A Physical and Moral Agent,
1860–1914

Within Victorian and Edwardian culture, cricket served as a metaphor for a wide range of equally significant and interrelated social objectives. The relationship between physical and mental health, the maintenance of appropriate standards of morality, the cultivation of 'manly' character, British cultural and racial superiority and British martial superiority were all linked to the encouragement of cricket. If anything, these themes were more accentuated in Britain's colonies where the standard rhetoric was for a long time coloured by equally strong concerns over the quality of the new society in relation to the ideal of the 'mother country'. Indeed, the earliest observers of New Zealand cricket, if not always the players, were seldom content that the game should merely be played in the fledgling settlements. They were as much concerned with the 'form' of the game on the field and the manners and mores this helped to shape off the field. While the nature of the New Zealand rhetoric displayed certain key differences to other parts of the Empire, it was nevertheless pursued with an equally determined conviction.

Health and Muscular Christianity

Aside from classical Greece, from whence they drew so much inspiration, there have been no more acutely health-conscious people than the Victorians. Under their tutelage, physiology and psychology emerged as separate approaches to medicine, and physical training became a vital component of overall physical culture. On the one hand, there was a utilitarian pragmatism aimed at providing a counter to various social ills.[1] Primary among these were alcoholism and sexual immorality – the former of which certainly became a subject for New Zealand commentators. But above all else, the new 'mania' for health stressed the interdependence of a healthy body and a healthy mind. Without achieving the former, one could not hope to possess the latter – or, as David Newsome neatly expresses it, 'I act therefore I am'.[2]

It was inevitable that a powerful alliance emerged between health and organised sport. Indeed, both Bruce Haley and Keith Sandiford have suggested that the Victorian preoccupation with health was an essential means of rationalising the place of sport in society. Earlier nineteenth-century fears that sport may contribute to delinquency and to an uneasy blurring of social class distinctions were replaced by an idealisation of the role of sport in the quest for higher human excellence. As Haley explains, sport provided a way of 'reconciling the pleasure of bodily self-awareness with the duty of moral self-improvement'.[3]

To the obsession with health, Thomas Hughes, Charles Kingsley and a proliferation of cricketing clerics added an important religious dimension – 'muscular Christianity' – that stressed the bond between sport, manliness and godliness. Precisely what was meant by 'manliness' in Victorian terms is not always easy to define. Honesty, maturity and a strong sense of moral duty were certainly paramount, as was Kingsley's emphasis on robust energy and physical vitality.[4] Keith Sandiford summarises the movement in these terms:

> The Victorians revived the medieval concept of the chivalrous knight and emerged with the notion of the Christian cricketer. Godliness and Manliness, spiritual perfection and physical power, became inextricably interwoven. It was not likely, in their view, that a feeble body could support a powerful brain.[5]

Cricket, above all other sports, was the vehicle through which muscular Christianity was articulated. As the oldest of the formalised English games, it was conceived as the one least tainted by vice and human foibles.[6]

Inevitably, both the spiritual and physical metaphors also fused with notions of imperial virility and unity. The qualities required of an archetypal sporting Christian were just those required to maintain the frontiers of empire. Furthermore, implicit is an explanation of the perceived cultural and racial superiority of Britons over other Europeans.[7] While many commentators were obliged to acknowledge the military and commercial abilities of rival European nations and empires, especially France and Germany, they had no hesitation in claiming that it was a superior attitude to, and execution of, athleticism which elevated Britain to its primacy in world affairs.

The New Zealand Ideology

Any discussion of the metaphors associated with cricket in New Zealand rests largely in a secular and imperial context. As Chapters 8 and 9 will show, the vast majority of rhetoric was inspired by the visits of English and Australian touring teams and the implications that their presence held for imperial unity. Yet there is almost no sign of an independent religious or literary tradition underpinning New Zealand cricket. Like all colonies, New Zealand took time to develop its own strata of middle-class intellectuals

FIGURE 4

Burke's Pass Sloggers, 1871–72. This team of South Canterbury runholders contained numerous English public school old boys and Oxbridge graduates. (Canterbury Museum: Ref. 13690)

FIGURE 5

The Canterbury and Otago teams pose in front of the pavilion built to mark the visit of Parr's All England XI to Dunedin in January 1864. The match between these two teams on 27 February is recognised as the first first-class match in New Zealand. (Weekly Press photo, Canterbury Museum: Ref. 8915)

FIGURE 6

The Canterbury team, 1906–07. This team defeated the MCC by seven wickets – but lost the return fixture by 236 runs. T.W. Reese, author of the two-volume history *New Zealand Cricket*, is second from the left in the back row. (Weekly Press photo, Canterbury Museum)

FIGURE 7

Christ's College XI, 1879. Christ's College made a significant contribution to Canterbury cricket from the 1860s onwards – providing perhaps one-third of all provincial players by 1914. The master in this group is Canon F.A. Hare – devoted cricket coach and College chaplain. (Christ's College Collection)

capable of articulating such ideas. More surprisingly, there is a marked absence of sustained comment on the game from the churches. Certainly, F.A. Hare was a determined cricketing cleric at Christ's College and there were a number of church-based teams in the mid-week and suburban cricket competitions that emerged during the first decade of the twentieth century. There are, though, no obvious signs of a pronounced eulogising of the game from the pulpit or from the pens of the clergy.

The only explanation that presents itself here, and it is certainly not a comprehensive one, relates to the relatively loose grip of religion over colonial New Zealand society. A degree of religious earnestness appears in some of the early settlement schemes – most obviously in the ideals of Presbyterian Otago and Anglican Canterbury – and the majority of New Zealand colonists claimed to be at least nominally Christian. But church attendance during the nineteenth century was not high, being lower than both Britain and the Australian colonies, and there is evidence in the new colonial setting of far less deference to the traditional authority of the churches.[8] Yet this is not to suggest that the influence of the churches should be entirely underestimated, hence the absence of recorded comment on cricket is, therefore, surprising.

Without doubt, the elite secondary schools (to be discussed in the next chapter), provide the richest source of moral cricketing metaphors. Beyond these institutions one is reliant upon the press – a source that demands close scrutiny in terms of both its reflection and diffusion of opinion. Of greater significance are the limits of the ideology itself. The New Zealand emphasis on 'manly' sporting values employs the same brand of Victorian chauvinism and quasi-medical determinism that prevailed in Britain. Women's cricket, far more than any other sport played by women, was criticised and marginalised as a threat to the masculine construct, and the version which was played in New Zealand was marked by rigid bounds from which it departed at its peril. At the same time New Zealand cricket lacks the racial dimension familiar to so much of what was embodied by muscular Christianity in other parts of the British Empire. While a number of Maori players made a quite visible contribution to the growth of New Zealand rugby before 1914 – and were received with predictable Victorian sentiment – only a select few played cricket at a competitive level. Equally, and in view of the limitations on working-class cricket outlined in the previous chapter, one cannot be at all sure that either the moral or imperial ideology penetrated working-class consciousness to any significant degree. Thus, when subjected to the trinity of race, gender and class, the publicly visible face of New Zealand cricket – that which conveyed its imperial and international themes – was somewhat less than representative.

Physical and Mental Abilities

The most common rhetoric attached to New Zealand cricket during the mid-nineteenth century stressed the physical and mental attributes required on the field as a metaphor for qualities of life off it. As the *New Zealander* reflected during Wellington's first visit to Auckland in December 1862:

> [T]he very training and education necessary to the acquisition of knowledge of it demand[s] a keen and sharp discipline of brain, eye and hand, which imparts a consequent influence upon the moral character, inspiring confidence in difficult situations, suggesting resources in danger, exciting a laudable ambition to excel, and an energy in the performance of every duty.[9]

Viewed from a military standpoint, those who had been trained properly on the cricket field would ultimately be the fittest, bravest and most skilled soldiers. In a similar vein, *The Press* heralded the visit of George Parr's All England XI to Christchurch in February 1864 by reminding its readers that the object of all games lay not in winning, but in the healthful benefits to be derived from participation:

> The object is of course worthless, but the habits of discipline induced in attaining it last a man for life, not only by hardening the muscles and strengthening the nerves, and expanding the lungs, and making the whole man a nobler and more perfect animal, capable of attaining to a far higher degree of physical enjoyment, but still more by accustoming him to habits of self-denial and self-sacrifice for a cause in which his selfishness is utterly lost.[10]

Kingsley and Hughes could not fault the emphasis on steadiness, discipline and the need for a perfect harmony between body and mind. Nor could they have faulted the *New Zealand Times* in January 1882 when it speculated on the reasons for cricket's primacy over other games:

> How this game became the national sport of Englishmen is difficult to say. Perhaps it may have been because no other creates in so high a degree a demand for all the qualifications produced by first-class physical training, strength, and speed, the harmonious action of eye, hand and foot, quickness of eye, courage and endurance, capacity for individual resource, with complete subjection to discipline.[11]

As we will see later, the *Times* could be equally forthright about a Wellington representative team that consistently failed to match these objectives in its encounters with English and Australian tourists.

Promoting good health was obviously balanced by the desire to prevent bad health. Here, cricket was presented as a deterrent to the mid-Victorian proclivity for excessive drinking and smoking. The *New Zealand Herald*, moved by the proliferation of new clubs in Auckland at the end of 1865, provided an unequivocal endorsement of cricket as a counter to disease and excess:

> [I]t at once becomes a powerful antagonist to disease – a strong opponent of over-indulgence and the too free use of alcoholic stimulants as aid to digestion, and a benefit to society. It is therefore justly entitled to the support of all fathers of families and those who have the training and education of our youth, and we trust that it will ever continue to enjoy the popularity which it has now acquired.[12]

In February 1867, C.B. Borlase, MHR and soon-to-be President of the United Wellington CC, informed a dinner for the visiting Nelson team that 'Cricket is a manly game, and it is very much better that young men should devote their time to it than spend it in public houses or like places'.[13] It was perhaps selective morality that allowed Borlase to turn a blind eye to the well documented extravagances of cricketing dinners and the considerable patronage given to the game by publicans in many New Zealand towns.

In Presbyterian Dunedin the *Otago Daily Times* was no less concerned with the temperate habits of cricketers, but also felt that sports such as cricket, football and golf would go some way to negating certain consequences of industrialisation. The mechanisation of the workplace had reduced the physical emphasis in labour to the point where man had become 'the finger adjusting the machinery of science, rather than the strong arm creating results by its own muscular energy'. It was therefore vital to encourage sport and physical exercise among Dunedin youth, an objective that would be greatly aided by early closing, the Saturday half-holiday and the better climate.[14]

As ever in the course of such discussions, some of the strongest rhetoric was reserved for those who appeared to take no interest in sport. During a sometimes heated debate on 'manly exercise' in the Christchurch *Press* during August 1867, 'Dumb Bells' mounted a scathing attack on the sedentary and effeminate recreational activities of many clerks and non-sportsman:

> It is true that some of them find great amusement in arraying their persons in gorgeous apparel and slowly perambulating the streets for the purpose of displaying the same, carefully avoiding however the more frequented ... thoroughfares lest ... some speck of mud should chance to light upon their boots or a collision with some misguided chimney-sweep should disarrange the elaborate adjustment of their neckcloth or the graceful disposition of their coat tails.

To counter such activities, the development of muscle among the youth of Christchurch depended on the encouragement of football and rowing, cricket in summer and a gymnasium for all weathers.[15] While some questioned the gloomy prognosis of 'Dumb Bells' as to the true state of sporting patronage in Christchurch, none questioned his basic criticism of the non-sportsman or his general assumption of a link between manly character and physical exertion.[16]

Significantly, cricket worked – or was believed to work – as a physical and moral agent because it was held to be accessible to all classes, a view sometimes maintained in the face of obvious contradictions. During the difficult years of the early 1880s, when working-class cricketers were frequently in dispute with the Otago Cricket Association, the *Otago Daily Times* could still insist that the game was untrammelled by class distinctions:

> Self-control, patience, perseverance, are all requisite to efficiency in cricket. Class prejudices are broken down, and the power of working with others for a common object, so necessary to success in life, is fostered. Above all, cricket accustoms boys and men to be fair, and not to take mean advantage however close may be the contest.[17]

Two years later *The Press* offered a similarly egalitarian opinion when welcoming a visiting Australian team. It claimed that cricket was a very democratic game because it was not necessarily expensive. 'Persons of all sorts and conditions in life meet on the cricket field, on equal terms, and enjoy themselves without a thought about social distinctions'.[18] Given that expense was perhaps the greatest impediment to New Zealand cricket even at the highest level, such observations tell more of prevailing idealism than prevailing reality.

It was not simply that cricket embraced so many qualities essential to a physically robust and morally pure being, it was at the same time uniquely English. While other nations may have been capable of competing in commercial volume or technological innovation, all of them lacked the quintessential elements of athleticism which ensured the durability of such a large British Empire.

At the beginning of the 1860/61 season, the *Lyttelton Times* informed its readers that cricket was one of the prime distinguishing features between Britain and her traditional antagonists – France, Russia and Germany:

> It is a curious fact that foreigners, though they copy English sports and aim at doing them in English style, have never attempted to introduce the game of cricket into their several countries. The Frenchman, the Russian and the German all hunt, shoot and race, and try to carry out the sport after the English model, though they all fail more or less in the attempt; but who ever saw one or other able to handle a bat decently, or send the near stump flying with a ripping round hander, or even catch or throw a ball in any other style than that peculiar one adopted by young ladies when they attempt the game.[19]

When the Tasmanian team arrived in Dunedin in February 1884 the *Otago Daily Times* was moved to an equally xenophobic summary:

> Continental nations are unable to understand how Englishmen can play at games with such earnestness. Without quoting the hackneyed saying of the Duke of Wellington, we may say that the lessons cricket teaches are just those features which distinguish the British character in every department of life and have made our national pride not altogether empty.[20]

No doubt these views were reinforced by the volume of international cricket being played. Tasmania were the fifth touring team to visit New Zealand in seven years, and three more were to arrive before the end of the decade.

When, during the Australian tour of 1905, the *New Zealand Herald* discussed the Englishness of athleticism, it went so far as to appropriate American football and Canadian lacrosse as conclusive proofs of the British origin of the North American population. But what was more revealing to the *Herald* was the lack of sporting credentials displayed by those outside the British Empire:

> Other European nations have never developed the taste for these things in any considerable degree, and even when brought into intimate contact with our own people, they are slow to do so. The Latin races of Europe have no national out of door games of mingled skill and endurance in which all classes of the people can join, and even the Teutonic and Slavonic races develop such a taste but slowly, so that it is hardly an exaggeration to claim such games, with all that they imply, as a heritage of our own. Nor is it easy to estimate fully the value of a heritage of this kind either to the individual or to the society which possesses it ... Even in a country like America, where there is a mixture of races, the popularity of cricket has suffered because it appeals but little to the instincts of the French race in Canada and the Germans and other European races that form so large a percentage of the population of the United States.[21]

These sentiments, expressed in 1905, were little removed in form or meaning from those of 1860. Half a century of development in New Zealand cricket had altered much in the shape and scale of the game but had not apparently altered its ideological significance.

Devoting more space to this rhetoric would add volume but not variety. Suffice to say, the basic terms of the moral metaphors used to frame and contextualise New Zealand cricket remained uniform over time and place. Moreover, there is no indication of any challenge to it, while in Britain there was a strong current of anti-athleticism that manifested itself even at Eton and other public schools.[22] As the next chapter will reveal, the only comparable attitude evident in New Zealand was a conventional desire to keep the sporting ethos in proportion, and especially to direct school sport away from the excesses of competitiveness.[23]

Maori Cricket

Besides the tempering of athletic and competitive rhetoric, there are other more overt constrictions on the New Zealand cricketing metaphor – not least the lack of any form of racial dimension. In India, the West Indies and parts of Africa sport held a crucial mediating and harmonising role between indigenous and colonising cultures. Even in Australia efforts were made by missionaries and various colonial administrators to encourage cricket among the various Aboriginal communities.[24] There is, though, no evidence of any deliberate cultivation of Maori cricket for similar purposes.

The process of European colonisation and acculturation was certainly not favourable to traditional Maori games and pastimes. Given that the various physical activities and contests that may be classified as sport were very much integrated within the rituals and routines of daily life, it follows that these were substantially eroded amid broader changes to Maori society during the nineteenth century. As the noted Maori scholar and politician Sir Peter Buck (Te Rangihiroa) observed during the late 1940s:

> The old Maori games have practically disappeared and been replaced by games learned from Pakeha children. In the change, the public schools have been a great influence, particularly schools attended by both races. This is seen in skipping and in swings. Tops have survived because they are used by European children, but the old chants which accompanied them have been forgotten.[25]

At present we know far too little about early Maori sporting interactions with Europeans. Yet it seems much too simple to suggest that they simply replaced one set of sporting inclinations with another – not least because the rural base and socio-economic disposition of the Maori population did not lend itself to an easy embrace of organised sport or a visible presence within it. Most Maori belonged to scattered rural communities and were engaged in farming and a variety of seasonal labouring occupations: only 11.2 per cent were urbanised by 1936 and 19 per cent by 1945. It was not until the late 1960s that Maori became a predominantly urban people.[26] The size of the Maori population was also a factor. By 1890 Europeans outnumbered Maori by 14 to 1, and the Maori population reached an estimated low point of 42,113 in 1896 before a gradual increase to 56,987 by 1921.[27] Furthermore, as secondary education was not compulsory, very few Maori were exposed to the sporting nurseries that emerged in New Zealand's elite secondary schools. By 1935 only 8.4 per cent of Maori aged 13 to 17 were attending secondary schools of any kind.[28]

Although there was an obvious Maori presence in rugby from the late nineteenth century, even this may be rather exaggerated. Despite claims that Maori had a natural affinity for a game that allowed expression of the 'warrior spirit', the best evidence is that participation was confined to those tribal areas that experienced the most harmonious relations with European society and to those individuals within them who enjoyed greater socio-economic parity. Early Maori players and teams are drawn very largely from the tertiary educated and occupationally professional.[29] Many other Maori remained at a distance from the sporting currents of European society until well after the turn of the twentieth century.

Against this background, the considerable urban bias of New Zealand cricket, the difficulties the game encountered in rural areas and the impediments to working-class participation outlined in the previous chapter, were substantially more applicable to Maori. Moreover, even those who were inclined towards the game were probably in a more tenuous position than their rural European counterparts in terms of sustaining the expense of cricket ground developments. At a purely speculative level, there is also a line of argument to suggest that rural Maori may have preferred rugby to cricket because it was not only cheaper to play but also corresponded more to the preferred rhythms of communal daily life and work patterns based on concerted bursts of group effort rather than more drawn-out activities that shifted the focus to individual performances. But it is ultimately impossible to test the validity of such ideas, and they are prone to become shrouded in rather dubious anthropology and selective sampling – as they have done in other attempts to link 'race' with performance and preference in sport.[30]

Whatever the explanation is, quantifying even the limited Maori involvement in cricket is a matter for some speculation. It is quite likely that Maori players participated in some of the earliest games arranged by missionaries during the mid 1830s. Beyond this there are only isolated references – and most of these from North Canterbury. There was a keen Maori following for cricket in the vicinity of Kaiapoi, Rangiora and Rapaki during the 1870s and 1880s. Yet the only formally reported match was in January 1883, when the Kaiapoi United CC defeated the 'Native' club.[31]

Surprisingly, in light of Buck's reference to the role of schools in the decline of Maori games, there seems to have been very little cricket played at the leading Maori secondary schools – St Stephens Native School and Te Aute College in Hawke's Bay. Te Aute, under the headmastership of John Thornton, 1878–1912, subscribed to many familiar English public school values and the Te Aute students association (Kotahitanga) was also a firm advocate of integration into European sport. As late as 1902 Thornton suggested that Maori should be encouraged to pursue more gentlemanly activities such as cricket and tennis, rather than rugby which was violent, caused injuries and aroused too much of a fighting spirit. The college was certainly invited by the NZCC to participate in the first tournament for the Heathcote Williams Challenge Shield in 1908. But there is no mention of a school cricket XI until at least the 1920s and, moreover, there is no mention of the game anywhere in the history of St Stephens.[32]

As for prominent individual Maori cricketers, the six first-class players who appeared prior to 1920 were all very much part of urban European society. John Grey (Jack) Taiaroa (1862–1907), the son of Hori Kerei Taiaroa, Ngai Tahu leader and MHR, was educated at Otago Boys' High School and became a solicitor in Hastings. He was a member of the first New Zealand rugby team to tour Australia in 1884, set a New Zealand long jump record during the 1880s and represented Hawke's Bay as a batsman throughout the 1890s.[33] Another Maori player, Paraire Henare Tomoana (c.1874–1946), educated at Te Aute College and later to become a noted Maori composer, writer and translator, played once for Hawke's Bay in 1903.[34]

Another cricketer with strong rugby connections was William Thomas 'Tabby' Wynyard (1862–1938). Educated at Devonport School, Auckland, Wynyard finished his career as district manager of the New Zealand Department of Agriculture in Wellington. He developed as a fine all-round sportsman, representing Auckland and Wellington at athletics and rugby during the 1880s and 90s as well as being an accomplished billiards player, cyclist, golfer and oarsman. A member of the New Zealand Native Football team that toured Britain and Australia in 1888–89, Wynyard also represented New Zealand in Australia in 1893. His first-class cricket career consisted of 12 matches as a batsman for Wellington and Auckland from 1882/83 to 1907/08. He was later a committee member of the Auckland Cricket Association.[35]

Wiri Aurunui Baker (1892–1966), a product of Wellington College, played as a batsman in 34 matches for Wellington between 1912 and 1930 and twice for New Zealand against New South Wales in 1923–24.[36] His brother, George, another Wellington College old boy, played four times as a batsman for Wellington in the 1919/20 and 1920/21 seasons. Another player of Maori descent, Thomas Grace, also played two matches for Wellington in 1911/12 and 1913/14.[37]

John Hopere Wharewiti Uru (1868–1921), educated at Tuahiwi in North Canterbury and at Te Aute College, was a farmer and native land agent who served as MHR for Southern Maori 1918–21. He represented Canterbury at rugby, was a captain of the North Canterbury Mounted Rifles and a member of the Maori contingent to Queen Victoria's Diamond Jubilee celebrations in 1897 and the Australian Commonwealth celebrations in 1901. As a fast bowler, Uru took nine wickets in his first game for Canterbury against Hawke's Bay in 1894, but none in his only other appearance against Wellington during the following season.[38]

Although Uru, Wynyard and Taiaroa were relatively prominent public figures, none of the Maori first-class players could be said to have left an enduring legacy to New Zealand cricket. As urbanisation gathered pace during the mid twentieth century, softball rather than cricket became the preferred sport for many Maori, although the reasons for this choice have yet to be explored. While it is difficult to be certain, it seems that no other players of Maori ancestry entered New Zealand first-class cricket until the early 1980s. Adam Parore became the first Test cricketer of Maori ancestry in 1990.

The Emergence of Women's Sport

If the limited racial dimension of New Zealand cricket was in large part a question of geography and demography, the delineation of gender roles was entirely deliberate. As much as the ideal of cricket was concerned with physical and moral harmony, it retained in New Zealand a strong Victorian chauvinism. The expedient of sport for men was, for women, absolutely secondary to the ideals of domesticity and femininity.

The prevailing Victorian attitude to women's sport has been extensively discussed elsewhere.[39] Broadly speaking, Victorian opposition to women's sport was couched as a quasi-medical concern for the preservation of their maternal function. Vigorous sporting endeavour was believed to pose a grave threat to reproductive capability. Moreover, within prevailing maxims of modesty and decorum, sport was both ungraceful and unfeminine. From this stemmed a more practical impediment, whereby accepted norms of dress – voluminous skirts and tight sleeves in particular – posed immediate difficulties for all but the most sedate forms of exercise.[40]

Only with the spread of higher education for girls and women during the last third of the nineteenth century, and a shift on the part of the medical profession to embrace the notion that healthy mothers were necessary to produce healthy offspring, was there acceptance of physical activity as a necessary component of female development. In ideology and organisation many of the Victorian girls' public schools closely followed the model of their male counterparts.[41] There were, however, clear limitations to this. The sports available to women and girls tended to be those such as tennis, croquet, golf and, later, hockey and cycling, that were either individual or less traditionally associated with an overtly male domain. These were sports commonly pursued as social rather than competitive activities within a private sphere such as one's family or school.[42]

Despite the positive sporting model provided by the girl's public schools, the idea of organised, competitive team sport for women remained anathema to male sporting administrators throughout the nineteenth century. One suspects that their reactions were as much a concern with preserving ideals of domesticity and femininity as preserving the integrity of their own games from 'aping' by female players.[43] In this vein there were especially vitriolic reactions to proposals for a women's rugby tour of New Zealand in 1891. One critic suggested that the tour would involve a 'degradation of womanhood to pander to a depraved public taste for the sake of getting money'.[44]

Despite claims from the promoter of the team, Nita Webbe, that her players would respect and strictly adhere to the rules of the game, the Auckland *Star* flatly condemned the venture: 'It is true that there have been some very popular "kickists" on the stage, and female performers in the circus are a good "draw" but the popular taste is still elevated enough to insist upon grace and beauty in such exhibitions by female athletes'.[45] The tour did not eventuate.

When, after 1900, women did gravitate towards team sports in greater numbers, they tended towards those such as basketball (later called netball) and hockey that possessed a less pronounced masculine heritage. Women's hockey showed a marked increase in New Zealand – from one club in 1897 to ten provincial associations affiliated to the New Zealand (Lady's) Hockey Association by 1908. Netball emerged around 1906 and was well established in girls' schools by 1914. The New Zealand Basketball Association was established in 1924 to govern the activities of a number of already existing provincial associations.[46]

As the oldest and most popular of team sports – and that which was most strongly associated with the cultivation of masculine physical and moral values – cricket posed particular problems during the nineteenth century for women interested in playing it. Georgian women had played cricket as early as 1745 and there was regular reporting of fixtures involving 'rustic' women in Hampshire, Surrey and Sussex throughout the century. At the same time, women of the higher classes were also attracted to the game and their fixtures became great social occasions. Considerably larger numbers of women also patronised the game as spectators. However, these levels of involvement had almost entirely disappeared by the Victorian era as the links between sport and manly virtue created a sharp contrast with orthodox notions of feminine weakness. The revival in England began in the late 1860s with isolated play in girls' schools and as a mixed recreation among middle-class families. The first female club was the aristocratic White Heather CC, formed in 1887, and the game took a stronger hold in the girls' public schools during the following decade. There was also a boost from the 'Original English Lady Cricketers', a semi-professional group who played exhibition matches during the early 1890s. But the latter were obliged to play under assumed names as a counter to strong objections against female professionalism. Moreover, the volume of women's cricket remained very minimal and peripheral and was confined largely to unmarried middle-class women. None of the Oxford women's colleges had a cricket XI by 1914.[47]

Women's Cricket in New Zealand

The diffusion of women's cricket in New Zealand followed almost exactly the pattern established in Britain. In so far as cricket secured any sort of hold, it was not until the early twentieth century, and then only in a select few of the leading girls' secondary schools. Moreover, this activity was

circumscribed by the same range of medical and moral objections characteristic of its revival in England.

As we have seen already, the first role for women in New Zealand cricket
was as spectators. The fledgling clubs of the 1840s and 50s regularly
expressed a desire for the presence of 'ladies' at their fixtures. To cater for
the next generation of female spectators, in 1883 William Outhwaite published *The Ladies Guide to Cricket, by a Lover of Both, with a Glossary of
Technical Terms and Cricket Slang and the Laws of Cricket*. In so far as this
lengthy and predictably patronising account of the game suggested that
cricket might actually be played by women in 'ladies schools', it advocated
'soft-ball' cricket rather than the conventional form.[48]

The first reference to women playing cricket in New Zealand was to a
'Ladies' cricket match' at Greytown in the Wairarapa on New Years Day,
1867.[49] In 1886 'eleven Marahau girls' challenged eleven of Riwaka (near
Nelson) to a game 'any time they like. Dinner and dance provided. All welcome.' The response from Riwaka is not reported.[50] There were apparently
several games played in the Waikato during the late 1880s, and clubs briefly
appeared in Picton and Kimbolton, and at Tikohino near Waipawa, during
the early 1890s.[51]

The most consistent growth seems to have been in Auckland. In
November 1890 the *New Zealand Graphic* reported on a growing interest in
cricket: 'About the suburbs already one is frequently coming across merry
parties of girls in light summer dresses, armed with bats and wickets, just as
we have been accustomed to seeing them the last few years with tennis racquets and shoes'.[52] It seems, however, that this devotion to the game was
short-lived.

Team cricket also gained a foothold. There were active teams in
Greymouth and Westport by 1907, and T.W. Reese makes reference to a fixture between Canterbury and Wellington women soon after the turn of the
century – although this cannot be substantiated.[53] Indeed, progress outside
the schools was slow and sporadic. There were no active club competitions
in any of the main centres until the 1920s and the first provincial cricket
associations, Auckland and Otago, were not formed until 1928. Canterbury
followed in 1931, Wellington in 1932, Wanganui and Southland in 1933 and
the New Zealand Women's Cricket Council in 1934.[54]

The atmosphere surrounding much of the earliest participation in cricket
by women was one of festivity and of a social rather than sporting objective.
A match involving members of Chirstchurch's Lancaster Park CC in March
1888, in which the men used broomsticks and the women bats, was held in
conjunction with an 'at home' given by the 'lady members'. Many of
Christchurch's leading citizens were present for an occasion which also
included tennis, an ample afternoon tea and regular interludes from the
Addington Brass Band.[55] In Auckland in 1891 'thirteen venturesome
damsels' played 'seven gentlemen batting left-handed with broomsticks'.[56]
In October 1895, at Bannockburn, Central Otago, a team of women defeated

the local club (bowling left-handed and batting with broomsticks) by 55 runs. Among the more unconventional dismissals noted by the Bannockburn *Argus* were 'skirts before wickets', 'improved before wickets' (?) and one player who retired in order to attend her baby.[57] In Wellington at the beginning of the 1902/03 season there was a 'Ladies match and tea party' on the Wellington College ground to raise funds for survivors of the *S.S. Elingamite* shipwreck. The two teams were drawn from J.C. Wilkinson's Musical Comedy Company.[58] In none of these instances was the game of a character or intent to prompt any real concern for the fabric or integrity of cricket.

Efforts by women to engage in cricket of a more serious nature drew a rather different response from critics. Writing to the *New Zealand Graphic* on 18 October 1890, 'Property' declared that cricket was not 'at all a suitable game' for ladies. The game involved too much undignified activity, and it was 'most ungraceful [to see] young ladies, or even middle aged dames, who ought to know better, flying after a cricket ball'. No woman looked 'nice' when she was running.[59] Others, while not ignoring the feminine aesthetic, suggested that cricket was a positive disadvantage to women and girls on 'physiological' grounds. As William Chapple, a prominent Wellington doctor, argued in 1894:

> It promotes *esprit de corps*; it favours manly and womanly relationships with competitors; it is practised in the open air and is exhilarating, recreative and attractive. The end of physical training in women, however, differs to some extent from that in men. The erect carriage, the graceful movements, the proportional frame, the personal deportment, the graceful gait, the unblemished hands – these are all attributes that are more valuable in women than in men, and they are attributes that should be valued, considered, and developed by any system of training that lays claim to physical education in women. However fascinating cricket may be as a sport amongst girls, it undoubtedly favours an ungainly gait, a stoop, an asymmetry, contracted shoulders and irregular and awkward movement of the arms.[60]

There is an obvious contradiction between these 'irregular and awkward' characteristics and the stance of successive generations of schoolmasters who promoted cricket as a means of physical and moral refinement for boys. Chapple's apparently altruistic 'physiological' concerns seem little more than antagonism towards female encroachment on a stringently male domain.

In light of such objections, women's cricket made its greatest progress away from the public arena in the more cloistered environment of the girls' secondary schools. Wellington Girls' College, Wanganui Girls' College, Woodford House in Hawke's Bay and Mt. Eden College in Auckland were all playing reasonably regular cricket before 1900.[61] They were joined during the next two decades by Auckland schools such as St Cuthberts, Diocesan High School and Auckland Girls' Grammar School, and by Southland Girls' High School.[62] Despite, or perhaps because of, the strong traditions of Canterbury in other spheres of the game, its girls' schools do not seem to have adopted cricket until the early 1930s.[63]

Attitudes to cricket within the girls' schools were mixed. While some regarded it as a rather peripheral activity, others made strenuous efforts to improve their standard of play. *The Addastrian*, the Wanganui Girls' College magazine, observed in 1903 that 'Cricket, unlike hockey, is not a game in which girls as a rule can excel. Practice may make us good batswoman, nature has made us fair fields, but nothing seems to make us expert over-arm bowlers.'[64] Seven years later the same source was able to observe a degree of improvement:

> Cricket has certainly improved, and girls show more spirit than formerly, but most of us require to cultivate bravery enough to meet the ball when it comes flying through the air. Why not meet the thing with a fixed face, and not show one's back, or try to double up into half one's natural size? However, girls are growing braver.[65]

By 1916 there were 106 girls in the College cricket club, and annual matches were arranged with Palmerston North Girls' High School.[66]

A cricket ground was provided at Southland Girls' High School by 1916, and, although there was a shortage of equipment and opposition, the school magazine was positive about the prospects for cricket by 1920. 'Knowing as we do the contempt of a masculine mind for a feminine attempt at games, we consider it a great tribute to our bowlers that their "overarms" frequently draw forth exclamations of approval from admiring small boys'.[67]

But it was Auckland where the greatest progress was made – under the guidance of Sarah Heap. Although the precise nature of her qualifications was never made clear, Heap acquired a reputation as an expert drill mistress and established the first comprehensive system of physical training for secondary school girls in New Zealand. She taught primarily at Auckland Girls' Grammar School and the Auckland Teachers' Training College, but was at various times involved with most of the other Auckland girls' secondary schools and with the Young Women's Christian Association (YWCA).[68] These connections assisted the development of regular inter-school fixtures after 1914 – especially between Auckland Girls' Grammar and Diocesan High School – and to games between pupils and old girls.[69]

The new sense of dedication and confidence surrounding physical education and sport at Auckland Girls' Grammar is revealed in the comment of the Headmistress, Miss Butler, when presenting a bat to a member of the 1st XI:

I am only fearful that, seeing an embryo W.G. Grace in one of my school's daughters, Mr Tibbs will want her to play for the boys' school ... The boys may be scornful about a girl getting 101 runs, and ask who the bowler was. Well, she was a very good bowler, and one of a visiting team who came determined to conquer.[70]

Aside from the existing strength of the Auckland Grammar School 1st XI, one suspects that Mr Tibbs had stronger reasons for not recruiting the player concerned.

Patterns of Diffusion

It is quite apparent, then, that any discussion of the positive moral values ascribed to cricket in New Zealand must be conducted within clear parameters of race and gender – and one must be equally cautious about its class dimensions. The last two chapters have demonstrated the social and demographic factors that contributed to middle-class predomination in representative cricket. It is by no means certain that responses to the ideology associated with the New Zealand game were any more inclusive.

Some of the earliest work on the diffusion of sporting ideologies, such as W.F. Mandle's writings on cricket and Australian nationalism, tended to deal only with the broadest and most observable interactions, such as those between the Australian colonies and the mother country. Yet it is vital to move beyond a monolithic approach, which assumes a united response to the transplanted ideology, to discover what became of sport outside formal middle-class institutions. For, as Richard Cashman points out, the monolithic approach places too great an emphasis on consensus while minimising the realities of sporting conflict within colonial society between such groups as officials, players, promoters and business interests.[71]

The study of working class ideology and opinion, especially beyond an organised political element, is always circumscribed by scarcity of sources and the danger that some of what survives is a record of behaviour interpreted by and for middle-class eyes. Nevertheless, one does not have to look far in either Britain or her colonies for evidence that the working class embraced organised sport without embracing the middle-class ideals that underpinned it.

Contrasting responses to the tour of the 1888–89 New Zealand Native Football Team are a useful starting point. While their matches against the elite rugby clubs of southern England attracted a certain amount of imperial rhetoric and a much more acute awareness of the predominantly Maori composition of the team, such themes were almost entirely absent from coverage of the matches against working-class teams in Yorkshire and Lancashire. Theirs was an essentially immediate and localised outlook divorced from the exigencies of imperial policy and the ideals attached to sport by the middle class.[72]

Of course, the north/south dichotomy revealed by the native team tour was only a minor symptom of a much deeper rift that culminated in the formation of the Northern Union (later Rugby League) at the end of 1895. Northern rugby, Welsh rugby and the professionalisation of football are perfect demonstrations of the working class appropriating bourgeois sport to suit the demands of their own culture. While many early clubs were founded with middle-class finance and patronage, Stephen Jones suggests that

> the working class was able to take out of games those elements, rituals and values which fitted into their own culture. Bourgeois control within governing bodies did not necessarily mean that sport was a vehicle of assimilation whereby canons of decorum, order and sportsmanship were simply refracted downwards into the working class.[73]

Indeed, increasing spectator misconduct at football matches from the late nineteenth century onwards was further proof that so-called respectable ideals did not survive in translation.[74]

Although there was no major schism in English cricket, there was nevertheless a considerable disparity between the philosophy of the upper middle class who controlled the first-class game and those who experienced cricket through the northern and midland leagues. Whereas first-class administrators apparently made very little effort to maximise the appeal or financial viability of their game,[75] the scheduling of league matches and the playing styles they demanded were geared firmly to the recreational patterns and demands of working-class players and spectators. As Jeffrey Hill explains, 'league cricket did not embody the very public display of social authority and deference that was a necessary accompaniment of the first-class game, and most clearly evident in the relationship between gentlemen amateurs and working class professionals'.[76]

The diffusion of cricket throughout the Empire reveals similar ideological discontinuities in terms of the tension between cultural imperialism and indigenous subversion. Although much Indian cricket followed the model epitomised by K.S. Ranjitsinhji and the 'Chief's Colleges' that sought to replicate English public school ideals, others subverted the game for their own purposes. Many Princes played for personal aggrandisement, conspicuous consumption or political status – all objectives far removed from the purest amateur idealism.[77]

In terms of class issues, Australia witnessed the greatest transformation of values. During the 1880s and again in 1912 there were acrimonious power struggles between middle-class officialdom and the more professional objectives of many players.[78] More indicative of working class sentiment were the gambling and barracking traditions that developed among Australian spectators. Both were criticised as antithetical to middle-class norms, and gambling was largely suppressed by the 1880s. But despite middle-class criticism of the taunting of visiting teams, and fears that barracking would translate into more overt disruption of the game, it has endured as an integral part of the Australian game. After the Test series of 1897–98, the England captain, Andrew Stoddart, maintained that crowd intimidation played a significant role in his team's defeat. In this he was generally supported by Australian officials, but the practice remained fairly close to the surface of Australian cricket – and emerged in its strongest form during the 'Bodyline' series of 1932–33.[79]

Aside from a noticeable gambling fraternity at interprovincial matches during the 1860s and 70s, of whom many were undoubtedly middle class, one struggles to find obvious examples of the ideological subversion of cricket in New Zealand. Indeed, later chapters will suggest that New Zealand representative cricket was as close to the English amateur ideal as any in the Empire. Yet the disputes within Otago cricket during the early 1880s and the class distinctions which marked the composition of many clubs within the main centres confirm that currents of class difference were present in the New Zealand game. Likewise, although the formation of the various suburban cricket leagues and associations were in part a response to the impediments to working-class cricket posed by the prevailing social structure, they also catered to a less formal and structured cricketing tradition which was somewhat at odds with the establishment game.

How far these demarcation lines can be extended to specific colonial working-class interpretations of muscular Christianity and the imperial sporting fabric is a moot point. But there is enough in the English and Australian examples – and in a growing body of scholarship on New Zealand rugby – to suggest that the monolithic approach is equally unrepresentative of New Zealand cricket. Given that accounts of New Zealand working-class sporting ideology are scarce to say the least, rather than assume that middle-class hegemony was comfortably maintained one must always be conscious of the potential – but not well-documented – limitations on the rhetoric of muscular Christianity and sporting imperialism.[80]

The pervasiveness of the message also has more practical limitations. Given that the vast majority of writing on New Zealand cricket, both descriptive and critical, is contained in newspapers, it is worth reflecting on how widely these were circulated. Ross Harvey has calculated that the circulation of newspapers as a percentage of total population rose from 7.2 per cent during the 1840s to 11.6 per cent in 1862–63, a peak of 14.6 per cent during the early 1870s and 11 per cent by 1881.[81] The figures for larger towns and for the four main cities, where newspapers could be more easily circulated, are obviously higher. Moreover, there is no way of calculating the number of individuals who read each newspaper. The available evidence, though, hardly suggests saturation coverage. In 1862 the *Otago Daily Times* produced *c.*7,000 issues daily to an Otago provincial population that reached 49,000 by 1864. At the same time the thrice weekly *Lyttelton Times* was producing

1,500–2,000 copies and *The Press* had a daily circulation, which amounted to 5,000 copies per week for a Christchurch population of *c.*5000 and a total Canterbury population of *c.*32,000. By 1881 the *New Zealand Herald* was producing 6,750 copies daily for an Auckland city population of *c.*31,000 and a provincial population of *c.*100,000. The widely circulated *Otago Witness* produced 7,250–8,500 copies weekly to a Dunedin population of 40,000 and an Otago population of 134,000; the *Otago Daily Times* offered 4,000–6,000 daily to the same market. The circulation of *The Press* in 1882 was 5,000 daily for a Christchurch population of 26,000 and a provincial population of 112,000.[82] On this basis, it is doubtful whether the ideological tracts on New Zealand cricket reached an especially wide audience.[83]

Therefore, notions of sport as a moral metaphor were largely the property of an educated elite who exercised a disproportionate influence over New Zealand cricket. It is the nature of this influence in the context of the expanding network of New Zealand secondary schools that we will turn to next.

Notes

1. J.A. Mangan and J. Walvin, 'Introduction' in J.A. Mangan and J. Walvin (eds), *Manliness and Morality: Middle-Class Masculinity in Britain and America 1800–1940* (Manchester, 1987), p. 5.
2. D. Newsome, *Godliness and Good Learning* (London, 1961), p. 197; B.E. Haley, *The Healthy Body and Victorian Culture* (Harvard, 1978), pp. 3–4.
3. Haley, *The Healthy Body*, p. 258; Sandiford, *Cricket and the Victorians*, p. 34.
4. Newsome, *Godliness and Good Learning*, pp. 195–7; See also, N. Vance, *The Sinews of the Spirit: The Ideal of Christian Manliness in Victorian Literature and Religious Thought* (Cambridge, 1985), pp. 1–28.
5. Sandiford, *Cricket and the Victorians*, p. 36.
6. Ibid., pp. 42–3.
7. Newsome, *Godliness and Good Learning*, p. 200.
8. Belich, *Making Peoples*, pp. 437–40; H. Jackson, 'Churchgoing in Nineteenth Century New Zealand', *New Zealand Journal of History*, 17, 1 (1983).
9. *New Zealander*, 20 Dec. 1862, p. 5.
10. *The Press*, 17 Dec. 1863, p. 2
11. *New Zealand Times*, 25 Jan. 1882, p. 2.
12. *New Zealand Herald*, 4 Dec. 1865, p. 5.
13. *Wellington Independent*, 19 Feb. 1867, p. 4.
14. *Otago Daily Times*, 26 Sept. 1863, p. 5.
15. *The Press*, 1 Aug. 1867, p. 2.
16. Ibid., 2 Aug. 1867, p. 2; 9 Aug. 1867, p. 2; 20 Aug. 1867, p. 2.
17. *Otago Daily Times*, 2 Feb. 1884, p. 2
18. *The Press*, 1 Dec. 1886, p. 4.
19. *Lyttelton Times*, 19 Sept. 1860, p. 4.
20. *Otago Daily Times*, 2 Feb. 1884, p. 2.
21. *New Zealand Herald*, 11 Feb. 1905, p. 6.
22. See for example, C. Dewey, '"Socratic Teachers": Part 1 – The Opposition to the Cult of Athletics at Eton 1870–1914', *International Journal of the History of Sport*, 12, 1 (1995); J.A. Mangan, *Athleticism in the Victorian and Edwardian Public School*, rev. ed. (London, 2000), pp. xxxiv–xxxvi.
23. For example, *New Zealand Herald*, 2 Sept. 1907, p. 6.
24. See: J.A. Mangan, *The Games Ethic and Imperialism* (London, 1986); B. Whimpress, *Passport to Nowhere: Aborigines in Australian Cricket 1850–1939* (Sydney, 1999).

25. Quoted in R. McConnell, 'Maori, the Treaty of Waitangi and Sport: A Critical Analysis' in Collins, *Sport in New Zealand Society*, p. 229.
26. M. King, 'Between Two Worlds' in Rice, *Oxford History*, p. 289.
27. Ibid., p. 286.
28. Ibid., p. 289.
29. Ryan, *Forerunners*, pp. 22–9.
30. There are numerous summaries of this debate in works on the sociology of sport.
31. J. Herries Beattie, *Traditional Lifeways of the Southern Maori* (Dunedin, 1994), p. 466; *Lyttelton Times*, 24 Jan. 1883, p. 4.
32. K. Tyro and K. Scarlett, *Te Aute College 125th Anniversary 1854–1979* (Pukehou, 1979); R.J. Walker, *Ka Whawhai Tonu Matou: Struggle Without End* (Auckland, 1990), pp. 174–5.
33. R.H. Chester and N.A.C. McMillan, *The Encyclopedia of New Zealand Rugby* (Auckland, 1981), p. 195.
34. A. Ballara and N. Huata, 'Paraire Henare Tomoana' in C. Orange (gen. ed.), *DNZB: Vol.3* (Wellington, 1996), pp. 534–6.
35. Ryan, *Forerunners*, pp. 139–40.
36. L. McConnell and I. Smith, *The Shell New Zealand Cricket Encyclopedia* (Auckland, 1993), p. 15.
37. A.H. Carman, *Wellington Cricket Centenary 1875–1975* (Wellington, 1975), pp. 119–25.
38. Scholefield, *Dictionary, Vol.1*, p. 413; Reese, *New Zealand Cricket 1841–1914*, pp. 317, 319.
39. See, for example: J.A. Mangan and R.J. Park, *From 'fair sex' to Feminism: Sport and the Socialization of Women in the Industrial and Post-Industrial Eras* (London, 1987); S. Fletcher, *Women First: The Female Tradition in English Physical Education, 1880–1980* (London, 1984).
40. Coney, *Standing in the Sunshine*, p. 238.
41. K.E. McCrone, 'Play up! Play up! and Play the Game! Sport at the Late Victorian Girl's Public Schools' in Mangan and Park, *From 'fair sex' to Feminism*, pp. 97–129.
42. Coney, *Standing in the Sunshine*, p. 238; M.A.E. Hammer, 'Something Else in the World to Live For: Sport and the Physical Emancipation of Women in Auckland, 1880–1920' (MA thesis, University of Auckland, 1990), pp. 4–37.
43. Hammer, 'Something Else in the World', pp. 38–9.
44. Quoted in ibid., pp. 37–8.
45. Quoted in ibid., p. 38.
46. Ibid.; S.A.G.M. Crawford, '"Ones Nerve and Courage are in very Different Order out in New Zealand": Recreation and Sporting Opportunities for Women in a Remote Colonial Setting' in Mangan and Park, *From 'fair sex' to Feminism*, p. 175; J. Nauright and J. Broomhall, 'A Woman's Game: The Development of Netball and a Female Sporting Culture in New Zealand 1906–70', *International Journal of the History of Sport*, 11, 3 (1994), pp. 391–6.
47. Sandiford, *Cricket and the Victorians*, pp. 43–4; K.E. McCrone, *Sport and the Physical Emancipation of English Women 1870–1914* (London, 1988), pp. 141–8.
48. W. Outhwaite, *The Ladies Guide to Cricket, by a Lover of Both, with a Glossary of Technical Terms and Cricket Slang and the Laws of Cricket* (Auckland, 1883), p. 5.
49. *Seventy Five Years of Cricket*, p. 5.
50. N. Joy, *Maiden Over: A Short History of Women's Cricket* (London, 1950), p. 31. There is some possibility that this challenge was made in 1896, not 1886.
51. Neely and Neely, *The Summer Game*, p. 44; Coney, *Standing in the Sunshine*, p. 239.
52. Quoted in Hammer, 'Something Else in the World', p. 40.
53. Reese, *New Zealand Cricket 1914–33*, p. 112; Neely and Neely (*The Summer Game*, p. 67) provide a photograph of a game in Hagley Park *c*.1900, but there is no evidence that this was the same fixture.
54. Else, *Women Together*, p. 434.
55. Newspaper clipping, 7 March 1888, Wilding Papers, Canterbury Museum Library.
56. Hammer, 'Something Else in the World', p. 40.
57. *Banockburn Cricket Union 1895–1995* (Bannockburn, 1995).
58. Neely, *100 Summers*, p. 63.
59. Quoted in Hammer, 'Something Else in the World', p. 39.
60. W.A. Chapple, *Physical Education in our State Schools* quoted in Hammer, 'Something Else in the World', p. 41.
61. Coney, *Standing in the Sunshine*, p. 242; P. Taylor, 'The Development of Sport and Physical Exercise in Single-Sex Girls' Secondary Schools in New Zealand Between 1877 and 1914' (research essay, University of Canterbury, no date), pp. 26–7.

62. Hammer, 'Something Else in the World', pp. 99, 105, 108, 112; C. Smith, 'Control of the Female Body: Physical Training at Three Secondary Schools, 1870–1920' (BA hons research essay, University of Otago, 1993), p. 47.
63. B. Peddie, *Christchurch Girls' High School, 1877–1977* (Christchurch, 1977), p. 117. There was apparently no cricket at Christchurch Girls' High School until 1937, and not again until 1946.
64. Quoted in Taylor, 'The Development of Sport and Physical Exercise', p. 26–7.
65. Quoted in ibid.
66. G. Abbott (ed.), *Wanganui Girls' College, 1891–1991* (Wanganui, 1991), p. 45.
67. Quoted in Smith, 'Control of the Female Body', p. 47.
68. C. Macdonald, M. Penfold and B. Williams (eds), *The Book of New Zealand Women* (Wellington, 1991), pp. 279–80; Hammer, 'Something Else in the World', p. 117.
69. Hammer, 'Something Else in the World', pp. 108, 117, 175.
70. Ibid., p. 114.
71. R. Cashman, 'Cricket and Colonialism: Colonial Hegemony and Indigenous Subversion?' in J.A. Mangan (ed.), *Pleasure, Profit and Proselytism: British Culture and Sport, at Home and Abroad, 1750–1914* (London, 1988), pp. 261–2.
72. G.J. Ryan, 'The Originals: The 1888–89 New Zealand Native Football Team in Britain, Australia and New Zealand' (MA thesis, University of Canterbury, 1992), pp. 48–67, 101–37, 164–6.
73. S. Jones, *Sport, Politics and the Working Class: Labour and Sport in Inter-War Britain* (Manchester, 1988), pp. 24–5. See also H. Cunningham, *Leisure in the Industrial Revolution* (London, 1980), pp. 128–9.
74. See W. Vamplew, 'Sports Crowd Disorder in Britain, 1870–1914: Causes and Controls', *Journal of Sport History*, 7, 1 (1980).
75. K.A.P. Sandiford and W. Vamplew, 'The Peculiar Economics of English Cricket Before 1914', *British Journal of Sports History*, 3, 3 (1986), pp. 286–311.
76. Hill, pp. 69–73.
77. Cashman, 'Cricket and Colonialism', p. 264.
78. Ibid., p. 262; D. Montefiore, *Cricket in the Doldrums: The Struggle Between Private and Public Control of Australian Cricket in the 1880s* (Sydney, 1992).
79. Cashman, 'Cricket and Colonialism', pp. 264–7.
80. See: L. Richardson, 'The Invention of a National Game: The Struggle for Control', *History Now*, 1, 1 (1995); G.T. Vincent, '"A Tendency to Roughness": Anti-Heroic Representations of New Zealand Rugby 1890–1914', *Sporting Traditions*, 14, 1 (1997).
81. R. Harvey, 'Economic Aspects of Nineteenth-Century New Zealand Newspapers', *Bibliographical Society of Australia and New Zealand Bulletin*, 17, 2 (1993). I am particularly grateful to Luke Trainor for providing this reference and additional figures relating to it.
82. Figures derived from Harvey, 'New Zealand Newspapers', pp. 59–60; C.J. Gibson, 'A Demographic History of New Zealand' (Ph.D. thesis, University of California, Berkeley, 1971), pp. 34–5, 51–2, 73.
83. When considering this subject one could also embark on a lengthy discussion as to the extent to which the press created or reflected public opinion on these matters.

5

Perpetuating the Straight Bat:
Cricket and the Schools, 1860–1914

Once the founding generation of New Zealand cricketers ceased to be active, there is a question as to how the next generations – most of them New Zealand-born – were introduced to the mores of the game and the hierarchies of the leading clubs. In short, how was the middle-class domination of New Zealand cricket sustained after the 1870s in the face of widespread social change at other levels of society?

Much of the answer can be found in the educational and athletic ideals of the English public schools and the network of colonial secondary schools that sought to replicate them from the late 1860s onwards: Christ's College, Wellington College, Wanganui Collegiate, Auckland Grammar School, Nelson College, Otago Boys' High School, Christchurch Boys' High School and Waitaki Boys' High School. Although the New Zealand schools contained no more than 3 per cent of New Zealand's school-age male population in 1901, they made a quite disproportionate contribution to club and first-class cricket, providing perhaps one-third of all Auckland and Canterbury players before 1914 and a considerable number of Otago and Wellington players. There were, however, also limits to this influence at both ends of the educational spectrum. In terms of primary schooling, which constituted the education limit for the majority of the population, cricket did not maintain a strong presence. Equally, but for rather different reasons, it did not become established within New Zealand's fledgling university colleges.

Before proceeding to an examination of these varied responses to cricket within New Zealand's educational institutions, it is essential to consider the more general impact of games on their English equivalents.

The English Public Schools

The sporting values that came to underpin the New Zealand education system were firmly rooted in an ideological shift that overtook the English education system during the mid nineteenth century. Even before the dubious academic standards and indiscipline of the public schools were considered by the Clarendon Commission in 1864, headmasters such as Charles

Vaughan at Harrow and Hely Hutchison Almond at Loretto had conceived an important new role for sport. They realised that organised sport and controlled leisure time outside the classroom was essential for control inside it. Thus, compulsory sport was introduced during the 1850s and quickly grew to include inter-school competition. Schools spent considerable sums on expanding their playing fields, hiring professional cricket coaches and evolving a structure where sporting rather than academic prowess was a sure path to success.[1]

Symbolic of these moves was the publication of Thomas Hughes' *Tom Brown's Schooldays* in 1857. Hughes' emphasis on sport perfectly conveyed and created a popular fashion. It showed that what had begun simply as a component of discipline was rapidly becoming an end in itself. Participation in games, and especially team games, could teach boys the principles of cooperation and interaction that would be paramount for life in business, the professions or the military.[2] Indeed, there is ample evidence to establish a link between sporting prowess and recruitment to the highest levels of public service. Sir Ralph Furse, responsible for Colonial Office recruitment to the Colonial Service 1910–50, made it clear that he desired staff not with superior academic credentials but with a solid second class honours and an Oxbridge blue. Nowhere is this more demonstrably apparent than the Sudan Political Service, where admission carried such a bias towards sportsmen that the Sudan became known as 'the land of blacks ruled by blues'.[3]

By the last third of the nineteenth century the public school system was being carefully replicated throughout the British Empire. Staffed almost exclusively by British-born masters, schools such as Harrison College in Barbados and the leading 'Chief's Colleges' of India such as Rajkumar College, Rajkot, were firmly dedicated to producing young men who subscribed to the ideals of Empire and to British modes of thinking and playing.[4] Even in North America, where cricket went into a significant decline after the Civil War, the game was an important part of the curriculum at Upper Canada College, and in both the United States and Canada there was a sustained market for *Tom Brown's Schooldays*.[5]

The New Zealand Elite Schools

It is impossible to know how many New Zealand colonists came from an English public school background. Figures were not kept and impressions are complicated by the erroneous tendency of some historians to characterise much of the nineteenth-century colonial elite as a predominantly English gentry.[6] It is clear, though, that educational attainment did emerge as a mark of social status. As one example, numerous sons of Canterbury and Hawke's Bay runholders were sent 'home' to England for school and university, as much for purely educational purposes as for cultural and intellectual reinforcement against the isolation of colonial life. Yet, as local schools were established, they became the preferred destination for sons of the colonial wealthy – although a number were still sent for 'finishing' at an Oxbridge college.[7]

It is very evident that the New Zealand elite schools tried to operate on the English model and that they played a crucial role in transmitting English cultural values to New Zealand. They fashioned a homogenous educational and social philosophy that stressed the primacy of an English cultural, moral and imperial ethos and reinforced a long-standing colonial nostalgia for the familiar social institutions of 'home'.[8] To this end, A.E. Campbell in *Educating New Zealand*, one of the volumes commissioned in 1940 to mark the centenary of European settlement, concluded that 'the historical principle of maintaining cultural continuity played a greater part in forming the education system of New Zealand than did the geographical principle of adaptation to a new environment'.[9]

This is not to suggest an immediate and wholesale adoption of the English model. As Gary McCulloch observes of Auckland Grammar School, 'imperial ideals and the trappings of tradition helped to conceal the fact that the school's character and role had in reality adapted quickly to its colonial setting'.[10] For all schools there were decades of fluctuating rolls and economic hardship before they could begin to consolidate and expand – and, in many respects, the New Zealand schools were quite distinct from their English counterparts due to their quite diverse social and theological origins and varying profiles within their local communities; most also claimed more egalitarian foundations and eventually became secular institutions endowed by the state.

Whatever their stated objectives, their teaching staff were drawn from the same narrow band of Oxbridge graduates and public school old boys. The first instinct of Christ's College until the early 1930s was to eschew local candidates in favour of advertising for its headmasters in England.[11] In time, though, these men were reinforced by their own carefully trained pupils and a clear pattern of recruitment from within the existing structure. For example, after six years as a teacher at Christ's College, Christchurch, Joseph Firth left to assume the headmastership of Wellington College in 1891. Two years later, C.F. Bourne relinquished the headmastership of Auckland Grammar School to take up the same position at Christ's College. There were other features that drew the schools together. By the end of the nineteenth century all of them had adopted the English prefect and house system, and most had adopted a school uniform – or at least a tie. More importantly, every school had established a magazine within which the sporting and other activities of the school were recorded and its ethos expressed in articles by masters and old boys.[12]

Educational reforms during the early twentieth century made little impact on these traditions – other than to gradually increase the number of New Zealand boys who were exposed to them. George Hogben's efforts as inspector general of schools and secretary of education to impose a more vocational curriculum on the classically academic proclivities of the schools and such far-reaching initiatives as the extension of free secondary education after 1902 were met with stiff resistance. Wellington College, in particular, simply refused to cooperate with the new regime. A. de Bathe Brandon, Chairman of the College Board of Governors, stated in 1908 that 'it is the duty of the Board to preserve the Wellington College as the institution contemplated by its founders'. He warned that submission to the free place scheme would involve the school in a 'moral suicide'.[13]

The Christ's College Tradition

As with certain of their English and colonial counterparts, it seems that the New Zealand schools took a few years to fully embrace the athletic ideal. Martin Crotty explains that a number of the Australian boys' secondary schools founded in the late 1840s and 1850s underwent a discernible shift from 'godliness and good learning' to athleticism. Without the impetus of a strong athletic tradition, their early priorities were intellectual knowledge and religious education, and little emphasis was placed on the physical development of boys or on the more secular components of character formation implicit in organised sport. These elements only emerged from the mid 1870s with the arrival of a generation of headmasters and masters more firmly grounded in the athletic ideology of Oxbridge and the English public schools that had taken hold from the 1850s.[14]

In similar fashion, the sporting terrain of the New Zealand schools appears relatively quiet until the 1870s. In part this may be a reflection of spartan facilities, but in all of the schools there appears to be a turning point in which one particular individual injected athletic life into a previously dormant institution. As with many things in New Zealand cricket, this transition first occurred in Christchurch.

Although it was founded at the end of 1850 with clear intentions to replicate the English public school model, Christ's College was very much a rudimentary colonial outpost during its first decade. Although it was allocated ground for cricket and football as early as July 1852, there is no evidence of organised school games until 1859. By the following year the college had established its own cricket ground in Hagley Park and regular matches were being played between the Ist XI and Fellows of the College and between such teams as 'Past and Present College' and 'The World'. By the mid 1860s a close relationship had also developed between College and the United Canterbury Cricket Club, resulting in the school paying substantially less than the working-class Albion CC for rent of facilities in Hagley Park. While the first headmaster, Henry Jacobs, was certainly an enthusiast for games playing, it is clear that the early organisation of cricket, football and athletics was very much the preserve of the boys who formed games committees and strictly regulated conduct among members of the respective clubs.[15]

W.C. Harris, headmaster 1866–73, laid much of the groundwork for a more coherent sporting tradition before ill health forced his resignation. But it was his successor, Charles Carteret Corfe, headmaster 1873–88, who left the greatest mark. Educated at Elizabeth College, Guernsey, where his father was principal, he took a BA in Mathematics from Cambridge and compiled a formidable sporting record. An Athletics blue, he also played cricket and rowed for Jesus College. Arriving at Christ's College in 1871, Corfe played for the UCCC and contributed some outstanding innings for Canterbury during the 1870s. He was a regular competitor at Canterbury Athletics Association meetings and was still winning titles during the mid 1880s.[16] At Christ's College, Corfe initiated the annual school sports and inter-school sports exchanges, supervised the building of the first gymnasium and swimming pool and the development of a new cricket ground. But he was a victim of politicking by conservative elements within the Christ's College board of governors, some of whom maintained that the College ought to be administered by a classically trained cleric rather than a mathematician. He was forced to resign in 1888, and turned his considerable abilities to reviving the fortunes of Toowoomba Grammar School, Queensland. Later, he undertook various relieving positions throughout Australasia – including a period at Christ's College during the First World War.[17] When Corfe died in 1935 the *Christ's College Register* was unequivocal in its praise of his contribution:

> [I]t was Mr Corfe who fired the imagination of the scholars, broadened their activities, impressed their receptive minds and fitted them to take their places in any company of the world's youth. He had a keen sense of his own responsibility, and both by example and by precept he created a similar sense in the minds of his boys. He knew what he was doing when he inculcated in his boys the love of games for their own sake and when he taught them that it was the quest and not the quarry that was important.[18]

This was high praise indeed for one who had departed from the college in somewhat acrimonious circumstances.

Corfe's successor, Francis Augustus Hare, headmaster 1888–93, possessed far less athletic ability but no less dedication to the cause. Educated at St Columba's, Dublin, and Emmanuel College, Cambridge, Hare came to New Zealand in 1872 as private secretary to the governor, Sir James Ferguson. Appointed to Christ's College in 1877 as chaplain and teacher of classics and divinity, he served as headmaster before reverting to the chaplaincy.[19] Hare took the College XI on its first tour to Timaru, Oamaru, Palmerston and Dunedin in 1878 and remained a passionate advocate of cricket: 'season after season found him daily at the nets … He had peculiar skill in detecting and developing latent talent and rejoiced exceedingly when he found the making of a good lob-bowler'. In 1882 Hare was instrumental in securing the services of the first professional cricket coach, W.J. Pocock, for two afternoons a week. He was followed after 1900 by the former Australian Test batsman, Charles Bannerman, H. Ellis from New South Wales, J.D. Lawrence, Canterbury and New Zealand, and various English professionals. Under Hare's guidance a new ground and pavilion were established in Hagley Park and a full-time groundsman employed to maintain them.

Perhaps Hare's greatest contribution was the establishment in 1884 of the *Christ's College Sports Register*, a detailed chronicle of current sporting performances and the achievements of old boys. It is revealing that the first College magazine took sport as its primary focus rather than the activities of the whole school. Indeed, it was to provide successive headmasters and old boys with a forum to philosophise on the importance of sport. The September 1884 issue contained a long letter from William Pember Reeves, future Minister of Labour and New Zealand Agent-General to London, on the subject of 'Cricket Practice for Beginners'; 'A Day at Olympia' in June 1886 provided numerous classical allusions in its account of a cricket match between Greeks and Romans; and the following year, an old boy writing on 'The Necessity for Systematic Gymnastic Exercise' stressed that education aimed only at the development of the intellect was incomplete – physical exercise and organised sport needed to be encouraged among all boys, regardless of ability.[20]

The sentiments expressed in the *Register* helped to create a superior sense of 'mission' in the attitude of Christ's College cricketers to their role in local cricket. As the *Register* lamented after a mediocre 1884/85 season: 'Until the school Eleven shows itself decidedly superior to the ordinary second elevens as still to be met in Christchurch, it will neither fulfil completely its mission of improving the standard of cricket here, nor will it repay the pains and trouble that have been expended in coaching it for some years past'.[21] After further disappointing performances at the end of 1885, the *Register* offered the intriguing suggestion that the higher purpose of college cricketers was being stifled by the standards of their opponents:

It is the misfortune, at any rate it is the lot, of a colonial school eleven to have to play for the most part against cricketers who do not usually set them quite the examples of style in batting and bowling which boys do well to copy. In England, the public school elevens are not only carefully coached on their own grounds, but during the early part of the summer are systematically fitted against teams of batsmen and bowlers, among whom are often gentlemen players of science and repute. Example, says the proverb, is better than precept. At any rate it is more often followed. Now without wishing to speak severely of a style as seen in the ordinary run of second eleven players in Christchurch, it may be safely affirmed that any youngster playing with or against them, will see quite as much to be avoided as to be imitated. Yet it is against second elevens that Christ's College cricket is almost entirely played.

FIGURE 8

Christ's College XI, 1896. In contrast to the XI of 1879, this team wore a distinct College cricket blazer – symptomatic of the many efforts by New Zealand elite schools to replicate the conventions of their English public school counterparts. (Christ's College Collection)

FIGURE 9

Cricket at Sydenham Park, 1914. Unlike many working-class suburbs, Sydenham – the 'Model Borough' – established good public recreational facilities during the 1890s. (Canterbury Museum: Ref. 1607)

To remedy this problem, Wednesday afternoon matches were instituted between the college XI and teams combining leading Canterbury players and aspiring college colts.[22] Nevertheless the XI still finished near the bottom of the local cup competition on several occasions during the next decade.

If they could not forge their reputation on the field, college cricketers certainly contributed a great deal to developments off it. College old boys such as Thomas Condell, T.D. Harman, Arthur Ollivier and George Tapper were prominent on the Canterbury Cricket Association committee, while the Harman brothers, Tapper and Reginald Vincent, among others, gave long service to the New Zealand Cricket Council.

By the mid 1890s the sporting facilities of Christ's College were such as to draw a more than favourable comparison from an English visitor to New Zealand. The college gymnasium, swimming baths and playing fields were as good as any in England. Indeed, one observer eulogised: 'The Canterbury people like to hear it called the "Eton of New Zealand", but it is Rugby rather than Eton. A leading feature in the school system is the attention paid to the physical side of education, to which the Canterbury people attach great importance'.[23] By 1914 Christ's College had produced at least 57 first-class cricketers for Canterbury, Hawke's Bay, Otago, and the universities of Oxford and Cambridge.[24] Curiously, the college also produced the first New Zealand team to take the field in England. In June 1885, under the name 'Oxford Maoris', a team comprising Christ's College old boys resident at Oxford took the field against the King Sutton CC; whether they played any other games is not known.[25]

Such a sporting reputation was jealousy guarded and threats to it were not easily tolerated. When the Revd E.C. Crosse succeeded as headmaster in 1920 he attempted to raise the academic standard of the school and reduce its sporting emphasis. Yet the tone of his prize-giving speeches throughout the 1920s reveals that while Crosse disparaged rugby as 'a dragon with claws which feeds on the young' he reserved a certain fondness for cricket and tennis and never intended that they should be the object of his criticism.[26] Although he remained for a decade, he steadily alienated the Old Boys Association and eventually resigned due to ill health. His successor, R.C. Richards, was an old boy and athlete. A.E. Flower, 1897–1937, and T.W.C. Tothill, 1923–60, were other long-term masters who took a considerable interest in sport. Tothill went on an exchange to Uppingham in 1929, after Harold Lusk, Auckland, Canterbury and New Zealand opening batsman, had been exchanged with Rugby in 1913.[27]

Firth of Wellington

If Christ's College had the strongest sporting tradition of the New Zealand elite schools, Wellington College lost little by comparison. After struggling for its first quarter century, Wellington began to make dramatic progress during the 1890s – progress due almost entirely to a headmaster who had been trained in the Christ's College tradition of Corfe and Hare. Indeed, just as Corfe was at the head of the English generation of sporting headmasters in New Zealand, so Joseph Firth was unchallenged among the first New Zealand-born generation.

Born in Wellington in 1859, Firth won a scholarship to Nelson College in 1873 and became a pupil-teacher in 1875. After representing the school at athletics, cricket and football, and as captain of cadets, he was a junior master at Wellington College 1881–86, and took 32 wickets in 5 matches for Wellington during the early 1880s. Appointed gymnastics master at Christ's College in 1886, he took a BA at Canterbury College before returning to Wellington College as headmaster in 1891.[28]

Before Firth's arrival, sport at Wellington College had languished, perhaps as much due to a lack of facilities as a lack of interest on the part of the teaching staff.[29] Cricket had been sporadic throughout the 1870s, although a match was played against Nelson College in 1878. Fortunes increased during Firth's first period of service during the early 1880s and there were numerous matches involving pupils, masters and old boys.[30] But standards slipped again after his departure, leading *The Wellingtonian* of May 1891 to roundly condemn the cricketers for their failure to practise and inability to put a full XI in the field at any time during the 1890/91 season.[31]

From 1891 Firth set about raising funds to build a gymnasium and turn the College's surplus of rough land into quality playing fields. As one old boy recalled, 'The Boss loved the Lower Ground. He spent hours after school with a bottle of concentrated sulphuric acid and a piece of tubing and burnt out the dandelions, docks and other weeds. He immersed himself in the literature of grass cultivation, and he became an authority on the question.'[32] Firth also led by example as a player, dominating the batting and bowling of the XI during the 1890s, boxing with his pupils, and regularly throwing his 6 ft 5 in frame into school football matches.[33] Accordingly, *The Wellingtonian* now found much to admire. Cricketers were praised for their enthusiasm in practice and energy on the field, while 'lounging' non games players were attacked mercilessly.[34]

While Firth valued sport, he valued sportsmanship even more, especially in team games where the right sort of 'corporate spirit' could be engendered. As his close friend and biographer, Sir James Elliott, surmised:

> Firth aimed at the development of the complete man, and would have placed first, character and personality; second, scholarship; and third, sport … Firth looked upon games for boys not only as physical exercise but also, and mainly, as moral and mental training. He had no wish to make football matches and cricket matches a public spectacle for idle thousands; a source of revenue for promoters, and astute gamblers. Mob hysteria which at times sweeps like a wave over New Zealand for

attainment of 'football supremacy of the world' would have been a
sorry spectacle for Firth. He remained all through the days of his manhood a grown-up, game-playing boy, and kept that spirit and outlook.[35]

Thus, Firth was able to keep sport in perspective, to view it as a component
of the wider education system rather than an end in itself. During a debate
on the role of school sport in 1907 he explained the careful balance of
his position:

> The schoolmaster's work lies very largely in the classroom, and his
> efforts are directed towards the boys' acquisition of knowledge and
> still more towards the training of the boys' minds; these things do not,
> by any means, sum up his work and anxieties, for there is a much more
> important thing than either – the boy's character. An important means
> by which to influence the boy in the right way, to get more closely in
> touch with his feelings, to give him opportunities for developing his
> individuality and his manly qualities – among which I rank highly use-
> fulness and self-sacrifice – is afforded by school games and athletics.
> Of course these things may be allowed to occupy too much of the boy's
> attention and thought – they may be regarded as the only things desir-
> able – but at this school very strenuous efforts are made to prevent play
> assuming too important a place.[36]

Warnings against the excesses of sport may have come less from Firth than
from his college board of governors. In August 1907 the board expressed
concern at the consequences of college teams playing in club football after
a local team had been suspended for its bad language in a match against the
college, and the Chairman advised Firth that college teams should only play
matches against other schools and not against local clubs.[37] The matter
appears to have been taken no further.

As much as it was a positive element in the building of character, sport
was equally, in Firth's considered opinion, a counter to the perceived evils
of masturbation and other adolescent vice:

> That Satan finds work for idle hands is an ever present difficulty for the
> schoolmaster whose aim should be to keep hands and minds busy with
> healthy occupation. It is true that at times the boy attaches too much
> importance to athletics, but the danger he thus incurs is a grain of sand
> to the mountain of danger that threatens the boy who, slack in his class-
> work, takes no part in the athletic side of school life. His mind wan-
> ders, and assuredly it does wander. It does not roam over the clean
> fields of health and the playing of games, but wades through the
> garbage of the gutter of idleness.[38]

Firth had been careful to include his familiar warning against excessive devotion to sport, but there was no escaping its importance as a device for social and moral control. By the time ill health forced his retirement in 1920, Wellington College had established a consistent reputation as an academic and sporting institution of high regard – both within New Zealand and among all the public schools of the Empire.[39]

Wanganui Collegiate School

One of Wellington College's most frequent opponents from the late 1890s was Wanganui Collegiate School, which established a very similar cricketing tradition. The first sporting initiatives at the school were taken by George Richard Saunders, a Cambridge undergraduate and talented athlete whose ill health forced him to come to New Zealand in 1876. He presented the first sporting colours, based on the dark blue and black of his own Gonville College, and raised £40 to clear a ground for cricket and purchase equipment. Around 1880, Saunders took the XI to Marton to play St Stephen's Parish School.[40]

His efforts were sustained by Bache Wright Harvey, headmaster 1882–88. A graduate of St John's College, Cambridge and a curate of various New Zealand parishes before his arrival at Wanganui, he was awarded a doctorate in divinity shortly before his death in 1888. Harvey oversaw the rapid expansion of cricket, rowing, rugby and tennis during the 1880s – with cricket especially attracting much attention from the local press. An 1883 letter to the Wanganui *Collegian*, signed 'Esprit de corps', suggested that arrangements should be made to photograph the XI, as it was common in England to photograph teams who had brought honour to the school. Two years later, arrangements were made for a cricket triangular between Nelson College, Wanganui Collegiate and Wellington College, but had to be abandoned when the latter was unable to travel.[41]

Sport at Wanganui Collegiate, though, received its greatest boost from Walter Empson. Educated at Charterhouse and Trinity College, Oxford, he worked variously on Canterbury sheep stations, as a banana grower in Fiji and as secretary to the Canterbury Jockey Club before joining the collegiate staff in 1884 and serving as headmaster 1888–1909. He quickly introduced the prefectorial system and placed many other institutions of the school – and sporting ones in particular – in the hands of the boys. Indeed, Empson's philosophy is quite apparent from a report to the Wellington Diocesan Synod in 1889, in which he stated that 'success in sport may not be an infallible test of a school's well-being, but there can be little doubt that decadence in this respect is an almost certain proof that all is not as it should be'. In 1901 Empson instituted the Loretto uniform of shorts and open-necked flannel shirts – soon to become standard in New Zealand schools; he was president of the New Zealand Cricket Council in 1900–01.[42]

Auckland Grammar School

Auckland Grammar School had a sporadic cricket club from its foundation in 1869, but inadequate facilities and the onset of economic depression during the early 1880s ensured that the school failed during its first two decades to develop the institutions typical of an English public school. The arrival of C.F. Bourne as headmaster in 1882 marked a steady revival. A product of St John's College, Oxford, Bourne used sport and extramural activities generally to foster what he regarded as a much needed 'tone' and 'school feeling'. In 1885 he persuaded the board of governors to hire two good wickets in the Auckland Domain. His idealisation, though, of the public school model was not always matched by the social and economic realities of a colonial school in which facilities were spartan and attendances sporadic. After several clashes with Auckland Grammar's governors, Bourne left in 1893 to succeed F.A. Hare as headmaster of Christ's College, a move he regarded as a 'professional promotion' to a school better suited to his English ideals.[43]

Bourne's successor, J.W. Tibbs CMG, headmaster 1893–1922, has been described by the school historian as belonging to the long tradition of 'great Victorian autocrats who ran their schools almost single-handed and moulded them to conform with their own theories'. He was a distinguished graduate of Keble College, Oxford, and taught mathematics at Auckland Grammar from 1885. Under his direction the school expanded to become the second largest secondary institution in Australasia – its role of nearly 700 in 1914 placing it behind only Sydney Grammar School. To maintain the 'tone' established by Bourne, Tibbs created a school cadet corps, generated new enthusiasm for the Old Boys Association and inaugurated a strong tradition of employing like-minded old boys as teachers. The playing fields were also significantly expanded and S.P. Jones, veteran of 12 Tests for Australia, was employed as cricket coach. There were four school XIs by 1913, and Tibbs had solicited sufficient contributions from old boys to initiate regular matches against Christchurch Boys' High School, among others. By 1914 the school had provided at least 40 – almost a third – of all Auckland representative cricketers.[44]

James Drummond, headmaster 1923–28, demonstrated, as Firth had, that New Zealanders possessed a considerable appreciation of the public schools ideal. Educated at Auckland Grammar – where he excelled at athletics and rugby – and at the University of Auckland, he expressed a determination to run the school along the lines of such institutions as Winchester. Like Firth, he had no time for those who allowed sport to dominate academia, but prized it as an essential adjunct. Nevertheless, after 1923 sport was almost compulsory.[45]

Nelson College

Cricket at Nelson College can be traced to at least 1860, when several matches were played against town teams. However, progress was not consistent until the 1880s, when the arrival of William Justice Ford, principal 1886–89, made a significant sporting impact. Educated at Repton and Cambridge, Ford was regarded as one of the hardest-hitting batsmen in England and played frequently for Cambridge, Middlesex and the MCC. Before moving to New Zealand he was a master at Marlborough College and later taught at Leamington College. A prolific writer on sport during his last years, he compiled histories of both Middlesex and Cambridge cricket.[46]

Soon after Ford's arrival the *Nelsonian* devoted four pages to 'Cricket as it is and as it was'. His performances as both player and coach ensured a period of prosperity for Nelson College cricket that lasted well beyond his brief term as principal. The season of 1893/94 was concluded with a formal 'cricket dinner', while a *Nelsonian* editorial of April 1895 referred to cricket as 'this manifestation of *esprit de corps*'. By 1901 cricket was under the astute guidance of C.H. Board, a college old boy who represented both Nelson and Otago at cricket and rugby and completed an MA at the University of Otago. There were eight school XIs by 1903, and the 1st XI possessed blazers which included a badge with the school colours.[47]

Otago Boys' High School

Otago Boys' High School had the weakest cricketing tradition among the elite New Zealand schools – due in no small part to the perennial Dunedin problem of a lack of suitable grounds. An XI was active within a year of the foundation of the school in 1863, but cricket had all but disappeared during the early 1870s as players shifted allegiance to the better facilities of the Dunedin CC. Under Dr William Macdonald, a product of Edinburgh University who served as rector 1878–85, there was a much-needed boost to all sports, with the figure of at least 100 cricketers by 1880 a sure indication of this.[48]

The prevailing emphasis, though, remained with club cricket. The *Otago High School Magazine* of November 1885 implied a certain loyalty to the Carisbrook CC who allowed the school to use their ground. School cricketing fortunes remained low, and the XI was criticised in March 1887 for its carelessness and lack of enthusiasm. Cricket was not strong in 1898 due to the presence of too many 'loafers' among the boys, and it had reached a very low ebb by November 1900. In August 1902 the *Magazine* criticised a lack of spectator support from non-players.[49]

In reality, the prognosis was less gloomy. A regular fixture was played with Christ's College from 1886, and in 1896 £80 was raised to develop a new school cricket ground. Under the direction of Alexander Wilson, a graduate of Aberdeen University who was rector 1895–1906, cricket began to flourish. From 1903 the school employed former Australian Test player Harry Graham as coach – with almost immediate results. They had, however, won only 6 of 46 encounters with Christ's College by 1934.[50]

Waitaki Boys' High School

Otago's nearest cricketing neighbour, Waitaki Boys' High School, Oamaru, had an active cricket team from its foundation in 1883, and the first issue of the *Oamaruvian* urged compulsory cricket for the following season. Matches were initiated against Timaru Boys' High School in 1886, Otago Boys High School in 1887 and Christchurch Boys' High School in 1894. Much of the credit for this growth is due to Algernon Charles Gifford and S. Gilbert. Gifford, born in Oamaru and educated at Denstone College, Staffordshire, and St John's College, Cambridge, assumed a position at Waitaki soon after its foundation. Gilbert, a talented cricketer, was a product of Manchester Grammar School and King's College, London.[51]

After Gilbert's departure during the early 1890s, Waitaki cricket went into decline, but had revived again by 1903. There was always a problem with the development of suitable grounds and with finding suitable opposition within a comparatively rural area. When the local Oamaru club competition declined after 1907 – and particularly during the First World War – the school was starved of opponents.[52]

Under Frank Milner, Waitaki's most famous rector (1906–44), cricket again flourished. Educated at Nelson College and the University of Canterbury, Milner was an ardent imperialist and educational innovator, regarded by certain of his contemporaries as the New Zealand equivalent of Thomas Arnold.[53] In his writings, Ian Milner vividly recalls both school cricket and the fascination that pupils held for the distant game of England during his father's rectorship:

> Empire sentiment apart, England at cricket, was the father of us all, Ashes in hand or no. A veteran like W.G. Grace was a dynastic figure.... I had my Jack Hobbs of Surrey and England and Bert Sutcliffe, Yorkshire and England ... After I'd straightened out the cream and green-covered mag, which had travelled twelve thousand miles into my hands, the first thing was to see how many Jack had made against Lancashire or Kent three months or more previously.[54]

Whatever Milner's subsequent career as an active socialist – and his implication as a KGB agent during the 1950s, there was no mistaking the imperial and public school ideology which dominated his youth.

Inter-School and University Cricket

While all of the elite secondary schools were developing a more or less similar ideology, and there were some regular interchanges – Christ's College
and Otago Boys' High, Wanganui Collegiate and Wellington College –
attempts to bring all of them into regular contact in the manner of the regular public school exchanges were less successful. In March 1908
E.H. Williams, founding president of the New Zealand Cricket Council,
offered the Heathcote Williams Challenge Shield for competition between
the leading schools. The Council initially proposed to award the Shield after
a tournament between Auckland Grammar, Christchurch Boys' High,
Christ's College, King's College (Auckland), Otago Boys' High, Te Aute
College, Timaru Boys' High, Wanganui Collegiate, Wellington College and
other schools to be approved – a category which presumably included
Nelson College, strangely absent from the original list.[55]

When King's, Otago and Wanganui announced that they were unable to
participate in a national tournament, an alternative series of regional tourna-
ments was suggested. This met with a similar lack of success and there were
eventually only two confirmed entries for the competition – Christchurch
Boys' High School and Christ's College. The former won the match and was
duly awarded the Shield in December 1908. Christ's College challenged
again during the following season, as did Auckland Grammar, but there was
no interest from any other school. When the Cricket Council attempted to
revive interest in the Shield in October 1913, it stressed that only three
schools had ever participated.[56] Although no reasons for such apathy were
ever given, it is likely that the major impediment was financial.

This failure to create an enduring and widespread competitive spirit
among the schools is matched by a lack of tradition once cricketers left
school. Certainly, there were clear relationships between schools and clubs,
such as that between Christ's College and the United Canterbury CC or
between Otago Boys' High School and Carisbrook. But only Wellington
College appears to have developed a specific old boys cricket club before
the 1920s.[57] At the same time, there was little university cricket in New
Zealand. In large part this was due to the small number of students, and especially the small number of matriculated (full-time) students. The University
of Otago boasted 167 male students in 1891, 203 in 1900 and 313 in 1910,
and the roll of the University of Canterbury peaked at 387 in 1891, declined
to 224 by 1900, before climbing to 399 in 1910 – perhaps only three-quarters of whom were male.[58] As a summer sport played outside university
term-time, cricket was not well placed to take advantage of the limited sense
of student community that existed before the 1920s.

Under the influence of Professor George Sale, the University of Otago
had an active cricket club from 1871, but its existence was sporadic during
the 1870s and it lapsed completely between 1879 and 1895. A challenge to
Canterbury College in October 1877 prompted the immediate formation of

a cricket club in Christchurch. But much as the members supported the idea of establishing a regular fixture with Otago, the secretary regretted that they were unable to do so:

> They considered ... that in order to give the match a truly collegiate character, the players should be confined to matriculated Students, and they regretted that owing to the fact that Canterbury College then possessed only fourteen matriculated Students, of whom some two or three were ladies, and some three or four others incapacitated through age and other infirmities from actively pursuing the noble art of cricket, they would be unable to place an eleven in the field that season; they hoped, however, to be able to do so in the following year.

By the time Canterbury felt able to accept the challenge at the end of 1879, the Otago club had lapsed.[59]

Although Canterbury College played some matches against Christ's College and Christchurch Boys' High School, it was not until the end of 1907 that arrangements for inter-varsity cricket came to fruition. Canterbury met Otago and Victoria University College (Wellington) annually until 1914 and an inter-Island fixture was played in April 1914. An informal meeting of university cricketers held at Easter 1911 also resolved to arrange matches involving Auckland, and to invite a team from Sydney University to tour New Zealand; neither of these proposals amounted to anything.[60]

Cricket and the Primary Schools

Further important questions arise concerning the fate of those at the other end of the social and educational scale. Without exception, the curriculum of the elite schools placed a strong emphasis on the utility of sport, and to a greater or lesser degree all of them served as nurseries for representative cricket. Given the nature of their composition and the middle-class bias of New Zealand cricket, it follows that the educative and recreative values of the schools had a strong bearing on the fabric of the game at the highest levels. Yet this needs some qualification. The number attending secondary schools in 1901 was perhaps 3,000 (*c.*1,800 boys and *c.*1,200 girls) – or 3 per cent of the eligible age group. This increased to only 25 per cent by 1939. Auckland Grammar, which always had the largest roll, probably had no more than 350 boys at any time prior to 1900. Wellington College peaked at 145 in 1882, declined to 60 in 1891 but climbed to 140 in 1893 as Firth began his work; by 1912 he had guided 2,836 boys through the school. Nelson grew slowly to a peak of 202 in 1908, and Waitaki averaged 196 per term during the following year. At best, less than 10 per cent of New Zealand males received any secondary education prior to 1914, and a large proportion of these attended district High Schools for only one or two years.[61]

What, then, was the extent of cricketing and recreational guidance provided for the majority of the population during their years at primary school?
The pioneering 1877 Education Act certainly did not neglect the physical
needs of pupils:

> In Public schools provision shall be made for the instruction in military
> drill for all boys, and in such of the schools as the Board shall from
> time to time direct provision shall also be made for physical training
> and whenever practicable there shall be attached to each school a play-
> ground of at least a quarter of an acre.[62]

Although organisational difficulties created an initial apathy to military drill,
it was well established in the primary school curriculum by the mid 1880s;
in 1887 a Nelson schools Inspector described it as 'a potent moral as well as
physical factor in bringing up an alert well-poised and readily obedient
race'.[63]

From 1893 the Government made available, free of charge, members of
the permanent artillery to act as drill instructors. The programme peaked
around the turn of the century, especially when initial British enlistments for
the South African war revealed disturbingly low standards of health and fitness. Drill was increasingly seen in quasi-medical terms. If applied correctly
it would assist normal physical development and cure physical defects. To
this end, many of the exercises were taken directly from the *Imperial
Handbook of Infantry Training*.[64]

The crucial difference between military drill for primary schools and the
public school ethos of codified sport lay in the type of discipline they sought
to create. As Colin McGeorge explains, 'One had been originally designed
to teach working class children to be obedient to external authority; the other
fostered co-operation but also provided opportunities for initiative and
leadership'.[65] But one significant disadvantage of the drill system for primary schools was that it made no provision for girls, and it was gradually
superseded by a 'Swedish' exercise programme for both sexes. Moreover,
the military onus was partially removed from teaching staff when the 1909
Defence Act merged school cadets under the new system of compulsory
military training.[66]

Games and athletics in the conventional sense were much slower to take
hold in the primary education system. Although the 1885 regulations for the
inspection of schools included 'supervision at recess', school inspectors
were not strictly required to comment on this aspect and teachers generally
showed little interest. The decision of the Malvern School Committee in
1887 to provide cricket gear for boys and tennis racquets for girls was the
exception rather than the rule.[67]

Perceptions of 'larrikinism', caused by children congregating on the
streets, prompted a reassessment of the wider role of schools from the early
1890s. Perceived to be at greatest risk of delinquency were young children

of the urban poor and those who had finished their compulsory education at the age of 12 but were unable to work under the terms of the Factories Act, which set the lower age limit at 14. Among other things, efforts were made to raise the school leaving age to 14 in harmony with the Factories Act, to strictly enforce the compulsory attendance clauses of the Education Act and to legislate on the out-of-school activities of children. Of this third area of effort, various – unsuccessful – local body attempts were made to impose curfews on children.[68]

Parallel to the rise of the kindergarten movement catering for pre-school children, the schools embarked upon what Brian Sutton-Smith has described as a gradual 'taming of the playground' during the 1890s. School committees began to fence their playing areas and install playground equipment, and teachers assumed a much more active role in the supervision of games. Whereas 'supervision at recess' had been largely ignored in 1885, examination candidates for the D and E teaching certificates in 1899 were required to comment on the dictum that the playground is an 'uncovered schoolroom'. Inspectors began to make more detailed comments on the matter, and the initial requirement to 'supervise' became one to 'organise'. In 1913 the inspection heading was changed to 'supervision in recess and organisation of school games'. At the same time, the 1912 Amendment to the Education Act formally substituted a physical training system for both sexes instead of school cadets. Under a syllabus issued by R. Garlick, the Director of Physical Education, physical training was to be allocated a definite place in the timetable of every school, and teachers were to be properly trained in its execution.[69]

Responding to an address by R. Darroch to the Wellington Public Schools' Cricket Association in October 1911, the *Lyttelton Times* strongly endorsed his call for compulsory school sport and noted with pleasure the efforts that were now being made by teachers:

[U]ntil games are made compulsory in the schools, the self-sacrificing labours of the teachers cannot attain the full measure of the success which will be their best reward. Even in New Zealand, proud as we are of our athletic prowess, the practice of athletics is by no means so widespread as it ought to be. There are far too many lookers-on. They play their part – and a very necessary part it is – in the development of sport; but the enthusiastic 'barracker' too often expends his energies in developing his vocal chords at the expense of the rest of his body, while he takes no opportunity to learn the moral lessons which are taught in the thick of the struggle. The preponderance of lookers-on, it seems to us, has been due very largely to the failure of school training to inculcate in the minds of boys and girls a proper love of healthy exercise and in some measure also to the neglect of sport bodies to provide for the wants of the growing youths immediately after their school days were over. Happily both the schools and the sport bodies have been mending their ways, and the good work they have done furnishes an excellent reason for some official recognition of their labours. Of course there will be strong and weak, expert and less expert players in the games when they are made compulsory in the schools, but it will be the aim of the sympathetic teacher to encourage the children to learn on the playing fields just as readily as in the class-rooms. It is the early encouragement that is needed to fit them for a better part in later life than that of looking on.[70]

In the manner of the public schools, the advocacy of games had shifted beyond a mechanism of social control to a realisation that they could impart moral benefit and bring prestige to a school.

By the early twentieth century large inter-primary school athletic meetings were being held in all of the main centres and schools' athletic associations were established to administer school sport. Typical of these was the Canterbury Public Schools Amateur Athletics Association established in July 1900. The Association constitution contained strict amateur clauses – including a ban on any pupil who may compete for cash in sports outside its jurisdiction – and it aimed to 'remove the suspicion ... that the teachers interest in their pupils is only superficial and ceases as soon as the actual schoolwork is over'. The Association took over the control of primary schools cricket from the Canterbury Cricket Association and established an extensive programme of inter-school athletics meetings. By 1903, 3,000 pupils were attending the annual sports at Lancaster Park in a programme that included 52 events for boys and 32 for girls.[71]

Perhaps surprisingly, a publication entitled the *School Journal* lent very little weight to the prevailing ideology. Established in May 1907, the *Journal* consisted of three parts, each directed at a different educational level up to Standard Six. It was undeniably conservative and a strong advocate of the British Empire, but its attention to sport is minimal. Part III of the first issue contained a letter from a New Zealand Rhodes Scholar, probably Otago and All Black wing Colin Gilray, outlining his visit to Winchester School and idealising the self discipline of the English public school games system. The following year an article on 'The Citizen and the State' used an analogy revolving around the duties of sports club members to explain the obligations of citizens to society. Thereafter, the *Journal* printed articles on the history of cricket in 1921 and 1929 and another, 'The Game of Empire', in 1927 that extolled the virtues of discipline, fair play and teamwork.[72]

How much specific emphasis the primary schools placed on cricket above other summer sports is a relevant point. The expense of equipment, the demands of space and ground quality undoubtedly militated against the formal organisation of the game in some areas. Indeed, there are no accounts of enduring inter-primary school competitions and traditions in the period before 1914. But it is equally apparent, given the passion and determination displayed by adult New Zealanders, that generations of children pursued the game with varying degrees of rudiment and improvisation. Moreover, there were teachers aplenty who encouraged them. Although few public school old boys became primary teachers, many products of New Zealand institutions certainly did. Moreover, the teachers training colleges that were formalised after 1905 encouraged sport among their students and established links with university and local clubs.[73] Herbert Milnes, founding principal of Auckland Teachers Training College 1905–16, was an unyielding advocate of games and exercise in the best English tradition and did not hesitate to lead his trainees by example.[74] Perhaps some of his protégés contributed to one of the few moments of cricketing success for New Zealand against Australia when a strong New South Wales Teachers XI was defeated by New Zealand Teachers at Auckland in 1912.[75]

There is no question that the English public school athletic ideal was successfully replicated in New Zealand. In the main centres, and at Nelson, Waitaki and Wanganui, an important nursery was created for provincial and national teams. Above all else, boys of whatever ability were imbued with an ideal that stressed a multiplicity of values for sport beyond individual athletic prowess. They may have been a minority of the population but they came to influence cricket in their post-school years as a group of well trained and well connected proselytising agents. In this respect New Zealand cricket could hardly have been better served. Yet, at the same time – as the following chapters reveal – there were structural and demographic impediments that dictated a course for New Zealand cricket quite beyond their control.

Notes

1. Holt, *Sport and the British*, pp. 75–83; Newsome, *Godliness and Good Learning*, pp. 81–2; T.J.L. Chandler, 'Games at Oxbridge and the Public Schools, 1830–80: The Diffusion of an Innovation', *International Journal of the History of Sport*, 8, 2 (1991), pp. 171–2.
2. Holt, *Sport and the British*, pp. 80–3.; Newsome, *Godliness and Good Learning*, p. 203.
3. A. Kirk-Greene, 'Badge of Office? Sport and his Excellency in the British Empire', *International Journal of the History of Sport*, 6, 7 (1989), pp. 220–32. Of the 300 members of the Sudan Political Service, 93 obtained Oxbridge blues for sport.
4. Stoddart, 'Sport, Cultural Imperialism and Colonial Responses', pp. 654–5; K. Sandiford and B. Stoddart, 'The Elite Schools and Cricket in Barbados: A Study in Colonial Continuity', *International Journal of the History of Sport*, 4, 3 (1987), pp. 334–41; C.L.R. James, *Beyond a Boundary* (London, 1963); J.A. Mangan, 'Eton in India: The Imperial Diffusion of a Victorian Educational Ethic', *History of Education*, 7, 2 (1978).
5. Mangan, *Games Ethic and Imperialism*, p. 155. See also J.S. Branthwaite, 'American Cricket From its Beginnings, Through the Philadelphian "Golden Age" to its Death' (MA thesis, University of Canterbury, 1993), pp. 20, 22, 26.
6. See Chapter 1, n.34.
7. Campbell, *Story of Napier*, pp. 307, 311–14, 319–31; Eldred-Grigg, *Southern Gentry*, pp. 80, 83, 115–19.
8. G. McCulloch, 'Imperial and Colonial Designs: The Case of Auckland Grammar School', *History of Education*, 17, 4 (1988), p. 257.
9. A.E. Campbell, *Educating New Zealand* (Wellington, 1941), p. 6.
10. McCulloch, 'The Case of Auckland Grammar School', p. 262.
11. D.G. Hamilton, *College!: A History of Christ's College* (Christchurch, 1996), p. 400.

12. The main magazines were: *The Grammarian* (Auckland Grammar School); *Christchurch Boys High School Magazine*; *Christ's College Register*; *Nelsonian* (Nelson College); *Otago High School Magazine*, *The Oamaruvian* (Waitaki Boys High School); *The Collegian* (Wanganui Collegiate School); *Wellingtonian* (Wellington College).
13. H. Roth, *George Hogben: A Biography* (Wellington, 1952), pp. 110–16.
14. M. Crotty, *Making the Australian Male: Middle-Class Masculinity 1870–1920* (Melbourne, 2001), pp. 31–73.
15. *School List of Christ's College from 1850 to 1935* (Christchurch, 1935), pp. 461–76; Hamilton, *College!*, pp. 33–4, 44–7.
16. C.C. Corfe, obituary, *The Christ's College Register*, Aug. 1935, pp. 93–5.
17. Hamilton, *College!*, pp. 78, 114–8, 129–37, 143–5.
18. *The Christ's College Register,* Aug. 1935, p. 93.
19. Hamilton, *College!*, pp. 109–11, 160–3; *School List of Christ's College*, pp. 324–6.
20. *Christ's College Sports Register*, Sept. 1884, p. 26; June 1886, pp. 7–11; D.A. Wood, 'Athleticism: A Study with Particular Reference to Christ's College' (research essay, University of Canterbury, 1985), pp. 24–6.
21. *Christ's College Sports Register*, June 1885, p. 8.
22. Ibid., Feb. 1886, p. 33. See also Hamilton, *College!*, pp. 109–12.
23. R.E.N. Twopeny, *Pictorial New Zealand* (London, 1895), pp. 220–1.
24. *School List of Christ's College*, passim.
25. Reese, *New Zealand Cricket 1914–33*, p. 115.
26. *Christ's College Register*, April 1931, p. 428.
27. Wood, 'Athleticism', pp. 20–1, 27–8.
28. A.W. Beasley, 'Joseph Firth' in Orange, *DNZB, Vol.2*, pp. 142–3.
29. H.A. Heron, *The Centennial History of Wellington College* (Wellington, 1967), p. 27.
30. F.M. Leckie, *Early History of Wellington College* (Wellington, 1934), pp. 277–85.
31. *The Wellingtonian*, 2 May 1891, p. 5.
32. Quoted in Sir J. Eliott, *Firth of Wellington* (Wellington, 1937), pp. 188–9.
33. Derived from *The Wellingtonian*, 1891–95.
34. For example: ibid., 30 April 1892, p. 8; 8 Dec. 1893, p. 6; April 1897, p. 11; April 1901, p. 11.
35. Eliott, *Firth of Wellington*, p. 178.
36. Ibid., pp. 183–4.
37. *New Zealand Herald*, 2 Sept. 1907, p. 6.
38. Eliott, *Firth of Wellington*, pp. 183–4.
39. Heron, *Centennial History of Wellington College*, pp. 55–6.
40. A. Sangster, *Pathway to Establishment: The History of Wanganui Collegiate School* (Wanganui, 1985), pp. 38–9.
41. Ibid., pp. 48–9.
42. Ibid., pp. 55–6; B. Mackay, 'Walter Empson' in Orange, *DNZB: Vol.2*, pp. 132–3.
43. K.A. Trembath, *Ad Augusta: A Centennial History of Auckland Grammar School 1869–1969* (Auckland, 1969), pp. 63–95, 73, 87.
44. Ibid., p. 96, 105, 132, 150, 172, 206, 383–9; *100 Not Out*, pp. 209–16.
45. Trembath, *Ad Augusta*, pp. 209–18.
46. J.K. McKay and H.F. Allan (eds), *The Nelson College Old Boys Register* (Nelson, 1956), p. 537; B. Green (comp.), *The Wisden Book of Obituaries* (London, 1986), pp. 274–5.
47. *Nelsonian*, 5, 3 (Sept. 1886), pp. 65–9; 9, 1 (May 1894), p. 15; 10, 1 (April 1895), p. 2; 16, 3 (Dec. 1901), p. 96; 18, 3 (Dec. 1903).
48. T.D. Pearce and R.V. Fulton, *Otago High School Old Boys Register* (Dunedin, 1907), n.p.; Crawford, 'A History of Recreation and Sport', p. 185.
49. *Otago High School Magazine*, 3, 1 (March 1887), p. 8; 14, 1 (April 1898), p. 8; 16, 3 (Nov. 1900), p. 130; 18, 2 (Aug. 1902), p. 52.
50. Scholefield, *Dictionary*, *Vol.2*, p. 520; *Otago High School Magazine*, 20, 4 (May 1904), p. 15; *School List of Christ's College*, p. 461f.
51. K.C. McDonald, *History of Waitaki Boys' High School, 1883–1933* (Wellington, 1934), pp. 54–5, 106–7.
52. Ibid., pp. 126–7, 156–7, 205–6.
53. I. Milner, *Milner of Waitaki: Portrait of The Man* (Dunedin, 1983), pp. 9–10.
54. I. Milner, *Intersecting Lines: The Memoirs of Ian Milner* (Wellington, 1993), pp. 49–50.
55. NZCC, Committee Minutes, 17 March 1908; 'Special Minutes', 11 June 1908.

56. NZCC, Committee Minutes, 29 Sept. 1908; 12 Dec. 1908; Management Committee Minutes, 16 Sept. 1909; 25 Oct. 1909; *Otago Witness*, 29 Oct. 1913, p. 53.

57. Both High School Old Boys and Old Collegians were admitted to the Christchurch senior competition in 1923–24. See CCA, Annual Report, 1924.

58. S. Elworthy, *Ritual Song of Defiance: A Social History of Students at the University of Otago* (Dunedin, 1990), p. 161; W.J. Gardner, E.T. Beardsley and T.E. Carter, *A History of the University of Canterbury 1873–1973* (Christchurch, 1973), p. 471.

59. G.J. Griffiths, *Otago University at Cricket: Its History, Records and Statistics* (Dunedin, 1978), pp. 4, 7; *Canterbury College Review*, No. 10, Oct. 1901, p. 10.

60. *Canterbury College Review*, No. 37, June 1911, p. 49; Reese, *New Zealand Cricket 1914–33*, p. 589.

61. Trembath, *Ad Augusta*, p. 132; Heron, *Centennial History of Wellington College*, p. 31; McKay and Allan, *Nelson College Old Boys Register*, p. 156; McDonald, *History of Waitaki Boys*, p. 198.

62. Quoted in A.G. Butchers, *Education in New Zealand* (Dunedin, 1930), p. 13.

63. Ibid., p. 86; C. McGeorge, 'Schools and Socialisation in New Zealand 1890–1914' (Ph.D. thesis, University of Canterbury, 1985), vol. 1, pp. 244–5.

64. Butchers, *Education in New Zealand*, p. 86; McGeorge, 'Schools and Socialisation in New Zealand', pp. 244–5.

65. McGeorge, 'Schools and Socialisation in New Zealand', p. 245.

66. Butchers, *Education in New Zealand*, pp. 86, 233–5.

67. McGeorge, 'Schools and Socialisation in New Zealand', p. 121.

68. Ibid., pp. 97–9.

69. B. Sutton-Smith, *A History of Children's Play: New Zealand 1840–1950* (Wellington, 1982), pp. 43–61, 176–200; McGeorge, 'Schools and Socialisation in New Zealand', pp. 118–25; Butchers, *Education in New Zealand*, pp. 233–5.

70. *Lyttelton Times*, 7 Oct. 1911, p. 8.

71. *NZ Referee*, 18 July 1900, p. 40; 1 Aug. 1900, p. 43; 9 Oct. 1901, p. 41; 4 Dec. 1901, p. 33; 2 Dec. 1903, p. 52; McGeorge, 'Schools and Socialisation in New Zealand', p. 246.

72. E.P. Malone, 'The New Zealand School Journal and The Imperial Ideology', *New Zealand Journal of History*, 7, 1 (1973); *School Journal*, Pt. III, May 1907, p. 12; Pt. III, Feb. 1908, p. 19; Pt. III, Feb. 1921, p. 25; Pt. III, June 1927, p. 134.

73. McGeorge, 'Schools and Socialisation in New Zealand', p. 248.

74. J.A. Mangan and C. Hickey, 'A Pioneer of the Proletariat: Herbert Milnes and the Games Cult in New Zealand', *International Journal of the History of Sport*, 17, 2/3 (2000).

75. Reese, *New Zealand Cricket: 1841–1914*, pp. 546–7.

6

Uniting Distant Communities:
Interprovincial Cricket, 1860–1914

During the last quarter of the nineteenth century the quite separate cricketing entities that had existed in each province crystallised into more homogenous forms. By 1900 the provincial cricket associations were similarly composed, governed by similar constitutions and administered almost identical club competitions. Fixtures between the major provinces expanded from 12 during the 1860s to 81 during the 1890s. In addition, contacts between the various minor cricket associations grew rapidly after 1890.

However, the dramatic growth of New Zealand cricket provides a clear example of conflict between Victorian idealism and economic expediency, a conflict that was, more often than not, able to be resolved in favour of idealism. The New Zealand school system succeeded in creating a native-born generation who idealised the moral and muscular qualities of cricket every bit as much as their English counterparts. Yet the game they administered was never economically viable. The provincial cricket associations quickly discovered that high ideals and influential patronage were no cure for crippling financial problems, inadequate facilities and intransigent local body politicians. In many instances, the associations were obliged to supplement their incomes from activities unrelated to cricket. Any major expenditure on essentials such as ground development, equipment or the hiring of professional coaches was almost certain to produce years of debt-ridden anxiety.

Reconciling the ideal and the reality of New Zealand cricket produced a colonial version of what Keith Sandiford and Wray Vamplew have termed the 'peculiar economics' of English cricket. The game was such an essential component of the Victorian psyche that its preservation could, and did, lead its administrators to fiscal manoeuvring of a sort that would have been anathema to the commercial world in which many of these same men prospered. Thus, an account of the struggle for uniformity and formalisation within New Zealand cricket is much more than an examination of pioneering provincial teams and determined administrators. It is as much about the pervasive values that allowed them to keep going in the face of so much economic unreality.

The fiscal impediment was not the only challenge to the ideal during this period of relative growth. Those who welcomed interprovincial cricket during the 1860s as a means of establishing a sense of unity between diverse and isolated settlements, and for reinforcing the fabric of 'Englishness' that underpinned the colony as a whole, were to be substantially disappointed. A close analysis of the interprovincial programme up to 1914 reveals haphazard arrangements, antagonistic provincial rivalries and disproportionate contributions from some provinces – especially from Canterbury. In some respects the provincial interaction appeared to become more rather than less difficult by 1914.

Interprovincial Beginnings

The perceived importance of cricket as a means of fostering intercommunity relations is reflected in the speed with which the first challenges were issued. Both Nelson in 1844 and Otago in 1848 made overtures to play Wellington at a time when neither settlement had more than a single fledgling club. Unfortunately, these challenges arrived during an equally lean time for Wellington cricket and were never acknowledged.[1] The next challenge, from Auckland, began life on a similarly uncertain footing. Although Wellington cricket was only just emerging from a long period of inactivity, a challenge in January 1860 was willingly accepted. The *Wellington Independent* felt that 'Such interchanges of courtesy are calculated to engender the kindliest feelings, and deserving of being on all occasions promoted'.[2] Such courtesy did not extend to firm arrangements, and the arrival of the Auckland team in mid March took their hosts entirely by surprise. On an unprepared ground, with several of their best players out of town, Wellington lost New Zealand's first – and decidedly low-key – interprovincial match by four wickets.[3] Nonetheless, the *Independent* was again encouraging in its review: 'The result will no doubt be a wholesome stimulus to all the lovers of this national game, and next year when the return match is played, we may hope for better things'.[4]

In customarily haphazard fashion, it was December 1862 before the return match was arranged. Moreover, its outcome demonstrated the clear differences between Auckland and Wellington cricket at this time. Under the auspices of Auckland's recently formed United Cricket Club, no pain or expense was spared in organising the match. A good, if isolated, ground was prepared at Newmarket. The band of the 40th Regiment was engaged to play and a match dinner was arranged – with a rather preclusive 15s admission charge. As the *New Zealander* enthused, 'Every endeavour has been used to render this, in the truest acceptation of the term, a provincial festival'.[5]

Wellington failed to match the occasion in every respect. After being dismissed for only 13 during a 39-run loss to Nelson on the first leg of their journey, they succumbed for 22 in each innings against Auckland to lose by 108 runs. Another loss to Nelson followed on the return journey. Auckland critics condemned the apparent lack of 'upper class' patronage for cricket in Wellington, suggesting that professional coaching was needed. Further, there was widespread criticism of Bromley, the Wellington umpire, who was replaced during the match.[6] Yet the final verdict on proceedings was broad-minded and encouraging:

> We did not anticipate such a crowning result, and although we hope that Auckland may always bear the belt, we would have been quite as well pleased had Wellington given her a harder tussle. We heartily congratulate the conquerors on their victory, expressing at the same time our commendation of the pluck and good feelings of the vanquished. It is such meetings as these that are to be desired to abate provincial prejudices, and to begat provincial kindliness. We have much to respect in each other, much to learn, and much to impart. May the opportunities be frequent and productive of mutual good will.[7]

But the reality, as outlined in Chapters 1 and 3, was that interprovincial travel and communication – especially in the North Island – remained difficult and slow throughout the nineteenth century. Auckland did not play again for another eleven years – until its ground-breaking southern tour in 1873.

As a retrospective indication of the haphazard nature of these early encounters, they are not deemed first-class in terms of the definitions adopted by the Imperial Cricket Council in 1947. First-class fixtures are dated from the inaugural meeting between Canterbury and Otago in February 1864 – surprisingly early given the subsequent struggles of the New Zealand game. Colonial first-class cricket had begun with a fixture between Victoria and Tasmania in February 1851. New South Wales entered the fray in 1856, South Australia in 1877 and Queensland and Western Australia in 1893. Caribbean fixtures were inaugurated with British Guiana's visit to Barbados in February 1865. There was no first-class cricket in South Africa until the first Test match against England in March 1889, with interprovincial fixtures beginning in 1890. India followed in August 1892 when Europeans played Parsees as a prelude to matches against Lord Hawke's touring team. First-class cricket reached Rhodesia in 1905 and Ceylon in 1926.[8]

Canterbury and Otago – An Enduring Rivalry

The only series of New Zealand interprovincial first-class matches to be sustained was that between the neighbouring provinces of Canterbury and Otago. This can be explained in terms of both relative geographical proximity and the altogether more deliberate approach taken by the influential cricketing elites of Christchurch and Dunedin. As a prelude to the visit of George Parr's All England XI in February 1864, a tournament was staged in Dunedin between Canterbury, Otago and Southland. This marked the first of

56 meetings between Canterbury and Otago during the 50 years until the outbreak of war in 1914. The fixture was always the most widely reported and keenly debated in New Zealand cricket. Team selections were a subject for much speculation, and numerous column inches were devoted to the current play and to results of previous encounters.[9] The intensity of public interest may also be judged from the amount of money changing hands on the sidelines. Individuals and newspapers frequently organised 'Calcutta Sweeps' in which substantial amounts were invested on the highest score in an innings or the outcome of a match.[10]

From the outset the Canterbury/Otago fixture was intended to replicate elite English traditions. A committee composed of Edward Stevens and H.P. Lance (Canterbury), and John Kissling, James Fulton and Gibson Turton (Otago), agreed in 1865 that the two provinces should adopt the Oxbridge playing colours – the dark blue of Oxford for Canterbury and light blue of Cambridge for Otago.[11] Explicit emphasis was also placed on the social and political importance of the fixture – not least in an *Otago Daily Times* editorial of 14 February 1866, almost certainly penned by its cricketing editor and future New Zealand Premier, Julius Vogel.

> It brings people together in a friendly unformal manner – the very thing which should be most carefully cherished in a society of waifs and strays like that of a colony. It is the isolated conditions of individuals that is the greatest bar not only to good society, but to good government. It unites Otago, for instance, against Canterbury, but unites it in a courteous, chivalrous, generous antagonism … Nor is it a small thing that cricket draws men from one province to another. Whatever our Canterbury friends may think of our climate, let us hope that they will depart not without feeling that they were very welcome, and not without discovering that Dunedin has attractions sufficient to induce them on their next visit to make arrangements for a longer stay.[12]

The spirit of gentlemanly camaraderie and healthy rivalry that was thought to prevail between Canterbury and Otago is in sharp contrast to the tensions between Auckland and Wellington, or the constant bickering with umpires that marred the Nelson/Wellington matches of the 1880s. In contrast, Canterbury and Otago remained on uniformly harmonious terms: the jubilee fixtures in 1914 were accompanied by veterans matches between earlier participants and lengthy press accounts of the cricketing history of the two provinces.[13]

Interprovincial Expansion

With the Canterbury/Otago link firmly established, the next major contribution to the fabric of interprovincial cricket was an Auckland tour to

Christchurch, Dunedin, Wellington and Nelson in November and December 1873. In practical terms, the tour did not make a lasting impact. Auckland only played one other game in the proceeding nine years, and the Canterbury/Otago and Nelson/Wellington fixtures did not increase in frequency. Yet by providing a common standard from which all provinces could measure their performances, Auckland served to raise the profile of interprovincial cricket. At the same time, the tour produced a more acute appreciation of the potential of cricket in bringing the isolated settlements together. More than one editorial expressed the hope that cricket would establish common reference points in a disparate colony dogged by provincial antagonism and precarious communication.

When Auckland's southern tour was first mooted at a meeting held on 14 June 1873 it was argued that even a moderately unsuccessful venture would be of considerable advantage in reviving Auckland cricket. To the contrary, critics insisted that any tour should come after the revival, rather than as a catalyst for it. There was only a muted response from Auckland clubs to the tour proposal, and it lapsed for several months until taken up by W.F. Buckland and J. Mumford, two of Auckland's best players. Even then, the endeavour only gained momentum when it became apparent that overtures to Wellington and the South Island had been successful. With Otago guaranteeing £40 and Canterbury £25, Auckland subscriptions raised £170 in six weeks. Cricketers in the Thames goldfields area also took a strong interest, with one, W.W. Robinson, eventually appointed captain of the touring team.[14]

True to custom, the team selection was a signal for bickering and complaints that those chosen were not practising hard enough. For their part, the team objected to a practice match against an Auckland CC XI – declaring that a XVI would make for a more even encounter. In response, several talented players who were unable to tour objected to being part of a XVI.[15]

The *New Zealand Herald* also viewed the tour with a certain degree of diffidence. It suggested that Auckland was perhaps being over-ambitious in conducting such a major tour. But neither would it be justifiable to criticise those who had put so much energy into the venture. Whether it succeeded or failed was somewhat secondary to the role it might play in bringing Auckland and the rest of the colony closer together:

> We are extremely glad to think that it is our cricketers who have inaugurated a series of matches which we trust will be of yearly recurrence. It is by intercourse such as this and similar matches generate, the distant communities are brought closer together, and become more intimately connected in friendly relationship. Auckland from Otago and Christchurch is at this present moment as far distant socially as it is in miles, and if by means of these annual cricketing matches a more intimate social relationship than at present existing is established, the representative team who proceed south today will be entitled to the best

thanks of the community, whether they return as conquerors or as defeated men.[16]

The focus on both geographical and social distance confirms that despite two decades of dramatic expansion there was a continuing perception of New Zealand as a collection of unconnected settlements.

In terms of playing ability, the initial pessimism of many Aucklanders proved groundless. The team defeated Canterbury by 7 runs, Otago by 4 wickets, Wellington by 3 wickets and Nelson by an innings and 56 runs. The *Herald* happily reported considerable public interest in the matches. Large crowds frequently gathered at its Auckland office for the latest telegraph news, and the victory over Canterbury was celebrated in the streets. When the team returned to Auckland they were conveyed from Onehunga by coach to be greeted by a large Queen St crowd and accompanying band; the Thames players received an equally enthusiastic reception.[17]

To the *New Zealand Mail* the value of the tour lay in a positive comparison with W.G. Grace's team then touring Australia. While the 'amateur' Grace was paid £1,500 for the tour, New Zealanders could be content that a spirit of genuine English amateurism had pervaded their cricket and enhanced the quality of society as a whole.

> The visit of the Auckland team round the colony a few months ago, and the interest which the various matches played with them excited amongst the lovers of cricket, have had a healthful effect upon the progress of the game generally. Their visit was of a nature very different from that of the now famous All England Eleven in Australia, and the effects have been different in proportion. There, where the conduct and tone of all the matches in which the Englishmen have played have been the subject of not very complimentary allusions both by the press and private persons, the result of a tour which was to infuse an altogether new spirit into the game of cricket, has been to produce a hearty dislike of the mention of the name, which will take some time to wear off, and an ennui in all matters relating to it very different from what the bargaining promoters promised. In New Zealand the genuine love for the game, and the fair spirit in which it was played by all throughout, have made just the opposite impression, and, instead of a relapse, there has been rather a new life exhibited.[18]

There is no evidence that the Auckland tour, or any subsequent interprovincial venture, owed anything to the ambition of commercial speculators.

At a time when provincial unity and cooperation ran a poor second to political and economic rivalry and antagonism, cricket emerged as a rare tonic. Unfortunately, this did not translate into a sustained or balanced programme of matches. Tables 3 and 4 reveal some major disparities within the fabric of interprovincial contacts.[19] After its 1873 tour, Auckland received a

TABLE 3

NEW ZEALAND PROVINCIAL TEAMS ON TOUR, 1864–1914

Home venue	A	C	HB	N	O	S	T	W	Total
Visiting team									
Auckland	–	10	4	1	7	–	–	10	32
Canterbury	10	–	3	–	28	–	1	14	56
Hawke's Bay	3	2	–	–	2	–	2	11	20
Nelson	–	–	–	–	–	–	–	8	8
Otago	5	28	3	–	–	1	–	4	41
Southland	–	–	–	–	1	–	–	–	1
Taranaki	1	–	3	–	–	–	–	–	4
Wellington	9	14	10	8	3	–	–	–	44

TABLE 4

OVERALL PARTICIPATION IN NEW ZEALAND FIRST-CLASS CRICKET

	1860s	1870s	1880s	1890s	1900s	1910s	Total	%*
Australia	–	–	–	–	4	14	18	6.5
Auckland	–	4	9	20	20	18	71	25.6
Canterbury	6	12	19	32	31	24	124	44.7
Fiji	–	–	–	6	–	–	6	2.1
Hawke's Bay	–	–	5	20	15	8	48	15.5
Ld Hawke XI	–	–	–	–	7	–	7	2.5
MCC	–	–	–	–	11	–	11	3.9
Nelson	–	5	11	1	–	–	17	6.1
NSW	–	–	–	17	–	–	17	6.1
New Zealand	–	–	–	3	6	4	13	4.7
North Island	–	–	–	1	1	–	2	0.7
Otago	6	11	14	23	25	16	95	34.2
Queensland	–	–	–	5	–	–	5	1.8
D. Reese XI	–	–	–	–	–	1	1	0.4
South Island	–	–	–	–	2	–	2	0.7
Southland	–	–	–	–	–	2	2	0.7
Tasmania	–	–	4	–	–	–	4	1.4
Taranaki	–	–	1	7	–	–	8	2.9
Wellington	–	6	22	27	26	21	102	36.8
W. Coast (NI)	–	–	1	–	–	–	1	0.4

* The final column of this table refers to the percentage of all games in which each team played – and is calculated on the basis that two teams participated in each game, hence the percentages add up to 200%.

visit from Canterbury in December 1877, but had no other first-class cricket until it toured south in November 1882. Thereafter, Auckland visited the South Island in 1885, 1889, 1893, 1901, 1906, 1907, 1912 and 1914. With the advantage of geographical proximity, Wellington and Nelson enjoyed more frequent contact. Nelson crossed Cook Strait in February 1864 and Wellington returned the visit in February 1867. They met on 23 occasions (including 16 of Nelson's 17 first-class matches) before Nelson declined from first-class status after 1892.[20] By the end of 1890 Wellington had also played two matches against the relatively close Hawke's Bay, but had only travelled to Christchurch twice and Auckland once. During the next 25 years they visited Canterbury 12 times and Auckland 8, but did not play Otago in Dunedin until December 1894 and not again until December 1904. Otago did not travel to the North Island until a four-match tour in December 1892, repeated in December 1899. In total, they played only 12 matches in the North Island up to 1914, by which time 56 of their 95 first-class matches had been against Canterbury. We will see in the next chapter that the inter-changes between the various minor cricket associations emerging during the late nineteenth century were similarly uneven.

Canterbury, the first cricketing province to tour outside New Zealand when it sent a team to Victoria in 1878–79, was not immune to the vagaries of interprovincial contact. By 1905 Canterbury had only visited Auckland on five occasions, although the lure of reclaiming the Plunket Shield – an interprovincial challenge trophy inaugurated in 1906 – produced five more trips during the next decade. By 1914 Canterbury had participated in slightly more than half of all interprovincial matches and 45 per cent of all first-class matches played in New Zealand. Certainly, the Canterbury/Otago fixture – which constituted one-fifth of all first-class matches – ensured that Canterbury played more first-class cricket than other provinces. Only during the 1880s, when Wellington and Nelson met annually, did any province play more matches than Canterbury in a particular decade.

There were several other initiatives, from both the Canterbury Cricket Association and private sources that aimed to increase the frequency of interprovincial contacts. At the end of 1884 the CCA arranged for both Auckland and Otago to visit Christchurch as part of a 'Cricket Carnival'. Due to a lack of funds and available players the Auckland Cricket Association declined to send a team. However, an unofficial representative team was eventually assembled, and they succeeded in beating Otago by five wickets at Lancaster Park in the only interprovincial match to be played on neutral ground. Plans for a similar meeting involving Nelson and Otago during the next season came to nothing.[21] But a 'Canterbury Wanderers' team did visit Nelson in 1889 – losing by an innings – and another toured the North Island in 1892.[22]

Given these disparities at interprovincial level, there were a surprising number of tours and matches between clubs. Lancaster Park (Christchurch) and Carisbrook (Dunedin) met frequently during the 1880s and 90s; the former also played Oamaru and South Canterbury, among others.[23] The Midland Canterbury CC toured the West Coast in 1891 and established a regular fixture with the Midland CC of Wellington.[24] After 1907 the New Zealand Nomads CC embarked on frequent tours throughout New Zealand. Based in the Rangitikei district, this club consisted almost exclusively of English public school and New Zealand elite school old boys who were able to fund the tours privately.[25] Indeed, all of the club tours were private ventures and involved well-established middle-class clubs.

When a comparison is made with Australian first-class cricket (Tables 5 and 6), the disparities of the New Zealand game become still more dramatic. Without the frequency of touring teams enjoyed by Australia, the extent of New Zealand's first-class cricket programme lagged well behind from the 1880s onwards. Yet the limitations on domestic cricket are more striking. Until the end of the nineteenth century, New Zealand had seven provinces active in first-class cricket. Australia, with far greater distances to overcome, had six colonies.[26] Furthermore, while New South Wales, South Australia and Victoria had established a regular interchange by the late 1880s, that between New Zealand teams was erratic to say the least.

The Failure of Idealism

Why did New Zealand fail to establish a coherent programme of inter-provincial cricket before 1914 and thus fail to match the idealism of the early 1870s? To a large degree the explanation is economic. The single greatest problem faced by all provincial cricket associations revolved around their inability to develop grounds and secure revenue from them. Without this revenue they were in no position to cover the expense of assembling interprovincial teams or embark on interprovincial tours. In the first instance the obstacles were bureaucratic. When these were removed, there was still the problem of accumulating sufficient funds for expensive development and maintenance.

TABLE 5

FIRST-CLASS MATCH COMPARISON: NEW ZEALAND AND AUSTRALIA

	New Zealand	Australia
1850/51–58/9	–	9
1859/60–68/69	6	11
1869/70–78/79	19	22
1879/80–88/89	43	89
1889/90–98/99	81	111
1899/00–08/09	74	145
1909/10–14/15	54	108
	277	495

Non first-class New Zealand inter-provincial matches: 1860s, 6; 1870s, 5; 1880s, 1.

TABLE 6

FIRST-CLASS MATCHES SEASON-BY-SEASON: NEW ZEALAND AND AUSTRALIA

	NZ	A		NZ	A
1859–60	(1)	1	1887–88	3	19
1860–61	–	1	1888–89	2	8
1861–62	–	2	1889–90	10	5
1862–63	(3)	1	1890–91	2	5
1863–64	1(1)	1	1891–92	6	12
1864–65	1	–	1892–93	5	10
1865–66	1	1	1893–94	15	8
1866–67	1(1)	1	1894–95	12	20
1867–68	1	1	1895–96	9	9
1868–69	1	2	1896–97	11	8
1869–70	1(1)	1	1897–98	8	19
1870–71	1(1)	2	1898–99	3	15
1871–72	1	1	1899–00	6	11
1872–73	1(1)	3	1900–01	7	7
1873–74	5(2)	–	1901–02	5	17
1874–75	2	2	1902–03	9	13
1875–76	2	2	1903–04	7	22
1876–77	2	3	1904–05	8	11
1877–78	3	3	1905–06	7	12
1878–79	1	5	1906–07	13	12
1879–80	3	2	1907–08	6	26
1880–81	2	6	1908–09	6	15
1881–82	2	10	1909–10	12	15
1882–83	6(1)	10	1910–11	5	25
1883–84	10	5	1911–12	7	24
1884–85	7	11	1912–13	5	17
1885–86	3	4	1913–14	16	16
1886–87	5	14	1914–15	9	10

( ) = non first-class inter-provincial match.

Clearly, the provincial cricket associations encountered major obstacles to their attempts to derive revenue from representative cricket. Various pieces of legislation culminating in the 1877 and 1881 Public Reserves Acts enshrined a series of restrictions on the use of public recreation grounds and particularly on the ability to enclose them and charge admission. What this tends to reflect is a colonial reaction against the sort of privilege and patronage in Britain which severely restricted access to playing spaces and recreational amenities. One can see a similar pattern in New Zealand game laws, which were always far more liberal than their British antecedents.[27] Among other things, the Public Reserves Act stated that local bodies had no power to lease any reserve that had been set aside for the purpose of public health or recreation. Such reserves could be:

enclosed, laid out, and planted, and there may be erected thereon any buildings for ornamental purposes, but not for making any profit there-from:

> Provided always that no disposition shall be made in respect of any such reserve whereby the public shall be excluded from the free access thereto.[28]

Unable to cover costs by charging admission, the provincial cricket associations were at the mercy of public subscriptions and donations. With no obligation to do so, the public were seldom very obliging.

The long-running exchange between the Otago Cricket Association and the Dunedin City Council is typical of the difficulties faced by cricketers. Deputations from the Association in 1879 and 1880 requested that the Council make improvements to the Southern Recreation Ground. As the most frequent users, the cricketers felt that they had certain rights to protect the ground for their own use. Moreover, as the OCA was willing to contribute funds for development, it was felt that the area should be reserved exclusively for sport.[29] Not only did the City Council Reserves Committee reject any move to restrict access to the only public recreation area in south Dunedin, they denied the entire premise that more cricket grounds were needed.[30] Such a verdict is clearly at odds with the basis of conflict between the OCA and D&SCA outlined in Chapter 3.

In search of a compromise, a subcommittee of the OCA – reporting at the Annual General Meeting in October 1880 – recommended a petition to Parliament to give the City Council power to lease. Having collected information from all other cricket associations in Australasia, the subcommittee concluded that Dunedin had the smallest area for cricket and on the least liberal terms. The OCA did not expect the right to exclude the public or charge them for admission, but did expect the right to protect the playing surface from other users. Others at the same meeting complained bitterly that the Association had derived no gate revenue from the last five interprovincial matches in Dunedin. Yet the Council again affirmed its inability to restrict the use of public property.[31] Most probably, it was also reluctant to be seen as favouring the demands of one particular interest group over many others.

Some of the problem was resolved in January 1882 with the floating of the Carisbrook Ground Company. With a private ground it was at least possible to derive gate receipts, but the relationship between the Company and the OCA was seldom harmonious. Dominated by conflicts of interest among Company shareholders who were also active members of the OCA, there was constant wrangling over the terms of the lease and the percentage of revenue to be derived by each body from interprovincial matches. The situation became so difficult that Carisbrook was abandoned in favour of the Caledonian ground for the Canterbury match in 1890, but this facility was lost when the Phoenix CC disbanded during the same year. The OCA was still searching for an alternative ground to Carisbrook in 1892.[32]

With a wider range of influential patronage to draw on, Canterbury cricketers sought a more direct and comprehensive solution: the establishment of their own private ground. After a public meeting on 8 May 1880, at which A.M. Ollivier, E.C.J. Stevens and others outlined the necessity of a self-supporting ground to be used by a variety of sports, the Canterbury Cricket and Athletic Sports Company Ltd was floated with £4,500 capital derived from 450 £10 shares. Within a year of land being purchased from the Lancaster estate, a ground had been established with a seven-foot perimeter fence, stands, terraces, a cinder track, cricket ground, tennis courts and bowling greens.[33]

Meanwhile, the visit of the 1881 Australian XI highlighted a familiar problem with the Public Reserves Act when a large attendance at Hagley Park yielded a gate of only £150. The *Lyttelton Times*, though, saw a solution close at hand: 'The generosity of people who are not compelled to pay for their pleasure, is always a precarious thing to depend on; and it is with satisfaction, therefore, that lovers of the game watch the progress to completion of the new private ground'.[34] However, all was not so simple. Costs, especially for the pavilion, stands and drainage, greatly exceeded expectations, with the result that Harman and Stevens, Christchurch's leading estate agents, had to negotiate a £4,000 loan. By the end of 1882 the annual interest on the account was £260 with another £150 required to pay for a groundsman and maintenance. It was 20 years before the one and only cash dividend was paid to original investors. In the meantime all Canterbury sporting bodies – and the Canterbury Cricket Association especially – operated under the shadow of huge liabilities.[35]

After years of wrangling between the Company and the various sports using Lancaster Park, the CCA moved to purchase the ground for £10,000 in February 1904. After the Canterbury Rugby Football Union refused to join them in the venture, the CCA issued debentures and accepted responsibility for a £4,000 mortgage, but high interest payments and limited returns again prompted requests to the CRFU for assistance, which they accepted in 1911. Only in 1920, when fundraising in the context of a post-war euphoria for sport yielded £12,000, was Lancaster Park finally free of debt.[36]

Wellington cricketers could at least claim a degree of support from the City Council in their efforts to develop the 'canal basin' swamp into a cricket ground, but they were no less impeded by financial constraints and restrictive legislation. After securing a lease from the Wellington Town Board in 1866, the cricketers, in conjunction with the Caledonian Society, spent a considerable sum surveying and draining the ground. But bureaucracy inevitably intervened when another proposal was put before the Town Board to build a road through the centre of the Basin. Strong representations from influential cricketers, and in the cause of public recreation generally, eventually saw the road proposal withdrawn and the swamp transformed into the Basin Reserve by early 1867 – ten years after the scheme had first been mooted.[37] A grandstand, financed by the issue of £10 debentures, was soon erected. However, a heated public meeting in April 1876 recommended that the Basin should be opened for wider public access with paths and walkways. The reply from the cricketers – that the public had only taken an interest in the area once it had been developed – seemed to meet with the approval of the City Council. They worked closely with the newly formed Wellington Cricket Association on further improvements and drainage during the next five years.[38]

The greatest obstacle, though, was posed by Wellington footballers. A letter to the *Evening Post* after the Australian XI cricket match in 1881 lamented the abominable state of the ground, suggesting that it would remain so until cricketers gained more exclusive use. In similar fashion, a *New Zealand Times* editorial complained that cricketers were spending £150 annually on the ground only to have their efforts ruined by footballers.[39] Efforts by the City Council in 1884 to restrict winter activities resulted in an acrimonious Supreme Court case as the footballers failed in a challenge to the legality of their exclusion from a public reserve. Finally, a new Deed was gazetted for the Basin Reserve on 18 December 1884.[40]

The struggle for control continued well into the twentieth century. In 1888 the WCA complained bitterly to the City Council when the Wellington Football Club was again given permission to use the Basin Reserve for their annual sports,[41] and again in 1907 when the Council allowed lacrosse, hockey and football on the ground. Meanwhile, proposals for ground improvements had been put on hold while the Council considered a proposal to put a tramway through the ground. Thankfully for the cricketers, this was abandoned.[42] In the 1990s proposals had advanced to the point of advocating a tunnel under the ground.

While Auckland never suffered the ground limitations of the other main centres, local cricket was not without its share of problems. During the 1860s and 70s the Auckland Domain Board was constantly short of funds, but encountered strong protests whenever it sought to increase its revenue by charging admission to matches or by leasing grazing rights. Only when the Domain came under the control of the Auckland City Council in 1884 were funds made available to develop it properly.[43] But, as the area was not specifically designated for cricket, local games were often cancelled to make way for athletics, cycling and race meetings. Thus the Auckland Cricket Association began searching for a private ground in 1901.[44] This search lasted for more than a decade, for it was not until 1912 that the ACA finally completed negotiations and financing for the control of Eden Park – which hosted its inaugural first-class game in 1913. Inevitably the costs of developing the ground greatly exceeded expectations – not least the members' stand built at a cost of £1,835 – and by 1921 the ground trustees still required £8,000. Only when a joint agreement was made with the Auckland Rugby Union in 1926 did the Park begin to prosper.[45]

Although much less is known, it is evident that the expenses of ground development also afflicted the minor cricket associations – bodies that possessed even less financial resources to cover them. Despite considerable development expenditure by cricketers, the first ground in Napier was annexed for the building of the Provincial Council chambers. That which followed in the late 1870s was too small to cater for either a high standard of cricket or the safety of the buildings around it.[46] Finally, in September 1881, a Napier Recreation Ground Company was formed to lease a new ground from the Napier Borough Council. Although the ground was soon developed and remained as the headquarters of the Hawke's Bay Cricket Association until 1913, it also incurred considerable debts. The Company exceeded its budget by £445 during the first year and was eventually obliged to transfer its interests back to the Borough Council. No dividend was ever paid, and investors recovered less than half of their original capital.[47] Similarly, when neighbouring Manawatu cricketers purchased land for a ground from the Palmerston North Borough Council during the early 1890s they were unable to afford the upkeep and the ground was eventually returned to the control of the Council.[48]

The Implications of Indebtedness

Aside from the pressures it placed on provincial cricket associations at a local level, the Public Reserves Act contained particularly damaging implications for international cricket. By presenting a strong discouragement to English touring teams the Act greatly undermined the growth of New Zealand cricket during a crucial period of the 1880s. Alfred Shaw, promoter of several English touring teams, recalled that 1,000 Aucklanders refused to pay at the England XI match in 1882 as the ground was a public reserve. With no other ground available, 'We had no option but to play the match as arranged, and keep out those who thought we could afford to travel from England and play cricket without charge for their edification and amusement'. In Wellington it was estimated that as many spectators were watching the game from vantage points outside Newton Park as were inside the ground. An attempt to obscure their view by erecting sacking above the fence was thwarted by Wellington wind.[49]

Something of a vicious circle was completed by the attitude of the provincial cricket associations. Debt-ridden and deprived of income from interprovincial cricket, they saw the popularity of touring teams as an ideal opportunity to make amends. A letter from James Lillywhite to the secretary of the Auckland Cricket Association in November 1886 made it clear that their ambition had backfired:

> Our team very much wished to visit you, but it is out of the question on such conditions. Why on earth they [the provincial cricket associa-

tions] should want twice as much as the Melbourne and Sydney people I cannot imagine. I should have thought they would have welcomed the English teams to New Zealand without any plunder, if only to improve their cricket, as visits to Australia improved Australian cricket in such a marked manner; but your authorities think otherwise, and by heavy blackmail they put a veto on our visit.[50]

The implied tension in this conflict between the supposed missionary role of touring cricket teams and the financial manoeuvring which surrounded them will be considered later. The more immediate impact was that, aside from three matches by C.A. Smith's team in March 1888 and one by a touring English football team, no English touring teams visited New Zealand from 1882 until 1902–03. During the same period, Australia hosted nine English teams and dispatched nine to England.[51]

Certainly, two full-strength Australian teams played five matches each in New Zealand in 1886 and 1896 and the plethora of visits from other Australian teams meant that New Zealand witnessed the same number of touring teams – 21 – as Australia before 1914. But as the last three chapters will explain, most of these teams were of a quality, reputation and public appeal vastly inferior to those who ventured to Australia. Indeed, when Lord Hawke's England XI finally arrived in December 1902 the *New Zealand Herald* was quick to suggest that local cricket had been stunted by a lack of such visits. Unlike Australia, which had been able to maintain high standards through regular contacts with English teams, New Zealand's isolation and inability to furnish the necessary financial guarantees had prevented 'our cricketers from being aroused to emulation by formidable antagonists'.[52]

The much-needed amendment to the Public Reserves Act came in 1885. In pure form the provisions of the new Act gave sporting bodies exactly what was required. Local councils were now able to lease reserves for up to three years and to sanction the building of pavilions and stands. More importantly, for a maximum of ten days in any year sporting bodies were allowed to enclose such reserves and charge for admission. Any charge was not to exceed one shilling per day for the ground or ten shillings for the grandstand, with an extra one shilling for each horse or vehicle; such charges could not be demanded on more than three days consecutively. Finally, local bodies were able to regulate which games were played on the reserves. In particular, they had the power to prohibit any game that would damage the reserve in such a way as to prohibit the playing of any other game.[53] This final clause was especially useful to cricketers in restricting the activities of footballers.

By allowing the establishment of permanent facilities and permitting sports bodies to generate revenue from their fixtures, the new Act was far more flexible than its predecessor. Yet the advantages for cricket were largely cosmetic. Potential access to grounds was one thing, having the resources to use that potential was quite another. The 1881 Act had prompted Canterbury, Otago and Wellington to plunge their resources into private ventures that were to burden them long after the 1885 Amendment. With no cash reserves the cricket associations were not in any position to take immediate advantage. We will see shortly that demographic factors also conspired against them.

Without a regular diet of touring teams to attract paying spectators, New Zealand cricket simply did not have the revenue-producing opportunities that enabled Australian expansion. At no time did any of the cricket associations have a sufficient surplus of funds to contemplate long-term development or regular interprovincial touring, nor did they have the funds to compensate players for loss of earnings during such tours. It was, therefore, difficult to secure the quality of teams necessary to make interprovincial cricket attractive to the paying public. Moreover, an erratic interprovincial programme did nothing to sustain the sort of public interest and enthusiasm for cricket necessary to draw spectators to games on a consistent basis. Even the Plunket Shield, introduced in 1906 as a focal point for interprovincial cricket, failed to solve the problem. As matches were played on a challenge basis and on the home ground of the holder, the opportunities for all associations to profit were limited. Such windfalls as they did have – from specific fundraising activities or the rare profits from English and Australian touring teams – were quickly absorbed during subsequent years on day-to-day running costs.

Peculiar Economics

The provincial association finances outlined in Table 7 are cash balances only. They take no account of significant long-term liabilities, especially for ground development, that all associations carried at various times. Yet it is clear that the line between profit and loss was a very fine one, and that failure during one season could severely restrict opportunities for the next. After posting a healthy profit on their match against Australia in 1881, Canterbury were left heavily in overdraft after the rain-ruined Tasmanian tour three years later. Bad weather caused a loss on the England matches in March 1888, and the New South Wales tours of 1894 and 1895–96 both produced heavy losses for the province that had done most to organise them. Indeed, only one touring team – Lord Hawke's England XI in 1902–03 – matched financial expectations: Canterbury increased its bank balance by £190 and Otago by £150. Auckland also profited from the Australian team of 1905, but Canterbury was back in overdraft by the end of the same season. Following the MCC tour of 1906–07, marked by extravagance on the part of the tourists and a lack of public enthusiasm for their mediocre performances, all of the major associations were left with substantial overdrafts.[54]

As testimony to the financial limitations of New Zealand cricket, the escape from debt was frequently through avenues totally unrelated to the

TABLE 7

FINANCES OF PROVINCIAL CRICKET ASSOCIATIONS, 1876–1914

	ACA	CCA	OCA	WCA
1876	–	–	–	+£1.10.0
1877	–	–	–	+£3.18.3
1878	–	+£47.12.0	–	–
1879	–	+£74.9.10	+£10.7.6	+£27.16.0
1880	–	–	+£66.11.6	–
1881	–	+£115.15.6	–	–
1882	–	–	–	–
1883	–	+£25.12.2	+£1.6.10	+£3.0.6
1884	+£7.4.0	–£57.12.5		(–c.£75)
1885	+£1.0.7	(-£155.15.6)	–£23.19.0	(–£36.18.11)
1886	+3.13.10	£0.0.0	–	–£51.19.10
1887	+£2.16.10	–	+£0.7.10	+£36.1.0
1888	+£5.16.4	–£8.3.11	+£18.17.5	+£26.4.9
1889	+£5.9.4	+£8.4.7	+£6.16.10	+£30.5.1
1890	–	+£10.5.9	+£-.9.4.	–
1891	+£4.0.3	+£27.19.9	+£4.17.0	–
1892	+£10.15.8	+£3.4.11	+£2.17.4	–
1893	+£10.1.8	+£9.18.1	+£1.1.4	–
1894	+£7.18.9	–£21.11.2	+£14.11.4	–
1895	+£6.15.6	+£12.6.10	+£3.2.7	–
1896	–	–£20.9.5	+£85.13.1	–
1897	+£5.7.8	+£32.19.10	+£86.10.6	+£33.2.1
1898	+£0.7.8	+£48.0.4	+£72.18.3	+£18.9.6
1899	+£20.5.9	+£10.13.3	+£44.16.3	–
1900	+£19.5.2	+£2.18.0	+£0.3.3	+£34.10.9
1901	+£5.13.9	–£21.2.0	+£60.12.10	+£14.11.0
1902	+£34.17.9	+£1.1.11	+£55.1.0	+£27.11.9
1903	–£9.8.11	+190.5.6	+£207.3.5	+£22.5.2
1904	+£103.14.9	+£88.7.6	+£110.18.4	+£10.13.0
1905	+£175.6.1	–£12.15.3	+£121.2.10	+£52.2.10
1906	+£19.0.3	+£3.11.9	+£79.18.5	+£41.2.11
1907	–£210.8.8	–£71.4.6	–£199.17.8	–£167.8.2
1908	+£43.15.2	–£58.7.7	–£100.4.10	–£166.18.6
1909	+£6.8.0	–£10.11.6	+£183.3.1	–£196.16.0
1910	+£4.2.5	+£35.1.4	+£127.11.2	–£241.12.3
1911	–£58.19.9	+£52.11.11	+£74.18.7	–£227.3.11
1912	–	+£136.3.7	+£42.1.10	–£152.18.3
1913	–£133.0.6	+£29.17.7	–£32.-.11	–
1914	–	–	–£38.6.5	–

( ) = excess of liabilities over assets.

game. From its formation in 1875 to the announcement of its first profit in 1887, the Wellington Cricket Association estimated that it had spent £2,590.5s.7d on the development and maintenance of the Basin Reserve. Association finances were so precarious in 1879 that a concert committee was formed to help clear debts: they raised £44. The Wellington Amateur Dramatic Club repeated the gesture in 1883 after the failure of a call for all players to give 5s to develop the Basin Reserve.[55] When the situation had again deteriorated by 1900, the WCA was rescued by the Wellington Rugby Football Union and the Athletic Park Ground Company, who staged a benefit match to raise funds. A decade later the WCA was back to an overdraft of £227.3s.11d after the failure of an Art Union lottery organised to help clear debts. The Association complained that only 717 of 5,000 tickets had been sold, most of them to non-players. The WCA president, Sir F.H.D. Bell, threatened to resign unless players took a more active role in securing the future of the Association.[56]

As its cricket activities continually produced losses, the WCA was forced to take direct action. At the beginning of the 1911/12 season the Association announced a levy of 1s on every senior player and 6d on every junior player for each Saturday on which they played. It was hoped that this would net the Association £150 for the season, but the scheme did not meet with general satisfaction, and failed to address a wider problem. The Annual Report of 1913 lamented the fact that a scarcity of interprovincial matches was placing great financial strain on the WCA. In response, Daniel Reese organised a Canterbury XI to play Wellington at the end of the 1913/14 season.[57]

Despite its far more ambitious interprovincial programme, or possibly because of it, the Canterbury Cricket Association was financially no better off than Wellington. In 1886, after declaring a balance of £0.0s.0d, the CCA organised a two-day fundraising fête at Lancaster Park that included a well-patronised tennis tournament. Within two years, and carrying an overdraft of £8.3s.11d, the CCA announced that it could not afford to pay the travel and accommodation expenses of leading players. Consequently a weak team consisting of players could afford the trip was sent to Dunedin for the interprovincial match.[58] The Association's debts were finally cleared in 1895, but the Annual Report of 1898 again stressed the need for income generating schemes. Arrangements were made in 1901 to amalgamate with the Canterbury Lawn Tennis Association for a floral fête, but it was cancelled amid mourning for the death of Queen Victoria. No such consideration existed when the event was tried again in 1909, but it ended disastrously. Initial plans for an Anniversary Day floral fête to reduce the CCA overdraft were postponed due to bad weather, so the fête was held the following week – and made a £40 loss. Some of this was recouped by a performance from the Christchurch Comedy Club, which raised £10.18.6, and an Art Union lottery in 1910, which produced a very healthy £241.3.5. In 1911, though, a public subscription was still required to send the Canterbury team to Auckland for a Plunket Shield challenge. Their victory signalled a gradual financial recovery, but the CCA was still saddled with debts relating to the purchase of Lancaster Park in 1904.[59]

Cricket in Otago was as much of a financial failure as anywhere in the country, but the Otago Cricket Association was somewhat more successful with its fundraising activities. After a £6 loss on the Canterbury visit at the beginning of 1886, a benefit game recouped £3.11s for the Association. The following year, a benefit match organised by the Otago Rugby Union returned £14.15s.3d. When wet weather caused losses on the Fiji, Southland and Wellington matches in 1895, the response was an 'Otago Cricketers Association Japanese Fair and Art Union', which raised £132. At the beginning of the next season a concert raised £20 to send the provincial team to Christchurch. Over a decade later, in 1909, money was still very much an issue, with a £100 overdraft wiped out by an Art Union lottery that raised £302.[60]

Finance was again the overriding factor when a conference was finally called in July 1912 to establish a formula for regular interprovincial cricket. Meeting in Wellington on the initiative of the OCA, delegates considered proposals to change the Plunket Shield from its existing challenge format to a tournament similar to that of the Australian Sheffield Shield. After lengthy debate the plan was rejected as impractical and potentially bankrupting. Instead, it was decided that Canterbury and Wellington should play each province annually, Auckland and Otago to meet every two years, and Hawke's Bay to secure matches by individual arrangement. The NZCC would claim 5 per cent of takings from each match, and the visiting team 30 per cent.[61]

Inevitably, the scheme hit a snag when Auckland and Canterbury disagreed over how it ought to be started. Having toured south during 1911–12, Auckland was reluctant to do so during the 1912/13 season. Canterbury was unwilling to visit Auckland unless it could secure a greater proportion of the gate than the agreed 30 per cent. It was not until the following season that the *Otago Witness* could safely announce that a more regulated interprovincial interchange had been set in place.[62]

Judged purely in business terms, it is reasonable to suggest that none of the provincial cricket associations should have survived beyond their first decade. Wellington did not return a profit during its first 12 years, Canterbury sustained 5 successive losses during the 1880s, and Auckland's bank balance did not exceed £10 during its first 9 years. Efforts to sustain cricket at any level – local, interprovincial or international – represent a considerable economic anomaly, especially during the economic depression of the late 1880s. Moreover, it was an anomaly perpetuated by some of the most prominent members of New Zealand's commercial elite: E.C.J. Stevens accumulated a fortune in excess of £290,000 from his activities as a commission and estate agent in Canterbury and W.H. Levin, President of the Wellington Cricket Association 1880–93, enjoyed a long career at the head of a business empire originally established by his father.[63] Naturally, one must ask why this economic unreality was allowed to continue and whether any genuine effort was made to alter it.

FIGURE 10

Crowd at Lancaster Park, 1903. These spectators were almost certainly watching the fixture between Canterbury and Lord Hawke's XI. The apparel gives some idea of the sense of occasion which always surrounded the visits of touring teams – and English teams in particular. (Weekly Press photo, Canterbury Museum: Ref. 3208)

FIGURE 11

Daniel Reese (1879–1953). A left-handed batsman, slow bowler and superb fielder, Reese was undoubtedly the best New Zealand player prior to 1914. He captained Canterbury and New Zealand, played for Essex and W.G. Grace's London County side, and later served a long tenure as president of the New Zealand Cricket Council. (Weekly Press photo, Canterbury Museum: Ref. 14800)

FIGURE 12

E.C.J. Stevens (1837–1915). Although he played for Canterbury as a batsman, Stevens' greater contribution to cricket was as an administrator. He initiated the formation of the Canterbury Cricket Association in 1877 and represented numerous provinces as a delegate to the New Zealand Cricket Council until his death. (Canterbury Museum: Ref. 2433)

The situation in English cricket during the same period – and well into the 1960s, for that matter – is most instructive. The vast majority of cricket clubs were not economically viable. Indeed, the editor of the *Athletic News* was moved to observe in 1886 that 'It would be difficult … to point to a cricket club which did not get into debt. It is one of their brightest privileges.' What income they had was derived from membership subscriptions and gate money, with a select few able to augment this by renting their grounds to other sports such as athletics and football.[64] As a profit-making enterprise, English first-class cricket was a failure. The majority of county clubs were sustained only by the generosity of patrons and members. For example, Lord Sheffield spent a vast sum supporting Sussex during the 1880s and 90s, while the Duke of Devonshire frequently liquidated Derbyshire debts that stood as high as £1,000 in 1887.[65] At a local level, many cricket clubs only survived because of their dual existence as football clubs. In 1900, Sheffield United drew a £1,755 profit from football but sustained a £521 loss on its cricket activities.[66]

As an explanation, Keith Sandiford and Wray Vamplew argue that the esteem in which Victorians held the game determined that 'so far as cricket finances were concerned, on many occasions emotion superseded economics'.[67] The county clubs and the MCC gave very little attention to maximising profit prior to 1914. They did, moreover, nothing to popularise county cricket as a spectacle by reducing the number of drawn games – which had reached nearly 40 per cent by 1900; nor did they attempt to reduce the lack of competitiveness that accompanied the increasing ascendancy of bat over ball. Frequent proposals to assist bowlers by modifying the lbw law or by widening the wicket were all rejected.[68] As Sandiford and Vamplew conclude:

> Many of the game's traditional supporters were willing to subsidise the sport for reasons of civic pride, county allegiance, or even national jingoism. Basically cricket was so much an integral element of English ritual, mores and tradition that it was not viewed simply, or even primarily, as a business proposition.[69]

In short, although English cricket was not economically viable in its existing form, there was virtually no effort to alter it in order to attract more paying spectators.

New Zealand administrators were conditioned by a similar approach. Drawn as they were from the English public school system or its New Zealand clone, they were never prompted to question the manners and forms of the game as articulated by the MCC. Unlike Australia, where some minor alterations were made to the length of the over, the duration of matches and the follow-on,[70] there is no evidence of either the provincial cricket associations or the NZCC making any attempt to alter the fabric of the game or to make any specific allowances for local conditions. There is ample evidence, especially in attempts by Otago to tour the North Island during the late nineteenth century, of proposed interprovincial tours being abandoned due to lack of funds,[71] but no sign of a reduction in the determination to continue trying to stage them or much thought given to restructuring New Zealand cricket.

No doubt the inferior standard of New Zealand cricket contributed to the reluctance of administrators to tamper with the fabric of the game. In rugby, which obtained a considerable degree of international success prior to 1914, the reverse was the case. There was agitation from the highest echelons of New Zealand rugby to reform the game both on and off the field, especially after the all-conquering 1905 All Black tour of Britain, and the Otago Rugby Football Union was not alone in presenting a far-reaching plan aimed at faster play with greater public appeal. In particular, New Zealand's perseverance with its own radically different scrum formation and with the playing of a wing-forward caused considerable friction with British rugby until its abolition in 1931. Interpretations of various playing and administrative laws remain a source of debate.[72]

In a sense, the economic position of New Zealand cricket was even more extreme than that of English cricket. Although the scale of activities by the provincial cricket associations was minute compared to the obligations of the English counties, there were at the same time no aristocratic patrons blessed with the resources of Lord Sheffield nor any professional football clubs with a substantial spectator base to assist with liquidating debts. As a general rule, it seems that the New Zealand wealthy of the nineteenth century were little disposed to philanthropy and saw little need of it as a key to establishing their identity within the colony. There was a sense in which the making of money, rather than the giving away, was a greater indicator of worth in both senses of the term. Those who were inclined to charitable activities frequently possessed a specific political, religious or ideological agenda. Moreover, such charity as was dispensed tended to be directed towards 'serious' and 'deserving' objectives – churches, benevolent societies and the like.[73] The attitude of Ross and Glendining, prominent Dunedin merchants, is instructive. In 1892 the firm's Christchurch office was rebuked for having given £2 for a cricket match and making similar donations previously. Christchurch was ordered to 'in future, please give no subscriptions at all without reference to us, and only refer to us such applications as we are likely to approve of for what seem to be necessitous cases calling for legitimate help. All amusements can be declined right off.'[74]

Certainly, there is ample evidence of the colonial wealthy involving themselves in the administration of cricket and of their making the largest contributions to the public subscription lists that were frequently used to raise funds for tours. Such contributions, though, were only a fraction of colonial wealth in comparison with some of the benevolence displayed in English cricket. More to the point, they were not disproportionately large in comparison to those made by many other, less wealthy citizens, and there is no evidence to be found in the balance sheets of the provincial cricket associations of donations from the wealthy.

New Zealand Cricket Crowds

Finally, we must consider the limited opportunities for revenue that could be derived from the potential spectator base in New Zealand – and especially as a comparison with the much greater levels of urbanisation and evidence for crowds in eastern Australia.

The discovery of gold in New South Wales and Victoria in 1851 triggered dramatic population expansion in Eastern Australia. Sydney grew from 54,000 in 1851 to 138,000 in 1871, 400,000 in 1891 and 648,000 by 1911. Melbourne increased from 29,000 in 1851 to 191,000 in 1871, 493,000 by 1891 and 593,000 by 1911. In terms of British cities, only London, Birmingham, Glasgow, Liverpool and Manchester were larger. Although Adelaide and Brisbane did not benefit so directly from an influx of gold seekers, they had reached 169,000 and 141,000 respectively by 1911. Perth, as a consequence of the Western Australian goldrush of the 1890s, stood at 107,000.[75] In contrast, the largest New Zealand city in 1871 was Auckland with 22,370; in 1891 Dunedin led with 45,869 but Auckland had the largest population once again by 1911 with 102,676 – 20,000 more than its nearest rival.[76]

Australia's dramatic urban growth was reflected in its cricket crowds. H.H. Stephenson's England XI attracted at least 25–30,000 for its match against a Melbourne XVIII in 1861 and another 30,000 in Sydney. Numbers for the first four Test series in Australia increased from a daily average attendance of 4,750 for the eight days of the first two Tests in March 1877 to 12,124 for the 14 days of the four Tests of 1882–83, with a number of individual days producing crowds of 15–20,000. Although Test match crowds declined in response to the glut of English touring teams later in the 1880s, they were again reaching a daily average in excess of 12,000 by the mid 1890s. The best individual day prior to 1914 was 37,997 spectators at the SCG on the second day of the fourth Test against England in February 1902. Attendances at intercolonial fixtures and those against touring teams were also frequently in excess of 10,000 per day.[77] However, the daily average for the two first-class fixtures played by the 1899 New Zealand team in Australia was only 571, a figure which rose to 2,400 per day for the 1914 team. The reasons for such lamentable interest will be discussed in Chapter 9.

Attendances at cricket were in turn exceeded by those for football. The semi-professional Australian Rules competition in Melbourne was attracting crowds in excess of 10,000 for club matches by the early 1880s, with some leading clubs drawing as many as 25,000 every Saturday; Grand Final attendances at the MCG reached 54,463 by 1912. Rugby was also capable of attracting large crowds: in 1907, 52,000 saw New South Wales play New Zealand in Sydney. Furthermore, because Australian grounds were dual-purpose facilities, sporting bodies had no shortage of revenue for improvements to the playing surface and the building of substantial new grandstands and scoreboards.[78]

Similarly comprehensive details for New Zealand have proved elusive – and especially so for interprovincial fixtures. To a large extent we are reliant on the match reports compiled by T.W. Reese and on the assumption that where Reese saw fit to mention the size of the crowd it was considered to be significant. On this basis, figures that are available for touring teams give some indication of both the largest nineteenth century crowds and the disparity with Australia. The 'tolerably numerous' crowd on the second day of Canterbury's match against Parr's All England XI in February 1864 amounted to only 1,500 people; the same fixture against Lillywhite's team in 1877 attracted 15,000 for the whole match. The following year, 6,000 were present on the last day to witness the Canterbury XV defeat Australia, and another 6,000 attended the first day of the much-anticipated second meeting of the two teams in February 1881.[79] In short, the few attendances considered worthy of note are little different from the *average* Australian figures for the 1870s. More to the point, in view of the inability to charge admission after 1877, they represent a relatively small number from which to secure donations: we have seen already the considerable disappointment with the £150 gate for the tour match of the 1881 Australians in Christchurch.

In absolute terms, the best attendances for the most popular and profitable touring team in New Zealand – Lord Hawke's England XI of 1902–03 – are well short of comparable Australian figures. The opening match of the tour against Auckland drew a 'capital attendance' of 5,000 on Boxing Day 1902. Later matches against Canterbury and Wellington both attracted 16,000 spectators over three days and that against Otago drew a Dunedin record of 5,600 on the first day. Two years later, 8,000 were present on the second day for Auckland's match against a full-strength Australian team, there was a 'capital attendance' of 5,000 on the first day in Dunedin and an estimated 10,000 – surely a record for a single day in New Zealand prior to 1914 – turned out on the first day in Wellington.[80] Yet the tour as a whole made a loss.

As proportions of population these attendances compare more than favourably with Australia. Based on the 1901 populations of the two cities, crowds of 5,600 for Dunedin in 1902 or 8,000 for Auckland in 1905 represent *c*.10.7 and 11.9 per cent respectively, and the 10,000 in Wellington in 1905 represents an exceptional 20.2 per cent. By comparison, the 37,997 record for Sydney in 1902 represents 7.7 per cent of the 1901 city population. Yet there are two significant caveats to the New Zealand figures. Firstly, they are only very isolated gleanings – and rounded estimates at that – for individual days and matches. They do not, therefore, represent the vast bulk of first-class fixtures for which the attendances are not considered worthy of mention. Neither do they take account of the likelihood, to be discussed in the next chapter, that the colder New Zealand climate contributed to more lost playing days than in Australia. Secondly, from this much smaller revenue-producing spectator base, New Zealand administrators were faced with many basic operating costs – such as ground preparation, player travel and accommodation – that are likely to have been no different in magnitude to those of eastern Australia.

Certainly, rugby, with a shorter duration that was more conducive to working-class spectatorship, was drawing consistently larger crowds from the 1880s onwards. Crowds of 5,000 attended several matches by the first two New South Wales touring teams in 1882 and 1886, and 7,000 saw Wellington play a British team in 1888. The 1908 Anglo-Welsh team attracted in excess of 10,000 to a number of provincial matches and 23,000 to the Test match in Dunedin. By the 1920s attendances for internationals averaged 35,000,[81] but these levels of patronage were also small by Australian standards.

The initial reluctance of the provincial rugby unions to commit themselves to financing ground developments such as those at Lancaster Park and Eden Park perhaps serves as a reminder that although these bodies were relatively wealthy in relation to New Zealand cricket, they were far from being absolutely wealthy in their own right. There is certainly no evidence of combined clubs whereby rugby subsidised cricket in the manner of many English football clubs.

Despite these obstacles, the cricket associations stuck determinedly to their objectives. Indeed, as later chapters will show, they continued to tackle the expense of English professional coaches and English touring teams when cheaper options presented themselves in Australia. Quality of cricket, not economy of cricket, was the abiding principle. It was against this background that the NZCC struggled to establish continuity after 1894.

Notes

1. *Nelson Examiner*, 16 March 1844, p. 6; *Otago News*, 13 Dec. 1848, p. 1.
2. Quoted in *Southern Cross*, 10 Feb. 1860, p. 3.
3. Reese, *New Zealand Cricket 1841–1914*, p. 143.
4. *Wellington Independent*, 20 March 1860, p. 3.
5. *New Zealander*, 6 Dec. 1862, p. 4; 10 Dec. 1862, p. 3.
6. Ibid., 20 Dec. 1862, p. 5.
7. Ibid., 10 Dec. 1862, p. 3.
8. P. Griffiths (ed.), *Complete First-Class Match List Volume 1 1801–1914* (London, 1996).
9. For example, see: *Weekly Press,* 3 Jan. 1885, pp. 7–8; *The Press*, 17 Dec. 1898, p. 3; 19 Dec. 1898, p. 2; 20 Dec. 1898, p. 2.
10. Grant, *On a Roll*, pp. 40–42.
11. Reese, *New Zealand Cricket 1841–1914*, pp. 34–7. After the formation of the NZCC, Auckland claimed prior right to the dark blue. Disgruntled Cantabrians then adopted the red and black of Jesus College Cambridge – the college of C.C. Corfe, headmaster of Christ's College.
12. *Otago Daily Times*, 14 Feb. 1866, p. 4.
13. *New Zealand Referee*, 24 Dec. 1913, p. 85. To qualify for inclusion, a player had to have represented his province at least 20 years earlier.
14. *Auckland Cricketers Trip to the South: A Complete History of the Late Successful Tour ... 1873–4* (Auckland, 1874), pp. 5–6; *New Zealand Herald*, 10 Nov. 1873, p. 3.
15. *New Zealand Herald*, 13 Oct. 1873, p. 2; 14 Oct. 1873, p. 2; 4 Nov. 1873, p. 2.
16. Ibid., 14 Oct. 1873, p.2.
17. Ibid., 21 Nov. 1873, p. 2; 4 Dec. 1873, p. 3; 8 Dec. 1873, p. 3.
18. *New Zealand Mail*, 21 March 1874, p. 20.
19. All details concerning the frequency of interprovincial matches are derived from Reese, *New Zealand Cricket 1841–1914*.
20. Nelson's only other first-class match was against Auckland in December 1882.
21. *Weekly Press*, 29 Nov. 1884, p. 10; 6 Dec. 1884, p. 8; 20 Dec. 1884, p. 11; OCA, Annual Report, 1886.
22. Reese, *New Zealand Cricket 1841–1914*, p. 109.
23. See, for example: *Lyttelton Times*, 2 Jan. 1882, p. 5; *The Press*, 20 Dec. 1891, p. 3; 3 April 1893, p. 3; 9 Nov. 1893, p. 3.
24. See, for example: *The Press*, 13 Jan. 1891, p. 3; 2 Jan. 1893, p. 3.
25. Reese, *New Zealand Cricket 1914–33*, pp. 105–7.
26. New Zealand: Auckland, Canterbury, Hawke's Bay (1882–1921), Nelson (1874–92), Otago, Taranaki (1883–98), Wellington. Australia: New South Wales, Queensland, South Australia, Tasmania, Victoria, Western Australia.
27. McDowall, *Gamekeepers of the Nation*, pp. 1–10.
28. *New Zealand Statutes*, 1881: 45. Vic., No.15. See also 1854: 18. Vic., No.7; 1862: 26. Vic., No.15; 1877: 41. Vic., No.36.
29. Tait, 'History of the Otago Cricket Association', p. 43; OCA, Annual Report, 1879; *Otago Daily Times*, 17 March 1880, p. 3.
30. *Otago Daily Times*, 22 Sept. 1880, p. 3.
31. Tait, 'History of the Otago Cricket Association', pp. 46–9; OCA, Annual Report, 1880; *Otago Daily Times*, 1 Oct. 1880, p. 3.
32. Tait, 'History of the Otago Cricket Association', pp. 49, 61–2; OCA, Committee Minutes, 30 Sept. 1892.
33. T.W. Reese, *History of Lancaster Park, Christchurch* (Christchurch, c.1935), pp. 1–6.
34. *Lyttelton Times*, 24 Feb. 1881, p. 6.
35. Reese, *Lancaster Park*, pp. 7–10.
36. Brittenden, *100 Years of Cricket*, p. 18; *The Press,* 18 April 1904, p. 6; 3 May 1904, p. 5; 26 Sept. 1904, p. 8.
37. *Wellington Independent*, 21 Nov. 1865, p. 5; 11 Dec. 1866, p. 3; 25 Dec. 1866, p. 3; 12 Jan. 1867, p. 5.

38. Neely, *100 Summers*, pp. 18–19.
39. Ibid., p. 25.
40. Ibid., p. 29.
41. *New Zealand Times*, 22 Sept. 1888, p. 5.
42. WCA, Annual Report, 1903, 1904, 1907.
43. Bush, *Decently and in Order*, p. 167.
44. ACA, Annual Report, 1901.
45. *100 Not Out*, pp. 123–9.
46. Cane, *Cricket in Hawke's Bay*, pp. 11–12, 15.
47. Reese, *New Zealand Cricket 1914–33*, p. 584.
48. Ibid., p. 586.
49. A.W. Pullin, *Alfred Shaw: Cricketer: His Career and Reminiscences* (London, 1902), p. 74; *New Zealand Times*, 7 Feb. 1882, p. 2.
50. Pullin, *Alfred Shaw*, p. 96.
51. R. Webster (comp.), *First-Class Cricket in Australia: Vol.1 1850/51–1941/42* (Melbourne, 1991), passim.
52. *New Zealand Herald,* 18 Dec. 1902, p. 4.
53. *New Zealand Statutes*, 1885: 49. Vic., No.29.
54. All financial details are derived from the Annual Reports and Balance Sheets of the Auckland, Canterbury, Otago and Wellington cricket associations and the NZCC.
55. WCA Annual Report, 1879, 1883, 1887; Neely, *100 Summers,* p. 28.
56. WCA Annual Report, 1900, 1911; Neely, *100 Summers*, pp. 78–9.
57. *Otago Witness*, 25 Oct. 1911, p. 60; WCA Annual Report, 1913; Reese, *New Zealand Cricket 1841–1914,* p. 576.
58. *Weekly Press*, 19 Nov. 1886, p. 10; *New Zealand Referee*, 26 Jan. 1888, p. 115.
59. CCA, Annual Report, 1895, 1898, 1901, 1909, 1910; CCA, Committee Minutes, 10 Jan. 1901, 31 Jan. 1901.
60. OCA, Annual Report, 1886; 1887; 1895; 1896; 1909.
61. NZCC, General Meeting Minutes, 25 April 1912, 23 Sept. 1912; *New Zealand Referee*, 17 July 1912, p. 87.
62. *The Press*, 24 Sept. 1912, p. 8; *Otago Witness*, 29 Oct. 1913, p. 53.
63. R. Nicholls, 'Nathaniel William Levin' in Oliver (ed.), *DNZB, Vol.1*, pp. 239–40; G. Miller, 'Edward Cephas John Stevens' in Oliver (ed.), *DNZB, Vol.1*, pp. 407–8.
64. Sandiford, *Cricket and the Victorians*, p. 56.
65. Ibid., pp. 65–6.
66. Ibid., p. 57. See also J. Williams, *Cricket and England: A Cultural and Social History of the Inter-War Years* (London, 1999), pp. 162–8.
67. Sandiford and Vamplew, 'Peculiar Economics of English Cricket', p. 311.
68. Ibid., pp. 313–6.
69. Ibid., pp. 323–4.
70. Webster, *First-Class Cricket in Australia*, 'preface – a Chronology of Australian Laws', n.p.
71. See, for example: *New Zealand Herald*, 26 Sept. 1885, p. 6; OCA, Annual Report, 1886.
72. S. O'Hagan, *Pride of Southern Rebels: History of Otago Rugby* (Dunedin, 1981), p. 70; G.T. Vincent and T. Harfield, 'Repression and Reform: Responses Within New Zealand Rugby to the Arrival of the "Northern Game", 1907–8', *New Zealand Journal of History*, 31, 2 (1997).
73. McAloon, *No Idle Rich*, pp. 143–70.
74. G.R. Hercus to Christchurch office, 28 Mar 1892, Ross and Glendining Letterbook 9, quoted in ibid., p. 158.
75. C. Forster, *Australian Cities: Continuity and Change* (Melbourne, 1995), p. 9.
76. See Chapter 3, Table 2.
77. R. Cashman, *'Ave a Go Yer Mug! Australian Cricket Crowds from Larrikin to Ocker* (Sydney, 1984), pp. 11–68; R. Cashman, *Australian Cricket Crowds: The Attendance Cycle – Daily Figures, 1877–1984* (Sydney, c.1984), pp. 26–35, 72–80, 134–56.
78. Cashman, *'Ave a go Yer Mug!*, pp. 40–44.
79. *The Press*, 9 Feb. 1864, p. 2; Reese, *New Zealand Cricket 1841–1914*, pp. 186, 194, 211.
80. Reese, *New Zealand Cricket 1841–1914*, pp. 414–23, 439–40.
81. R.H. Chester and N.A.C. McMillan, *The Visitors: The History of International Rugby Teams in New Zealand* (Auckland, 1990), pp. 18, 22, 31–2, 50, 83–4, 91, 98; A. Manley, 'Antidote to Depression: Rugby and New Zealand Society 1919–39' (Dip. Arts thesis, University of Otago, 1991), pp. 24–7.

7

A Fragile Edifice:
The New Zealand Cricket Council,
1894–1914

During the 1890s cricket reached the peak of its influence within New Zealand sport and took its greatest steps towards unity. There were more interprovincial matches and more touring teams than ever before; the first representative New Zealand team took the field in 1894 and embarked on its first tour of Australia in 1899; numerous local and regional cricket associations were formed beyond the four main centres; and associations also emerged to cater for the mid-week and social cricketer. Most importantly, though, a meeting in Christchurch on 27 December 1894 established the New Zealand Cricket Council as a central administrative body. At the end of the century cricket was a national game – perhaps *the* national game.

The task of forming a cricket council for New Zealand was approached with idealism and enthusiasm. The Council set itself wide-ranging objectives, and there was no shortage of Victorian sporting gentlemen possessed of the necessary influence to carry them out. Yet by 1914 the Council was embroiled in bitter controversies with its provincial components, and more than one element of the press insisted that a centralised administration was not in the best interests of New Zealand cricket. In practical terms, the Council inherited the financial problems that so severely restricted the provincial associations. At the same time, its efforts to select New Zealand teams and to coordinate overseas touring teams established a convenient staging ground for provincial antagonisms and self-interest. Ultimately, the NZCC could never be any more effective than the sum of its provincial parts allowed it to be.

The aims of the NZCC were also limited by the fact that it did not have a viable product to promote. Interprovincial cricket became competitive and an interesting public spectacle in so far as there were keenly contested encounters between teams of equal ability – or lack thereof. But the reality – shown most clearly when New Zealand teams entered the international arena – was a standard far below that in any other major cricketing country. Victories were few and only achieved against opposition that was second- or third-rate by the prevailing standards of England and Australia. Within a decade of the formation of the Council, cricket had been superseded by rugby as the 'national game' – a title which owed as much to the numbers playing and supporting rugby as to its increasing prominence within public consciousness.

Thus, what was in many respects the period of greatest formalisation and advancement for New Zealand cricket was at the same time the period of its greatest decline in relative importance. This contradiction produced a good deal of theorising among contemporary observers. Climatic conditions, the extent of urbanisation and geographical isolation were common explanations that must now be considered carefully, as should the dramatic expansion and success of rugby. Did the popularity of rugby really reduce support for cricket as many believed? Whether real or imagined, all theories about the state of New Zealand cricket are relevant in that they contributed to a generally pessimistic perception of the game and the role of the NZCC within it.

The New Zealand Cricket Council

Pessimism was far from the minds of those who set out to establish the NZCC in 1894. Earlier proposals for a central administrative body arose from attempts to organise 'combined New Zealand' teams in 1867, 1875, 1882, 1886 and 1889. Prior to the visit of the 1886 Australian team, the Wellington Cricket Association circulated a letter suggesting that a match be played between the North and South islands with a view to selecting a New Zealand team to play against the tourists. The WCA felt that the best way to manage this proposal would be through the establishment of a single controlling body. Their suggestions were rebuffed, though, by the other provincial associations on the basis of both a lack of time and the financial strain it would impose on them.[1]

It was more than seven years before a New Zealand team finally took the field – against New South Wales in Christchurch on 15 February 1894. The initiative for this match came from the Canterbury Cricket Association, which guaranteed the venture and appointed A.M. Ollivier as sole selector of the New Zealand team.[2] Within four months Canterbury administrators had determined to put the organisation of New Zealand teams, and cricket generally, on a more collective footing. In June 1894 T.D. Harman and L.A. Cuff of Christchurch, the latter of whom had captained the first New Zealand team, drafted rules for a New Zealand Cricket Council and circulated these to all provincial cricket associations.[3] Their motives in taking this initiative may have been as much defensive as altruistic: for its trouble in organising the first New Zealand match, the CCA was now £21.11s.2d in overdraft. Moreover, there had been complaints from both Otago and Wellington regarding Ollivier's selection of five Canterbury players in the New Zealand team.[4]

To describe the first meeting of the Council on 27 December 1894 as a great coming together of New Zealand cricket administrators is rather deceptive. All but 3 of the 12 delegates were Cantabrians holding proxy votes for the various cricket associations; this would remain the formula for the next two decades. Under the chairmanship of Edward Heathcote Williams, a Hawke's Bay solicitor and runholder who was later elected first president, the meeting outlined six objectives aimed at establishing stability and promoting New Zealand cricket.

In addition to a general intention to advance the game of cricket throughout New Zealand, the NZCC accepted responsibility for: the arrangement of all colonial and 'foreign' cricket tours and matches in New Zealand and New Zealand representative teams touring overseas; the arrangement of all interprovincial matches; the settling of all disputes and differences between provincial cricket associations; and the adoption of all rules and amendments passed by the MCC.[5] The meeting also determined that Auckland, Canterbury, Otago and Wellington would pay a two-guinea subscription and provide two delegates to the Council, with other associations to pay one guinea and provide one delegate. Interprovincial matches would be arranged at the annual general meeting, and the Council conformed to the New Zealand Rugby Football Union decision to adopt a silver fern leaf badge as the playing insignia of its representative team.[6]

However, all was not entirely smooth for the NZCC. In an ominous sign for the future, delegates rejected three aspects of Cuff and Harman's draft constitution. After a lengthy debate they refused to consent to the Council having sole power to appoint umpires for interprovincial and intercolonial matches or its deriving a percentage of gate takings from these matches, or that the New Zealand team should be chosen by one selector each from the North and South Island.[7] The provinces, then, were certainly determined to maintain a degree of autonomy.

In accordance with its objectives, the NZCC dispatched W.S. Wanklyn of Christchurch to Australia in 1895 to negotiate for a possible New Zealand tour and to attract Australian teams to New Zealand. In the latter respect he was successful in that the first officially sanctioned New South Wales team arrived at the end of the year, followed by Queensland during the following season.[8] At the time of the first annual general meeting in October 1895, *The Press* was quick to spot the advantage of a cricket council:

> We hope that now that our cricketers have the advantage of a general body to make arrangements for them, it may become the regular thing for New Zealand cricketers every other year to meet on Australian ground the elite of Australian cricket while in the alternate years we may be visited by one or more Australian teams.[9]

Such promise produced more disappointment than satisfaction over the next two decades. For the moment, though, the NZCC steadily drew the minor cricket associations under its control: Westland had joined by 1898, Hamilton, Manawatu, South Canterbury, South Otago, Wairarapa and Wanganui had all affiliated by 1903, Marlborough and North Taranaki by 1905, and Buller and Poverty Bay by 1909.[10]

The office holders of the NZCC were collectively an influential group. The first president, Edward Heathcote Williams, was the driving force behind Hawke's Bay cricket and president of the Hawke's Bay Cricket Association 1892–1931. From a wealthy family of farmers and orchardists, and educated at the Church of England Grammar School, Auckland, Williams established a very successful legal practice in Hastings. He served further terms as NZCC president in 1913–14 and 1919–25.[11] Beyond its Christchurch base, Williams exerted the greatest influence on the NZCC during its first four decades. His successors, F.H.D. Bell, Frederick Wilding, A.E. Whitaker and Alfred Hanlon were all prominent lawyers and provincial sporting figures. They were followed by George Cleghorn, proprietor of a large medical practice in Blenheim, and Walter Empson, the Rector of Wanganui Collegiate School.[12]

Yet how much control the president actually exerted is a moot point in that the position was rotated yearly among the various cricket associations, and day-to-day business rested with the secretary and treasurer in Christchurch. Of these men the most important were George Tapper, T.D. Harman, Reginald Vincent and F.C. Raphael. Tapper was educated at Christ's College and became manager of the Bank of New Zealand in Christchurch. Thomas De Renzy Harman, a Christ's College-educated lawyer with an extensive background in Anglican Church affairs, was also a fine all-round sportsman. He was a Canterbury cricket and rugby represen-

FIGURE 13

Frederick Wilding (1853–1945). A multi-talented sportsman who played for Canterbury for two decades, Wilding was president of the Canterbury Cricket Association from 1907 to 1923 and three times president of the New Zealand Cricket Council. (Weekly Press photo, Canterbury Museum: Ref. 14803)

tative, a talented golfer and several times holder of the New Zealand long jump record. Reginald Vincent was a solicitor and sometime president of the Christ's College Old Boys' Association. It was F.C 'Tim' Raphael, though, who did more than anyone to shape the course of the Council during his 14-year secretaryship 1901–14. A Christchurch-educated real estate agent, his strong personality and organisational skill were at the centre of numerous patriotic and fundraising endeavours in Christchurch, especially during the First World War.[13]

In addition to this permanent Christchurch influence, the constraints of travel and communication also dictated a Canterbury domination of NZCC proceedings. After providing three-quarters of the delegates to the first meeting, Canterbury supplied 6 of 11 to the annual general meeting of 1898, 6 of 9 in 1901, 9 of 27 in 1903, 13 of 16 in 1905 and 9 of 17 in 1909.[14] Certainly, most of these delegates held proxy for other associations and were bound in their response to set agenda items, but one might wonder at the range of views expressed in more informal discussions.

Surprisingly, very little effort was made to challenge this Canterbury domination or to follow the example of other sports and move the NZCC from Christchurch to a central location in New Zealand. At the inaugural meeting of the New Zealand Rugby Football Union in 1892 there was much debate before it was decided to establish the headquarters of the Union in Wellington, New Zealand's geographical centre. The Otago delegate expressed particular objections to what he felt would become simply a Wellington organisation administered by proxy votes, but the majority opinion declared Wellington to be the only feasible location for all delegates to attend. For similar reasons, the New Zealand Lawn Tennis Association also transferred its headquarters from Napier to Wellington during the early 1890s.[15]

It was not until 1910 that there was even any suggestion that the administration of New Zealand cricket should be moved. In a letter to the Wellington Cricket Association, E.H. Williams suggested that the development of New Zealand cricket would be assisted by moving the NZCC to Wellington. Nonetheless, after a heated debate, the WCA rejected the proposal.[16] It seems that not even an association that was normally one of the strongest critics of the NZCC was willing to question the traditional mantle of Christchurch as the spiritual home of New Zealand cricket.

The NZCC and the Provinces

With hindsight, the most significant achievements during the first two decades of the NZCC's existence were the inauguration of the Plunket Shield for interprovincial first-class cricket in 1907 and the Hawke Cup for minor associations in 1911, and the establishment of a representative programme for New Zealand teams – including tours to Australia in 1899 and

1914. However, despite these achievements the debates surrounding all of these events reveal that the NZCC was really no more secure than the sum of its fragmented and financially vulnerable constituents. Consequently, there were several instances in which the NZCC either failed completely or had its objectives severely compromised by interprovincial rivalries.

One of the NZCC's earliest resolutions – to hold an inter-island fixture in every season when New Zealand was not playing – was stifled by a lack of finance. A game was planned for the end of the 1901/02 season but was cancelled owing to lack of funds, the inability of many players to gain work leave and the inability of the NZCC to cover the basic expenses of others. Most leading players were again unavailable during the following season, but the game was played nevertheless. With a lack of 'star' players, it drew a small crowd and sustained an £89 loss. In 1907 another scheme was adopted for a match between Auckland, the Plunket Shield holders, and the rest of New Zealand, but this too was abandoned when the NZCC could secure only three players from Wellington and none from Canterbury or Otago. A more ambitious proposal at the end of 1910 to stage two inter-island matches, with one involving minor association players, was abandoned as being too expensive.[17] The second inter-island match was finally played in 1922 and the third in 1935.

Another problem arose when the Plunket Shield was introduced in 1907. After the NZCC accepted the offer of an interprovincial challenge shield from the Governor, Lord Plunket, it became involved in a protracted debate as to who should be the first recipient. Many felt the Shield should be awarded to Auckland as the recent MCC touring team had regarded them as the best provincial team in the country. A motion to this effect was lost by ten votes to six, and the Shield was eventually awarded to the Canterbury team because of their performances during the previous season and good record against the tourists. This decision caused objections from Auckland, who claimed that it was unfair that they would now have to challenge for the Shield in Christchurch when Canterbury already owed them a visit. Auckland, though, eventually agreed to a challenge in Christchurch, and justified their earlier claims to the Shield with an innings victory.[18]

The Council also struggled to match its ambitions for international tours. While it was not encumbered with the sort of ground development debts that hung over Canterbury and Wellington, its revenue-earning capacity was even more limited by the fact that international tours were far less frequent than interprovincial fixtures and far more expensive to stage. Moreover, as the NZCC's original proposal to derive a percentage of gate takings from interprovincial matches had been rejected, it had virtually no income during seasons when there were no international tours. As Table 8 reveals, even when there were international tours they were not necessarily lucrative: only the tour by Lord Hawke's England XI in 1902–03 returned a very substantial profit.[19] This, though, was quickly absorbed by large losses on the inter-island match and tours by Australia and the MCC.

TABLE 8

NEW ZEALAND CRICKET COUNCIL: FINANCIAL POSITION, 1895–1914

1895	+£1.0.0	
1896	+£56.15.5	profit on New South Wales tour of New Zealand
1897	+£131.14.9	
1898	+£140.2.10	
1899	+£4.4.8	loss on New Zealand tour of Australia
1900	–£24.2.6	loss on Melbourne Cricket Club tour of New Zealand
1901	–£28.1.2	
1902	–£25.12.2	
1903	+£505.18.11	profit on Lord Hawke's England XI tour
1904	+£227.15.9	loss on inter-island match
1905	+£135.19.2	loss on Australian tour of New Zealand
1906	+£60.19.0	loss on Melbourne Cricket Club tour of New Zealand
1907	+£21.19.9	loss on MCC tour of New Zealand
1908	–£85.13.6	repayment of MCC tour guarantees of provinces
1909	–£68.18.1	
1910	+£84.13.2	profit on Australian tour of New Zealand
1911	–	
1912	+£197.1.5	
1913	+£247.3.10	
1914	+£7.7.11	loss on Sims' Australian XI tour of New Zealand and New Zealand tour of Australia

Without cash reserves the Council could only guarantee the expenses of touring teams by securing smaller guarantees from the provincial associations – which were really no better off. Moreover, as Chapter 9 will show, the Council was also frequently in conflict with provincial associations which seemed to feel that their financial guarantees entitled them to equal representation in New Zealand teams and a greater say in the running of the game generally.

Inevitably, when the NZCC did attempt to secure its own financial position it was met with strong criticism from the provinces. 'Touchline' of the *New Zealand Free Lance*, a persistent critic from 1909 onwards, condemned the failure of the NZCC to reach terms with the Wellington Cricket Association for its proposed fundraising match against the New Zealand team when they returned from Australia in 1914. The NZCC apparently wanted too great a share of gate takings:

The Cricket Council, in my opinion, once again failed to rise to the occasion and in their chase after the mighty dollar were [sic] left lamenting their exaltation of the financial side to the detriment of the real purpose of playing the game of cricket in the Dominion. This is one more instance to add to the many laches of the Council, and they make a goodly total at this history of their career. As the Council comes of age next year, probably the individual members of that body will display more wisdom, with their extra responsibilities than they have in the days that are past.[20]

Certainly, Wellington's finances were precarious, but those of the NZCC were no better. With a heavy loss looming from the Australian tour, and more to come from the visit of Arthur Sims' Australian XI to New Zealand, the cash balance was only £7 at the end of the 1914 season.[21]

The sentiments expressed by 'Touchline' are as much parochial as symptomatic of a conception of 'amateur' cricket that owed far more to idealism than pragmatism. In 1909 he had accused Canterbury of placing a higher value on playing ability than coaching ability in its search for a professional coach. Ignoring the value of Albert Trott in Hawke's Bay during the 1890s and Albert Relf in Auckland from 1907 as both players and coaches, 'Touchline' insisted that the role of the Plunket Shield was to improve the standard of New Zealand cricketers, not to provide a theatre for imports. A few months later the NZCC strengthened an earlier resolution that all coaches playing in Plunket Shield matches must meet a strict residential qualification.[22]

Ironically, though, it was 'Touchline', writing after New Zealand's 162-run loss to Australia at the Basin Reserve in March 1910, who offered one of the most succinct contemporary analyses of the problems facing administrators:

> It is all very well for some people to say that we in New Zealand cannot play cricket for nuts; it is very easy to advise that capable coaches are a necessity to lift us up out of our present low state, and it admits of no contradiction that the wickets on which our cricketers are compelled to show their capabilities are not all they should be. No one with even a superficial knowledge of the playing of cricket in this Dominion will deny any of these things, but a casual glance at the balance sheets of the Cricket Associations in New Zealand will convince that they are one and all at their wits end to know how to make ends meet year after year.[23]

'Touchline', however, remained unable to make the connection between the problem of finance faced by the provincial cricket associations and the same problem faced by the NZCC as their controlling body.

The New Zealand Playing Standard

Undoubtedly, the best efforts of the NZCC were dogged by provincial rivalries – some of them petty and some of them understandable in terms of trying to protect their own precarious positions. There are, though, two other factors – and a deceptively significant third – that had an important bearing on the fortunes of the New Zealand game and the viability of the product that the NZCC was trying to promote. Firstly, even allowing for financial and administrative limitations, the playing standard in New Zealand was so dramatically inferior to that in all other major cricketing countries as to demand further explanation in its own right. Secondly, the consistent failure of efforts to improve cricket beyond the four main cities meant that the 'talent base' of New Zealand representative teams was effectively confined to one-third of the adult male population. Thirdly and finally, while the summer game languished New Zealand rugby was establishing a niche as one of the strongest sporting institutions in the world. Cricket, therefore, inevitably emerged unfavourably in comparisons between the two. Nonetheless, one must ask whether there is really any reason why progress in rugby should have hindered that in cricket.

A comparison of results with Australia gives a good idea of the extent to which New Zealand cricket teams struggled. From 1877 to 1914 Australia won 36 and lost 40 of 95 Test matches against England. Following the war the balance would swing significantly in Australia's favour. Against all first-class opposition, touring teams in Australia won 91, lost 53 and drew 25 of their 169 matches.[24] By contrast, New Zealand representative cricket teams won 4, lost 13 and drew 1 of their first-class matches prior to 1914. They did not play a Test match until 1930. Against first-class opposition, touring cricket teams in New Zealand won 43, lost 10 and drew 15. Of the losses, three were sustained by Tasmania in 1883–84, two by Fiji in 1894–95 and two by the weak MCC side of 1906–07; most of the draws were caused by bad weather. Of the 175 matches played by all touring teams, 114 were won, 12 lost and 49 drawn. The two non first-class losses were by Australia against a Canterbury XV in 1878 and a Wanganui XXII in 1881.[25]

The overall weakness of cricket within New Zealand is given further definition when one considers that several of the most successful players were products not of the local environment, but were Australian born and received their cricket training before coming to New Zealand. For example, Charles Boxshall of Melbourne was the best wicketkeeper in New Zealand prior to 1914; Thomas Cobcroft, captain of the 1895–96 New South Wales touring team, captained the 1899 New Zealand team to Australia; Charles Richardson had the same honour against Lord Hawke's XI in 1903, having scored the first century for a New Zealand team – 114 not out against the Melbourne Cricket Club – in 1900; both Syd Callaway and Jack Saunders played Test cricket for Australia before representing New Zealand; and Joseph Lawton was a professional from Warwickshire who served four seasons as Otago coach.[26]

Even allowing for 'imported' players, it is doubtful whether New Zealand was ever able to field its best team. The inability of many players to gain or afford work leave meant that original selections were changed constantly. Four of the 13 players selected for the 1899 tour of Australia were unable to accept the invitation, as was one of their nominated replacements.[27] The demands of business curtailed other careers. Leonard Cuff and Herbert DeMaus, among the leading batsmen of the early 1890s, departed for Tasmania and Fiji respectively at the peak of their powers. A decade later, Daniel Reese and Arthur Sims were absent from New Zealand for significant periods. The case of the Otago off-spinner Alec Downes was noted in Chapter 3; his inability to take work leave meant that he played only 6 of New Zealand's 18 first-class games up to 1914.[28] Not even the most influential patronage could sustain the fortunes of the NZCC against these odds.

Cricket and Climate

Aside from economics, the most frequent contemporary explanation for the retarded growth of New Zealand cricket relates to climate. In this context Andrew Hignell has provided a fascinating examination of the impact of weather patterns – especially rain – on the fortunes of English county cricket. For New Zealand, George Griffiths also presents a climatic argument that certainly merits wider consideration than his original application of it to cricket in Otago.

Among other things, Hignell argues that the wetter county seasons contributed to the financial vulnerability of the counties as games were abandoned and gate money lost. At the same time, and remembering that wickets remained substantially uncovered before 1981, a number of surveys suggest a correlation between lower batting and bowling averages during wet seasons. Wet or damp wickets and outfields assisted bowlers and hindered run scoring, while 'sticky' wickets – those drying after rain – often made batting conditions quite treacherous. Conversely, in dry and sunny summers batsmen thrived and bowlers toiled.[29] Interestingly, three of the wettest seasons since 1890 – 1927 (10th), 1931 (1st) and 1958 (4th) – were seasons encompassing the first, second and fifth New Zealand tours to England!

Cricket was too firmly established in English tradition ever to 'give in' to the weather. Yet, as Griffiths argues, the elements may have been a determinant on sporting preferences in new colonies, and perhaps also in Scotland and Ireland. In the heat of India and the West Indies cricket was the natural choice; unsurprisingly, a more vigorous contact sport such as rugby gained almost no following – although soccer gained a level of support. In Australia and South Africa, with somewhat more temperate climate in the main areas of settlement, both winter and summer sports flourished. In New Zealand, where the climate is closer to English conditions, winter sport held a distinct advantage over summer sport. In an endeavour to explain the struggle of Otago cricket at representative level, Griffiths points to several disadvantages for cricket in the most southerly, and therefore coldest, of New Zealand's main cricketing provinces. He argues that the climatic impediment to cricket is not simply rainfall but temperature also. While areas such as Queensland have a higher average rainfall than Otago, the average temperature of the Australian states is much higher. It is, then, the combination of rain and cold that contributes most to damp, inferior pitch conditions.[30]

Although Griffiths' argument is not reinforced with precise meteorological data, the broad validity of it and the applicability to New Zealand of the kinds of correlations identified by Hignell can be seen in a statistical comparison of batsmanship between New Zealand and Australia, as set out in Table 9. This reveals substantial differences in the scores of batsmen. In theory, at least, there is no reason why batsmen in New Zealand and Australia should not have had the same chances to succeed against bowling of a relative standard to their own play. Thus one is drawn to the conclusion that bowlers in New Zealand operated under a considerable advantage from damp wickets and atmosphere.

The very low instance of scores in excess of 300 during the nineteenth century is particularly noticeable. That Canterbury compiled 9 of the 17 that were made is as much a reflection of the greater skill of its players as the efforts of administrators to establish first-class facilities at Hagley Park and Lancaster Park. Equally revealing are the figures for the period after 1900, when one-third of all Australian first-class innings – but only one-eighth of those in New Zealand – exceeded 300. Moreover, of the 57 New Zealand scores in excess of 300 during this period, 20 were made by touring teams.

If figures from the entire history of New Zealand interprovincial cricket to the end of the 2000/01 season are incorporated, the pre-1914 period assumes an even more dramatic perspective:

- 78 of the first 100 completed provincial team innings (not all first class) produced scores less than 100, as did 49 of the next 100 (all first-class). The Australia figures (all first class) are 58 of 100 and 14 of 100.
- Of the ten highest team innings completed by Auckland, Wellington, Canterbury and Otago, only two – by Auckland in 1907 and 1910 – were compiled prior to 1914.
- Of the lowest completed innings by these teams, Auckland compiled 6 of 10 prior to 1914, Wellington 12 of 13, Canterbury 11 of 14, and Otago 9 of 11.
- 12 of the 14 lowest 2-innings aggregates by one team in a New Zealand first-class match were made prior to 1900.
- Eight of the nine lowest innings totals in New Zealand were made prior to 1914; the other was 26 by New Zealand against England in 1955.
- Six of eight New Zealand first-class games completed in a single day occurred prior to 1900. The Auckland vs. Fiji match in 1948 involved three declarations after lengthy rain delays.

TABLE 9

FREQUENCY OF FIRST-CLASS TEAM INNINGS EXCEEDING 300 IN AUSTRALIA
AND NEW ZEALAND, 1850/51–1914/15*

AUSTRALIA

	1850/51–1898/99	242 matches	911 innings
	1899/00–1914/15	253 matches	927 innings
Total	1850/51–1914/15	495 matches	1,838 innings

	1850/51–1898/99		1899/00–1914/15		Total 1850/51–1914/15	
300–399	99	10.9%	168	18.2%	267	14.5%
400–499	44	4.8%	84	9.0%	128	7.0%
500–599	13	1.4%	37	4.0%	50	2.7%
600–699	4	0.4%	13	1.4%	17	0.9%
700–799	1	0.1%	3	0.3%	4	0.2%
800–899	2	0.2%	3	0.3%	5	0.3%
900+	–	–	1	0.1%	1	0.1%
300+	163	17.8%	309	33.3%	472	25.7%

NEW ZEALAND

	1859/60–1898/99	149 matches	552 innings
	1899/00–1914/15	128 matches	479 innings
Total	1859/60–1914/15	277 matches	1,031 innings

	1859/60–1898/99		1899/00–1914/15		Total 1859/60–1914/15	
300–399	13	2.3%	41	8.6%	54	5.2%
400–499	4	0.7%	9	1.9%	13	1.3%
500–599	–	–	4	0.8%	4	0.4%
600–699	–	–	3	0.6%	3	0.3%
300+	17	3.0%	57	11.9%	74	7.2%

Scores in excess of 300 made by touring teams: Australia, 91 of 472 (19.2%); New Zealand, 21 of 74 (28.4%).

* Figures include all team innings begun in first-class matches – whether complete, incomplete, declared or abandoned – and include those where a score in excess of 300 was not possible due to match circumstances, such as a team requiring less than 300 to win in a fourth innings.

By so greatly restricting opportunities for batsmen and placing bowlers at a deceptive advantage, New Zealand pitch conditions did nothing to assist local players in developing the technique necessary to counter the superior skills of touring teams. Australian players – and Warwick Armstrong especially – frequently observed that New Zealand cricket would only improve in relation to the quality of its pitches. Frank Laver suggested in 1905 that better quality soil should be imported from Australia, while M.A. Noble added that there was little to be gained from playing on surfaces that were unfair to batsmen and offered no challenge to bowlers.[31]

The damp, slow New Zealand wickets did nothing to assist representative players in their preparations for the tours of Australia in 1899 and 1914. Daniel Reese was in no doubt that the failure of many batsmen was directly attributable to a lack of experience on hard, fast wickets. Unaccustomed to the confidence engendered by scoring runs in good batting conditions, an unnecessary inferiority complex developed among local players. Indeed, Australian bowler and frequent New Zealand tourist Hugh Trumble reinforced this view with the observation that 'he would be inclined to back the New Zealanders, if they were batting at the nets'.[32]

The NZCC and the Minor Associations

Another significant impediment to the growth of New Zealand cricket derived from the distribution of the population. The financial implications of this have been discussed already in terms of the lack of population from which to derive essential revenue. Others saw a more direct impact on the quality of players. As the *New Zealand Herald* concluded prior to Auckland's encounter with Australia in February 1905:

> The settlement of New Zealand – and we have every reason to congratulate ourselves upon the fact – has not tended to centralise population as it has for the most part in the colonies that now form the Commonwealth; and without a large and somewhat centralised population it is hardly possible to obtain many first-rate exponents of such a game as cricket. What cricket was in Australia forty years ago, when the early English teams played fifteen or eighteen representatives of Melbourne or Sydney, and secured an easy victory, that the game is necessarily at our New Zealand centres today. The process of attaining first-rate skill in the game has taken thirty years in Australia, even with a centralised population, and it may reasonably be expected to take longer here.[33]

A *Press* columnist also pointed out that such a scattered population was not conducive to any form of professional cricket and that the game was not therefore played on a sustained basis.[34] Given that the total European population – the New Zealanders most likely to play cricket – of the four main cities increased from only 23.32 per cent in 1881 to 31.52 per cent in 1911, this is a sound explanation. By comparison, Sydney in 1901 contained 37 per cent of the New South Wales population, Melbourne contained 41 per cent of Victorians and Adelaide 39 per cent of South Australians. By 1911 Sydney had increased to 47 per cent, Melbourne to 45 per cent and Adelaide to 41 per cent. The more important factor, though, as we saw in the previous chapter, was the considerably larger total population of the Australian cities.[35]

The de facto dominance of the four main cities cannot, of course, be attributed to neglect by the NZCC or the administrators of its constituent minor associations. As discussed in Chapters 2 and 3, the runholders of South Canterbury, Hawke's Bay and the Wairarapa could display the same English public school or middle-class credentials as their counterparts in Christchurch or Wellington and they had lent their patronage to the formation of ten minor cricket associations by 1898.

Yet no amount of administrative prestige and energy could easily overcome the financial, logistical and geographical obstacles that confronted cricketers outside the main cities. Inter-district and inter-association matches grew very slowly. Although Otago played Southland in 1864 and South Canterbury a decade later, it was not until Manawatu hosted Wanganui at Feilding in March 1894 that a major match occurred without the involvement of a first-class province.[36] With the exception of Nelson's visits to Wanganui in 1881 and Taranaki in 1897, and Taranaki's visit to Nelson in 1901, all minor association matches prior to the inauguration of the Hawke Cup in 1911 were between neighbouring teams.[37]

The Hawke Cup, presented to the NZCC by Lord Hawke in 1910, did not produce an immediate improvement in the volume of minor association cricket. A tournament to determine the first holder prompted Southland to meet South Canterbury in Dunedin and Nelson to tour the lower North Island in 1910–11, and for the teams in that region to engage in more frequent exchanges. Yet Southland's tenure as holders of the Hawke Cup produced only one challenge in two years, and the NZCC was obliged to arrange another tournament in 1913 to prevent the competition becoming moribund. South Auckland won the tournament, then promptly lost the Cup to Wanganui. Only during the early 1920s did a more consistent pattern of matches develop between the minor associations.[38]

Furthermore, the relatively peripheral position of minor associations and smaller conurbations is attested to by the fact that only five players from outside the four main cities were selected for New Zealand teams prior to 1914: William Robertson was selected from Southland in 1896, having previously played for New Zealand whilst resident in Christchurch; Hugh Lusk from Napier played four matches from 1897 to 1903; Bernard McCarthy of Taranaki played two matches in 1903; and Chester Holland of Taranaki and Len McMahon of Poverty Bay played one match each in 1914. It is particularly revealing that Hawke's Bay's 48 first-class matches produced only 1 New Zealand selection. During the 1920s and early 1930s another six players gained representative honours from minor associations, but none enjoyed a lengthy career for New Zealand.[39]

The Rise of Rugby

As a winter game, rugby was never in direct competition with cricket for popular support and patronage, and in that sense its fortunes have no bearing on those of the NZCC. Nonetheless, if an innings and 358 run loss to Australia at Wellington in March 1905 was close to the nadir for New Zealand cricket, the zenith of a rugby phenomenon that had been building since the 1880s occurred at the end of the same year. The 1905 All Black tour of Britain, France and North America in which the New Zealanders scored 976 points to 59 and lost only 1 – still disputed – match to Wales, remains the benchmark for any discussion of the historical significance of sport in New Zealand.[40] This success cannot be ignored and raises obvious questions as to why New Zealand cricket did not prosper to the same extent.

Although the first game under rugby rules was not apparently played in New Zealand until May 1870, growth was rapid thereafter – from 7 representative fixtures in 1880 to 19 in 1887, 29 in 1889 and 121 for the decade 1880–89, in addition to 38 by touring teams. During the next 10 seasons another 245 matches were played between teams drawn from 16 provincial rugby unions, with another 18 matches involving touring teams. The decade after 1900 produced 402 inter-union matches and 36 by touring teams, with an inter-Island match played annually from 1902.[41] This compares with a total of 277 first-class cricket matches for the entire period 1864–1914, sporadic fixtures between first-class provinces and minor associations and between neighbouring minor associations from 1894 onwards. Moreover, rugby growth also produced considerable international success. From 1884 to 1914 representative New Zealand rugby teams, at home and on tour to Australia and the British Isles and France, won 118, lost 7 and drew 4 of their matches. By comparison, Australian and British touring teams in New Zealand won 42, lost 53 and drew 6 against all opposition.[42]

Explanations for the disparity in growth and success between rugby and cricket are complicated by the weakness of much of the existing historiography of New Zealand rugby. In the work of Jock Phillips and a legion of uncritical devotees one finds a characterisation of rugby as the epitome of rural, colonial masculinity. The effort, cooperation and egalitarianism required of pioneers in taming a rugged landscape supposedly produced an especially tough New Zealand male 'type' ideally suited to the combative demands of the rugby field.[43] The pervasiveness of these connections is enhanced by Phillips' contention that rugby spread rapidly into rural areas and was securely entrenched as the 'national game' by the early 1880s, a situation 'confirmed' by his thrice misprinted – and often recycled – claim that there were 50,000, rather than 5,000, affiliated rugby players in New Zealand by the mid 1890s.[44] Consequently, the 'Phillips school' places a great deal of emphasis on the characteristics of 'frontier' masculinity as a counterpoint to sedentary urbanity, femininity and domesticity.[45]

Yet such arguments are not grounded in any systematic analysis of the social and geographical origins of New Zealand rugby players – and especially of the All Blacks. They fail to recognise the disjuncture between mythology and actuality and leave a deceptive impression that contemporary explanations for the successes of 1905 – especially the rural dimension – contain much truth. As I have argued elsewhere, with the benefit of a comprehensive statistical analysis it is clear that New Zealand rugby – and the upper echelon of the game in particular – has always been disproportionately urban and rather more middle-class than egalitarian in character. All Black teams, as the most visible international face of the game, were dominated by players from the provincial teams of the four main cities who were far more likely than the population as a whole to have attended elite educational institutions and secured professional occupations. At no time have farmers, or the rural sector generally, exerted a dominant influence over New Zealand rugby.[46] Furthermore, while the fledgling game of the 1870s was certainly a fairly physical activity, this is clearly not true of the more 'scientific' rugby emerging in New Zealand from the 1880s. Rule changes, or local interpretations of them – especially the development of the wing-forward and 2-3-2 scrum formation, shifted the emphasis from brute force in prolonged forward exchanges to a dependence on skill and speed in open play.[47]

Certainly, the mythology remains vitally important as an embodiment of entrenched perceptions and stereotypes about the essential characteristics of New Zealand society and its transition from colony to nation. It is undeniable that the performances of the 1905 All Blacks were the subject of immense colonial pride and no small amount of political interest and opportunism. Premier Richard Seddon was quick to seize on the tour as a means to strengthen New Zealand's profile within the Empire – to say nothing of his own increasingly vulnerable Liberal Government.[48] There is also much to ponder and explain in the enduring nostalgic fascination of New Zealand rugby followers and media with anachronistic rural imagery. Yet as the key elements of the mythology epitomised by reactions to 1905 were a product of the success of rugby rather than a causal factor of that success, it follows that they have nothing to offer as a coherent explanation for the prominence and success of rugby and the relative failure of cricket. More to the point, there is no recorded instance of any suggestion that cricketers, despite their failings, were any less manly than their rugby counterparts. Indeed, Chapters 4 and 5 have shown that the nexus between cricket and manliness was very secure.

Therefore, New Zealand rugby did not surpass cricket in importance because of any greater ability to 'make men'. Rather, it prospered because –

relatively speaking – it was better able to overcome key obstacles to sporting growth. In many respects rural rugby encountered the same obstacles of geography, demography and transience that constricted cricket beyond the four main cities.[49] Unlike cricket, though, rugby did not face the impediments of climate in that it required neither good weather nor a dry and manicured surface and the finance to produce and maintain one. Additionally, it was far less time consuming and demanded nothing in the way of expensive equipment – thus making it more accessible to a wider range of participants constrained by long working hours, comparatively low pay, or both. What is required is less a further investigation of the relationship between rugby and cricket and more an investigation of the pre-eminence of rugby in New Zealand over other football codes – such as soccer and Australian Rules – that shared its comparative advantages in relation to cricket.

A comparison with sporting development in Australia also gives some perspective to the increasingly uneven relationship between cricket and rugby in New Zealand. More favourable climatic conditions, a revenue-earning spectatorship and regular visits from English teams ensured that cricket flourished throughout Australia. At the same time, the eastern colonies all possessed active and lucrative football fraternities, albeit in quite different forms. By the 1890s Victorian rules in Melbourne and Adelaide and rugby in Brisbane and Sydney were far more advanced in relation to Australian cricket than New Zealand cricket was in relation to rugby.[50] The progress of Australian football and rugby, though, does not appear to have had an adverse affect on the development of Australian cricket. In light of this, then, there is nothing to suggest that the dominance of rugby or any football code in New Zealand should, of itself, have been detrimental to the progress of cricket.

Other Theories of Failure

In the early twentieth century, contemporary analysis of the state of New Zealand cricket offered several other explanations for the struggle it faced. After New Zealand's Basin Reserve 'Test' loss to Australia in March 1910, the *Evening Post* hinted that, as well as systematic coaching, an injection of youth would also assist the New Zealand team:

> Cricket in New Zealand has been a proper step child: allowed to hustle for its own existence and work out its own salvation as best it might. And to-day [sic] we have a New Zealand representative team composed mostly of men who have been playing a second rate game for years, simply for the lack of the necessary assistance. It is a bad sign to see a predominance of middle aged (in a cricket sense) men battling for their country on the cricket field: it indicates that the youngsters are not worthy.[51]

FIGURE 14

Schoolboys from French Farm, Banks Peninsula, 1882. Despite the difficulties of transport and communication, there was no shortage of enthusiasm for cricket in rural areas. (Canterbury Museum: Ref. 13692)

A month later the *New Zealand Times* expressed a similar opinion while also pointing to a failure in translating cricketing enthusiasm from the generations of colonists to the native born. The *Times* complained that there was no longer a strong English public school tradition in New Zealand cricket. Control of the game had shifted to New Zealanders, 'who, it must be confessed, have been content to play in a more or less languid manner and to take no pains to foster cricket among the young'.[52] This, however, stands more as a matter of perception than fact. Many of the leading administrators were products of New Zealand's elite schools, and others such as Bell, Stevens and Wilding possessed English experience.

Among the more inventive theories on offer was a contention in Canterbury that declining fortunes for cricket were due to the rise of lawn tennis. A *Press* editorial during the Australian XI match against Canterbury in December 1886 argued that cricket had become too slow to sustain public interest and that the elite were shifting their patronage to tennis. Tennis required less space, fewer players and less practice time, thereby enabling more people to play it proficiently. It also involved a player more constantly than the enforced idleness imposed by some parts of a cricket match. There was no likelihood that the English would ever abandon cricket, but its laws perhaps required modification if it was to remain as the leading sport of the Empire. The *Press* summed up its point of view as follows: 'We do not wish to decry cricket or to make out that tennis is a superior game. We only assert our belief that if it be true that cricket is less popular than it was, it is largely owing to the increased popularity of tennis.' Interestingly, though, the frequency with which prominent cricketers such as C.G. Gore, R.D. Harman and Frederick Wilding collected New Zealand tennis titles tends to suggest that the two games were quite compatible.[53]

Wilding, for one, did concede that tennis and other sports imposed certain limitations on cricket. Interviewed during Australia's tour of New Zealand in 1905, he suggested that tennis, bowling, motoring and horse racing especially had all taken potential players from cricket and limited the opportunities for practice among many existing players:

> I say this without wishing to attack racing or any other sport. In the old days every race day was used for the purposes of a cricket match. Of late years our players have had far less match practice than in the old times, and no amount of net practice will make up for the loss of match practice. Our cricketers are as strong, as active, as keen-sighted, and possess equally good natural qualifications as Englishmen or Australians, but they lack the nerve which men can only acquire by being put to the supreme test of frequent important matches.[54]

Of course, the rise of other sports was as much a phenomenon in Australia as New Zealand. Wilding was therefore quick to endorse Armstrong and Laver's views on the sub-standard quality of New Zealand grounds.[55]

Evaluating the NZCC

Irrespective of their accuracy, the various explanations for the comparative failure of New Zealand cricket embody an acute awareness that the game had fallen well short of expectations. Implicit in this was a feeling that the NZCC had failed in its role as a central administrative body.

Certainly, the Council had failed in many of its objectives and was not assisted by the jealousies of its provincial constituents. In this light it is tempting to wonder whether a more progressive and cooperative group of administrators at all levels may have been able to take the game further. Would a move to Wellington have been of benefit to the NZCC in terms of providing a centralised and accessible body and one free from the traditional dominance of Canterbury? Of course, the answers to these questions are purely in the realm of speculation. The administration of Australian cricket, though, may offer some clues.

The Australasian Cricket Council, established in 1892, never came to terms with the existing influence of the Melbourne Cricket Club and the New South Wales Cricket Association, nor could it contend with the reluctance of the players to relinquish their traditional financial control of international tours. Accordingly, the Council was wound up in January 1900. The Australian Board of Control for International Cricket (ABCIC), formed in May 1905, became another forum for bitter personal and interstate rivalries. Acrimony reached a peak in 1912 with a fist fight between Peter McAlister, a former Test player and keen supporter of the Board, and Clem Hill, Australia's star batsman and a strong advocate of player control, during a selection committee meeting. Subsequently, six leading players, including Hill, refused to join the 1912 tour to England. It was not until October 1914 that the ABCIC could boast of a full complement of state cricket associations as members.[56]

Yet this fractious environment did not stifle the development of a very high standard of club and first-class cricket and the fashioning of an international record that became a strong component of Australia's emerging national identity prior to 1914. In short, and if we also consider the points made in the last chapter about the failure of English administrators to address the parlous economic position of the game, a case can be made that a high standard of cricket can and does emerge despite the best efforts of administrators. On balance, therefore, it is reasonable to conclude that the NZCC struggled with a number of factors largely beyond its control – as we have seen in this chapter.

Some astute observers clearly understood the obstacles facing the NZCC in particular and New Zealand cricket in general. Nevertheless, it remains to consider how such sustained failure was interpreted within a sporting ideology that conceived cricket in relation to questions of eugenics, moral metaphors, imperial unity and, in the Australian context, emergent nationalism.

Notes

1. ACA, Annual Report, 1886; OCA, Annual Report, 1886. The origins of a representative New Zealand team are fully discussed in Chapter 9.
2. D.O. Neely, R.P. King and F.K. Payne, *Men in White: The History of New Zealand International Cricket 1894–1985* (Auckland 1985), p. 35.
3. *New Zealand Referee*, 26 June 1894, p. 26.
4. See Chapter 9.
5. *New Zealand Referee*, 3 Jan. 1895, p. 27.
6. Ibid.
7. Ibid.
8. Neely, *100 Summers*, p. 49.
9. *The Press*, 18 Oct. 1895, p. 4.
10. NZCC, Annual Report, 1898, 1903, 1905, 1909.
11. Cane, *Cricket in Hawke's Bay*, pp. 15–55.
12. Gardner, 'Francis Henry Dillon Bell', pp.34-6; F. Hall, 'Frederick Wilding', in Orange (ed.), *DNZB: Vol. 2*, pp.576–77; G.G. Hall, 'Alfred Charles Hanlon' in Orange (ed.), *DNZB, Vol.2*, pp. 192–3; R. Wright-St Clair, 'George Cleghorn' in Orange (ed.), *DNZB, Vol.2*, p. 90.
13. *CNZ*, Vol.3, p. 262; *The School List of Christ's College from 1850 to 1935* (Christchurch, 1935), pp. 122, 147; T.D. Harman, obituary, *The Press*, 24 April 1950, p. 8; F.C. Raphael, obituary, *The Press*, 20 May 1940, p. 9.
14. NZCC, Annual Report, 1895, 1898, 1901, 1903, 1905, 1909.

15. A.C. Swan, *History of New Zealand Rugby Football: Volume 1 1870–1945* (Auckland 1992), pp. 113–4; P. Elenio, *Centrecourt: A Century of New Zealand Tennis* (Wellington, 1986), p. 3.
16. WCA, Annual General Meeting Minutes, 28 Sept. 1910; Neely, *100 Summers*, p. 78; See also *Christchurch Times*, 12 Dec. 1931, p. 12.
17. NZCC, Annual Report, 1904; Committee Minutes, 21 Dec. 1901; 22 Jan. 1902; 21 Nov. 1907; 17 March 1908; Management Committee Minutes, 24 Oct. 1910; 3 Nov. 1910.
18. NZCC, Special Committee Minutes, 2 Oct. 1906; Committee Minutes, 18 April 1907; 15 May 1907; Annual General Meeting Minutes, 19 Oct. 1907; *Otago Witness*, 22 May 1907, p. 58.
19. As set out in the previous chapter, not only was it expensive to bring touring teams to New Zealand, especially from England, but a much smaller urban population than in Australia dictated that there would always be a smaller revenue-producing spectatorship to cover much the same basic cost as that faced by Australia.
20. *New Zealand Free Lance,* 24 Jan. 1914, p. 19.
21. NZCC, Annual Report, 1914.
22. *New Zealand Free Lance*, 10 Oct. 1909, p. 19; *New Zealand Times*, 8 Feb. 1910, p. 10.
23. *New Zealand Free Lance*, 9 April 1910, p. 18.
24. Webster, *First-Class Cricket in Australia*, passim.
25. F. Payne and I. Smith (eds), *The 1997 Shell Cricket Almanack of New Zealand* (Auckland, 1997), pp. 334–5; Neely et al., *Men in White*, pp. 35–58.
26. McConnell and Smith, *Encyclopedia*, passim.
27. Neely, et al. *Men in White*, p. 40.
28. McConnell and Smith, *Encyclopedia*, pp.25, 33, 37, 128, 134.
29. Hignell, *Rain Stops Play*, pp. 113–70.
30. Griffiths, 'History of Otago Cricket', n.p.
31. F. Laver, *An Australian Cricketer on Tour* (London, 1905), p. 104; Reese, *New Zealand Cricket 1841–1914*, pp. 118–19; *Otago Witness*, 22 March 1905, p. 56; *Australasian*, 19 March 1910, p. 718; 21 March 1914, p. 649.
32. D. Reese, *Was it all Cricket?* (London, 1948), pp. 390, 395; Reese, *New Zealand Cricket 1841–1914*, p. 116; *Otago Witness,* 8 Oct. 1913, p. 54.
33. *New Zealand Herald,* 11 Feb. 1905, p. 6.
34. *The Press*, 6 Feb. 1903, p. 2.
35. Forster, *Australian Cities*, p. 9.
36. Although Hawke's Bay had not obtained first-class status when it played Poverty Bay in 1878–79, it was to do so in 1882.
37. Derived from Reese, *New Zealand Cricket 1841–1914*, passim.
38. McConnell and Smith, *Encyclopedia*, p. 206.
39. Reese, *New Zealand Cricket 1914–33*, p. 590.
40. See, for example, Sinclair, *A Destiny Apart*, pp.143–55.
41. Swan, *History of New Zealand Rugby Football*, pp. 1–170.
42. Chester and McMillan, *Encyclopedia of New Zealand Rugby*, pp. 379–82, 397–9; Chester and McMillan, *The Visitors*, pp. 17–101.
43. J.O.C. Phillips, 'Rugby, War and the Mythology of the New Zealand Male', *New Zealand Journal of History*, 18, 2 (1984); Phillips, *A Man's Country?*, pp. 86–130. See also: J. Nauright, 'Sport, Manhood and Empire: British Responses to the New Zealand Rugby Tour of 1905', *International Journal of the History of Sport*, 8, 2 (1991); J. Nauright, 'Colonial Manhood and Imperial Race Virility: British Responses to Post-Boer War Colonial Rugby Tours' in J. Nauright and T.J.L. Chandler (eds), *Making Men: Rugby and Masculine Identity* (London, 1996); S.A.G.M. Crawford, '"Muscles and Character are there the First Objects of Necessity": An Overview of Sport and Recreation in a Colonial Setting – Otago Province, New Zealand', *British Journal of Sports History*, 2, 2 (1985), pp. 112–8.
44. Barclay, 'Trends in New Zealand Sport from 1840 to 1900', p. 21; Phillips, *A Man's Country?*, p. 88; rev. ed. (Auckland, 1996), p. 88; J.O.C. Phillips, 'The Hard Man: Rugby and the Formation of Male Identity in New Zealand' in Nauright and Chandler, *Making Men*, p. 71. Fifty thousand affiliated players in 1890 would have constituted 59% of the New Zealand male population aged 15–30. There is no evidence that even 5,000 players is a reliable figure.
45. Phillips also directs a sustained focus on the nexus between success in sport and war as key components of an emerging New Zealand nationalism during the early years of the twentieth century. The qualities of colonial manliness revealed by the All Blacks in 1905 were the same as allowed New Zealand soldiers to excel in the South African war and to cling valiantly to the Gallipoli

peninsula under unrelenting Turkish fire in 1915. See, in particular, Phillips, *A Man's Country?* (1987), pp. 108–22.

46. Ryan, 'Rural Myth and Urban Actuality'. See also my 'The End of an Aura: All Black Rugby and Rural Nostalgia Since 1995', forthcoming.

47. Ryan, *Forerunners*, pp. 114–16; Chester and McMillan, *The Visitors*, p. 41. Geoff Vincent also argues that pre-1914 New Zealand rugby presents a highly contested terrain in terms of the translation of middle-class sporting ideals from Britain to a colonial setting. The New Zealand game was marked by different interpretations of the playing laws, a more commercial imperative and flexibility in interpreting the amateur ethos – all elements that were anathema to the English public school founders of the game and that would bring New Zealand sharply into conflict with the British Isles after 1905. See also: Vincent, '"A Tendency to Roughness"'; G.T. Vincent, 'Practical Imperialism: The Anglo-Welsh Rugby Tour of New Zealand, 1908', *International Journal of the History of Sport*, 15, 1 (1998); G. Ryan, '"A Lack of Esprit de Corps": The 1908–09 Wallabies and the Legacy of the 1905 All Blacks', *Sporting Traditions*, 17, 1 (Nov. 2000), pp. 39–55.

48. See T.N.W. Buchanan, 'Missionaries of Empire: 1905 All Black Tour' (research essay, University of Canterbury, 1981), p. 22.

49. Ryan, 'Rural Myth and Urban Actuality', pp. 52–7.

50. See, for example: G. Blainey, *A Game of Our Own: The Origins of Australian Football* (Melbourne, 1990); T.V. Hickie, *They Ran with the Ball: How Rugby Football Began in Australia* (Sydney, 1993).

51. *Evening Post*, 29 March 1910, p. 6.

52. *New Zealand Times*, 30 March 1910, p. 4.

53. *The Press*, 1 Dec. 1886, p. 4; Elenio, *New Zealand Tennis*, p. 184.

54. *New Zealand Referee*, 23 March 1905, p. 53.

55. Ibid.

56. P. Derriman, *True to the Blue: A History of the New South Wales Cricket Association* (Sydney, 1985), pp. 103–7; C. Harte, *A History of Australian Cricket* (London, 1993), pp. 174–202, 222. Despite the name, there is no evidence that any New Zealand province or the NZCC was ever invited to join the Australasian Cricket Council.

8

Humble Imitators at these Distant Antipodes: The Imperial Connection in the Nineteenth Century

From the arrival of George Parr's All England XI in February 1864 to the departure of Arthur Sim's Australian XI in March 1914, New Zealand retained a fascination with touring cricket teams that generally transcended any notion of victory or even of competitive play. During these five decades provincial and national teams secured only 12 victories from 175 matches against touring teams. Of these, three were against Tasmania, two against Fiji and two against the weak MCC team of 1906–07. Almost two-thirds of the fixtures pitted touring teams against local XVs, XVIIIs or XXIIs. No English team played on even terms until 1902–03, and New Zealand did not meet Australia on even terms until 1905. What, then, was so peculiarly important and attractive about these tours?

TABLE 10

TOURING TEAMS IN NEW ZEALAND, 1864–1914

		First-class				All matches			
		P	W	L	D	P	W	L	D
1863–64	G. Parr's England XI	–	–	–	–	4	3	–	1
1876–77	J. Lillywhite's England XI	–	–	–	–	8	6	–	2
1877–78	Australia	–	–	–	–	7	5	1	1
1880–81	Australia	–	–	–	–	10	6	1	3
1881–82	A. Shaw's England XI	–	–	–	–	7	5	–	2
1883–84	Tasmania	4	–	3	1	7	2	3	2
1886–87	Australia	–	–	–	–	5	2	–	3
1887–88	C.A. Smith's England XI	–	–	–	–	3	–	–	3
1888–89	English Football Team	–	–	–	–	1	–	–	1
1889–90	New South Wales	5	4	–	1	7	6	–	1
1893–94	New South Wales	7	4	1	2	8	4	1	3
1894–95	Fiji	6	2	2	2	8	4	2	2
1895–96	New South Wales	5	3	1	1	5	3	1	1
1896–97	Australia	–	–	–	–	5	3	–	2
1896–97	Queensland	5	3	1	1	8	4	1	3
1899–00	Melbourne CC	–	–	–	–	7	6	–	1
1902–03	Lord Hawke's England XI	7	7	–	–	18	18	–	–
1904–05	Australia	4	3	–	1	6	4	–	2
1905–06	Melbourne CC	–	–	–	–	10	8	–	2
1906–07	MCC	11	6	2	3	16	10	2	4
1909–10	Australia	6	5	–	1	9	7	–	2
1913–14	Sim's Australian XI	8	6	–	2	16	8	–	8

There is a considerable literature documenting the role of sport generally and cricket especially as a mechanism of cultural power that was crucial to the maintenance of continuity within the British Empire and subsequently as a means through which distinct colonial and then national identities were expressed.[1] The strongest focal points in this process were the regular interchange of touring teams. While the tours were not evenly distributed or timetabled, they provided a yardstick by which the colonies could easily measure their standards and progress against those of the mother country. During these tours, the rhetoric of muscular Christianity that normally accompanied Victorian cricket was transformed into broader statements encompassing collective racial and social qualities and the shared culture of the British Empire. By 1900 13 English teams had been sent to Australia, 2 to India, 2 to the West Indies, 4 to South Africa and 12 to the United States. Of the touring teams to Australia, four carried on to New Zealand. The first separate tour of New Zealand, by Lord Hawke's England XI, came in 1902–03. In return, one Aboriginal and ten white Australian teams toured England, along with one South African, three American, one Canadian, one West Indian and two Parsee teams. The first tours between colonies were visits by various Australian teams to New Zealand; 14 such tours took place between 1878 and 1914. Australia also visited South Africa, the first tour taking place in 1902–03 and reciprocated in 1910–11.[2]

In many respects, New Zealand reveals a conventional response to touring teams. The anticipation and expectation that accompanied the hosting of English touring teams in 1864, 1877 and 1882, and equally the criticism that ensued when standards were not met, leaves no doubt that imperial cricket contacts were a crucial part of the process by which New Zealand sought to establish its niche within the Empire. To perform honourably on the field was a means of informing those at 'home' that New Zealand had inherited and maintained requisite standards of Englishness.

In other ways, though, the New Zealand response is not straightforward. Firstly, as we will see later in this – and the following – chapter, the most frequent cricketing contacts – and calamities – were not against the mother country but against colonial Australian teams. While much may be said of cricket and the British Empire, it is also important to examine an intercolonial dimension and the place of cricket within late-nineteenth-century conceptions of colonial and imperial federation. Secondly, as Chapter 10 will explain, New Zealand cricket displayed few, if any, signs of the transition to a more aggressive strain of colonial assertiveness and, later, emergent nationalism characteristic of the Australian game. Yet, at the same time rugby became, initially, an assertion of New Zealand's contribution to the Empire, and, later, a component of a more independent New Zealand identity during the twentieth century. That the obvious disjuncture between the broad explanations for the success of rugby and their lack of applicability to cricket was never examined, let alone reconciled, by any contemporary

FIGURE 15

Lord Hawke's XI vs. Canterbury, Lancaster Park, 1903. Although the tourists won all of their matches convincingly, Canterbury's loss by 133 runs represented a better performance than most. (Weekly Press photo, Canterbury Museum: Ref. 3209)

FIGURE 16

Muff cricket match, Lancaster Park, 1884. This group is typical of the many unusual matches that were played in aid of various charities during the late nineteenth century. (Canterbury Pilgrims' and Early Settlers' Association Collection, Canterbury Museum: Ref. 9499)

observer of the two games highlights the limitations of much of the New Zealand sporting rhetoric of the time.

Anglo-Australian Cricket

Early cricket tours to New Zealand are best understood in the context of Anglo-Australian cricketing relations. The Australian progression from deference to assertiveness provides a benchmark against which to judge New Zealand reactions and performances and in which to consider New Zealand's failure to follow Australia along the same cricketing path.

The first English tours of Australia in 1861–62 and 1863–64 are clear examples of tutelage. The term refers both to the deferential sense among colonists that they were little more than transplanted English who stood only to learn from the superiority of the mother country and to improve by her example, and to an appreciation that the real value of tours lay not in notions of possible colonial victory but in the reinforcement of British cultural hegemony and the imperial bond.

When H.H. Stephenson's English team reached Melbourne in December 1861, one observer called it 'a most audacious thing of the colonists to challenge the finest players in the world and to imagine that they could teach their respected grandmother'.[3] Later in the tour the *Sydney Morning Herald* put matters into a more accurate perspective:

> In inviting you to visit us we had no idea of testing our skill against yours – that would be simply absurd; but we were desirous of having you here to witness British skill in the noble game of cricket. It is a comfort to know that we are beaten by our own countrymen. They can not find foreigners to beat our cricketers, our masters come from the old country.[4]

Although the tourists lost two matches against XXIIs in Victoria, these achievements were not attributed to Australian skills or superior numbers. Rather, 'One long clatter of knives and forks followed by the usual popping of corks' had taken its toll.[5]

However, a series of victories during the 1870s, first by New South Wales and Victorian XVIIIs in 1873–74 and then by an Australian team on even terms in 1877, along with the successes of the first Australian teams to visit England in 1878, 1880 and 1882, prompted a noticeable shift from deference to colonial self-assertion. These performances helped to subdue earlier fears concerning the blight of convictism in Australian settlement and possible physical deterioration in a hot southern climate. Indeed, they acted in an overt fashion to highlight a healthy climate, open spaces and an apparently egalitarian social order as the keys to Australian prosperity.[6] Yet, rather than being stridently nationalistic or anti-English, these sentiments were part of a middle-class Anglo-Australian ideal that stressed Australia's strength within – as opposed to independence from – the Empire.[7] Moreover, a decade of setbacks on the field during the 1880s, and bitter politicking off it between administrators and players, served to dilute excessive optimism.

It was not until the 1890s that Australian cricket was to regain its status and embark on a gradual shift from colonial assertiveness to emergent nationalism.[8] As working-class, and especially Irish working-class elements within Australia came to see certain tenets of imperialism as little more than English nationalism, cricket – and the regular battles for the Ashes in particular – assumed centre stage in a rhetoric of democracy, independence and Australian cultural distinctiveness.[9] While a thorough commitment to anti-imperial nationalism might logically have disposed Australians against essentially English institutions such as cricket, the movement instead derived rewards from beating the mother country at its own game. Early in 1898, when political federation of the Australian colonies was by no means a certainty, the radical Sydney *Bulletin* responded to Australia's victory over Andrew Stoddart's English touring team with the observation that 'This ruthless rout of English cricket will do – and has done – more to enhance the cause of Australian nationality than could ever be achieved by miles of erudite essays and impassioned appeal'.[10]

George Parr's All England XI

By the terms of the Australian model, New Zealand cricket never made it beyond the 1860s.

It is, moreover, ironic that the starting point for New Zealand's entry into the wider world of cricket was in Dunedin – the settlement with the least coherent cricketing tradition during its formative years. Shadrach Jones, a local entrepreneur who was building his fortune on the injection of capital and population caused by the recent Otago gold discoveries, was quick to see the potential of enticing George Parr's All England XI to venture across the Tasman Sea after it had played in Melbourne during the 1863/64 season.

The possibility that Parr's team would visit New Zealand was voiced as early as July 1863. While there was little realistic interest from the struggling cricketing communities of Auckland, Wellington and Nelson, large public meetings were soon being held in both Dunedin and Christchurch to rally support and finance the tour. In Dunedin rapid progress was made towards developing the Dunedin CC's rather unsatisfactory ground, and by the end of November tour funds were such as to allow a tender for the enclosure of the ground with 600 yards of 7-foot-high paling fence and the building of a 375-foot-long grandstand. On completion, opinion was expressed that the facilities were as good as those in Melbourne.[11]

Such unprecedented public support for cricket was in sharp contrast to the apathy and lack of funds that had dogged the Dunedin CC only two years earlier. From this position it embraced an acute awareness that the successful staging of tour matches would be a valuable advertisement for the colony in general and for the South Island settlements in particular. As *The Press* put it on 17 December 1863, Canterbury was not especially concerned with Shadrach Jones and his financial speculation on the tour:

> The honour of the settlement is the main point of importance to us. It is not a game of play we are engaged in. It is not a spectacle for the amusement of fair ladies, idle men and boys out for a holiday. A match of this kind means and involves a great deal more, without which it is an empty show costing a great deal of money.[12]

Six days later the same source pointed more explicitly to the impressions that the performances of New Zealand cricketers might convey to an English audience:

> No option is left us now, we shall be posted in every newspaper in England either as a plucky set of fellows who, in the midst of the hard struggles of a settlers life, and the incessant grind of money-grubbing, have retained some of the manly tastes of our race, and some of the honourable pride which English lads delight to carry even into their amusements; or on the other hand we shall be charged with having fallen off as a community from the high standard of the old country, and with having exchanged pluck and activity for bounce and tall talk.[13]

Such apparently high stakes demanded the greatest attention to detail.

More than three months before Parr's team arrived in New Zealand, complaints began to surface in both Canterbury and Otago that the provincial cricketers were showing a lack of dedication to practice. On 20 November 1863 Jerningham Wakefield, the irascible son of the architect of systematic colonisation and himself a committee member of the original Christchurch CC, lamented that only two players were present in Hagley Park at 6 a.m. on a fine summer morning. However, he was reassured that a professional bowler, John Stevens, would soon be engaged to assist the team. On 17 December, though, *The Press* declared that 'the attempt to meet the All England Eleven on the cricket ground will be a disgraceful burlesque unless our players will determine to do their best, and take the means to do it'. This was followed by strong criticism of existing fielding standards, and a call to select the team immediately and appoint a captain.[14]

The efforts being made in Christchurch prompted concern in Dunedin that not enough was being done to prepare local players, and the *Otago Witness* pleaded for cricketers to follow the Canterbury example: 'Constant handling of bat and ball, vigorous exertion in active fielding, and utter abandonment of petty jealousies, are the requisites essential to achieve the much coveted success'. In response, 3,000 spectators attended a trial match between the Dunedin CC and Jones' XI on Boxing Day 1863.[15]

While the *Witness* alluded to 'coveted success', others took a much more pragmatic view. Realising that Canterbury had no hope of defeating the visitors, *The Press* suggested that far more value would be derived from their performance if judged in relative colonial terms:

> Of course the eleven will easily beat any twenty-two we can bring against them, but we shall not be playing against the eleven but against all the Australian colonies. The thing we should aim at is that the twenty-two of Canterbury should leave on record a score which shall show favourably against, if it cannot overtop, the score of any other twenty-two in the colonies.[16]

Certainly, there is ample evidence of English tours engendering strong rivalries between New South Wales and Victoria,[17] but a perusal of Australian sources reveals no similar concern with cricket as an indicator of New Zealand's place within the colonial hierarchy. This lopsided trans-Tasman cricketing relationship would become apparent from the late 1870s.

On New Year's Day 1864 *The Press* published a lengthy mock report of a match between England and Canterbury. Among other things, Canterbury were dismissed in 25 balls for one run – a leg bye 'awarded' from a ball which rebounded after breaking a batsman's leg. Batsmen were applauded for hitting the ball – even if caught, and two who survived four balls each were greeted with 'uproarious cheering'. Three batsmen were too scared to bat, four others left the ground completely and one went to the wicket wearing every pad possessed by the Canterbury Cricket Club. In response, England scored 300 for no wicket by lunch – including 114 runs from lost balls hit out of the ground. However, the match ended in a draw due to bad weather, and Canterbury thus became the first team in Australasia to draw with the tourists![18] To a slight degree this account was prophetic, in that the Canterbury XXII (all of whom batted) scored only thirty and 105, to lose by an innings and two runs.

Dunedinites approached their apparently inevitable defeat in slightly more measured tones. Referring to some of the particular 'stars' of the All England XI, the *Otago Daily Times* predicted a difficult time for the local team:

> You yourselves cannot expect, and of course nobody else nourishes the idea, that you have any chance of making much of a scene at the wicket against the terrific bowling of Tarrant and the teasing 'slows' of Tinley; nor can you hope that your own balls will be very hard to be kept off the stumps by a Hayward or a Carpenter.[19]

The address of welcome presented to George Parr on behalf of the 'Cricketers in Otago' was equally timid:

> As humble imitators at these distant antipodes of your famous deeds in
> England, we gladly hail the opportunity of witnessing the excellence to
> which your prowess has brought the manliest of English pastimes ...
> To look for anything like success in the forthcoming struggle, when
> pitted against the Champions of the world, would be presumptuous on
> our part, but you will be glad to learn that no exertion has been wanting
> to select the best twenty-two our province can boast of to take the field
> against you.

Taking a more constructive line, E.T. Gillon of the Tokomairiro CC stressed
that the visit would do much to stimulate interest in, and improve the standard of, Otago cricket.[20]

Behind the notion of tutelage was an unequivocal idealisation of all
things English and imperial. While a small group of cricketers and cricketing enthusiasts were destined to learn something practical from their
encounters on the field, in a far broader sense the tour was held to represent
a much wider bond of Empire and English characteristics. R.J.S. Harman, a
prominent Canterbury settler and sporting administrator, informed one of
Christchurch's numerous public meetings on arrangements for the tour that
it would be most important for local youth, 'as he most thoroughly believed
that cricket and other athletic games did much to keep up English "pluck",
and our character for hardiness and endurance'.[21] Two days later *The Press*
was moved to reprint a lengthy editorial from the *Otago Daily Times* in
which it was suggested that cricket could do more to highlight New
Zealand's place within the Empire and attract more British settlers than any
of the recent gold discoveries in Otago:

> Paltry as some may deem a mere game of bat and ball, and waste of
> time as others may declare it, it is none the less an absolute certainty
> that the press of London and the different counties has more encour-
> aging articles on this proof of colonial enterprise, than on the fact of
> our gold discoveries, for it shows us to be British still in both com-
> mercial daring and love of national pastime. Printed narratives of finds
> of monster nuggets are but casually glanced at by many thousands
> whose desires ... are irresistibly attracted to this hemisphere by the
> leading articles and paragraphs which tell them of English cricketers
> handling the leather and willow on Australian turf.[22]

In its own account, *The Press* also implied that it was cricket above all else
that would draw people along the ever-improving transport networks
between Britain and her colonies:

> The mere mention of the scheme affords an undeniable proof of the
> advancement of the colony, and also of the gradual lessening of the dis-
> tance which separates us from the Mother Country ... Such symptoms

of the growth of the colony are not to be mistaken, and auger [sic] well for the approaching establishment of the Panama route and the great increase to the prosperity of the settlement which will infallibly result there from.[23]

Yet there is a sense in which New Zealand waters posed a greater difficulty for imperial cricket than Panama or any other route. While the All England XI only played in Dunedin and Christchurch, it is nevertheless surprising that their activities attracted only minimal attention from the press in Auckland, Wellington and Nelson. Not a single editor saw fit to comment on the wider significance of the tour, or even to reprint editorial extracts from South Island sources. Most provided only match reports. One must therefore question the pervasiveness of the imperial sporting ideology. Was it really seen to be of significance to the whole colony, or only to those parts that were lucky enough to benefit directly from it?

Given the build-up to the tour, it is no surprise that the arrival of the All England XI in both Dunedin and Christchurch prompted considerable pageantry and conspicuous colonial display. In both towns, merchants, banks and government departments decided to emulate the Australian response by giving their workers at least a half-holiday on the days of the match. John Hardy, MPC for Tokomairiro, went so far as to provide his farm employees with horses so that they might travel to Dunedin for the game.[24]

To mark the arrival of the English team, the buildings of Port Chalmers, Otago, were decorated with flags, foliage and banners, as were many ships in the harbour. A marquee was also erected with capacity for 200 at a planned luncheon for the visitors. Unfortunately, the delayed arrival of the steamer from Melbourne until after midnight on a Saturday, and the prohibition against public welcomes on the Sabbath, meant that by the time Parr and his team were formally received on Monday strong winds and dust had destroyed the marquee and considerably reduced the gaiety of Port Chalmers. During the same weekend a large fire destroyed much of the commercial centre of Dunedin and the winds removed the roof of the newly erected grandstand.[25]

In light of these events, the reception for the team was all the more remarkable. After the firing of salutes, they were escorted from Port Chalmers to Dunedin in a seven-carriage entourage that included numerous public officials and the provincial brass band. In Dunedin the team were greeted by another large procession and attended a further reception at which George Parr was presented with an engraved address of welcome.[26]

At both Port Chalmers and Dunedin Parr responded to his hosts with familiar imperial enthusiasm:

> We have come a long way to meet you, not in untoward strife, I trust, but in true friendship. We are all brothers. We are all of the same old stock; and I believe that we are all brothers in loyalty, in language, in

religion, and in our love of the fine old English game ... Time and cricket bring distant parts of the world together; and now our colonies seem to be like only so many counties one to the other ...[27]

Other members of the team felt that the Dunedin reception was better than any received on previous tours to Australia, Canada or the United States. Indeed, William Caffyn had a clear memory of events 35 years later: 'We had a tremendous reception when we arrived. The people seemed to have fairly gone mad with excitement.'[28]

As with Dunedin, the reception for the team in Christchurch did not go at all according to plan. A delay in the arrival of the steamer from Port Chalmers meant that many of the large crowd assembled in Christchurch soon dispersed. Those who remained occupied their time by drinking most of the banquet champagne amid mock toasts and related festivities. Nevertheless, the eventual arrival of the English team was marked by a large procession and reception at the Christchurch Town Hall.[29]

Pessimistic predictions were ultimately justified. Otago were defeated by nine wickets, and by an innings in the return fixture, and Canterbury were also defeated by an innings. Only in the final match, a draw against a combined Canterbury and Otago XXII, were the tourists placed under any real pressure – conceding a first innings lead of 18 after being dismissed for 73. Much of the credit for this performance belonged to Thomas Wentworth Wills. The leading cricketer of Victoria, Wills travelled with the English team to New Zealand ostensibly to strengthen their opposition and thus prolong the matches in the interests of gate receipts. He secured 6 wickets for Canterbury and another 4 as captain of the combined team, as well as contributing 2 of only 15 double-figure scores from the 176 individual innings played against the touring team.[30]

In the end, the results of the tour do not matter. More important is the almost fanatical intensity of the reception that surrounded the All England XI. Here was proof for all to see that those who colonised New Zealand had successfully transplanted not only the formal, structural and political institutions of Britain, but also the informal institutions and social mores that underpinned them.

Lillywhite's and Shaw's All England XIs

It was a decade before another English team visited Australasia, in 1873–74, but negotiations failed to bring W.G. Grace's XI across the Tasman Sea to New Zealand. It was, therefore, January 1877 before a second touring team, James Lillywhite's All England XI, visited New Zealand. Importantly, they were the first to tour the whole colony – playing Auckland, Wellington, Taranaki, Nelson, Westland, Canterbury, Otago and Southland. Five of these encounters were won by an innings, Canterbury lost by only 24 runs, and the

Otago and Westland fixtures were drawn very much in favour of the visitors. Five years later, Alfred Shaw brought another English team to New Zealand after touring Australia. In addition to the four main centres, they played North Otago, South Canterbury and Waikato – winning five and drawing with Canterbury and Wellington when lack of time prevented almost inevitable innings victories.[31]

The various responses to Lillywhite's and Shaw's teams are instructive. On the one hand they placed the status of New Zealand cricket in sharp relief against that of Australia. For immediately after their victorious procession through New Zealand, Lillywhite's team crossed the Tasman to play, and lose, the first ever Test match. Within five years the Australians would fully confirm their transformation with victory against England on English soil. At the same time the tours provoked markedly different responses among the New Zealand provinces. Those provinces that were experiencing their first touring team exhibited the same traits of inferiority and deference as Canterbury, Otago and the Australian colonies had during the early 1860s. However, Canterbury, and to a lesser extent Otago, which were both experiencing their second tour, began to display an air of self belief and colonial assertiveness akin to that which was developing in Australia during the mid 1870s. Canterbury, with the benefit of a much stronger cricketing infrastructure than any other province, entertained some hopes of victory over Australian and English teams and came to embody the hopes of the colony as a whole. Yet Canterbury too was soon to fall well behind the rate of progress being made in Australian cricket, and the rest of New Zealand was to fall well behind the Canterbury standard.

As with Canterbury and Otago in 1864, Auckland and Wellington in 1877 were in no doubt about their responsibilities in hosting an All England XI. Despite unseasonably wet weather, Auckland preparations were well in hand at least a month before the tourists arrived. To assist efficient and regular practice, their team stayed together at the Ellerslie ground for several days prior to the match. In Wellington, special efforts were made to recruit the best players from outlying districts.[32]

Yet high public expectations also prompted strong criticism of the apparent disorganisation and apathy among players and the respective match committees. The Auckland team were reminded in no uncertain terms that they had an obligation to those who had provided the financial guarantee for the tour and that they were expected to perform in a manner that compared favourably with southern centres. In Wellington, the Basin Reserve trustees were lambasted for providing a sub-standard ground that would not reflect credit on the city.

In both cities the arrival of the All England team was marked by the obligatory large procession and brass band and by the firing of salutes. Prominent citizens and the Governor, the Marquis of Normanby, were conspicuous by their presence at the matches.[33] Beyond these self-conscious displays, expectations were not high. The *New Zealand Herald* declared that as the Auckland match would be an important learning experience for local cricketers, there was no disgrace in losing. In Wellington, the *New Zealand Times* hoped only that the local XXII would bat as well as Auckland. In this they failed miserably – scoring 31 and 38 compared with Auckland's 109 and 94. Referring to the Wellington performance as 'the slaughter of the innocents', the *Times* noted that there was much to learn from the Englishmen in a game that ought to be a 'study' rather than a 'farce'. The *Evening Post* added that the defeat would be the means of 'rousing our local players to more practice and energy'.[34]

At a luncheon for Lillywhite's team in Auckland, William Lee Rees, MHR and a cousin of the Grace family, employed familiar imperial rhetoric:

> He hoped that the visit of the cricketers to the Australasian colonies would help to strengthen the ties which bound England to her children in these far distant regions, where manly athletic games were practised with as much assiduity as on her own shores. The common love for these sports was one of the strongest links in the chain which connected the Mother Country with her offspring, a chain which, though light as silk, was strong as steel.[35]

Rees' juxtaposition of silk and steel is a valuable reminder that the sporting empire was implicit rather than explicit – a product of culture and ideology rather than of coercion and legislation.

Wellingtonians, for their part, revealed their clear understanding of the imperial connection when Alfred Shaw's England XI arrived in January 1882. Having prefaced its remarks with a comparison between English athleticism and French lethargy, the *New Zealand Times* expounded on the implications of cricket for the continuity of the Empire:

> A vast deal of good has been done by these cricketing visits to and from the Australian [sic] colonies. They have been the best advertisement of our prosperity and [the] energy these colonies could have had; they have shown, physically at least, there has been no deterioration in the British subjects of Her Majesty at this part of the world; and the friendly reception of the cricketers sent from either 'end of the earth' to the other has greatly strengthened the sentimental tie uniting England to her colonies and the colonies to England.[36]

The *Evening Post* reinforced this with a more assertive reminder of the power of cricket in actively promoting colonial interests to Britain:

> The fact that a dozen of the most renowned English players of England's great national game find it worthwhile to travel all the way to New Zealand and play matches in half-a-dozen different parts of the colony, tends to direct hither the attention of many classes who would otherwise no nothing of New Zealand but its name.[37]

The structural development of Auckland and Wellington cricket certainly lagged well behind that of the South Island during the 1860s and 70s, but there is nothing to suggest that their appreciation of the cultural and political significance of the game lost anything by comparison.

In many respects Otago approached the visit of Lillywhite's team in similar fashion to the North Island centres. While gold prosperity and an influx of talented Australians had considerably boosted its cricketing stocks during the mid 1860s – prompting its sponsorship of Parr's team and enabling five victories in seven years against Canterbury, Otago's decline was swift and dramatic. As clear evidence of this, it secured only one victory against Canterbury during the 1870s.

Otago's only real concession to its cricketing heritage was to field XVIII as opposed to XXII against the English teams of 1877 and 1882. Otherwise, it approached its task with a resigned air of inevitability. When, in December 1876, it was proposed to abandon the annual interprovincial fixture with Canterbury in order to concentrate on preparations for the tour match, H.F. Fish, later an MHR, argued that there was more to be gained from a competitive standard of cricket and long-standing obligations with Canterbury than a 'hollow' match against Lillywhite's team. When the tourists arrived in Dunedin, the Mayor made the customary announcement that although Otago would learn much, they stood no chance of victory. Indeed, many in Otago looked to Canterbury to redeem the performances of other provinces against Lillywhite's team, with the *Otago Daily Times* going so far as to declare that it would not be surprised if Canterbury achieved a victory.[38]

Such optimistic predictions are testimony to Canterbury's primacy within New Zealand cricket. The progress made by the province during the 1870s was in every way comparable with the transition occurring in Australia. After suffering a heavy defeat in 1864, a Canterbury XVIII lost to All England by only 24 runs in 1877, and a Canterbury XV defeated Australia by six wickets in 1878.

By the beginning of December 1876, 3 months before the arrival of Lillywhite's XI, Canterbury had selected a squad of 30 players with a view to initiating compulsory practices. Although wet weather severely restricted these plans, and internal bickering resulted in the resignation of some members of the match committee,[39] most observers were confident of a good Canterbury performance. On 23 February 1877 *The Star* outlined the significance of Canterbury's task as follows:

> Peculiar interest is attended to this match, for upon Canterbury the eyes of all cricketers in the colony are at the present moment turned. By common consent, our province is acknowledged to be unapproachable in the game at present, and it is the only one which has the remotest chance of coming off victorious. To it does every man in North and South look to uphold the honour of New Zealand, which has been so roughly treated upto the present time, and though it is hardly possible

that we shall prove the victors, yet the Englishmen themselves acknowledge that they have the hardest nut of all to crack when they reach Christchurch. So let our chosen ones keep a stout heart and a bold front; and let them go in with the determination to do their utmost, and then, if they are defeated, we may be sure the defeat will be an honourable one, and not a mere procession of crestfallen men, marching from the pavilion to the wickets, back again, and nothing more.[40]

While there was no victory to celebrate, the manner of Canterbury's narrow loss left much to praise. Whereas in 1864 the province had been too young and undeveloped for the match to be of any consequence, and most emphasis had been placed on the mere presence of an English team, *The Press* now suggested that better facilities and more numerous players gave Canterbury a standard quite comparable with that at 'home'. Moreover, 'It is proof, if any were needed, how this eminently national sport suits the genius of Englishmen in whatever part of the world they may locate themselves'.[41]

The Rise of Canterbury

The new confidence of Canterbury cricket proved well founded when the first Australian XI toured New Zealand during the following season. Canterbury originally proposed to meet the Australians on even terms. The visitors, conscious of prolonging the match in the interests of gate receipts, insisted on the usual XXII. A compromise was reached in which Canterbury fielded a XV, which then proceeded to dismiss Australia for 46 and 143. The Canterbury XV replied with 135 and 57 for 8 to achieve victory by 6 wickets.[42]

Reactions to this performance were more indifferent than ecstatic – as if victory by a New Zealand team was somehow beyond comprehension. *The Press* suggested that the Australians had taken Canterbury 'too cheap' as a response to their presumption in playing only 15 men. The *Evening Post* described the result as 'simply one of those phases of cricketing fortune by which the best teams are liable to be overcome'. Moreover, if the Wellington XXII was defeated by Australia after its defeat by Canterbury, such would reflect 'grave discredit' on Wellington cricket.[43]

Australian observers were ultimately no more encouraging. In its first report of the match, the *Australasian* suggested that the Canterbury victory 'shows us that cricket in that part of New Zealand at all events is not nearly so backward as we in Victoria are generally disposed to believe'. A week later, though, the same source attributed the result to bad pitch conditions, cold weather and the tiredness of the Australians after a long journey to Christchurch. Two further weeks later, the *Sydney Mail* appeared to concur with this less favourable view when referring to 'bad wickets, bad weather and bad umpiring'.[44]

Despite these muted responses, Canterbury lost no time in seeking to capitalise on its performance. In December 1878 a reasonably strong provincial team left for Australia to play against club sides in Hobart and Melbourne. Although most observers felt that the results of the tour would be somewhat secondary to the main purpose of establishing links with Victoria, *The Press* did raise some hope that a strong provincial team might pose a challenge to the Victorian XI.[45]

In Australia the team were commended for their enterprise in undertaking a venture that would hopefully be 'the prelude to many similar friendly encounters between the cricketers of Victoria and New Zealand'. 'A Bohemian', the cricket correspondent for the *Australasian*, felt that although one or two weak players reduced the reputation of the team as a whole, they generally had very little to learn from Australia in the art of playing cricket. At the end of the tour, *The Press* concluded that 'future cricketers of New Zealand will have every reason to be proud of the doings of the first team which left the shores of the colony to throw down the gauntlet to its more advanced neighbours'.[46]

Yet circumstances conspired against the Canterbury team. The competing attractions of the Australian XI, who were still playing matches after their return from England, and of Lord Harris's England XI, ensured that Canterbury remained very much on the periphery. They did not secure a match against Victoria, and the tour did very little to raise the profile of New Zealand cricket or the colony in general. Indeed, the lack of public interest contributed to severe financial difficulties. Funds had to be remitted from Christchurch to enable the team to return home, and, in a somewhat evasive reference to the outcome of the tour, the CCA passed a motion stating 'That this Association does not hold itself responsible for any criticism on matches or matters connected with cricket which appear in the local press, unless authorised by the Association'.[47] Furthermore, promises by Victoria and by several of its club sides to visit New Zealand during the 1879/80 season were not kept.

Canterbury's progress during the late 1870s was a microcosm of the process by which Australia had advanced from XXIIs to Test status. The response to W.L. Murdoch's 1881 Australian team highlights some significant parameters to the Canterbury and New Zealand outlook engendered by this progress. Unlike the 1878 Australian team that had come to New Zealand *before* their pioneering tour of England, Murdoch's 1881 team arrived fresh from an English tour in which they had eventually done much to build on the reputation of their predecessors. The difference between the two tours was not lost on the *Otago Daily Times*:

> As we expected, the present match excites more interest than that of 1878 when the public attended in but scant numbers. Yesterday, however, the attendance was capital … Many of them we believe were attracted by curiosity quite as much as by cricket – they wanted to see

the eleven colonials who have not only proved themselves 'the cricket monarchs of Pacific's main' … but very nearly of Atlantic's also.[48]

In short, an Australian team that had achieved successes on English soil was to be accorded a great deal more kudos than that of 1878 which had been something of an unknown quantity to the New Zealand public. While that team had beaten Lillywhite's XI in the first Test match, it had done so under Australian conditions and not at 'home'.

This attitude to the Australians is evident in Canterbury's preparations for the 1881 match. Some certainly felt that the victory of 1878 could be repeated by a team that had had more practice and contained equally talented players, but others argued that Canterbury should acknowledge the proven strength of its opposition and increase the size of its team from XV to XVIII or XXII.[49] What finally persuaded Canterbury to persevere with a XV was less a statement of faith in its ability as a sense that it had a moral duty to contest the match on the same terms as previously. As *The Star* put it:

> Having beaten the first Australians with fifteen, it would have shown a lamentable want of confidence – a most undeniable case of 'peake' – for the cricketers of Canterbury to have sent in eighteen. It remains for the Australians to prove that they can beat a fifteen of Canterbury before our boys surrender the position which they have achieved against them.[50]

Canterbury duly surrendered their position by an innings and 100 runs as the Australians scored 323, including a century from Murdoch. *The Star*, which had been one of the more confident pre-match advocates of Canterbury's prospects, now suggested that their heavy defeat may have been a good thing:

> There are those indeed who hold that a victory for Canterbury would have been a most unfortunate thing for cricket amongst us, and they do not hesitate to affirm that 'our boys' needed the sweet lessons of a rough adversity to teach them to be more constant in practice and more attentive to the niceties of the game.[51]

Clearly, then, from the highs of 1878 some Cantabrians had reverted to a deferential mindset akin to that of the 1860s.

When the next Australian XI arrived late in November 1886, there were generally gloomy predictions and no debate over the Canterbury decision to field XVIII. When the team managed a more than favourable draw, the *Lyttelton Times* remarked that 'If our cricketers have not quite conquered an Australian Eleven, they have quite conquered or reconquered their place in the public estimation here'.[52] Two more creditable draws against C.A. Smith's England XI during the following season ensured that Canterbury finished the decade in confident mood. Indeed, there were proposals for another tour of Victoria and Tasmania – this time involving Otago as well as Canterbury players. The plan only foundered when leading Canterbury players declared themselves unavailable for business reasons. A further proposal from the CCA to send a New Zealand team to New South Wales and Tasmania in 1893 also came to nothing.[53]

A Growing Malaise in the 1880s

In other New Zealand centres the stakes were not nearly as high as they were for Canterbury. Nonetheless, Australian tours were still occasions for a good deal of pageantry and display. Moreover, the vitriolic criticism frequently levelled at the best efforts of local players and officials – and more particularly at those members of the public who took little or no interest in cricket – reveals that the tours were regarded as neither peripheral nor merely sporting.

After Wellington's innings defeat to Australia in 1881, the *Evening Post* declared that 'the only "good all round" part of their batting as far as we could see was the imposing array of "round noughts" made'. The WCA was also condemned for the state of the Basin Reserve and for 'the spirit of exclusiveness and clubism' that hampered preparations for the match.[54] When Australia inflicted another heavy defeat on a Wellington XXII in 1886, it was announced that the public would soon tire of watching the humiliation of such an inept team. 'With a view to avoiding any future repetition of so melancholy a fiasco', the press called for the engagement of a professional coach to initiate the sort of improvements that had been made in Australian cricket during the 1860s.[55]

Dunedinites exhibited similar foreboding about their cricketers. When Tasmania arrived in February 1884, it was observed that while the standard of New Zealand cricket was not entirely beyond redemption, Otago would stand little chance of victory against the visitors, or any other touring team for that matter. 'Even at its best the climate of this colony is more favourable to the production of good wheat than good cricket, and we can never hope to send Home a team which will lower the colours of the MCC or meet with respectful consideration from All England'.[56] However, prior to Otago's match against the 1886 Australians, the press condemned the OCA for their decision to field a XXII: 'The match committee have chosen to play such a number against the Australian cricketers that the contest is robbed of all interest. If our men win, it is no honour; if they lose, it is a disgrace.' This approach was apparently symptomatic of a more general deterioration in the standard of Otago cricket: 'Our cricketers seem like the Bourbons – "they learn nothing and forget nothing", and to crown all, some indulge their effeminacy by playing such maudlin games as lawn tennis'.[57]

In Southland, both the public and local businesses were criticised for failing to contribute funds to guarantee the visit of the 1881 Australian team.

Their arrival, though, was attended by a great deal of excitement. A half-holiday was proclaimed and reduced rail fares were offered so that spectators from outlying districts could easily travel to Invercargill for the match. The significance of the tour to the fabric of the Empire was not lost on the *Southland Times*: 'In the old country they had done wonders; though representing only a mere handful of men, they had competed successfully against the representatives of the millions of Great Britain. They had done honour to the flag of Australia, and had made it respected all over the world.'[58] Unfortunately for Southland, though, they were visited by only 5 of the next 18 teams to tour New Zealand up to 1914.

Cricket and Australasian Federation

With the limited exception of Canterbury, the performances of New Zealand provinces against touring teams offered nothing to justify the sort of colonial assertiveness that characterised Australian cricketing relations with England from the late 1870s. To the contrary, some came to view cricket not as a means by which New Zealand might carve out its own distinct niche within the Empire, but as a bridge to federation with the Australian colonies.

Despite the prevailing myths of 'better stock', stronger Britishness and a sense of superiority over 'convict' Australia discussed in Chapter 1, the late nineteenth century was marked by a significant level of interaction between New Zealand and the Australian colonies. Many of those joining the New Zealand pastoral boom of the 1850s and the gold rushes of the 1860s came from Australia, and regular patterns of trans-Tasman labour migration continued thereafter – the numbers in each direction fluctuating according to the fortunes of the various colonial economies. Moreover, at an official level there was cooperation on such issues as mail services, shipping, cable communications and defence. All of these connections contributed to the shaping of a broad 'Australasian' identity and a tendency to group the 'seven colonies of Australasia' as a single entity within the British Empire.[59]

Ideas that New Zealand could formally federate with the Australian colonies were first aired during the early 1880s, mainly in the context of the consultative Federal Council, incorporating the Australian colonies, New Zealand and Fiji, which was established in 1886. Yet aside from a brief revival of interest during the Colonial Conferences of 1890 and 1891, and a belated flurry of activity in 1899 after the Australian colonies had committed themselves to Federation as the Commonwealth of Australia, there was little public or political support for the concept in New Zealand. Among the multiplicity of suggested reasons for New Zealand's failure to join are geographical distance and a reluctance to become enmeshed in a depressed Australian economy during the late 1890s. However, it is more likely – as mentioned in Chapter 1 – that an emerging sense of New Zealand national identity and a desire to preserve its distinct voice within the Empire played as great a part.[60]

Nevertheless, at a Christchurch reception for the 1881 Australian team, their captain, W.L. Murdoch, stressed that in playing for the honour of the Australian colonies, his team – drawn predominantly from New South Wales and Victoria – had always included New Zealand. There was already a South Australian in the team and therefore no reason why a New Zealander could not also accompany them to England 'so that it might be a thoroughly representative team of Australasia'.[61]

Other gestures followed in similar situations. At the end of 1895, for example, Wellington's *Evening Post*, the only New Zealand newspaper to sustain a campaign for colonial federation, suggested that visits by New South Wales athletes and cricketers were transcending the contradictions of existing attempts to federate at a political level:

> While politicians are in the same breath talking of drawing closer the bonds of unions between the colonies, and making hostile tariffs to drive them apart, there is a practical federation of the young generation in the field of athletics which will probably do much in moulding the future Federal opinions, and it is for this reason, as well as for the sake of the branches of sport concerned, that we especially welcome at this Christmas season the New South Wales Cricketers and the New South Wales Amateur Athletes.[62]

Ten years later, the *New Zealand Herald* took the visit of the 1905 Australians as an opportunity to remind its readers of an ultimate loyalty among the colonies and with Britain:

> The friendliness that is manifested, the common interests that are called forth, the very emulation that is excited between the branches of the same people keeps alive the feeling that we are one people and not strangers. This, more than many more seemingly important things, forms a real bond of union which may at least help to stand the strain which distance, and to some extent, perhaps, conflicting interests, may hereafter put upon the unity of the Empire.[63]

The reference to 'conflicting interests' suggests that the *Herald* was perhaps mindful of tensions between imperial and national aspirations. Australasian xenophobia, and particularly that directed towards Chinese, Japanese and Indians, manifested itself in a series of restrictive immigration measures that were very much at odds with the broader objectives of British strategic and diplomatic policy – especially a desire to align itself with Japan in order to keep Russia in check.[64]

As late as 1928 New Zealand prime minister Gordon Coates displayed his awareness of the importance of cricket to trans-Tasman relations. In an address to the departing Australian team, he said:

Visits such as these do an enormous amount of good. In fact they are essential in order that the representatives of either country can come into closer contact and understand the viewpoints of each other better. You know that in the political world today there is an effort to have some point round which representatives from all parts of the world can meet and discuss international problems … It would be difficult to draw comparisons, but, nevertheless, we can not underestimate the good visits of this kind bring with them.[65]

Ironically, this was the last Australian tour of New Zealand for 18 years.

Besides statements made at a largely gestural level, there were also some practical manifestations of this federal spirit. In 1896–97, after spectacular bowling success for Otago against Australia and Queensland, Arthur Fisher was invited to Melbourne for trials in the hope that he might play in the Test matches against A.E. Stoddart's England team. Notwithstanding his failure to impress in drier conditions, Fisher later claimed that he was not given a trial on the terms originally promised. Ultimately, the intercolonial jealousies so prevalent in Australian cricket prevented him from playing for Victoria or in any matches against the touring team – a snub that prompted a strong rebuke from the Dunedin press:

The matter is not a trivial one. Cricket has had no small share in bringing about the improved relationship between the colonies and the Mother Country, so that the interests of the game have come to possess an almost imperial importance. It is natural that New Zealand should desire this colony, if possible, to have a share in the international cricket tournament, and there were good grounds for thinking that Mr Fisher had shown himself worthy of, at all events, a thorough trial … Not to put too fine a point on it, he has been badly treated.[66]

A year later, when Fisher returned to Australia with the New Zealand team, he secured only one wicket for 179 runs. On a more promising note, Daniel Reese's sound batting for New Zealand against Victoria raised suggestions that he might play for 'The Rest' in a trial match against the 1899 Australians, but he failed to score in his next innings against New South Wales. Despite these false starts, as late as 1910 it was still being suggested that the development of New Zealand cricket might lead to players being selected for Australia.[67]

There is perhaps a misleading temptation to view these loose arrangements as a form of sub-imperialism whereby New Zealand was incorporated into the orbit of another colony. More likely, though, is that they were a simple matter of expediency. New Zealand did not hold Test status, and would not until 1930. If its individual players wished to play Test cricket, they were obliged to do so for England, Australia or South Africa. The relaxed attitude to international qualification rules that allowed

K.S. Ranjitsinhji to represent England during the 1890s, and several other players to represent two countries, provided a sound precedent for the Australian approach to New Zealand players. At the same time there were numerous precedents in other sports: an Australasian tennis team competed in, and dominated, the Davis Cup between 1907 and 1920; New Zealand and Australia also appeared under the Australasian umbrella at the Olympic Games in 1908 and 1912; and there were various other manifestations of Australasia in athletics and rugby league.[68]

Pragmatism and Idealism

Just as analysis in Chapter 4 highlighted the manner in which various moral metaphors were circumscribed by issues of race, gender, class and the simple diffusion of the sources that articulated them, the rhetoric that surrounded touring teams is open to exactly the same scrutiny. Moreover, there is an obvious contradiction between the objectives of the touring teams and the ideals ascribed to them by their hosts. Put bluntly, the aims of the English teams and most of the Australian teams were financial rather than imperial. George Parr, James Lillywhite and Alfred Shaw were all professional cricketers for whom the viability of an Australasian tour had to be assessed in monetary terms before any other. Players on the first tours to Australia in 1861–2 and 1863–4 received £250 and £475 respectively – although the 'money-grabbing' exploits of Parr's team acted to discourage Australian backing for a further tour until 1873. In 1876–77 Lillywhite was able to pay his players double their original guarantee, and two years later Lord Harris's party pocketed £500 each. On their first Australian venture as joint promoters in 1881–82, Lillywhite, Shaw and Arthur Shrewsbury recouped no less than £750 each followed by a substantially reduced, but still healthy, £150 in 1883–84.[69]

So determined did English cricketers become in their desire to capitalise on the Australian market that there was a team in the colonies for some part of every year from 1881 to 1888. This determination, though, did not always yield satisfactory results. A combination of intercolonial business rivalries and declining public interest after five tours in five years saw Lillywhite, Shaw and Shrewsbury lose £250 each on their third Australian venture in 1886–87 and as much as £1,200 when they and G.F. Vernon's touring team attempted to compete for the same Australian fixtures and spectatorship in 1887–88. 'The least that can be said of the blunder', recalled Alfred Shaw, 'is that it was such stupendous folly a similar mistake is never likely to occur again'.[70] Indeed, this marked the end of fully professional cricket tours to Australasia.

There can be no doubt that whatever higher moral ground New Zealand observers chose to take over the presence of a touring team, the tourists themselves were working to a more self-serving agenda. A report of the arrival of the 1878 Australians provided a damning contrast with the visit of Lillywhite's team during the previous year: 'They are very agreeable and gentlemanly in their manners – a point which was all the more noticeable in that the Englishmen were just the reverse'.[71] The English team encountered their greatest problems when wicket-keeper Edward Pooley was arrested after a brawl prompted by a betting scandal in Christchurch. Pooley had wagered with locals that he could predict the individual score of each member of the Canterbury XVIII. The odds were such that his prediction that each batsman would score zero was guaranteed to return a healthy profit, but Pooley's attempts to claim his winnings produced complaints that the bet was unfair. The resulting confrontation saw Pooley and the team's baggage man charged with assault and damage to property. When, after six weeks, the case was thrown out through lack of evidence, the public of Christchurch took sympathy and presented Pooley with £50 and a gold watch. Yet his detention in New Zealand had greater consequences, in that he was not able to play in the first ever Test match. He never played Test cricket and, as with a number of his professional contemporaries, fell on hard times and died in poverty in 1907.[72]

Murdoch's Australian team, while in Nelson in 1881, also encountered criticism:

> Individual members of the team might improve on acquaintance, and it may be that one or two are not in reality so boorish as they appeared. It is, however, generally supposed that travel gives polish; but if it has done so with several of the Australian team, we can only deplore their original roughness. We were led to consider the players as gentlemen when they went home, but now – they have become professionals in the money-making sense, but in another we have met better professionals.[73]

Perhaps the key to this impression of the team rests in the final remark concerning professionalism. In the quest for riches, the privately organised Australian teams of the 1880s were little different to their English counterparts.

New Zealand's inability to reconcile the pragmatic and idealistic objectives of touring teams undoubtedly contributed to its comparative cricketing isolation during the late nineteenth century. The refusal of Shaw, Shrewsbury and Lillywhite to bring English teams to New Zealand after 1882 stemmed entirely from their inability to negotiate terms with cricket authorities in New Zealand. Nonetheless, there were still enough tours around with which to fashion a coherent ideology – one that stressed the power of cricket to unite the Empire along common cultural lines, in terms of both the relationship with the mother country and that between colonies.

From this point onwards, New Zealand cricket showed a marked divergence from the pattern that characterised Anglo-Australian cricketing relations. Instead of building on the degree of colonial assertiveness evident in Canterbury's performances during the 1880s, New Zealand cricket fell victim during the 1890s to a pronounced inferiority complex and to internal politicking and posturing of a sort that ultimately precluded any role for cricket in the shaping of a distinct New Zealand identity.

Notes

1. See, for example: R. Cashman, *Patrons, Players and the Crowd: The Phenomenon of Indian Cricket* (New Delhi, 1980); Mangan, *Games Ethic and Imperialism*; J.A. Mangan (ed.), *The Cultural Bond: Sport, Empire, Society* (London, 1992); H.McD. Beckles and B. Stoddart (eds), *Liberation Cricket: West Indies Cricket Culture* (Manchester, 1995); A. Guttmann, *Games and Empires: Modern Sports and Cultural Imperialism* (New York, 1994).
2. Mandle, 'W.G. Grace', p. 355.
3. K.S. Inglis, 'Imperial Cricket: Test Matches Between England and Australia 1877–1900' in R. Cashman and M. McKernan (eds), *Sport in History: The Making of Modern Sporting History* (St Lucia, 1979), pp. 166–7.
4. Quoted in W.F. Mandle, *Going it Alone: Australia's National Identity in the Twentieth Century* (Ringwood, Vic., 1978), p. 27.
5. Quoted in ibid.
6. Ibid.
7. See R. Cashman, 'Symbols of Unity: Anglo-Australian Cricketers, 1877–1900', *International Journal of the History of Sport*, 7, 1 (1990).
8. See W.F. Mandle, 'Cricket and Australian Nationalism in the Nineteenth Century', *Journal of the Royal Australian Historical Society*, 59, Pt.4 (1973).
9. Cashman, 'Symbols of Unity', pp. 97, 109.
10. Quoted in Inglis, 'Imperial Cricket', p. 169.
11. *Otago Witness*, 3 Oct. 1863, p. 5; 24 Oct. 1863, p. 5; 6 Feb. 1864, p2; *The Press*, 27 Oct. 1863, p. 2; 10 Nov. 1863, p. 3; 28 Nov. 1863, p. 5; 16 Jan. 1864, p. 4.
12. *The Press*, 17 Dec. 1863, p. 2.
13. Ibid., 23 Dec. 1863, p. 2.
14. Ibid., 11 Nov. 1863, p. 2; 20 Nov. 1863, p. 3; 21 Nov. 1863, p. 2; 17 Dec. 1863, p. 2.
15. *Otago Witness*, 12 Dec. 1863, p. 5; 1 Jan. 1864, p. 3.
16. *The Press*, 17 Dec. 1863, p. 2.
17. See Montefiore, *Cricket in the Doldrums*.
18. *The Press*, 1 Jan. 1864, p. 2.
19. Quoted in ibid., 5 Feb. 1864, p. 3.
20. *Otago Witness*, 6 Feb. 1864, p. 7.
21. *The Press*, 10 Nov. 1863, p. 3.
22. Quoted in ibid., 12 Nov. 1863, p. 3.
23. *The Press*, 27 Oct. 1863, p. 2.
24. *Otago Witness*, 30 Jan. 1864, pp. 4–5.
25. Ibid., 6 Feb. 1864, p. 7.
26. Ibid.
27. Ibid.
28. *Daily Telegraph*, 2 Feb. 1864, p. 2; W. Caffyn, *Seventy One Not Out* (London, 1899), p. 207.
29. *The Press*, 8 Feb. 1864, p. 2.
30. Reese, *New Zealand Cricket 1841–1914*, pp. 183–7. The 176 innings included no less than 56 ducks.
31. Ibid., pp. 183–7, 218–22.
32. *New Zealand Herald*, 29 Dec. 1876, p. 3; 16 Jan. 1877, p. 3; *Evening Post*, 13 Feb. 1877, p. 2.
33. *New Zealand Herald*, 22 Jan. 1877, p. 2; 29 Jan. 1877, p. 2; 31 Jan. 1877, p. 2; *Evening Post*, 3 Feb. 1877, p. 2; 5 Feb. 1877, p. 2; 24 Feb. 1877, p. 2.
34. *New Zealand Herald*, 1 Feb. 1877, p. 3; *New Zealand Times*, 3 Feb. 1877, p. 3; 10 Feb. 1877, p. 3; *Evening Post*, 10 Feb. 1877, p. 2.
35. *New Zealand Herald*, 1 Feb. 1877, p. 2.

36. *New Zealand Times*, 25 Jan. 1882, p. 2.
37. *Evening Post*, 27 Jan. 1882, p. 2.
38. *Otago Daily Times*, 8 Dec. 1876, p. 3; 26 Feb. 1877, p. 3; 3 March 1877, p. 3.
39. *The Press*, 7 Dec. 1876, p. 2; 19 Feb. 1877, p. 3.
40. *The Star*, 23 Feb. 1877, p. 2. See also: 22 Feb. 1877, p2; *Lyttelton Times*, 6 March 1877, p. 6.
41. *The Press*, 1 March 1877, p. 2.
42. Neely et al., *Men in White*, p. 29; *The Press*, 19 Jan. 1878, p. 3.
43. *The Press*, 19 Jan. 1878, p. 2; *Evening Post*, 25 Jan. 1878, p. 2.
44. *Australasian*, 26 Jan. 1878, p. 108; 2 Feb. 1878, pp. 139–40; *Sydney Mail*, 16 Feb. 1878, p. 212.
45. *The Press*, 14 Sept. 1878, p. 2; 8 Feb. 1879, p. 3.
46. *The Australasian*, 11 Jan. 1879, p. 43; 25 Jan. 1879, p. 108; *The Press*, 8 Feb. 1879, p. 3.
47. Neely et al., *Men in White*, p. 30; CCA, AGM Minutes, 22 May 1879.
48. *Otago Daily Times*, 21 Jan. 1881, p. 3.
49. *The Press*, 24 Jan. 1881, pp. 3, 5; 26 Jan. 1881, p. 3; *Lyttelton Times*, 29 Jan. 1881, p. 4.
50. *The Star*, 28 Jan. 1881, p. 2.
51. Ibid., 2 Feb. 1881, p. 2.
52. *Lyttelton Times*, 2 Dec. 1886, p. 4.
53. *New Zealand Referee*, 24 Aug. 1888, p. 164; 14 Sept. 1888, p. 199; 2 Nov. 1888, p. 282; OCA, AGM Minutes, 28 Sept. 1893.
54. *Evening Post*, 9 Feb. 1881, p. 2; *New Zealand Times*, 9 Feb. 1881, p. 3.
55. *Evening Post*, 3 Dec. 1886, p. 2; *New Zealand Times*, 4 Dec. 1886, p. 2.
56. *Otago Daily Times*, 2 Feb. 1884, p. 4.
57. *Otago Witness*, 3 Dec. 1886, p. 26.
58. *Southland Times*, 7 Jan. 1881, p. 2; 10 Jan. 1881, p. 2; 15 Jan. 1881, p. 2; 19 Jan. 1881, p. 2.
59. See: R. Arnold, 'Some Australasian Aspects of New Zealand Life 1890–1913', *New Zealand Journal of History*, 4, 1 (1970); K. Sinclair (ed.), *Tasman Relations: New Zealand and Australia, 1788–1988* (Auckland, 1987).
60. K. Sinclair, 'Why New Zealanders are not Australians: New Zealand and the Australian Federal Movement, 1881–1901' in Sinclair, *Tasman Relations*, pp. 90–103; Belich, *Paradise Reforged*, pp. 49–52.
61. Quoted in *The Press*, 31 Jan. 1881, p. 3. The South Australian team-member is significant in this context because he came from outside the prevailing New South Wales/Victoria power base of Australian cricket.
62. *Evening Post*, 27 Dec. 1895, p. 2.
63. *New Zealand Herald*, 11 Feb. 1905, p. 6.
64. See, for example, L. Trainor, *British Imperialism and Australian Nationalism* (Melbourne, 1994), pp. 81–94, 159–62. Unsurprisingly, the Anglo-Japanese alliance of 1902 was not popular in Australasia.
65. *The Press*, 11 April 1928, p. 12.
66. A.H. Fisher, 'Cricketing Papers 1895–1970', 'Clippings Book No.1', Hocken Archives, Dunedin.
67. *Daily Telegraph*, 24 Feb. 1899, New South Wales Cricket Association (NSWCA), 'Cricket Book 1895/6–1912/13' (press cuttings), NSWCA Library, Sydney; *The Australasian*, 30 April 1910, p. 1088.
68. For a detailed discussion of the various sporting manifestations of 'Australasia' see R. Cashman (ed.), *Sport, Federation, Nation* (Sydney, 2001).
69. W.F. Mandle, 'The Professional Cricketer in England in the Nineteenth Century', *Labour History*, No. 23 (1972), p. 9; Pullin, *Alfred Shaw*, p. 116.
70. P. Wynne-Thomas, *Give me Arthur: A Biography of Arthur Shrewsbury* (London, 1985), pp. 63–68, 77–91; Pullin, *Alfred Shaw*, p. 101.
71. Quoted in *Sydney Mail*, 26 Jan. 1878, p. 117.
72. G. Cotter, *England versus New Zealand: A History of the Test and Other Matches* (Marlborough, Wilts., 1990), p. 19; Green, *The Wisden Book of Obituaries*, pp. 714–16.
73. *The Colonist*, 12 Feb. 1881, p. 3.

9

A Near but Distant Neighbour:
New Zealand and Australia,
1890–1914

It is easy to point to broad historical similarities between New Zealand and Australia. Yet from the 1890s relations were marked by an equally significant degree of divergence, which – along with fundamental differences – defeated hopes for colonial federation present in the last quarter of the nineteenth century. As elements within Australian society sought to draw away from Britain and forge a more distinct local identity, New Zealand, relatively speaking, remained circumscribed within a more conventional imperial role in which continued cultural and political links to Britain were paramount. Furthermore, the establishment of the Commonwealth of Australia in 1901, and New Zealand's refusal to join, increasingly acted to accentuate differences and erode notions of 'Australasia'. As the twentieth century progressed the two countries assumed a rather detached official relationship with only spasmodic cooperation on such issues as defence and trade.[1]

At the same time, the gap between cricketing standards in Australia and New Zealand increased. As Chapter 7 explained, New Zealand's failure to maintain cricketing parity is, in part, due to factors such as climate and economics, which were largely beyond the control of the NZCC. Yet there was also a propensity to sabotage even the limited resources that did exist. Rather than unity in a common purpose, the selection of New Zealand teams to oppose Australia provides a catalogue of provincial antagonism and vitriolic rivalry. On numerous occasions the best interests of New Zealand cricket and the NZCC were subsumed by the need to placate the provincial cricket associations.

The attitude of Australian cricket authorities is also crucial. As Anglo-Australian Test tours assumed much greater imperial/national proportions during the 1890s, the entire *raison d'être* for Australian cricket came to revolve around much higher financial, personal and political stakes than had earlier been the case. Against this background, New Zealand objectives were increasingly peripheral. As a result, they had much to gain from Australia, but little to offer.

Tours and Controversies, 1890–1910

In many respects, the 1890s was the most successful decade for New Zealand cricket. There were more touring teams than at any other time, the first New Zealand representative team was assembled in 1894 and the first New Zealand touring team visited Australia in 1899. Between 1894 and 1897 New Zealand provincial and national teams secured five of their ten first-class victories against touring teams prior to 1914. Underpinning these achievements was the emergence of the NZCC as a central administrative body. Yet improvements to the internal fabric of New Zealand cricket ultimately had little bearing on the wider public perception of the game. The reality for New Zealand was that the few victories were against weak or unrepresentative opposition. When the full strength of Australian cricket was encountered, especially in 1905 and 1914, it was clear that notions of progress were illusory.

New Zealand responses to Australian cricket were quite out of proportion with what was actually at stake. There was hardly an Australian tour of New Zealand between 1890 and 1914 that did not produce some degree of acrimonious local melodrama. Yet most of the touring teams either lacked representative strength or lacked unequivocal sanction from Australian cricket authorities. As New Zealanders approached their objectives and responsibilities with all the intensity normally reserved for an Anglo-Australian Test match, the Australians increasingly viewed New Zealand cricket as peripheral. On more than one occasion it was accorded a priority below that of local grade cricket.

The Australian teams of 1878, 1881 and 1886 were fully representative sides that were either proceeding to or returning from England. Yet, of the nine England-bound teams between 1888 and 1914, only those of 1896 and 1905 visited New Zealand. A strong Australian 2nd XI toured in 1910, and Arthur Sims' private team of 1914 was near enough to full representative strength – but not designated as an official Australian team. The remaining visits to New Zealand were by colonial or club sides: three by New South Wales, two by the Melbourne Cricket Club and one each by Queensland and the South Melbourne CC.

None of the three New South Wales teams during the 1890s can be regarded as in any way representative of that colony. The teams of 1890 and 1894, selected and managed by J.C. Davis – later the cricket correspondent for the Sydney *Referee*, failed to gain the sanction of the New South Wales Cricket Association (NSWCA). Indeed, the Association refused to play against the 1890 tourists prior to their departure for New Zealand as they had not been selected by the NSWCA.[2] Although official sanction was given to a team in 1895–96, the Association handled proceedings with a certain indifference to New Zealand interests. Without consulting the NZCC, they reduced the tour from six to four weeks to avoid a clash with the final rounds of Sydney grade cricket. Moreover, the team was very much a 2nd XI: 7 of the 12 players had no other first-class cricket outside the New Zealand tour. Additionally, in both 1894 and 1895–96 the Australian press were more inclined to refer to the tourists as 'Sydney' teams, implying that they were not fully representative of New South Wales as a whole.[3]

The controversy that surrounded the visit of the Australian team at the end of 1896 reinforces the feeling that New Zealand would only be accommodated if Australian domestic arrangements were not compromised. In August 1896 both New South Wales and Victoria informed the Australian team, which was then in England, that the players had a duty to appear in Sheffield Shield matches rather than undertake a proposed tour to New Zealand. This position was reinforced by the Australasian Cricket Council, which also criticised its New Zealand counterpart for negotiating directly with the management of the team rather than with authorities in Australia. Nevertheless, 'L.G.', the cricket correspondent for the *Australasian*, declared that the Council had no real basis for objecting to the tour and were only concerned that early season intercolonial matches would lose gate money if the leading players were still in New Zealand. Ultimately, the Council reneged when the team manager informed them that the players had unanimously decided to tour New Zealand.[4] However, Australian authorities would not compromise any part of their own lucrative programme to allow touring English teams to embark on short tours of New Zealand, and efforts by the NZCC to secure visits in 1892, 1895, 1898 and 1901 were therefore rejected.[5]

FIGURE 17

New South Wales vs. New Zealand, Lancaster Park, Christchurch, 1895. New Zealand achieved its first victory over a touring team by defeating New South Wales by 142 runs. L.A. Cuff and J.C. Lawton are batting. (J.J. Kinsey photo, Canterbury Museum: Ref. 8912)

The other colonial team to visit New Zealand during this period, Queensland in 1897, was not yet in the top flight of Australian cricket. Although granted first-class status in 1893, Queensland was not admitted to the Australian Sheffield Shield competition until 1926–27.[6] In short, there was very little contact between New Zealand and the highest echelon of Australian cricket and very little to suggest that Australian administrators gave a particularly high priority to the New Zealand game.

Despite this lack of mutual enthusiasm, the NZCC determinedly set about arranging tours and creating opportunities for its representative team. Plans for fully representative New Zealand teams dated back to 1875 when it was proposed to play a match between New Zealand and Australia at Auckland. The Wellington Cricket Association raised the idea again in connection with the 1886 Australian tour and with C.A. Smith's English team a year later. A further New Zealand team was proposed in connection with attempts to secure a visit from the Australian team after their tour of England in 1893.[7] When these latter plans fell through, the Canterbury Cricket Association – in consultation with delegates from Auckland and Otago – agreed to take full responsibility for arranging a match between New Zealand and J.C. Davis's 1894 New South Wales team, including sole responsibility for selecting the New Zealand team and carrying all financial risks involved with the venture.[8]

Far from prompting other provinces to rally around Canterbury, the initiative of the CCA drew immediate criticism. Three weeks before the New Zealand team was selected, Wellington's *Evening Post* complained that the South Island was 'running the whole show' and suggested that the Canterbury selector, A.M. Ollivier, was likely to select a predominantly southern team. The Wellington Cricket Association also criticised Ollivier for taking advice from persons other than the Wellington selection committee. In retort, the Christchurch-based *New Zealand Referee* defended the right of Ollivier to use his own methods as a selector and remarked that 'it would not be characteristic of Wellington, however, if they did not raise some objection'.[9]

When the New Zealand team was announced it contained five Canterbury players, with two each from Auckland, Wellington and Otago. The *Otago Witness* felt that this was a generally reasonable selection in view of the batting strength of Canterbury during the current season. Yet the Otago Cricket Association took an altogether different view – passing a motion criticising Ollivier's treatment of Otago players and his selection of the New Zealand team before the Otago fixture against New South Wales: 'As it is Mr Ollivier has offered a direct insult to Otago cricketers by implying that there are only two of their number whose claims for selection in a team representative of the colony are worthy of consideration'. The situation was made worse when one of the Otago players, Alec Downes, was unable to gain work leave for the match. The only Otago player who took the field was J.C. Lawton – the OCA's English professional coach. In place of Downes, a sixth Canterbury player was included in the New Zealand team and, consequently, Ollivier was further condemned for not attempting to secure the replacement player from Otago.[10]

Although it was never explicitly stated, reactions to the 1894 team – and to many later selections – point to the feeling in some quarters that a provincial quota had to be observed. In this, as in so much of the antagonism that surfaced among the provincial cricket associations, it seems that those who provided the financial guarantees that enabled tours to take place felt entitled to an equal share of representation in New Zealand teams. Certainly, the superiority of Canterbury – especially during the early 1890s – allowed it a greater share of players. Yet many of the comments from Auckland, Otago and Wellington indicate a feeling that national representation was a right rather than an honour. This being the case, the role of a New Zealand team as a focal point for the best cricket in the colony becomes somewhat problematic.

While some took the conventional attitude that the strongest possible team should be selected to carry the honour of the colony, others apparently felt that a team should not only represent New Zealand but be representative *of* New Zealand. This inclusive stance rested more on narrow-minded provincialism than an altruistic desire to encapsulate the whole fabric of New Zealand cricket within a representative team. Encouraging the idea of a quota was a way of ensuring that a province had at least *some* players in a New Zealand team. Almost without exception, the selection controversies were of a sort where Wellington critics demanded the inclusion of more Wellington players, or Otago critics did the same for their own favourites. Thus, it was not likely that a Wellingtonian would argue the claims of an Auckland or Canterbury player ignored by the selectors. No doubt each province would have provided more than its share of players if the opportunity arose.

In March 1910, when objections inevitably surfaced over the selection of the New Zealand team for the second 'Test' against Australia, the *Lyttelton Times* stressed that New Zealand needed to select teams without an eye to provincial quotas:

> Half the value of cricket depends upon the spirit in which it is played, and petty jealousies and local prejudices are always to be deprecated. The impending match is a New Zealand match, and Canterbury will be delighted by the successes of the representatives of other provinces, even if her own men should fail.[11]

Indeed, the Canterbury press was generally far less inclined to immerse itself in selection controversies than many of its counterparts. Yet this was not because Canterbury dominated New Zealand teams to anything like the extent that some critics implied. Of the 77 players who represented New Zealand up to 1914, 25 were selected from Canterbury, 20 from Auckland,

18 from Wellington, 11 from Otago and 1 each from Hawke's Bay, Poverty Bay, Southland, Taranaki and Wanganui.[12] It can hardly be said, then, that the Canterbury contribution was excessive, and neither was Wellington – always the strongest critic of New Zealand teams and the NZCC – substantially under-represented.

The problem, however, was that cold facts could not, in themselves, cut through the layers of entrenched provincialism that choked the notion of a single identity for New Zealand cricket. Even Canterbury contained elements that preferred to put provincial ahead of national interests. In November 1896 there were strong objections, for example, when the CCA decided to forgo a match against the visiting Australians in order to stage a New Zealand fixture in Christchurch. In a letter to *The Press*, W.H.K. Wanklyn, a Canterbury delegate to the NZCC, condemned the decision as an injustice to the young cricketers of Canterbury, as it was important for New Zealand cricket that as many players as possible learn from opposing the Australian team. Wanklyn also reminded other NZCC delegates of an earlier decision whereby a New Zealand fixture would only be arranged if it did not interfere with existing provincial arrangements. In another letter, 'Cricketer' attacked the NZCC for the procedure it had used to reverse the earlier decision (apparently only 5 of 16 delegates were present) and suggested that the New Zealand fixture was nothing more than an attempt by the Lancaster Park Ground Company to increase its profits. The same correspondent later suggested that the Company, the NZCC and the Christchurch Tram Company should reimburse the CCA for lost revenue – a point echoed by T.D. Harman, a long-serving Canterbury administrator.[13]

Certainly, one cannot deny the concerns of those who sought to protect the financial interests of the CCA, or any provincial cricket association for that matter. All of these bodies operated fairly close to the poverty line and could be excused for seeking to increase their revenue at every opportunity. Yet the proposed fixture would mark the first meeting between fully representative Australian and New Zealand teams, albeit on uneven terms – New Zealand were to field a XV. The willingness of Wanklyn and others to sacrifice this opportunity to satisfy much narrower Canterbury objectives suggests that there was a certain amount of local indifference to the principles that the visiting Australian team and its predecessors had come to symbolise – the role of cricket in forging a sense of colonial unity and identity.

Under the sobriquet 'One of the Public', another Christchurch correspondent outlined more pragmatic objections to a Canterbury rather than New Zealand fixture:

> Do the advocates of the Canterbury match think that a game (I cannot call it a match) between a team of eighteen, or, for that matter, eighty players of the calibre of those who so lately (mis)represented Canterbury v. Otago would attract any 'gate' at all? ... That a game against the visitors would be of great interest to the eighteen chosen

players is probable enough, and if they relied on themselves to pay for it, I would be silent.[14]

At the end of November 1896 a New Zealand XV put up a very creditable performance in losing to the Australians by only five wickets. Later in the same season, the WCA had no hesitation in forfeiting their provincial match against Queensland in favour of one involving New Zealand.[15]

However, the liberality of the WCA in 1896 was not matched by the same body in 1910. On the later occasion, Wellington's refusal to compromise with the NZCC almost brought about the cancellation of a tour by a strong Australian 2nd XI. The issues involved were presented in more straightforward financial terms than those of the 1890s, but they are an equally instructive lesson in the perils encountered by New Zealand cricket in its effort to present a united public face, capitalise on opportunities to play its neighbour and thereby strengthen an Australasian identity.

With very limited funds of its own, and a very limited direct income, the NZCC was entirely dependent on the provincial cricket associations pooling funds to finance touring teams. Of course, the associations were in an equally precarious position – and Wellington usually more so than most. Consequently, when the NZCC approached the WCA in August 1909 seeking its share of a guarantee for the forthcoming Australian tour, the request was declined. Wellington pointed out that it had lost heavily after guaranteeing £500 towards the MCC tour of 1906–07. Although the gate for its own match had been quite satisfactory, the return on its guarantee was severely depleted by gate failures in other areas. Now, in 1910, the Association was equally unwilling to cover the losses of others, but at the same time it did not expect anyone else to cover possible Wellington losses. To this end, the NZCC was informed that Wellington would provide a £100 guarantee for its own match against the Australians, but would contribute nothing to the pool.[16]

Wellington, though, had adopted a minority position. When the NZCC surveyed its other members as to the possibility of abandoning the pooling system, it received a unanimous endorsement of the status quo – especially from the minor (non first-class) provincial associations that had benefited considerably from the contributions provided by larger centres. As Wellington refused to alter its stance, it was excluded from the tour itinerary. However, this move prompted Auckland and Otago to threaten to withdraw from the pooling system unless Wellington was allocated a fixture. Moreover, only Canterbury agreed to provide extra funds to cover the shortfall caused by the missing Wellington guarantee. On 21 January 1910 the NZCC dispatched a cable to the Australian Board of Control informing them that the tour was off.[17]

From this position, how the tour was saved is not altogether clear. In a strong cable the Australian Board informed the NZCC that there would be 'future consequences' unless its internal disputes were resolved and the tour proceeded according to plan.[18] When the Australians arrived in New Zealand, they not only played the Wellington provincial team, but one of the two 'Test' matches was also staged at the Basin Reserve. The resurrection of the tour, though, did not prevent a scathing attack on the WCA by the *Lyttelton Times*. In a long editorial it suggested that the Wellington position was nothing more than a disruptive campaign to shift the headquarters of New Zealand cricket from Christchurch to Wellington, a city that already controlled New Zealand rowing, rugby and tennis: 'Whether the change should be made is a question for the devotees of the sport to decide, but in view of recent events we should not have much confidence ourselves in an administration body that derives its inspiration from the gentlemen who are dictating the present policy of the northern Association'.[19] The accuracy of such claims was offset when the WCA defeated a motion – promoted by E.H. Williams of Hawke's Bay – to move the NZCC from Christchurch. Nonetheless, it was the negative perception by the other provinces of Wellington's position that was ultimately more important than the facts of the matter.

Such displays of vitriol do not sit comfortably with the imperial and federal rhetoric that had greeted touring teams during the 1880s. There had always been a certain amount of rivalry as provincial XVIIIs and XXIIs compared their performances, but this was a rather more abstract notion than the interaction that was demanded of them after 1894. Instead of bringing men, colonies and the Empire closer together, efforts to select New Zealand teams between 1894 and 1914 frequently did more to drive them apart. Not that this was by any means unique to New Zealand: Australian cricket was marked by numerous intercolonial, selection and player disputes with much higher stakes than those in New Zealand. Yet interprovincial acrimony was only one part of a process that also included the practical impediments to cricket outlined earlier, the general lack of international success for New Zealand teams and the realisation that their few good performances were against decidedly second-rate opposition. When these elements are combined, a picture emerges as to why New Zealand cricket entirely failed to embrace popular imagination – to say nothing of cultural and political aspiration – in the manner of its Australian counterpart.

Interpreting Success and Failure

The lack of confidence and expectation in New Zealand cricket during the 1890s is most evident in the muted responses to rare moments of success. Neither the Canterbury victory over New South Wales in January 1894 nor those by New Zealand over New South Wales in January 1896 and Queensland at the end of the same year prompted anything by way of editorial observation or any suggestion that the results may offer a more general measure of New Zealand's standing in the world. Indeed, after the Canterbury victory the *New Zealand Referee* rather discouragingly observed that questions were inevitably being asked concerning the strength of the New South Wales team.[20] Two weeks later, when New Zealand sustained a generally unexpected loss to the same opposition, the *Lyttelton Times* assessed the tour in an equally gloomy perspective: 'We confess to an obstinate belief that were the elevens to meet again a close battle ought to ensue, but they will not meet again, and the result of their only encounter is that the second eleven of New South Wales has defeated New Zealand with almost ridiculous ease'.[21]

Somewhat perversely, New Zealand successes were greeted with more pleasure in Sydney than they were in New Zealand. Following the Canterbury victory, the Sydney *Referee* was decidedly magnanimous: 'In a match fought out under equal conditions, Welshmen will not be chagrined to hear that the New Zealanders have won. Such an ending will at once prove that the good old game is going ahead over there, and news of that kind will be sweet to us all.' Moreover, despite the reluctance of the NSWCA to sanction the 1894 tour, there was considerable praise for New Zealand cricket authorities and much hope that interchanges between the two colonies would be more frequent.[22] This pattern was repeated in 1895, when the Sydney press criticised the NSWCA for altering tour arrangements without consulting the NZCC – a body that had acted 'with a generosity which is rare among cricket officials'.[23] Additionally, when the touring team lost to New Zealand, the *Referee* again aligned itself with the wider cause of cricket:

> No one will accuse me of any lack of patriotic feeling for expressing a high sense of pleasure at the result of the game … [It] is welcome evidence that the good old game of cricket has some worthy exponents across the seas. To me the ability of New Zealand to beat this combination of Welshmen is a source of much joy … We have long since been able to look up to New Zealanders as the teachers of our footballers who favour rugby … And let us hope with all our hearts that the same improvement will mark their cricket through contacts with New South Wales.[24]

Although the New Zealand team had won two of its first three representative matches, the gulf between Australia and New Zealand was such as to allow this large degree of Australian complacency and paternalism. It is impossible to imagine an English victory being received in such welcoming terms.

The 1899 New Zealand Tour of Australia

One event – the 1899 New Zealand tour of Australia – neatly encapsulates the disparity of the trans-Tasman relationship. Whereas the first Australian

FIGURE 18

Opoho Cricket Club, winners of the Dunedin Junior Challenge Shield, 1899/1900. Opopho was one of the more skilful blue-collar cricket clubs in Dunedin during the 1890s. (Weekly Press photo, Canterbury Museum: Ref. 14798)

FIGURE 19

Wellington East Ladies Cricket Team, 1909. Nothing is known of how often this team played or who their opponents were. Suffice to say, they were given little support from the male cricketing community. (Weekly Press photo, Canterbury Museum: Ref. 14799)

tour of England in 1878 signalled a new epoch in Anglo-Australian relations, both on and off the field, the first New Zealand venture overseas was,
if anything, a backwards step for cricket. It accentuated provincial antagonism, almost bankrupted the NZCC and reinforced the prevailing sense of
inferiority.

Problems surfaced as soon as the New Zealand touring party was
announced in December 1898. Of the original selection, which comprised
two players from Auckland, three from Canterbury and four each from
Otago and Wellington, four withdrew for business reasons – three of whom
were Wellingtonians. Of their replacements, one also withdrew. Another
original selection, Alfred Clarke of Otago, was replaced shortly before the
team departed. The final tour party comprised five Canterbury players, three
each from Auckland and Otago, and two from Wellington.[25]

So many changes raised questions about the value of the tour. On
9 January 1899 Wellington's *Evening Post* warned that 'With men constantly dropping out, there seems to be such difficulties in the way of making
the trip. It will be absurd if it becomes necessary to send away a combination that is not representative of the colony's strength and, at the present
time, this contingency appears to threaten.' Two days later the WCA
expressed this concern in a formal motion: '... owing to so few of the original team being able to get away, this Association strongly recommends that
the tour be abandoned'. These concerns were echoed from the other side of
the Tasman Sea, with the Sydney *Daily Telegraph* commenting that 'It is a
pity the tour should be made with a team that [is] certainly not representative of a very weak cricket colony'.[26]

Despite the numerous changes to the team, much of the controversy that
surfaced during January 1899 was directed against some of the original tour
selections, especially Frank Ashbolt of Wellington, the son of Arthur
Ashbolt – the NZCC's sole selector. Even Wellington's *Evening Post* was
moved to question Ashbolt's selection – although only in terms of the exclusion of Earnest Upham, another Wellington player. 'Slip', the cricket columnist for the *Otago Witness*, declared that 'in the selection of this team such a
scandalous preference has been shown to cricketing mediocrity over merit,
that I should do outrage to my own feelings were I not to speak plainly on
the subject'. As to Ashbolt, 'Slip' suggested that he had deliberately avoided
the fixture between Wellington and Canterbury in which 'the hollowness of
his pretensions to a place in the New Zealand team would have been completely exposed by his bowling being slammed all over Lancaster Park'.[27] To
this the *New Zealand Herald* added its own condemnation of both Arthur
Ashbolt as a selector and the NZCC for appointing him:

> That such a state of affairs should exist seems to indicate a rottenness
> in the state of Denmark, or, in other words, that the system of
> entrusting the selection of a representative team in the hands of one
> man – and more particularly one not fully cognisant of the relative

merits of the cricketers of the colony – is a wrong one, and it is hoped that the New Zealand Cricket Council will profit by the present pointed illustration, as shown in the general dissatisfaction with which the selection has been hailed.

As it transpired, Frank Ashbolt contributed none for 72 and 48 runs in four innings in his two first-class appearances on the Australian tour. Nonetheless, although he did not play for New Zealand again, his 105 wickets at an average of 16.01 in 21 first-class matches suggest that he was far from being the least qualified cricketer to represent his country. Upham, who eventually made the New Zealand team as a replacement for one of the many original selections, also struggled in Australia – taking three wickets for 249 runs. However, at provincial level he was undoubtedly the best fast-medium bowler in New Zealand, with 265 wickets at 16.65 in a 17-year first-class career.[28]

The replacement of Otago's Alfred Clarke shortly before the team departed prompted a more complicated series of protests. Clarke, a member of the 1890 New South Wales team, shifted to New Zealand and represented his adopted colony against New South Wales and Australia in 1896. Yet his selection for the Australian tour was vetoed by the NZCC on the grounds of 'moral delinquency eight years previously'. While the Council made no further comment about the supposed offence, Clarke was reputedly asked to state that he was unavailable for the tour due to work commitments. This request, which would protect the Council from potential criticism, was refused.[29]

The ambiguity surrounding Clarke's exclusion moved the *Otago Witness* to question the value of the NZCC and of the general principle of centralised administration in sport. The view was expressed that there was too much petty jealousy and too many administrators 'on the make' who put their own interests before those of cricket.[30] The *Otago Daily Times* called for the Council to explain its position regarding Clarke so as to save further embarrassment to Arthur Ashbolt:

> If the team was selected on the merits of the players as players, the omission of Clarke would simply be an indefensible blunder. If considerations other than the merits of the players have been allowed to operate in the selection of the team, then the New Zealand Cricket Council should let the fact be known in order that the selector may be spared the harsh judgement to which the disregarding of the claims of the man who is perhaps the only really brilliant batsman in the colony will otherwise subject him.[31]

All things considered, this was an ominous beginning for a tour that was supposed to promote the virtues of the colony to an Australian audience.

As the team prepared to leave New Zealand in early February 1899, there were very mixed expectations. The *Otago Witness* suggested that while they would not win all of their matches, the team would not be disgraced. The *Evening Post* added that the tour was primarily an educational venture in which New Zealand was not expected to win – although recent performances against Australian touring teams suggested that they stood an even chance in the minor fixtures in Tasmania. Sounding the most pessimistic note, the *New Zealand Herald* doubted that they would even win in Tasmania. In Sydney, *The Leader* prophetically observed that as the Australian XI were playing three matches prior to their departure for England, the New Zealand tour should be postponed to avoid a clash of interests.[32]

If the tour preliminaries served to expose the factionalism and vulnerability of New Zealand cricket, the subsequent course of events was no more encouraging. In their minor matches the New Zealanders drew with South Tasmania and defeated North Tasmania by 150 runs, but in the two first-class fixtures, against Victoria and New South Wales, they lost heavily. The innings and 384 run loss to New South Wales remains New Zealand's heaviest defeat. Moreover, neither of the colonial sides was at full strength. Victoria was without five of its regular players – a fact that the *Referee* described as usual 'when the match is not absolutely first-class' – but nevertheless made their highest first-class total to that date.[33] New South Wales, although fielding its regular bowlers, gave opportunities to several promising batsmen – including one Victor Trumper, who responded with a double century.[34]

Financially and organisationally, the tour was a disaster. It lost in excess of £260 – reducing the bank balance of the NZCC from £140 to £4 and forcing the four main provincial associations to pay guarantees of £25 each to bail it out. L.T. Cobcroft, the former New South Wales player who captained the New Zealand team, attributed the loss to the bad timing of the tour. It coincided with racing carnivals in Tasmania and Melbourne and with the 'Test match' between the Australian XI and 'The Rest' in Sydney. Daniel Reese, during a 1913 interview with the Sydney *Referee*, said that he had many regrets regarding the 1899 tour, including the non-selection of several good young players and the bad organisation of the tour by the NZCC in that there were only four matches in seven weeks.[35]

The final stages of the tour were also marred by a controversy that reveals a good deal about the apparent attitude to New Zealand among Australian cricket officials. Several New Zealand players complained that they had not been treated with the courtesies normally accorded to visiting Australian colonial teams in Sydney. There was no formal welcome from the NSWCA when they arrived, and local officials later ignored them at a banquet supposedly held in their honour. Although members of the team had received tickets to the match between Australia and 'The Rest', they had been left to pay for their own lunches. In the words of one player, 'That we received scurvy treatment at the hands of the representative cricketing body of NSW admits to no question'.[36]

These feelings were certainly echoed in Sydney. At a sometimes heated special meeting of the NSWCA, J.C. Davis, organiser of two unofficial New South Wales tours to New Zealand, suggested that a New Zealand team ought to be treated with greater courtesy than visiting Australian teams, especially given the extreme hospitality extended to New South Wales teams in New Zealand. The secretary of the Association replied that they had done all that was required and were not in the business of running 'junkets' for touring cricketers. Nonetheless, a motion was proposed to donate the entire gross receipts from the New South Wales fixture (£116) to the NZCC as compensation for any discourtesy; an amendment to reduce this to £50 was lost amid claims from the Association that the public would regard any sum as 'conscience money'. It was finally resolved to review the matter at a meeting three months later.[37] Ultimately, the balance sheet of the NZCC indicates that no payment was ever forthcoming from the NSWCA.

There were few encouraging signs from the tour. Among New Zealand sources, only the *New Zealand Referee* offered faint hope that the team might benefit from their experiences: 'No one in this colony, I fancy, anticipated that the New Zealand team would win in Melbourne or Sydney, and the idea in playing the best teams in those places was to gain experience, and provided our men profit by the lesson, good must result from their tour'.[38] The *Sydney Mail* was also able to appreciate the value of the tour irrespective of its results:

> The trip has marked a new era in cricket in the southern hemisphere, and may justly be said to have completed the federation of the grand old English game in this part of the world. Therefore those who proposed the visit and those who carried it out are entitled to every congratulation on their sportsmanlike behaviour, especially as regards the manner in which they accepted their defeats.[39]

The most realistic verdict, though, is that offered by Don Neely in his monumental *Men in White*: 'Any sense of optimism carried by the team to Australia after home wins over New South Wales and Queensland had been blasted by the humiliating failures on the tour. The New Zealanders returned with the sober knowledge that they were mere novices in the world of cricket'.[40]

A Growing Disparity, 1900–1914

The twentieth century offered nothing to alleviate the malaise that descended over New Zealand cricket in 1899. As links between England and Australia flourished, and Ashes Tests drew increasingly large crowds amid what has been termed the 'Golden Age' of cricket, relations between Australia and New Zealand were little different to the notions of inferiority that had characterised earlier encounters.

Reactions to the Australian touring team of 1905 are typical of the prevailing outlook. The main point of debate was whether New Zealand teams would meet the visitors with odds or on even terms. Canterbury predictably decided to take the field with an XI, and opinion in Otago generally favoured an XI rather than XV on the basis that the extra fielders would inhibit the Australian batsmen and thus reduce the educational value of the match. As the *Otago Witness* explained, 'the object is not so much to beat the Australians ... but to see these masters of bat and ball, and to get from them an idea of how cricket should be played under fair and recognised conditions of the game. This is impossible if odds are persisted in'.[41] Whether the Otago XI felt suitably educated by their subsequent innings and 172-run defeat is a moot point.

The debate over odds was strongest in the North Island. In Wellington the *New Zealand Times* declared that the public were pleased with the abandonment of an 'ill-advised' plan to play only XI against the Australians: 'For eleven such players as those Wellington possesses to oppose the visiting combination would be the broadest comedy'.[42] The debate in Auckland was eventually resolved in similar fashion. Writing to the *New Zealand Herald*, 'Old Player' insisted that Auckland should field an XI as 15 fielders would curtail the style of the Australian batsmen. Moreover, Canterbury was fielding only XI, and Auckland was obliged to do likewise. Two days later, 'One of the Public' retorted that the Auckland Cricket Association ought to increase rather than decrease the size of its team. 'Playing 11 men only would be to court certain defeat, proclaim our self-conceit and stupidity, and reduce the contest to a ridiculous farce'.[43] Another correspondent stressed that the Australians would be required to put more effort into a match with a XV:

> The public will not go to the domain in any large numbers just to witness an exhibition of Australian cricket; but I am persuaded they will go in thousands to witness the grand match now that there is to be at least a semblance of equality in the contest, and had 18 local men been chosen, the attendance would be still larger.[44]

The Auckland XV were duly defeated by an innings and 160 runs, and Wellington were lucky to escape with a draw.

Despite these debates, the tour did mark the first occasion on which New Zealand met a full Australian team on even terms. Few, though, were willing to see this as a significant advance for New Zealand cricket. Prior to the first match in Christchurch, *The Star* offered a rather backhanded compliment to the NZCC for their decision to play on even terms, but questioned the status of the fixture:

> If New Zealand is to be treated to a vigorous whacking, then it is advisable that the process should be made as free from humiliation as possible. But, while we commend the authorities for selecting only eleven

men ... we think that they have made a mistake in dubbing the 'butchery' a 'Test' match. If as a joke it were calculated to inspire our representatives with confidence it would have its use. But it is much more likely to make them simply feel foolish.[45]

Rain enabled New Zealand to escape from the Christchurch match with a draw, but nothing could save them in Wellington as they lost by an innings and 358 runs. While New Zealand had not been expected to win, *The Press* complained that the manner of their loss was most unsatisfactory. Even the New Zealand fielding had declined to 'third grade' standard.[46]

In the end, the NZCC's use of the term 'Test match' was not as flippant as *The Star* had suggested. In 1948, the Imperial Cricket Conference belatedly granted Test status to New Zealand's match against Australia in 1946 – thus making it the first Test match between the two countries. At the same time New Zealand attempted to secure similar retrospective status for the two matches of 1905. This was rejected, in large part because Australia refused to alter its records.[47]

These defeats, and those against Warwick Armstrong's Australian 2nd XI in 1910, inevitably took their toll on public enthusiasm for international cricket. Indeed, the debacle against Armstrong's team in Wellington prompted the *New Zealand Times* to question the basic value of touring teams:

> The most they accomplish we should think is to afford the public an agreeable spectacle and show how unutterably inferior our cricketers are in skill. Beyond learning that they play the game very badly in comparison with Australians, the New Zealanders are not likely to derive much benefit from contemplation of their opponent's skill.[48]

Given New Zealand's abysmal record against Australian teams, such cynicism was only to be expected.

However, the NZCC was nothing if not determined. Despite the record of defeats, constant efforts were made to attract Australian teams to New Zealand and to arrange a regular interchange between the two countries. In 1899 and 1902 the Council tried to entice Australian teams to New Zealand after tours of England, and it was also suggested that one of the Ashes Tests might be played in Christchurch as part of the 1907 International Exhibition. Various proposals were also floated to bring New South Wales, South Australian and Tasmanian teams to New Zealand.[49] In April 1911 Edward Stevens stated that the greatest benefit to New Zealand cricket would be derived from regular contacts with Australia, rather than attempts to pursue English or South African teams. Frederick Wilding added that the ideal would be for New Zealand to tour Australia every five years, with New South Wales, South Australia, Tasmania and Victoria to visit in the alternate years.[50] None of these proposals amounted to anything.

However, progress was made in the other direction. After several false starts, another New Zealand team was finally dispatched to Australia in November 1913 – nearly 15 years after the previous visit. Yet, as with 1899, this tour served more as a measure of the rifts and animosities within New Zealand cricket and the disparity with Australia than as any tool for expressing notions of unity or development.

As with previous tours, the selection of the New Zealand team did not proceed smoothly. According to the *Otago Witness* the tour selectors had been instructed to focus on younger players and on the educational value of the tour – hence it was not strictly necessary to send the best team to Australia.[51] Thus, when the selected team included the 50-year-old Charles Boxshall and several other players over 30, the *Witness* accused the selectors of having no regard for the future of New Zealand cricket. As there was no hope of even the strongest New Zealand team competing with Australian State teams or doing anything to encourage greater Australian interest in New Zealand cricket, the game would have been better served by including those who stood to benefit most from the experience. Moreover, both the *Witness* and the OCA strongly condemned the lack of equity in the selection policy. They felt that the team should have been selected equally from each province in order to secure the widest possible benefit for the New Zealand game. To this end, Otago supporters also directed barbs at self-satisfied Cantabrians who saw no fault with the prevailing selection policy; Canterbury provided 7 of the 14 players.[52]

In terms of results the tour was only marginally better than its predecessor. New Zealand won 4 and drew 1 of its minor matches, secured a 12-run victory against Queensland and a draw in a high-scoring encounter with South Australia, but they lost to New South Wales by an innings and 247 runs and to Victoria by an innings and 110 runs.[53] Of the New South Wales match, Sydney critics could find nothing worthy of praise:

> There can be only one conclusion on the all round form of the match. New Zealand has not improved and at present is in quite another class – a lower one – to that of the best Australian teams. And it is really questionable whether a two days slaughter of this kind has any real practical value educationally for the keen, willing-to-learn, but mediocre islanders.[54]

'Felix' of the *Australasian* was equally candid about New Zealand's experience at the hands of Victoria, observing that the match 'was poorly attended and can only be set down as hopelessly one sided'.[55]

The financial outcome of the tour was also less than satisfactory. Although it made a £200 surplus on the fixtures in Australia, this was entirely absorbed by repayment of original guarantees from the provincial cricket associations. Moreover, the NZCC drew heated criticism when it was discovered that they had spent £210 on payments to players during the tour.

According to the OCA there had been no reference to any such payment proposal prior to the tour, and it was unlikely that the NZCC would have gained
unqualified support from the provincial cricket associations had they been
aware of such expenditure. 'Long Slip' of the *Otago Witness* was quick to
chastise the Council:

> The Council may preserve the right to do what it likes with its own
> funds, but it is inexcusable that the guarantees of affiliated associations
> should be used in such manner as the payment of New Zealand crick-
> eters on a tour of Australia without first notifying and acquiring the
> sanction of subscribing associations ... This is quite the latest Star
> Chamber act on the part of the New Zealand Cricket Council.[56]

The NZCC replied that reimbursement of players for loss of wages had long
been a part of its policy and that the prevailing rate of 5s per day could be
considered a bargain. Nonetheless, the ACA threatened to secede from the
NZCC and the OCA remained firm in its objections.[57]

A flurry of letters to *The Press* in June 1914 suggests that objections to
the Council's payment scheme rested more on a perception of its failure
to communicate rather than a sustained objection to the principle of player
payment. S.A. Orchard, the manager of the touring team, declared that
most cricketers were constantly 'on the make' and determined to extract
money from the Council at every opportunity. In reply, Daniel Reese,
the captain of the touring team, stated that his players had not asked for
the tour allowance, and the initiative for it had come entirely from the
NZCC. Personally, he was only in favour of payment to waged – but not
salaried – players.[58]

The dispute prompted the resignation of the entire NZCC Management
Committee and Tim Raphael, who had been secretary of the Council since
1899.[59] While most of the members of the committee, including Raphael,
soon found their way back to the Council, there was no sign of abatement in
the disharmony and provincialism that had surrounded the NZCC and its
representative teams during the previous two decades.

Immediately following the New Zealand tour, a strong, privately organised Australian team under the captaincy of Arthur Sims, philanthropist and
former New Zealand captain, toured New Zealand. As T.W. Reese put it, this
team 'veritably smashed their way through the Dominion' – recording
innings totals of 658 against Auckland, 653 against Canterbury, 709 against
Southland and an unprecedented 922 for 9 in a day against South
Canterbury.[60] Despite the very one sided matches, the calibre of the tourists
– Armstrong, Noble, Ransford and Trumper, among others – attracted strong
public interest. While the performances of New Zealand teams gave little
comfort, the pessimism of 1910 was replaced by a more familiar faith in the
educational value of touring teams. As the *Otago Witness* expressed the
cliché prior to the first 'Test' match, 'The question of victory or defeat will

be of comparatively little moment compared with educational values that such a match will have'.[61]

Although the Australian Board of Control had not sanctioned the tour, primarily because it was privately organised, they eventually decided not to oppose it. Moreover, it prompted them to finally set about formalising arrangements with New Zealand. In June 1914 the Board passed a motion agreeing to approach the NZCC in an effort to arrange regular tours between the two countries.[62] This represented a considerable advance on the position held by the New South Wales Cricket Association during the 1890s. The new initiative was halted until the early 1920s, though, by the outbreak of war.

The disparity that had emerged in trans-Tasman cricketing relations by 1914 was perhaps greater than it should have been. Certainly, there were climatic and demographic factors that gave Australian cricket a considerable advantage over that in New Zealand, as discussed in Chapter 7. Yet it is equally apparent that the chances of competing with Australia were undercut by repeated instances of provincial rivalry and vitriol. The precarious financial position of every provincial cricket association produced considerable reticence when it came to supporting the international objectives of the NZCC. As the gap widened between Australian and New Zealand standards, the Australians perceived that they had little to gain from an involvement with New Zealand cricket. Eventually, this attitude forced New Zealand to look much more towards England for its international opportunities and guidance. However, this was not a prospect to dishearten the NZCC – as we will see in Chapter 10.

Notes

1. See: Sinclair, *Tasman Relations*; A. and R. Burnett, *The Australia and New Zealand Nexus* (Canberra, 1978).
2. Webster, *First-Class Cricket in Australia*, pp. 143, 179; NSWCA, Minutes, 13 Jan. 1890.
3. Webster, *First-Class Cricket in Australia*, p. 209; *Sydney Mail*, 3 Feb. 1894, p. 247; 14 Dec. 1895, p. 1233; *Daily Telegraph*, 24 Oct. 1895, NSWCA press cuttings.
4. *New Zealand Referee*, 20 Aug. 1896, p. 31; 27 Aug. 1896, pp. 30–1; 3 Sept. 1896, p. 31; 10 Sept. 1896, pp. 30–1; 24 Sept. 1896, p. 31.
5. *New Zealand Referee*, 24 Oct. 1891, p. 26; 15 Nov. 1894, p. 33; NZCC, Committee Minutes, 21 Dec. 1901.
6. Webster, *First-Class Cricket in Australia*, pp. 178, 663.
7. *The Press*, 12 July 1875, p. 2; *New Zealand Herald*, 30 Sept. 1886, p. 6; *New Zealand Referee*, 20 Jan. 1888, p. 103; *The Press*, 12 Aug. 1893, p. 6.
8. *New Zealand Referee*, 4 Jan. 1894, p. 27.
9. Ibid., 11 Jan. 1894, p. 26; 8 Feb. 1894, p. 25.
10. *Otago Witness*, 15 Feb. 1894, p. 32; Neely et al., *Men in White*, p. 35.
11. *Lyttelton Times*, 24 March 1910, p. 6.
12. Figures derived from Reese, *New Zealand Cricket 1914–33*, pp. 590–3. Two players were selected for New Zealand teams from two different provinces – J.N. Fowke from Auckland and Canterbury, and W. Robertson from Canterbury and Southland.
13. *The Press*, 13 Nov. 1896, p. 3; 14 Nov. 1896, p. 5; 17 Nov. 1896, p. 6; 19 Nov. 1896, p. 6.
14. Ibid., 20 Nov. 1896, p. 6.
15. Neely et al., *Men in White*, pp. 38–9.

16. NZCC, Management Committee Minutes, 17 Aug. 1909; Special General Meeting Minutes, 2 Dec. 1909; *New Zealand Freelance*, 5 Feb. 1910, p. 18.
17. NZCC, Management Committee Minutes, 3 Dec. 1909; 13 Dec. 1909; 23 Dec. 1909; 30 Dec. 1909; 17 Jan. 1910; 22 Jan. 1910.
18. Ibid., 21 Jan. 1910.
19. *Lyttelton Times*, 26 Jan. 1910, p. 6.
20. *New Zealand Referee*, 8 Feb. 1894, p. 24.
21. *Lyttelton Times*, 19 Feb. 1894, p. 4.
22. *Referee*, 7 Jan. 1894, p. 8; 7 Feb. 1894, p. 8; 7 March 1894, p. 8.
23. *Sydney Telegraph*, 24 Oct. 1895, NSWCA press cuttings.
24. *Referee*, 8 Jan. 1896, p. 8.
25. Neely et al., *Men in White*, p. 40.
26. *Evening Post*, 9 Jan. 1899, p. 2; *New Zealand Mail*, 12 Jan. 1899, p. 22; quoted in Neely et al., *Men in White*, p. 40.
27. *Evening Post*, 31 Dec. 1898, p. 3; *Otago Witness*, 12 Jan. 1899, p. 36.
28. *New Zealand Herald*, 21 Jan. 1899, p. 6; McConnell and Smith, *Encyclopedia*, p. 40.
29. Neely et al., *Men in White*, p. 40; *Otago Witness*, 12 Jan. 1899, p. 36.
30. *Otago Witness*, 12 Jan. 1899, p. 36
31. *Otago Daily Times*, 7 Jan. 1899, p. 4.
32. *Otago Witness*, 2 Feb. 1899, p. 22; *Evening Post*, 16 Jan. 1899, p. 4; *New Zealand Herald*, 28 Jan. 1899, p. 6; *The Leader*, 21 Jan. 1899, p. 16.
33. *Referee*, 22 Feb. 1899, p. 8.
34. Neely et al., *Men in White*, pp. 40–2; Webster, *First-Class Cricket in Australia,* pp. 248, 258–9.
35. Neely et al., *Men in White*, p. 42; *Otago Witness*, 16 March 1899, p. 36; 8 Oct. 1913, p. 54; Daniel Reese quoted in *Otago Witness*, 8 Oct. 1913.
36. *Otago Witness*, 30 March 1899, p. 42; *New Zealand Referee*, 15 March 1899, p. 38.
37. *Daily Telegraph*, 21 March 1899, NSWCA press cuttings; NSWCA, Minutes, 30 March 1899.
38. *New Zealand Referee*, 1 March 1899, p. 33.
39. *Sydney Mail*, 4 March 1899, p. 531.
40. Neely et al., *Men in White*, p. 42.
41. *Otago Witness*, 25 Jan. 1905, p. 56.
42. *New Zealand Times*, 14 Feb. 1905, p. 4.
43. *New Zealand Herald*, 31 Jan. 1905, p. 9; 2 Feb. 1905, p. 7.
44. Ibid., 3 Feb. 1905, p. 7.
45. *The Star*, 9 March 1905, p. 2.
46. *The Press*, 20 March 1905, p. 6.
47. Harte, *History of Australian Cricket*, p. 412.
48. *New Zealand Times*, 30 March 1910, p. 4.
49. *Otago Witness*, 16 March 1899, p. 36; NZCC, Committee Minutes, 25 March 1902; 15 May 1906; 17 March 1908; Management Committee Minutes, 12 Dec. 1912; 6 May 1913.
50. NZCC, General Meeting Minutes, 27 April 1911.
51. *Otago Witness*, 10 Oct. 1913, p. 53.
52. Ibid., 22 Oct. 1913, p. 53; 29 Oct. 1913, p. 53.
53. Neely et al., *Men in White*, pp. 53–6.
54. Quoted in *Otago Witness*, 14 Jan. 1914, p. 52.
55. *Australasian*, 17 Jan. 1914, p. 131.
56. *Otago Witness*, 4 March 1914, p. 53; 25 March 1914, p. 52.
57. *The Press*, 11 May 1914, p. 8; 10 June 1914, p. 4. See also *The Press*, 31 Jan. 1905, p. 6, for a statement of NZCC policy regarding payment of expenses to players.
58. *The Press*, 10 June 1914, p. 4; 11 June 1914, p. 10; 12 June 1914, p. 9; 13 June 1914, p. 8; 18 June 1914, p. 7.
59. NZCC, Annual Report, 1914.
60. Quoted in Neely et al., *Men in White*, p. 57.
61. *Otago Witness*, 23 Feb. 1914, p. 53.
62. ABCIC, Minutes, 20 June 1914.

10

More English than the English: The Imperial Connection in the Twentieth Century

There is no doubt that a strong sense of imperial and intercolonial symbolism was associated with the middle-class stratum that dominated New Zealand cricket. Indeed, it is a theme that gained greater clarity because it was never subsumed by the expressions of assertive colonialism and, later, emergent nationalism that characterised Australian cricket. Indeed, quite the reverse was the case. Over time New Zealand's cricketing idyll became more firmly identified with that of distant England than neighbouring Australia. Despite the expense and logistical difficulties, the NZCC and the provincial cricket associations took every opportunity to entice English touring teams and players to New Zealand. Within this conception of the game, notions of victory or defeat became quite superfluous to concerns with 'form' and 'style' – and the truest form of cricket was deemed to be that pursued by Oxbridge and public school amateurs.

A catalogue of reactions to the tours by Lord Hawke's England XI in 1902–03 and the MCC in 1906–07 adds nothing new to the rhetoric of cricket and empire outlined in the previous two chapters. Rather, it serves to highlight the banality and shallowness of much of that rhetoric. For the enduring reticence of New Zealand cricket – and the various explanations for it – is in stark contrast to the increasing significance of rugby. We have seen already in Chapter 7 that rugby, and especially the 1905 All Black tour, was beginning to provide New Zealand with a similar focus to that of Australian cricket for promoting a more assertive nationalistic rhetoric in its relationship with the mother country – not least because it provided a reassuring contrast between the new colonial society and the supposed stagnation of Britain revealed in the 'physical deterioration' debates following the South African war. Very quickly, New Zealand rugby relations with Britain also foundered on some of the same clashes between middle-class sporting idealism and elements of colonial pragmatism and egalitarianism that had so perturbed Andrew Stoddart and his ilk in Australia during the mid 1890s. The New Zealand cricket elite, on the other hand, were still inclined in the 1930s to refer to themselves as 'transplanted Britishers'. They epitomised an element of the New Zealand psyche that sought to maintain close ties with Britain and that interpreted successes on the battlefield and the rugby field more as an affirmation of imperial vitality than a statement of separate New Zealand identity.

The point is that the obvious polarity between these two positions was never reconciled by contemporary observers and has been entirely ignored by subsequent scholars. In short, the achievements of New Zealand rugby have been seized upon by innumerable chroniclers of New Zealand's quest for 'national identity' as a vital component of its emergence.[1] Yet this interpretation ignores the fact that many of the columnists and editors who saw New Zealand rugby as a symbol of pride and independence were the same people who not only saw New Zealand cricket from an anglophile's perspective but interpreted its corresponding lack of success as proof positive that New Zealand as a whole was still firmly under the wing of the mother country. Tackling the multiple contradictions of New Zealand identity is well beyond the scope of the present work, but what follows is at least one part of the revisionist jigsaw.

English Touring Teams and the Amateur Tradition

Despite success in developing contacts with Australia, the ultimate goal of New Zealand cricket authorities was always to secure tours by English teams. The reaction of *The Press* in August 1878 to a proposed visit by Lord Harris's amateur England team is typical:

> Such a visit would do more real good to the noble game than almost any number of matches with professional players. The character of the game as played by the gentlemen of England and the players is vastly different and our colonial players would derive great advantage from a contest with the former, as their play is of the more brilliant character, combining as it does good defence with grand hitting powers.[2]

The tour failed to eventuate, as did numerous other attempts by Canterbury and the NZCC to entice touring teams during the 1880s and 90s. In 1897 the Council even extended an invitation to an English parliamentary cricket team – a prospect that the *New Zealand Referee* greeted with enthusiasm: 'since the Jubilee, most members of the Imperial Parliament feel their education incomplete until they have seen the Empire, and no more agreeable way presents itself than through the medium of the national game – cricket'.[3] This tour also failed to materialise.

When the NZCC received word that A.C. MacLaren's team would not be able to extend its Australian tour to include New Zealand in 1902, the decision was finally made to forego the Australian connection and arrange an English touring team exclusively for New Zealand. A letter was sent to the Yorkshire captain, Lord Hawke, requesting him to bring an English amateur team to New Zealand. The Council stressed that although cricket was the first priority, the tour would not be as businesslike as English visits to Australia, and would include opportunities for other recreation and sightseeing.[4]

When the tour was confirmed in April 1902, the NZCC could not disguise its pleasure: 'The Chairman [E.C.J. Stevens] thought that nothing could be better for New Zealand cricket than the visit of a team such as that now proposed, and speaking for himself, he would rather see a team of English amateurs than a professional team or one from Australia'.[5] The preference for an amateur team was no idle consideration. When Lord Hawke announced that he was having difficulty recruiting amateur players, and that the team should contain two professional bowlers, the Council passed a motion reaffirming its desire for a purely amateur team. This was a clear reflection of the strong middle-class and public school heritage of the upper echelon of New Zealand cricket's administration – and especially the Christ's College old boys who monopolised the CCA and NZCC. The Auckland Cricket Association also threatened to withdraw its financial guarantee for the tour if the team included any professional players and if they played any matches in Australia either before or after the New Zealand tour. It was felt that a visit to Australia would compromise both the New Zealand itinerary and the 'holiday' aspect of the tour. Eventually, Lord Hawke won both points: two professional bowlers were included, and the team played three first-class matches in Australia.[6]

Underpinning everything was a feeling that an English amateur team would bring about the 'salvation' of New Zealand cricket. Ignoring the Australian teams of the 1890s, Alfred Kidd, the Mayor of Auckland, said that Lord Hawke's team would give a considerable public boost to cricket – a game which had languished somewhat since the visit of Alfred Shaw's England XI twenty years earlier.[7] The 1902 NZCC Annual Report held similar hopes:

> There is reason to hope that the visit of a team of such high calibre will cause a revival in cricket throughout the colony quite equal to that in Australia after the visit of Lord Sheffield's team there. When we remember the apathy existing among the Australian cricketing public for some years prior to 1892–3 [sic] the hope is not too sanguine.[8]

Reference to Lord Sheffield's team is particularly fitting: his patronage of a team to Australia in 1891–92 was conceived as a deliberate contrast to the bitter financial wrangling and excessive competitiveness that had characterised the professional touring teams of the 1880s.[9]

The itinerary for Lord Hawke's team further suggests that the NZCC perceived them as missionary saviours rather than opponents to be challenged at every opportunity. Pelham Warner, who assumed the captaincy of the team when Lord Hawke was forced to withdraw, complained with hindsight that the itinerary contained far too many fixtures of dubious cricketing value. 'We had too many games against odds, against cricketers of the rustic and Salt Bush Bill type, and a better means of improving cricket would have been to have had more eleven a side matches'.[10] Similarly, the *Otago Witness* felt that the NZCC was subjecting the tourists to a large number of redundant fixtures – and for motives that were apparently more pecuniary than cricketing:

> Having got the team safely in the colony, the Council has proceeded to drag them round and force them to play all sorts of idiotic matches in all sorts of absurd places against innumerable hordes of back blocks cricketers simply and solely for the purpose of making money out of them, as if they were a team of performing tigers or a crowd of variety artists. At any rate we cannot credit the Council with the imbecility of thinking that the visitors will enjoy playing on concrete pitches, and knocking down an enormous number of wickets defended by Saltbush Bill and Clancy of the Overflow, and other wayback dwellers. The cricket of back blocks will not be improved, any more than a Kaffir would be improved by five minutes with the 'First Principles' of Herbert Spencer, and no reasonable man can imagine that the visitors will feel anything but a profound ennui at the silly matches. So the only conclusion must be that the Council is merely using its guests for the purpose of making money.[11]

Logic suggests that New Zealand, the weakest cricketing colony in Australasia, ought to have fielded its strongest teams against an English touring party described as being better than average county standard.[12] That only 7 of the 18 matches were first-class and on even terms suggests that the NZCC was more interested in fostering 'inclusive' cricket, wherein as many players as possible were exposed to the finer English traditions of the game, than 'competitive' cricket which would benefit its best players. As a basis for integrating cricket into notions of colonial identity, the New Zealand approach was amateur rather than Australian.

Australia during the same period was clearly moving away from an odds and 'up-country' itinerary to one that better served the higher, publicly visible aims of its cricket. Whereas Andrew Stoddart's touring team of 1894–95 played 12 first-class fixtures out of a total of 23, and 12 of 22 in 1897–98, the MCC side of 1903–04 had 14 first-class encounters on a 20-match tour; in 1907–08 18 out of 19 fixtures were first-class, and 14 of 18 in 1911–12. Even allowing that there were no Test matches to inflate the first-class content of its tours, the attitude of New Zealand administrators appears decidedly unambitious. Between 1864 and 1914, only 39 per cent of matches played by touring teams in New Zealand were first-class (68 of 175); for the period 1920–39 the figure rises to 45.5 per cent (61 of 134). The Australian figures are 26.3 per cent (57 of 216) for the period 1862–90,

59.9 per cent (106 of 177) for the period 1891–1914 and 75 per cent (137 of 182) for the period 1920–39.[13]

To some extent the amateur objectives of New Zealand cricket administrators are also evident in the off-field activities of touring teams. The original itinerary for Lord Hawke's team included a larger than usual number of 'leisure days', in part to satisfy the dedicated trout fishermen among the touring team. This itinerary was eventually altered by the tourists themselves in order to accommodate their more lucrative and competitive fixtures in Australia,[14] but the recreation that they did pursue in New Zealand was of a conventionally middle-class nature. In Auckland there was an 'Oxford and Cambridge dinner' attended by the Governor, Lord Ranfurly, and numerous other local dignitaries. The team were also entertained on two occasions at the Wellington Club and once at the Christchurch Club, as well as at race meetings and a privately guided visit to the Rotorua thermal district.[15] Yet, because of the financial position of the NZCC prior to the tour, the team were billeted in private homes rather than in hotels – a situation that left fewer opportunities than normal to mix with local players and the public.[16]

This sort of social round was not confined to Lord Hawke's team. Daniel Reese recalled that all of the Australian teams that visited Christchurch during the 1890s were entertained in extravagant fashion, either at 'Thorrington' by the wealthy Clark family or at 'Fownhope' by the Wilding family.[17] The 1906–07 MCC team were entertained in similar fashion. Among other things, they attended dinners at the Christchurch and Dunedin clubs, enjoyed a fishing party arranged by Sir John Hall – former premier and mayor of Christchurch – and toured Rotorua.[18] In short, there is a sense in which teams were received in a typically English 'country house' fashion that insulated them from contact with the wider public and, more importantly, those cricketers who were not of the requisite social class to participate in such activities. Perhaps without realising it, the pursuit of etiquette by New Zealand cricket officials counteracted their other desire to gain maximum educational value from touring players.

While the agenda of the NZCC differed from its Australian counterparts, it also ran contrary to strands of an independent colonial identity that were beginning to emerge in New Zealand. The reception for Lord Hawke's team in Auckland raised precisely this juxtaposition. Pelham Warner, perhaps the most dedicated cricketing imperialist of all, explained that the particular interest of his team in visiting the most distant colony of the Empire was in part related to New Zealand's contribution to the recently concluded Anglo-South African War:

> They had all been anxious to see New Zealand because the colony had sent no less than ten contingents, consisting of some 6000 men, to aid the mother country in the South African war. This was a great number,

but further than that the New Zealanders, according to those who had been to the war, had been unsurpassed in bravery and endurance.[19]

By the end of a tour in which his team won all 18 of their matches – including ten by an innings, it was surely clear to Warner that qualities of bravery and endurance did not extend to New Zealand cricket. Indeed, the colony that had done so much to enhance its imperial reputation on the battlefields of South Africa, and would soon do so again on the rugby fields of Britain, responded to the English tour with predictable humility. Only the *New Zealand Herald* offered any hint that New Zealand teams might be competitive against Warner's team:

> It goes without saying that this colony cannot place in the field, at any provincial centre, a team which can confidently hope to speed the Englishmen along with the beating our genuine good feeling teaches us would be for their betterment. But every place where they pitch their wickets can at least produce a team which will die hard and will make the visitors show us what they can really do in order to win.[20]

More typical is the debate that ensued in Wellington when the WCA decided to meet the tourists on even terms. The *Evening Post* offered the familiar argument that a XV would make the fixture rather more competitive and provide an important educational opportunity for a larger number of players.[21] 'The Hittite', cricket columnist for the *New Zealand Mail*, supported the WCA decision and pointed out that it was not necessary to play against the tourists in order to learn from them: 'To paraphrase old Milton, "they too can learn who only stand and gaze", and therefore the argument that fifteen players should be selected to play for Wellington so as to extend the educational influence of the game is so much piffle'.[22] At the end of the tour, after noting Warner's dislike for odds matches, the *Post* reaffirmed its earlier view:

> With all due respect to so distinguished an authority, we would ask him if it benefits the game to inflict a defeat of an innings and 230 runs on an opponent [Otago]? That, surely, cannot be called cricket, and a few such thrashings destroy the public interest in the game and damp the ardour of all but the most enthusiastic.[23]

Aside from Canterbury's loss by 133 runs, that of Wellington by ten wickets was the most creditable performance against the tourists by a provincial team.

Feelings in the South Island were no less pessimistic. Amid mortification that Otago's defeat by an innings and 230 runs had 'brought home so forcibly the decadence of our local cricketers', the *Otago Daily Times* urged the OCA to immediately acquire a professional coach.[24] The *Nelsonian*, though, saw a solution closer to home as it highlighted the role that the schools needed to play in raising the standard of New Zealand cricket:

> The lesson which the Englishmen have taught us in regard to our lamentable inefficiency in the art of playing this noble game ought to arouse an emulative spirit in every New Zealand lad. The triumphant career of these men throughout the entire length and breadth of New Zealand is a distinct slur on our athletic ability. It behoves us all to put forward our best energies in order to raise the standard of the game as we are all aware of the fact that the schools are the nurseries of the adult clubs. Then should an English team visit our shores once more it might encounter a reception which would debar even the most proficient of its members from retiring in order to go fishing.[25]

Not surprisingly, the NZCC concluded at the end of the tour that it was premature to consider sending another New Zealand team overseas, let alone to England.[26]

The playing results of the tour were somewhat irrelevant when set against its success in other respects. Lord Hawke's team completed what was far and away the most popular and profitable tour of New Zealand prior to 1914. The 1902/03 season in which they toured enabled the NZCC to convert a £25.12.2 overdraft to a credit balance of £505.18.11.[27] When one considers that most tours, including the star-studded Australian teams of 1881, 1896 and 1905, either lost money or struggled to break even, it seems that New Zealand spectators shared the predisposition of players and officials towards the best traditions of *esprit de corps* and English amateurism. Competitive cricket was not a priority.

'Form' rather than Victory

The lukewarm public response to the first MCC tour of New Zealand in 1906–07 only serves to clarify this idealisation of the English game. The tour produced the first defeats for any English team in New Zealand as the tourists lost to Canterbury by 7 wickets and to New Zealand by 56 runs. They also contested very even draws with Auckland and Wellington. In reality, though, this was one of the weakest teams ever sent to New Zealand, and the reaction to it left no doubt that the cultivation of a good 'form' of cricket was considered more important than the pursuit of victory. From this perspective, New Zealanders could derive no comfort from successes against sub-standard opposition. For international success to be considered worthwhile, it had to be achieved on even terms and against opposition who were able to 'play the game' in all senses of the term.

The selection of the MCC team was determined, in large part, by the performances of its predecessor. *Wisden* noted that the 1902/03 team had been too strong for the cricket to be especially interesting or valuable to New Zealand. The MCC tour was therefore an altogether more modest venture with no professional bowlers and less powerful batting. As the *Evening Post* noted at the end of the tour, 'The idea probably was to send a team which was good enough to win, but not so strong as to overwhelm its opponents, and if this were so then the strength of our cricket was pretty accurately gauged'.[28] Only 5 of the 15 tourists had played regular county cricket during the season before the tour, and of the three who subsequently played Test cricket, only J.W.H.T. Douglas enjoyed a lengthy career.[29]

While the composition of the team lent itself to competitive cricket, it did nothing to generate public enthusiasm. Whereas Lord Hawke's team had boosted the coffers of the NZCC by more than £500, the MCC tour lost the Council nearly £600, with gate receipts of £1,669 well short of the initial prediction of £2,500.[30] The New Zealand public were always far more interested in seeing cricketing 'stars' than well-contested encounters between lesser mortals. With the extensive coverage given to English cricket in the New Zealand press, the public were acutely aware of the standard and experience of the MCC team. Consequently, they were not likely to be lulled into false notions of success.

Neither the Canterbury nor the New Zealand victory generated any form of national or imperial sentiment. *The Press*, while recognising that a Canterbury victory, even against weak opposition, offered much encouragement to New Zealand cricketers, made no grander claims for its significance: 'Though a win is not everything in cricket … it counts for a good deal in moral effect, and should go far to counteract that unfortunate trait, occasionally displayed by our cricketers, of being bowled, or otherwise disposed of, before they get to the wicket'.[31] In a similar vein, the *Evening Post* rather tamely described the New Zealand victory at the Basin Reserve as the 'happiest event of the *last week* for many New Zealanders'. Only a small crowd was present to witness what was generally regarded as a fairly predictable outcome.[32] The vast majority of the New Zealand press paid it no editorial attention whatsoever.

Instead of embracing the successes of the tour, there developed a greater inclination to question its real value to New Zealand cricket. The *Otago Witness* criticised the NZCC for draining funds on an MCC tour when Australian teams with far more talent could be secured at one tenth of the cost. After the brilliance of the 1905 Australian team, the MCC had contained no celebrities and attracted little interest. Others questioned the priority and integrity of the tourists. F.C. Campbell, the President of the OCA, declared that it was disgraceful that a team of supposedly amateur gentlemen should exploit New Zealand hospitality in the manner of the MCC. The £48 in the NZCC tour accounts for washing bills and hotel tips was excessive, leaving Campbell with no desire to see another English tour on similar terms.[33] Percy May, the leading MCC bowler, made no secret of the fact that 'strenuous pleasure-seeking' sometimes had an effect on the performance of the team. Indeed, the prevailing theme of his account is of a tour in which the emphasis was as much social as sporting.[34]

Despite the failings of the MCC tour, and although the NZCC never abandoned its efforts to improve relations with Australia, it continued to direct its greatest energies towards Lord's. Every English tour of Australia saw strenuous attempts by the Council to persuade the tourists to play even a few matches in New Zealand. However, most of these proposals foundered on the refusal of the Australian Board of Control to curtail any part of its own itinerary in favour of New Zealand interests. There were particularly acrimonious exchanges over the 1928/29 MCC tour of Australia. The ABCIC bluntly rejected an NZCC request that the last match in Australia be cancelled to allow two matches in New Zealand, and they were equally abrupt in responding to a compromise whereby a small number of touring players might be released for a team combining MCC players and various of the English professional coaches already in New Zealand.[35]

These coaches provide another clear illustration of the stronger English influence on New Zealand cricket. Former Australian Test players Harry Graham, Jack Saunders and Albert Trott coached in Otago, Wellington and Hawke's Bay respectively, and Canterbury secured several Australian coaches in conjunction with Christ's College, but the provincial cricket associations generally preferred to tax their already strained finances with the extra expense of engaging professional coaches from England rather than Australia. Otago secured J.C. Lawton of Warwickshire during the early 1890s and Frank Shacklock of Nottinghamshire a decade later; Canterbury engaged Jim Phillips from Middlesex during the late 1890s and later obtained the services of Edward Humphreys of Kent; Jack Board of Gloucestershire succeeded Trott in Hawke's Bay; and Auckland had five English coaches during the period 1907–14, including Shacklock and A.E. Relf of Sussex and England. There was another influx during the mid 1920s.[36]

Wider public interest in English cricket was amply catered for by the New Zealand sporting press, and especially the *New Zealand Referee* and *Otago Witness*. From the 1880s onwards far more column inches were devoted to the English County Championship, public schools' cricket and the leading English club sides than to activities in Australia. Moreover, it was not uncommon for the major daily papers to editorialise on performances and developments within the English game. A case in point was the very pro-English sentiment that emerged from the New Zealand press during the bodyline controversy of 1932–33. *The Press* accused the Australian media of sensationalism, recalled the damage inflicted on England by Australian fast bowlers Jack Gregory and Ted McDonald in 1921, and praised the MCC for its strong condemnation of 'sweeping charges' made by the Australian Board of Control. Others suggested that bodyline was neither dangerous nor unplayable, and that the real fault lay in the techniques of Australian players.[37]

Disregarding the complaints against the ability and excesses of the 1906/07 MCC team, there is only one instance of serious conflict between New Zealand and English cricketing values. The perceived aloofness of A.C. MacLaren's MCC team in 1922–23 moved several observers to question the appropriateness of class and social distinctions in English cricket as models for the game in New Zealand. During a reception for the team in Christchurch, Daniel Reese, speaking on behalf of the NZCC, suggested that although the MCC was admired as a great institution, 'its constitution was not democratic enough to suit the ideas of cricketers overseas'.[38] Taking this theme further, the Christchurch *Sun* insisted that the MCC would be well advised to leave distinctions between amateurs and professionals at home as New Zealanders had no intention of treating the two groups differently. Moreover, in the lack of style, enterprise or spectator appeal shown by this predominantly amateur team, the *Sun* found an obvious explanation for England's heavy losses to Australia in 1920–21: 'English cricket needs to be "gingered up". It is wanting in imagination, courage and resource; virtues which are strongly characteristic of Australian play.'[39]

However, much of the controversy, and the apparently sharp reversal of attitudes to amateurism, can be traced to the personal tactlessness of MacLaren and the detached opportunism with which he viewed a tour that had been initiated to aid the recovery of New Zealand cricket after the Great War. Moreover, his team as a whole was not a social success. New Zealand player Eddie McLeod recalled that they had been 'a little bit off-hand … they didn't incline to mix with us'. That the NZCC also lost £900 on the tour cannot have assisted the prevailing attitude.[40]

Going Home

As with Australia, the ultimate measure for New Zealand cricket could only be found on the playing fields of England. Yet it is indicative of respective standards that it took New Zealand almost 50 years longer than Australia to send a team 'home'. E.G. Wynyard, captain of the MCC team, had extended an informal invitation in 1907 – prompting the *Otago Witness* to observe that 'At the first blush, however, it appears quite apparent that a New Zealand team would be very much outclassed in county cricket in the Old Country'.[41] Australian players such as M.A. Noble and Victor Trumper also stressed the need to send a New Zealand team to England.[42] Yet it was not until 1927 that a team finally departed.

This tour, and the first Test-playing tour in 1931, are instructive for lingering tones of tutelage and deference that reveal as much about the historical strength of New Zealand's cricket as about a prevailing attachment to Britain and the reluctance of the country to embark on the transition from colony to dominion status and free association. When the Statute of Westminster was enacted in 1931, removing the last vestiges of control from London and confirming the reality of New Zealand's shift from dominion to independent state, the measure was effectively ignored. Not until 1947, after 12 years of Labour government, was the Statute grudgingly adopted.[43]

Summarising prospects for the 1927 team, F.S. Ashley-Cooper, cricketing scholar and imperialist, declared: 'The Tour has been arranged, not with any idea of challenging our supremacy in the game, but from an educational point of view'. Former Test player Frank Mitchell added that the New Zealanders would receive a fond welcome in light of the efforts of the New Zealand Division during the Great War. When the team arrived in London in April 1927, their captain, T.C. Lowry – Cambridge blue and former Somerset player, informed the British Sportsmen's Club that his men were 'Britishers anxious to appear on the cricket map, and accordingly came Home not to beat the best sportsmen but to learn the rules as England taught them'.[44] At the end of the tour, the New Zealand High Commissioner, Sir James Parr, affirmed the underlying importance of the venture: 'The ties that held New Zealand and the home country together were ties of affection and loyalty which such visits helped to strengthen – such ties were stronger than written constitutions or bonds of steel. The team had played good cricket and had also been missioners of Empire'.[45] Contrary to predictions, New Zealand performed remarkably well – winning 7 and drawing 14 of their 26 first-class matches during a wet summer.

Four years later, although a Test match was scheduled for the first time, the conception of touring in England had not changed. Arthur Donnelly, the President of the NZCC, highlighted its dual objectives: 'They had come to England to improve the standard of the game in their own country and to promote, in some small degree, good feeling and understanding between the Mother Country and the most distant, but not least loyal, of the Dominions of the Empire'.[46] While going out of its way to praise the fine amateur spirit maintained by Lowry and his team in 1931, *Wisden* echoed Donnelly's sentiments: 'Representatives of one of our great Dominions beyond the seas, the New Zealanders looked upon the tour perhaps from a bigger point of view than the mere playing of cricket'.[47] *The Field* was rather more direct when it asked 'Who shall say that these new developments of enthusiasm for cricket do not play a modest part in the consolidation of imperial unity?'[48] At the end of the tour, the London *Truth* congratulated the New Zealanders for apparently bringing amateur ideals back to English cricket:

They have proved themselves genuine, wholehearted cricketers, playing the game in the truest and best tradition – a very different tradition from that which has been known in county cricket at times and in Australian tours often. They have had a purifying effect on the game over here. They have made sporting declarations popular. They have wiped out the old notion of 'playing for keeps'.[49]

It seems, then, that the New Zealand cricket fraternity had finally matched their own claims to be more English than the English.

The 'English' element that stemmed from Wakefieldian idealism in the mid nineteenth century remained strong in New Zealand cricket late into the twentieth century. Up to 1951, 19 of New Zealand's 22 Test matches were against England, and to the end of the 2000 English season it had played more than twice as many Test matches against that country as any other – amounting to 30 per cent of all of its Test matches.[50] Yet as much as this surely reflects the tastes of the NZCC, it must also be attributed to prolonged indifference on the part of Australia. From the late 1920s the Australian Board of Control adopted a very negative attitude towards the New Zealand game. A low point was reached in December 1930 when the ABCIC stated that while it was willing to assist New Zealand cricket by sending young players on development tours after the completion of the Sheffield Shield programme, sending more experienced men would unfairly deprive Australian clubs during important end-of-season grade games.[51] No Australian team toured New Zealand from 1928 to 1946, and there were only 6 visits in the 40 years following New Zealand's admission to Test cricket in 1929–30. Apart from the retrospectively recognised Test match of 1946, the two countries did not meet regularly at international level until 1973–74.[52] The Australian attitude prompted former Australian captain Vic Richardson to observe that 'the Marylebone Cricket Club has done more for cricket in New Zealand from a distance of 10,000 miles than the Australian Board of Control for International Cricket has done from 1500'.[53] Unlike those of a strong imperial ilk who inhabited Lord's and perhaps felt a moral obligation to sustain cricket in the most distant corners of the Empire, the pragmatists of the ABCIC realised that New Zealand had nothing to offer Australian cricket.

New Zealand defeated Australia for the first time in March 1974, and finally won a Test against England at the Basin Reserve, Wellington, in February 1978 – a century after the Australian victory against the MCC at Lord's had dramatically changed the fabric of imperial cricket. Although the age of empire had long departed, the victory was attended by much greater celebration than the first success over Australia. Indeed, some likened it to VE Day, others to New Zealander Edmund Hillary's conquest of Mt Everest.[54] Whatever the true magnitude of the performance – and New Zealand fell rapidly to earth with a heavy defeat in the next Test at Christchurch – it could at least be said that cricketing parity, regardless of its brevity, had at last been achieved with the one opponent who still mattered above all others.

Notes

1. See, for example: Phillips, 'Rugby, War and the Mythology of the New Zealand Male', pp. 108–22; Sinclair, *A Destiny Apart*, pp. 143–55.
2. *The Press*, 17 Aug. 1878, p. 3.
3. *New Zealand Referee*, 24 Oct. 1891, p. 26; 15 Nov. 1894, p. 33; 15 Sept. 1897, p. 36; 6 Oct. 1897, p. 30; 15 Dec. 1897, p. 33.
4. NZCC, Committee Minutes, 21 Dec. 1901.
5. Ibid., 26 April 1902.
6. Ibid., 18 Aug. 1902; 18 Sept. 1902; Special Committee Minutes, 30 Aug. 1902.
7. *New Zealand Herald*, 18 Dec. 1902, p. 6.
8. NZCC, Annual Report, 1902.
9. Inglis, 'Imperial Cricket', pp. 161–2.
10. P.F. Warner, *Cricket Across the Seas* (London, 1903), p. 140.
11. *Otago Witness*, 28 Jan. 1903, p. 53.
12. P.F. Warner, *My Cricketing Life* (London, 1920), p. 120.
13. Figures derived from Webster, *First-Class Cricket in Australia,* and Payne and Smith, *Cricket Almanack of New Zealand*, p. 333. The comparative figures are not affected by the definition of a first-class match – a definition that owes more to the accepted status and designation of the teams involved than their standard of performance.
14. NZCC, Annual Report, 1903.
15. Warner, *Cricket Across the Seas*, pp. 25, 27–35, 135.
16. Cotter, *England versus New Zealand*, p. 35.
17. Reese, *Was it all Cricket?*, pp. 22–3.
18. P.R. May, *With the MCC in New Zealand* (London, 1907), pp. 11–15, 29, 35, 55.
19. *New Zealand Herald*, 18 Dec. 1902, p. 4.
20. Ibid.
21. *Evening Post*, 19 Jan. 1903, p. 4.
22. *New Zealand Mail*, 7 Jan. 1903, p. 34.
23. *Evening Post*, 9 March 1903, p. 4.
24. *Otago Daily Times*, 19 Feb. 1903, p. 4; 24 Feb. 1903, pp. 4–5.
25. *The Nelsonian*, 18, 3 (Dec. 1903), p. 32.
26. NZCC, Annual General Meeting Minutes, 30 Sept. 1903.
27. NZCC, Annual Report, 1903.
28. *Wisden Cricketers Almanack 1908* (London, 1908), p. 503; *Cricket*, 25 May 1907, p. 108.
29. Cotter, *England versus New Zealand*, p. 36.
30. Ibid.; NZCC, Committee Report: MCC Tour 1906–07.
31. *The Press*, 29 Dec. 1906, p. 8.
32. *Evening Post*, 12 March 1907, p. 4, [the italics are mine]; *The Press*, 12 March 1907, p. 8.
33. *Otago Witness*, 24 April 1907, p. 58; 22 May 1907, p. 58.
34. May, *With the MCC in New Zealand*, pp. 10–11.
35. Harte, *History of Australian Cricket*, p. 311; MCC, Committee Minutes, 12 July 1909; 10 Oct. 1927; 3 Dec. 1928; ICC, Minutes, 20 May 1930; 25 July 1934; 15 June 1938.
36. Green, *The Wisden Book of Obituaries*, pp. 88, 473, 539, 708, 801; *100 Not Out*, pp. 115–19. Although Phillips was Australian-born, he was based in England.
37. See G.J. Ryan, 'Extravagance of Thought and Feeling: New Zealand Reactions to the 1932–33 Bodyline Controversy', *Sporting Traditions*, 13, 2 (1997).
38. Quoted in D. Kynaston, *Archie's Last Stand: MCC in New Zealand 1922–23* (London, 1984), p. 63.
39. Quoted in ibid., pp. 92–5, 135–6.
40. Ibid.
41. *Otago Witness*, 9 Jan. 1907, p. 56.
42. *Lyttelton Times*, 2 April 1911, p. 8.
43. Sinclair, *A Destiny Apart*, pp. 96–103; Holt, *Sport and the British*, pp. 231–3.
44. *The Cricketer: Spring Annual 1927* (London, 1927), pp. 20–5; *Cricketer*, 7 May 1927, p. 15; *The Times*, 7 May 1927, p. 6.
45. *The Times*, 17 Sept. 1927, p. 5.
46. Ibid., 26 Sept. 1931, p. 3.
47. *Wisden Cricketers Almanack 1932* (London, 1932), pt.2, pp. 1–6.

48. *The Field*, 27 June 1931, p. 937.
49. Quoted in Neely et al., *Men in White*, p. 130.
50. Payne and Smith, *Cricket Almanack of New Zealand*, pp. 395–6.
51. ABCIC, Minutes, 29 and 30 Dec. 1930.
52. Neely et al., *Men in White*, pp. 174, 465.
53. V.Y. Richardson, *The Vic Richardson Story* (Melbourne, 1967), p. 1.
54. Neely et al., *Men in White*, p. 503. For a discussion of the significance of Everest in the Imperial process, see G.T. Stewart, 'Tenzing's Two Wrist-Watches: The Conquest of Everest and Late Imperial Culture in Britain 1921–53', *Past and Present*, 149 (1995).

Conclusion

There is a common characterisation of 1914 as the end of cricket's golden age – a period in which cricket enjoyed huge popularity and fully established itself as a national pastime replete with an Edwardian ethos that stressed energy and elegance above all else. However, New Zealand cricket is rather different. If a metallic analogy is required, 1914 might be characterised as the end of cricket's iron age –the end of a gradual transition from primitivism to the brink of cricketing civilisation. The golden age, if there was one, might be found during the late 1920s and early 1930s, when provincial cricket was transformed by an unprecedented supremacy of bat over ball and various New Zealand players and teams began to make a mark on the fields of England. Alternatively, one might find it as recently as the early 1980s, when New Zealand fashioned a team that could consistently hold its own with all international opposition.

Yet, if one looks at the bare biographical details of those who established and administered New Zealand cricket, the relative failure of the game presents a major contradiction. There were patrons aplenty with the right mix of English public school and Oxbridge grooming, wealth and influential connections to ensure that cricket gained an early hold in the fledgling settlements of New Zealand. At the same time, though, there were obstacles that no amount of idealism and determination could overcome.

The formative years of New Zealand cricket owed most to the influence of the principles of systematic colonisation. The society envisaged by Edward Gibbon Wakefield placed a premium on the replication of English values, class relationships and social customs. Where these were applied most successfully – particularly in Canterbury during the 1850s – cricket prospered. As well as its recreational value, cricket served to enhance social cohesion and class delineation, to assist the integration of recent arrivals to the fledgling colonial settlements and, above all else, to perpetuate devotion to England and all things English.

The strongest cricketing structure in New Zealand evolved in Canterbury, where the systematic ideal was implemented with the greatest degree of success. The Christchurch Cricket Club and its successors fashioned a socially exclusive environment that was aimed as much at the playing of cricket per se as at a conspicuous display of the status of those who played. This middle-class emphasis was to persist throughout the nineteenth century, allowing only limited opportunities for identifiably working-class clubs and players.

In Wellington and Nelson during the 1850s where the systematic ideal fell well short of expectations, in Auckland where it never existed, and in Otago where it was executed by Scottish Presbyterians hostile to English influence, there was not an elite of sufficient numbers or social standing to sustain cricket on a regular basis. Certainly, the military in Auckland and Wellington continued their empire-wide encouragement of the game, as did gold prospectors in Otago. Yet none of these centres could match the level of elite patronage directed at the activities of the first Canterbury cricket clubs. All of them struggled to secure and develop grounds or to counter the apathy that so easily discarded cricket amid the multitude of other concerns and priorities facing a new society.

The three decades after 1870 encompassed the transition from isolated and disparate cricketing traditions in the various settlements to a basic uniformity, if not unity. By the mid 1880s the main centres possessed fairly similar competition and administrative structures. Provincial cricket expanded dramatically during the 1890s and the New Zealand Cricket Council was formed in December 1894. Nonetheless, the emergence of a much larger number and variety of cricket clubs also produced clear patterns of participation based on social class.

Despite growth in class participation, New Zealand cricket remained firmly under the administrative control of local social elites. One hesitates to suggest, though, that this was a product of deliberate social exclusion. While this played some part, middle-class domination was more to do with the social and economic structure of the colony as a whole. Long working hours, the rural base of much of the semi-skilled and unskilled population, and their lack of educational opportunities all militated against a significant level of working-class participation in representative cricket. To compensate for this, all of the main centres developed mid-week, suburban and trades based competitions. Only in Otago during the early 1880s, where the politics of individual personalities undoubtedly played a part, did the divisions between middle- and working-class cricketing interests produce significant conflict. Otherwise, one can assume that most cricketers were able to find an appropriate niche within the variety of teams and competitions that existed by the end of the nineteenth century.

The consolidation of an urban, middle-class game was reinforced by a strong contribution from New Zealand's elite secondary schools. Institutions such as Christ's College and Wellington College sought, exactly in the manner of the English public schools and their colonial clones in Australia, Canada, India and the West Indies, to use cricket as a means of fostering discipline and conformity within the schools and as training for the skills necessary to life outside them. Perhaps unsurprisingly, the elite schools made a disproportionate contribution to both provincial and national teams and to the administration of New Zealand cricket.

The schools were also instrumental in shaping a strong understanding of the wider meanings of Victorian cricket within New Zealand. Unlike India and Africa, where sport was a vital component in the subtle bridging of cultural differences between British administrators and indigenous elites, the nature of New Zealand race relations, and especially the rural distribution of the Maori population, precluded a role for conventional notions of muscular Christianity. Yet there is abundant evidence to show that New Zealand observers well understood the place of cricket within developing Victorian conceptions of the symmetry between a healthy body and a healthy mind. At the same time, they were equally fervent in their condemnation of those elements – and especially women's cricket – that threatened to pervert the prevailing ideology. In short, there can be no question, despite periodic complaints about declining public support for the game, that both the form and essence of Victorian cricket were successfully transplanted to New Zealand and transmitted to native-born generations.

Yet this structure, and the idealism that accompanied it, could not surmount a series of obstacles that ultimately restricted the growth and effectiveness of New Zealand cricket. A small population base, difficult transport and communication networks, and unfavourable legislation – such as the 1881 Public Reserves Act – determined that provincial and international cricket was never economically viable. As with most English counties and clubs, the provincial cricket associations were frequently obliged to derive their income from activities totally unrelated to cricket. There were few funds available to enable long-term planning or expansion – especially of good-quality grounds. Efforts to create a regulated programme of inter-provincial first-class matches foundered on similar problems.

Faced with these impediments, the provinces were inclined to guard their interests and resources carefully. As with the conflicts between the various Australian colonies and the Australasian Cricket Council during the 1890s, necessary self-interest frequently manifested itself as vitriolic rivalry. This seriously hindered efforts to foster a sense of unity and common purpose around the NZCC and the New Zealand representative team.

In this context, there is much scope to question the conventional Victorian notion of cricket as an agent of unity both between Britain and her colonies and between individual colonies. While there was no shortage of editors and public figures willing to espouse an imperial or federal rhetoric, the selection of every New Zealand team prior to 1914 prompted many of these same critics to abandon altruism in favour of chauvinism. One may also speculate as to whether many of the sentiments ascribed to cricket held any relevance to working-class cricketers – and especially to unskilled workers who were not subjected to the elite educational ethos or other sources, such as urban newspapers, that conveyed it. Indeed, if one considers that the heart of New Zealand cricket – the four main cities – contained less than one-third of the total European population by 1911, there is no sense in which the public face of cricket can be regarded as fully representative of New Zealand society.

The consistent failure of all New Zealand teams against international opposition naturally had its own impact. While the success of Australian cricket was able to obscure many of the divisions within it and enabled it to support themes of assertive colonialism and, later, emergent nationalism, New Zealand cricket remained bound by notions of deference and tutelage that emphasised the inferiority of the colony in relation to the mother country. Yet rather than seeking to find touring teams who were of comparable ability to New Zealand players, the NZCC deliberately tried to secure the highest quality English amateur opposition – teams that embodied both the best standard and form of cricket. Indeed, the idealisation of the English game remained a strong current in New Zealand cricket well into the 1930s. At the same time, relations with Australia deteriorated – in part a reflection of the growing disparity in the playing ability of the two countries, but perhaps also a New Zealand reaction to elements of brash professionalism in Australian cricket.

New Zealand cricket should have fallen victim to climatic factors, unreliable communications and the economic reality that constantly hindered the activities of the provincial cricket associations and the NZCC. That it did not is testimony to a powerful Victorian ethos that stressed the need to maintain and develop the game irrespective of cost. This was an ethos which determined that the most distant colony of the British Empire was also the one that guarded a traditional English form of cricket most jealously. Thus, a conscious and unrelenting effort was directed at making New Zealand cricket in the image of the English game.

Bibliography

Official Sources

New Zealand Statutes, 1881, No.15; 1894, No.32; 1905, No.43.
New Zealand Census of Population and Dwellings (Wellington, 1881–1911).

Official Cricket Sources

Auckland Cricket Association, Annual Reports/Annual Meeting Minutes, 1883–1914, various sources.
Australian Board of Control for International Cricket, Committee Minutes / Reports, 1905–51, Australian Cricket Board, Melbourne.
Canterbury Cricket Association, Committee Minutes/Annual Reports, 1877–1914, Canterbury Cricket Association, Christchurch.
Christchurch Cricket Club, Committee Minutes, 1864–65, Canterbury Cricket Association, Christchurch.
Imperial Cricket Conference, Minutes, 1909–39, MCC Library, London.
Marylebone Cricket Club, Committee Minutes/Annual Reports, 1906–39, MCC Library, London.
New South Wales Cricket Association, Minutes, 1889–1895, NSWCA Library, Sydney.
New South Wales Cricket Association, 'Cricket Book 1895/6–1912/13' (press cuttings), NSWCA Library, Sydney.
New Zealand Cricket Council, General Meeting Minutes/Management Committee Minutes/Special Committee Minutes/Annual Reports, 1894–1920, New Zealand Cricket Inc., Christchurch.
Otago Cricket Association, Annual Reports/Annual Meeting Minutes, 1877–1914, Hocken Library, Dunedin.
United Canterbury Cricket Club, Committee Minutes/Annual Reports 1866–71, Canterbury Cricket Association, Christchurch.
Wellington Cricket Association, Annual Reports/Annual Meeting Minutes, 1875–1914, various sources.

Manuscripts

Fisher, A.H., 'Cricketing papers 1895–1970', Hocken Archives, Dunedin.
Griffiths, G., 'A History of Otago Cricket', unpub., held by G. Griffiths,

(Dunedin, *c*.1976).

Macdonald, G.R., Canterbury Biographical Dictionary, Canterbury Museum Library, (Christchurch).

Neale, E.R., 'Memories brighten the eye (A century of Nelson cricket and other sports)', Nelson Provincial Museum, (Nelson).

Nelson Notables File/Biographical Files, Nelson Provincial Museum, (Nelson).

Wilhelm, W., Typescript notes on South Melbourne Cricket Club tour of New Zealand 1912–13, in possession of author.

Newspapers, Magazines and Periodicals

Auckland Weekly News (Auckland)
Canterbury College Review (Christchurch)
Christ's' College Register (Christchurch)
Conway's Australian Cricketers' Annual (Melbourne, 1876–77)
Cricket (London)
Daily Telegraph (Dunedin)
Evening Post (Wellington)
Evening Star (Dunedin)
Hawke's Bay Herald (Napier)
James Lillywhite's Cricketers' Annual (London, 1878, 1888)
John Lillywhite's Cricketers' Companion (London, 1878)
Lyttelton Times (Christchurch)
Nelson Examiner (Nelson)
Nelsonian (Nelson College, Nelson)
New Zealand Colonist & Port Nicholson Advertiser
New Zealand Cricketers Annual (Auckland, 1896–98)
New Zealand Free Lance (Wellington)
New Zealand Gazette and Wellington Spectator (Wellington)
New Zealand Government Gazette (Auckland)
New Zealand Herald (Auckland)
New Zealand Journal (Wellington)
New Zealand Mail (Wellington)
New Zealand Referee (Christchurch)
New Zealand Spectator and Cook Straits Guardian (Wellington)
New Zealand Times (Wellington)
New Zealander (Auckland)
Otago Daily Times (Dunedin)
Otago High School Magazine (Dunedin)
Otago Witness (Dunedin)
Southern Cross (Auckland)
Southland Times (Invercargill)
Spectator (Wellington)
Sydney Mail (Sydney)
Sydney Morning Herald (Sydney)
Taranaki Herald (New Plymouth)
The Australasian (Melbourne)

The Colonist (Dunedin)
The Colonist (Nelson)
The Cricketer (London)
The Field (London)
The Leader (Melbourne)
The Press (Christchurch)
The Referee (Sydney)
The Star (Christchurch)
Weekly Press and N.Z. Referee (Christchurch)
Wellington Independent (Wellington)
Wellingtonian (Wellington College, Wellington)
Wisden Cricketers Almanack (London, various)

Books

100 Not Out: A Centennial History of the Auckland Cricket Association (Auckland, 1983).
50 Years of Cricket, 1921–71: A History of the Wellington Mercantile Cricket League (Inc.) (Wellington, 1971).
Abbott, G. (ed.), *Wanganui Girls College, 1891–1991*, (Wanganui, 1991).
Acland, L.G.D., *The Early Canterbury Runs*, 4th ed., (Christchurch, 1975).
Adams, P., *Fatal Necessity: British Intervention in New Zealand, 1830–47* (Auckland, 1977).
Adelman, M.L., *A Sporting Time: New York City and the Rise of Modern Athletics, 1820–70* (Urbana, 1986).
Albion Cricket Club Jubilee Souvenir Programme (Dunedin, 1912).
Allan, R., *Nelson: A History of Early Settlement* (Wellington, 1965).
Andersen, J.C., *The Jubilee History of South Canterbury* (Auckland, 1916).
Arnold, R., *The Farthest Promised Land: English Villagers, New Zealand Immigrants of the 1870s* (Wellington, 1981).
Auckland Cricketers Trip to the South: A Complete History of the Late Successful Tour ... 1873–4 (Auckland, 1874).
Bagnall, A.G., *Wairarapa: An Historical Excursion* (Masterton, 1976).
Bannerman, J.W.H., *Early Cricket in Southland* (Invercargill, 1908).
Banockburn Cricket Union 1895–1995 (Bannockburn, 1995).
Beattie, J.H., *Traditional Lifeways of the Southern Maori*, edited by A. Anderson (Dunedin, 1994).
Beckles, H.McD. and Stoddart, B., (eds), *Liberation Cricket: West Indies Cricket Culture* (Manchester, 1995).
Belich, J., *The New Zealand Wars and the Victorian Interpretation of Racial Conflict* (Auckland, 1986).
Belich, J., *Making Peoples: A History of the New Zealanders from Polynesian Settlement to the end of the Nineteenth Century* (Auckland, 1996).
Belich, J., *Paradise Reforged: A History of the New Zealanders from the 1880s to the Year 2000* (Auckland, 2001).
Blainey, G., *A Game of Our Own: The Origins of Australian Football* (Melbourne, 1990).

Bohan, E., *Edward Stafford: New Zealand's First Statesman* (Christchurch, 1994).

Bose, M., *A History of Indian Cricket* (London, 1990).

Bowden, R., *Green Fields of Yesteryear* (Timaru, 1993).

Boyd, M., *City of the Plains: A History of Hastings* (Wellington, 1984).

Brittenden, R.T., *100 Years of Cricket: The History of the Canterbury Cricket Association* (Christchurch, 1977).

Broad, L., *Jubilee History of Nelson* (Nelson, 1892).

Brookes, B., Macdonald, C. and Tennant, M. (eds), *Women in History: Essays on European Women in New Zealand* (Wellington, 1986).

Burnett, A. and Burnett, R., *The Australia and New Zealand Nexus* (Canberra, 1978).

Burns, P., *Fatal Success: A History of the New Zealand Company* (Wellington, 1989).

Bush, G.W.A., *Decently and in Order: The Government of the City of Auckland 1840–1971* (Auckland, 1971).

Butchers, A.G., *Education in New Zealand* (Dunedin, 1930).

Butterworth, S., *Petone: A History* (Auckland, 1988).

Caffyn, W., *Seventy One Not Out* (London, 1899).

Campbell, A.E., *Educating New Zealand* (Wellington, 1941).

Campbell, M.D.N., *Story of Napier 1874–1974* (Napier, 1974).

Cane, F.F., *Cricket Centenary: The Story of Cricket in Hawke's Bay 1855–1955* (Napier, 1955).

Carman, A.H., *The Birth of a City: Wellington 1840–1843* (Wellington, 1970).

Carman, A.H., *Wellington Cricket Centenary 1875–1975* (Wellington, 1975).

Cashman, R., *Patrons, Players and the Crowd: The Phenomenon of Indian Cricket* (New Delhi, 1980).

Cashman, R., *'Ave a Go Yer Mug! Australian Cricket Crowds from Larrikin to Ocker* (Sydney, 1984).

Cashman, R., *Australian Cricket Crowds: The Attendance Cycle – Daily Figures, 1877–1984* (Sydney, c.1984).

Cashman, R., *The 'Demon' Spofforth* (Kensington, NSW, 1990).

Cashman, R., *Paradise of Sport: The Rise of Organised Sport in Australia* (Melbourne, 1995).

Cashman, R. (ed.), *Sport, Federation, Nation* (Sydney, 2001).

Cashman, R. and McKernan, M. (eds), *Sport in History: The Making of Modern Sporting History*, (St Lucia, 1979).

Cashman, R. and Weaver, A., *Wicket Women: Cricket and Women in Australia* (Sydney, 1991).

Cashman, R., Jobling, I.F., Moore, K. and O'Hara, J. (eds), *The Oxford Companion to Australian Sport* (Melbourne, 1992).

Chester, R.H. and McMillan, N.A.C., *The Encyclopedia of New Zealand Rugby* (Auckland, 1981).

Chester, R.H. and McMillan, N.A.C., *The Visitors: The History of International Rugby Teams in New Zealand* (Auckland, 1990).

Collins, C. (ed.), *Sport in New Zealand Society* (Palmerston North, 2000).

Coney, S., *Standing in the Sunshine: A History of New Zealand Women since they won the Vote* (Auckland, 1993).

Cooke, R. (ed.), *Portrait of a Profession: The Centennial Book of the New Zealand Law Society* (Wellington, 1969).

Costello, J. and Finnegan, P., *Tapestry of Turf: The History of New Zealand Racing 1840–1987* (Auckland, 1988).

Cotter, G., *England versus New Zealand: A History of the Tests and Other Matches* (Marlborough, Wilts., 1990).

Crotty, M., *Making the Australian Male: Middle-Class Masculinity 1870–1920* (Melbourne, 2001).

Croudy, B., *A Guide to First Class Matches Played in New Zealand 1863 to 1980* (London, 1981).

Cummings, I. and Cummings, A., *History of State Education in New Zealand: 1840–1975* (Wellington, 1978).

Cunningham, H., *Leisure in the Industrial Revolution* (London, 1980).

Daly, J.A., *Elysian Fields: Sport, Class and Community in Colonial South Australia, 1836–90* (Adelaide, 1982).

Dalziel, R., *Julius Vogel: Business Politician* (Auckland, 1986).

Darwin Keynes, R. (ed.), *Charles Darwin's Beagle Diary* (Cambridge, 1988).

Daunton, M.J., *Progress and Poverty: An Economic and Social History of Britain 1700–1850* (Oxford, 1995).

Derriman, P., *True to the Blue: A History of the New South Wales Cricket Association* (Sydney, 1985).

Dunning, E. and Sheard, K., *Barbarians: Gentlemen and Players: A Sociological Study of the Development of Rugby Football* (Canberra, 1979).

Eldred-Grigg, S., *A Southern Gentry* (Wellington, 1980).

Elenio, P., *Centrecourt: A Century of New Zealand Tennis* (Wellington, 1986).

Elliott, Sir J., *Firth of Wellington* (Wellington, 1937).

Else, A. (ed.), *Women Together: A History of Women's Organisations in New Zealand* (Wellington, 1993).

Elworthy, S., *Ritual Song of Defiance: A Social History of Students at the University of Otago* (Dunedin, 1990).

Fairburn, M., *The Ideal Society and its Enemies: The Foundations of Modern New Zealand Society, 1850–1900* (Auckland, 1989).

Fletcher, S., *Women First: The Female Tradition in English Physical Education, 1880–1980* (London, 1984).

Forster, C., *Australian Cities: Continuity and Change* (Melbourne, 1995).

Fraser, M., *New Zealand Parliamentary Record* (Wellington, 1913).

Friends of the Turnbull Library, *Edward Gibbon Wakefield and the Colonial Dream: A Reconsideration* (Wellington, 1997).

Galbraith, R., *Working for Wildlife: A History of the New Zealand Wildlife Service* (Wellington, 1993).

Gallaway, I.W., *Carisbrook Cricket Club Centennial History 1875–1975* (Dunedin, 1975).

Gardner, W.J., *The Amuri: A County History* (Culverden, 1956).

Gardner, W.J., *Colonial Cap and Gown: Studies in the mid-Victorian Universities of Australasia* (Christchurch, 1979).

Gardner, W.J. (ed.), *A History of Canterbury: Vol. 2 General History, 1854–76 and Cultural Aspects, 1850–1950* (Christchurch, 1971).

Gardner, W.J., Beardsley, E.T. and Carter, T.E., *A History of the University of Canterbury 1873–1973* (Christchurch, 1973).

Gillespie, O.A., *South Canterbury: A Record of Settlement* (Timaru, 1958).

Goldstein, W., *Playing for Keeps: A History of Early Baseball* (Ithaca, 1989).

Grace, R., *Warwick Armstrong* (Melbourne, 1975).

Grange Cricket Club 75th Anniversary (Dunedin, 1954).

Grant, D., *On a Roll: A History of Gambling and Lotteries in New Zealand* (Wellington, 1994).

Green, B. (comp.), *The Wisden Book of Obituaries* (London, 1986).

Grey, A.H., *Aotearoa and New Zealand: A Historical Geography* (Christchurch, 1994).

Griffiths, G., *The Mace's of Macetown, notes on some early arrivals in Otago, No.2* (Dunedin, 1969).

Griffiths, G., *King Wakatip* (Dunedin, 1971).

Griffiths, G., *W.G. Rees and his Cricketing Cousins, notes on some early arrivals in Otago, No.3* (Dunedin, 1971).

Griffiths, G., *Sale, Bradshaw, Wills, Manning and the 'Little Enemy', notes on some early arrivals in Otago, No.4* (Dunedin, 1971).

Griffiths, G., *Otago University at Cricket: Its History, Records and Statistics* (Dunedin, 1978).

Griffiths, P., (ed.), *Complete First-Class Match List Volume 1 1801–1914* (London, 1996).

Guttmann, A., *From Ritual to Record: The Nature of Modern Sports* (New York, 1978).

Guttmann, A., *A Whole New Ballgame: An Interpretation of American Sport* (Chapel Hill, 1988).

Guttmann, A., *Games and Empires: Modern Sports and Cultural Imperialism* (New York, 1994).

Haley, B.E., *The Healthy Body and Victorian Culture* (Harvard, 1978).

Hamer, D. and Nicholls, R. (eds), *The Making of Wellington 1800–1914* (Wellington, 1990).

Hamilton, D.G., *College!: A History of Christ's College* (Christchurch, 1996).

Harte, C., *A History of Australian Cricket* (London, 1993).

Hawkins, D.N., *Rangiora: The Passing Years and People in a Canterbury Country Town* (Christchurch, 1983).

Heron, H.A., *The Centennial History of Wellington College* (Wellington, 1967).

Hickie, T.V., *They Ran with the Ball: How Rugby Football Began in Australia* (Sydney, 1993).

Hight, J. and Straubel, C.R. (gen. eds), *A History of Canterbury: Vol.1 to 1854* (Christchurch, 1957).

Hignell, A., *Rain Stops Play: Cricketing Climates* (London, 2002).

Hinchcliffe, J. (ed.), *The Nature and Meaning of Sport in New Zealand* (Auckland, 1978).

Hobsbawm, E. and Ranger, T.O., *The Invention of Tradition* (Cambridge, 1983).

Holm, J., *Nothing but Grass and Wind: The Rutherfords of Canterbury* (Christchurch, 1992).

Holt, R., *Sport and the British: A Modern History* (Oxford, 1990).

Honey, J.R.deS., *Tom Brown's Universe* (London, 1977).

Hyland, T., *The Golden Jubilee of Domain Cricket* (Auckland, 1964).

Irvine-Smith, F.L., *The Streets of My City* (Wellington, 1948).

James, C.L.R., *Beyond a Boundary* (London, 1963).

Jones, S., *Sport, Politics and the Working Class: Labour and Sport in Inter-War Britain* (Manchester, 1988).

Joy, N., *Maiden Over: A Short History of Women's Cricket* (London, 1950).

Kirsch, G.B., *The Creation of American Team Sports: Baseball & Cricket, 1838–72* (Urbana, 1989).

Kynaston, D., *Archie's Last Stand: MCC in New Zealand 1922–23* (London, 1984).

Lash, M.D. (ed.), *Nelson Notables 1840–1940* (Nelson, 1992).

Laver, F., *An Australian Cricketer on Tour* (London, 1905).

Leckie, F.M., *The Early History of Wellington College* (Wellington, 1934).

Lemmon, D., *The Crisis of Captaincy: Servant and Master in English Cricket* (London, 1988).

Macdonald, C., Penfold, M. and Williams, B. (eds), *The Book of New Zealand Women* (Wellington, 1991).

Macdonald, K.C., *History of Waitaki Boys High School, 1883–1933* (Wellington, 1934).

Macdonald, K.C., *History of North Otago* (Oamaru, 1940).

Macdonald, K.C., *White Stone Country* (Oamaru, 1962).

Macdonald, K.C., *City of Dunedin: A Century of Civic Enterprise* (Dunedin, 1965).

MacKenzie, J.M., *Propaganda and Empire* (Manchester, 1985).

MacKenzie, J.M. (ed.), *Imperialism and Popular Culture* (Manchester, 1986).

Mandle, W.F., *Going it Alone: Australia's National Identity in the Twentieth Century* (Ringwood, Vic., 1978).

Mangan, J.A., *The Games Ethic and Imperialism* (London, 1986).

Mangan, J.A., *Athleticism in the Victorian and Edwardian Public School: The Emergence and Consolidation of an Educational Ideology* rev. ed. (London, 2000).

Mangan, J.A. (ed.), *Pleasure, Profit and Proselytism: British Culture and Sport, at Home and Abroad, 1750–1914* (London, 1988).

Mangan, J.A. (ed.), *The Cultural Bond: Sport, Empire, Society* (London, 1992).

Mangan, J.A. and Park, R.J. (eds), *From 'Fair Sex' to Feminism: Sport and the Socialization of Women in the Industrial and Post-Industrial Eras* (London, 1987).

Mangan, J.A. and Walvin, J. (eds), *Manliness and Morality: Middle Class Masculinity in Britain and America 1800–1940* (Manchester, 1987).

Manley, M., *A History of West Indies Cricket* (London, 1988).

Mann, S. (ed.), *Sydenham: The Model Borough of old Christchurch* (Christchurch, 1977).

Martin, J.E., *The Forgotten Worker: The Rural Wage Earner in Nineteenth Century New Zealand* (Wellington, 1990).

May, P.R., *With the MCC in New Zealand* (London, 1907).

May, P.R., *The West Coast Gold Rushes* (Christchurch, 1965).

McAloon, J., *Nelson: A Regional History* (Nelson, 1997).

McAloon, J., *No Idle Rich: The Wealthy in Canterbury and Otago 1840–1914* (Dunedin, 2002).

McConnell, L., *100 Summers at the Rec: The Centennial History of the Mataura Cricket Club* (Invercargill, 1984).

McConnell, L. and Smith, I., *The Shell New Zealand Cricket Encyclopedia* (Auckland, 1993).

McCrone, K.E., *Sport and the Physical Emancipation of English Women 1870–1914* (London, 1988).

McDowall, R.M., *Gamekeepers of the Nation: The Story of New Zealand's Acclimatisation Societies 1861–1990* (Christchurch, 1994).

McIntosh, P., *Sport and Society* (London, 1963).

McIntyre, W.D. (ed.), *The Journal of Henry Sewell 1853–7, Volume 1* (Christchurch, 1980).

McKay, J.K. and Allan, H.F. (eds), *The Nelson College Old Boys Register* (Nelson, 1956).

McLintock, A.H., *An Encyclopedia of New Zealand* (Wellington, 1966).

Melville, T., *The Tented Field: A History of Cricket in America* (Bowling Green, 1998).

Millar, D.P., *Once Upon a Village: A History of Lower Hutt 1819–1965* (Wellington, 1972).

Milner, I., *Milner of Waitaki: Portrait of The Man* (Dunedin, 1983).

Milner, I., *Intersecting Lines: The Memoirs of Ian Milner* (Wellington, 1993).

Mitchell, A., *84 Not Out: The Story of Sir Arthur Sims, KT* (London, 1962).

Montefiore, D., *Cricket in the Doldrums: the Struggle between Private and Public Control in Australian Cricket in the 1880s* (Sydney, 1992).

Morrison, J.P., *The Evolution of A City* (Christchurch, 1948).

Mulgan, A., *The City of the Strait: A Centennial History* (Wellington, 1939).

Nauright, J. and Chandler, T.J.L. (eds), *Making Men: Rugby and Masculine Identity* (London, 1996)

Neely, D.O., *100 Summers: The History of Wellington Cricket* (Wellington, 1975).

Neely, D.O., King, R.P. and Payne, F.K., *Men in White: The History of New Zealand International Cricket 1894–1985* (Auckland, 1985).

Neely, D.O. and Neely, P., *The Summer Game: The Illustrated History of New Zealand Cricket* (Auckland, 1994).

Newsome, D., *Godliness and Good Learning* (London, 1961).

Oamaru Cricket Club Centennial History 1864–1964 (Oamaru, 1964).

Ogilvie, G.B., *The Port Hills of Christchurch* (Wellington, 1978).

Ogilvie, K., *100 Years of Cricket in Temuka* (Temuka, 1984).

O'Hagan, S., *Pride of Southern Rebels: History of Otago Rugby* (Dunedin, 1981).

Oliver, W.H., (gen. ed.), *The Dictionary of New Zealand Biography: Vol.1 1769–1869* (Wellington, 1990).

Olssen, E., *A History of Otago* (Dunedin, 1984).

Olssen, E., *The Red Feds: Revolutionary Industrial Unionism and the New Zealand Federation of Labour 1908–1913* (Auckland, 1988).

Olssen, E., *Building the New World: Work, Politics and Society in Caversham 1880s–1920s* (Auckland, 1995).

Orange, C., *The Treaty of Waitangi* (Auckland, 1987).

Orange, C. (gen. ed.), *The Dictionary of New Zealand Biography: Vol.2 1870–1900* (Wellington, 1993).

Orange, C. (gen. ed.), *The Dictionary of New Zealand Biography: Vol.3 1900–1920* (Wellington, 1996).

Otago Cricket Association, *Otago Cricket Association Diamond Jubilee Celebrations: 1876–1936* (Dunedin, 1936).

Otago Cricket Association, *Centennial Souvenir Programme 1876–1976* (Dunedin, 1976).

Outhwaite, W., *The Ladies Guide to Cricket, by a Lover of Both, with a Glossary of Technical Terms and Cricket Slang and the Laws of Cricket* (Auckland, 1883).

Parnell Cricket Club: 75th Jubilee, 1884–85 – 1958–59 (Auckland, 1959).

Payne, F. and Smith, I. (eds), *The 1997 Shell Cricket Almanack of New Zealand* (Auckland, 1997).

Peake, J.F., *Statistics of New Zealand Cricket and Roll of Honour* (Christchurch, 1924).

Pearce, T.D. and Fulton, R.V., *Otago High School Old Boys Register* (Dunedin, 1907).

Peddie, B., *Christchurch Girls' High School, 1877–1977* (Christchurch, 1977).

Phillips, J.O.C., *A Man's Country? The Image of the Pakeha Male – A History* (Auckland, 1987).

Pinney, R., *The Early South Canterbury Runs* (Wellington, 1971).

Pinney, R., *The Early North Otago Runs* (Auckland, 1981).

Pitt, D. (ed.), *Social Class in New Zealand* (Auckland, 1977).

Plumptre, G., *The Golden Age of Cricket* (London, 1990).

Pointon, M.S. and Ogilvie, J.E., *From Paddock to Pavilion: A History of the First 100 Years of the Petone Cricket Club 1889/90 to 1989/90* (Wellington, 1990).

Pollard, J., *The Formative Years of Australian Cricket* (North Ryde, NSW, 1987).

Pollard, J. (ed.) *Six and Out*, enlarged ed. (Sydney, 1980).

Porter, B., *The Lion's Share: A Short History of British Imperialism 1850–1983* (New York, 1984).

Porter, F., *Born to New Zealand: A Biography of Jane Maria Atkinson* (Wellington, 1989).

Price, R., *An Imperial War and the British Working Class* (London, 1972).

Pugsley, C., *On the Fringes of Hell: New Zealanders and Military Discipline in the First World War* (Auckland, 1991).

Pullin, A.W., *Alfred Shaw: Cricketer: His Career and Reminiscences* (London, 1902).

Raphael, F.C. (comp.), *New Zealand Cricket Council 1895–1906: Roll of Honour* (Christchurch, 1906).

Reese, D., *Was it All Cricket* (London, 1948).

Reese, T.W., *New Zealand Cricket: 1841–1914* (Christchurch, 1927).

Reese, T.W., *New Zealand Cricket: 1914–33* (Christchurch, 1936).

Reese, T.W., *History of Lancaster Park* (Christchurch, *c*.1935).

Reynolds, P.E., *The Australian Cricketers' Tour Through Australia, New Zealand and Great Britain* (Cambridge, [1878] 1980).

Rice, G.W. (ed.), *The Oxford History of New Zealand*, 2nd ed. (Auckland, 1992).

Richards, E. (ed.), *The Flinders History of South Australia* (Adelaide, 1986).

Richardson, V.Y., *The Vic Richardson Story* (Melbourne, 1967).

Rogers, L.M. (ed.), *The Early Journals of Henry Williams* (Christchurch, 1961).

Roth, H., *George Hogben: A Biography* (Wellington, 1952).

Rules and Regulations of the Dunedin Cricket Club 1863–64 and 1864–65 (Dunedin, 1863/64).

Ryan, G.J., *Forerunners of the All Blacks: The 1888–89 New Zealand Native Football Team in Britain, Australia and New Zealand* (Christchurch, 1993).

Salmon, J.H.M., *A History of Gold Mining in New Zealand* (Wellington, 1963).

Salmond, A., *Two Worlds: First Meetings Between Maori and Europeans 1642–1772* (Auckland, 1991).

Salmond, A., *Between Worlds: Early Exchanges Between Maori and Europeans 1773–1815* (Auckland, 1997).

Sandiford, K.A.P., *Cricket and the Victorians* (Aldershot, 1994).

Sangster, A., *Pathway to Establishment: the History of Wanganui Collegiate School* (Wanganui, 1985).

Scholefield, G. (ed.), *Dictionary of New Zealand Biography: Vols 1 and 2* (Wellington, 1940).

Scholefield, G. (ed.), *The Richmond-Atkinson Papers, Vol.1* (Wellington, 1960).

Scotter, W.H., *A History of Canterbury: Vol.3 1876–1950* (Christchurch, 1965).

Seventy Five Years of Cricket: A History of the Wairarapa Cricket Association (Inc) 1894–1969 (Masterton, 1969).

Sinclair, K., *A Destiny Apart: New Zealand's Search for National Identity* (Auckland, 1986).

Sinclair, K., *A History of New Zealand* (Auckland, 1991).

Sinclair, K. (ed.), *Tasman Relations: New Zealand and Australia, 1788–1988* (Auckland, 1987).

Sissons, R. and Stoddart, B., *Cricket and Empire: The 1932–33 Bodyline Tour of Australia* (London, 1984).

Skelton, W.E., *Not Out … 75: The Official History of the Christchurch Suburban Cricket Association* (Christchurch, 1980).

Stannage, C.T. (ed.), *A New History of Western Australia* (Perth, 1981).

Stoddart, B., *Saturday Afternoon Fever: Sport in the Australian Culture* (North Ryde, NSW, 1986).

Stone, R.C.J., *Makers of Fortune: A Colonial Business Community and its Fall* (Auckland, 1973).

Stribling, J., *100 Years: Karori Cricket Club 1880–1980* (Wellington, 1980).

Studholme, E.C., *Te Waimate: Early Station Life in New Zealand* (Wellington, 1949).

Sutton-Smith, B., *A History of Children's Play: New Zealand 1840–1950* (Wellington, 1982).

Swan, A.C., *History of New Zealand Rugby Football: Volume 1 1870–1945* (Auckland, 1992).

Swanton, E.W. (ed.), *Barclays World of Cricket* (London, 1986).

Taylor, N.M. (ed.), *The Journal of Ensign Best: 1837–43* (Wellington, 1966).

The Cyclopedia of New Zealand: Industrial, Descriptive, Historical,

Biographical, Vols 1–6 (Wellington and Christchurch, 1897–1905).

The New Zealand Directory for 1866–67 (Wellington, 1867).

The School List of Christ's College from 1850 to 1935 (Christchurch, 1935).

'The Twelve', *Pavilion Echoes from the South, 1884–5* (Auckland, 1885).

Thompson, E.P., *Customs in Common* (Harmondsworth, 1991).

Thorns, D. and Sedgwick, C., *Understanding Aotearoa / New Zealand: Historical Statistics* (Palmerston North, 1997).

Tothill, T.W.C., *Canterbury Boys Cricket Association Golden Jubilee 1918–1968* (Christchurch, 1968).

Trainor, L., *British Imperialism and Australian Nationalism* (Melbourne, 1994).

Trembath, K.A., *Ad Augusta: a Centennial History of Auckland Grammar School, 1869–1969* (Auckland, 1969).

Tullett, J.S., *The Industrious Heart: A History of New Plymouth* (New Plymouth, 1981).

Twopeny, R.E.N., *Pictorial New Zealand* (London, 1895).

Tyro, K. and Scarlett, K., *Te Aute College 125th Anniversary 1854–1979* (Pukehou, 1979).

Underdown, D., *Start of Play: Cricket and Culture in Eighteenth-Century England* (Oxford, 2000).

Vamplew, W. and Stoddart, B. (eds), *Sport in Australia* (Melbourne, 1994).

Vance, N., *The Sinews of the Spirit: The Ideal of Christian Manliness in Victorian Literature and Religious Thought* (Cambridge, 1985).

Walker, R.J., *Ka Whawhai Tonu Matou: Struggle Without End* (Auckland, 1990).

Ward, A., *A Show of Justice: Racial 'Amalgamation' in Nineteenth Century New Zealand*, rev. ed. (Auckland, 1995).

Ward, R., *A Nation for a Continent: The History of Australia 1901–1975* (Richmond, Vic., 1977).

Warner, P.F., *Cricket Across the Seas* (London, 1903).

Warner, P.F., *My Cricketing Life* (London, 1920).

Waters, R.F. (ed.), *Land and Society in New Zealand: Essays in Historical Geography* (Wellington, 1965).

Webster, R. (comp.), *First-Class Cricket in Australia: Vol. 1 1850/51–1941/42* (Melbourne, 1991).

West, G.D., *The Elevens of England* (London, 1988).

Whimpress, B., *Passport to Nowhere: Aborigines in Australian Cricket 1850–1939* (Sydney, 1999).

Williams, J., *Cricket and England: A Cultural and Social History of the Inter-War Years* (London, 1999).

Wises NZPO Directory (Wellington, 1872–1910).

Wynne-Thomas, P., *Give me Arthur: A Biography of Arthur Shrewsbury* (London, 1985).

Articles

Armstrong, R.W., 'Auckland by Gaslight: An Urban Geography of 1896', *New Zealand Geographer*, 15, 2 (1959).

Bale, J., 'Sport and National Identity: A Geographical View', *British Journal of Sports History*, 3, 4 (1986).

Arnold, R., 'Some Australasian Aspects of New Zealand Life 1890–1913', *New Zealand Journal of History*, 4, 1 (1970).

Arnold, R., 'English Rural Unionism and Taranaki Immigration 1871–76', *New Zealand Journal of History*, 6, 1 (1972).

Binney, J., 'Christianity and the Maoris to 1840, a comment', *New Zealand Journal of History*, 3, 2 (1969).

Bradley, J., 'The MCC, Society and Empire: A Portrait of Cricket's Ruling Body 1860–1914', *International Journal of the History of Sport*, 7, 1 (1990).

Brown, D.W., 'Muscular Christianity in the Antipodes: Some Observations on the Diffusion and Emergence of a Victorian Ideal in Australian Social Theory', *Sporting Traditions*, 3, 2 (1987).

Campbell, J.D., '"Training for Sport is Training for War": Sport and the Transformation of the British Army, 1860–1914', *International Journal of the History of Sport*, 17, 4 (2000).

Cashman, R., 'Symbols of Unity: Anglo-Australian Cricketers, 1877–1900', *International Journal of the History of Sport*, 7, 1 (1990).

Chandler, T.J.L., 'Games at Oxbridge and the Public Schools, 1830–80: The Diffusion of an Innovation', *International Journal of the History of Sport*, 8, 2 (1991).

Clark, W.A.V., 'Dunedin at the Turn of The Century', *New Zealand Geographer*, 18, 2 (1962).

Connolly, C.N., 'Class, Birthplace, Loyalty: Australian Attitudes to the Bar War', *Historical Studies*, 18, 71 (1978).

Crawford, S.A.G.M., '"Muscles and Character, are there the first Objects of Necessity": an Overview of Sport and Recreation in a Colonial Setting – Otago Province, New Zealand', *British Journal of Sports History*, 2, 2 (1985).

Curson, P.H., 'Auckland in 1842', *New Zealand Geographer*, No.30 (1974).

Dewey, C., '"Socratic Teachers": Part 1 – The Opposition to the Cult of Athletics at Eton 1870–1914', *International Journal of the History of Sport*, 12, 1 (1995).

Fairburn, M., 'Social Mobility and Opportunity in Nineteenth-Century New Zealand', *New Zealand Journal of History*, 13, 1 (1979).

Gardner, W.J., 'The Foundation of Nelson and Canterbury: A Comparative Study', *Historical News*, 48 (1984).

Garrard, C.W., 'The School Playground – its Value', *New Zealand Schoolmaster* (Oct./Nov. 1902).

Harvey, R., 'Economic Aspects of Nineteenth-Century New Zealand Newspapers', *Bibliographical Society of Australia and New Zealand Bulletin*, 17, 2 (1993).

Hill, J., '"First-Class" Cricket and the Leagues: Some Notes on the Development of English Cricket, 1900–40', *International Journal of the History of Sport*, 4, 1 (1987).

Jackson, H., 'Churchgoing in Nineteenth Century New Zealand', *New Zealand Journal of History*, 17, 1 (1983).

Katz, M.B., 'Occupational Classification in History', *Journal of Interdisciplinary History*, No.3 (1972).

Kirk-Green, A., 'Badge of Office? Sport and his Excellency in the British Empire', *International Journal of the History of Sport*, 6, 7 (1989).

Lansbury, C., 'A Straight Bat and a Modest Mind', *Victorian Newsletter*, 49 (1976).

Maguire, J., 'Images of Manliness and Competing Ways of Living in late Victorian and Edwardian Britain', *British Journal of Sports History*, 3, 3 (1986).

Malone, E.P., 'The New Zealand School Journal and the Imperial Ideology', *New Zealand Journal of History*, 7, 1 (1973).

Mandle, W.F., 'The Professional Cricketer in England in the Nineteenth Century', *Labour History*, No.23 (1972).

Mandle, W.F., 'Games People Played: Cricket and Football in England and Victoria in the Late Nineteenth Century', *Historical Studies*, 15, 60 (1973).

Mandle, W.F., 'Cricket and Australian Nationalism in the Nineteenth Century', *Journal of the Royal Australian Historical Society*, 59, Pt.4 (1973).

Mandle, W.F., 'W.G. Grace as a Victorian Hero', *Historical Studies*, 19, 76 (1981).

Mangan, J.A., 'Eton in India: The Imperial Diffusion of a Victorian Educational Ethic', *History of Education*, 7, 2 (1978).

Mangan, J.A., 'Grammar Schools and the Games Ethic in the Victorian and Edwardian Eras', *Albion*, 15, 2 (1983).

Mangan, J.A., 'Christ and the Imperial Games Fields: Evangelical Athletes of the Empire', *British Journal of Sports History*, 1, 2 (1984).

Mangan, J.A. and Hickey, C., 'A Pioneer of the Proletariat: Herbert Milnes and the Games Cult in New Zealand', *International Journal of the History of Sport*, 17, 2/3 (2000).

McAloon, J., 'The Colonial Wealthy in Canterbury and Otago: No Idle Rich', *New Zealand Journal of History*, 30, 1 (1996).

McCulloch, G., 'Imperial and Colonial Designs: The Case of Auckland Grammar School', *History of Education*, 17, 4 (1988).

Moore, K., 'A Neglected Imperialist: The Promotion of the British Empire in the Writings of John Astley Cooper', *International Journal of the History of Sport*, 8, 2 (1991).

Nauright, J., 'Sport, Manhood and Empire: British Responses to the New Zealand Rugby Tour of 1905', *International Journal of the History of Sport*, 8, 2 (1991).

Nauright, J. and Broomhall, J., 'A Woman's Game: The Development of Netball and a Female Sporting Culture in New Zealand 1906–70', *International Journal of the History of Sport*, 11, 3 (1994).

Nobbs, K.J., 'History of the First Recorded Cricket Match in New Zealand', unknown source, Te Kauwhata, 1990.

Olssen, E., 'Mr Wakefield and New Zealand as an Experiment in Post-Enlightenment Experimental Practice', *New Zealand Journal of History*, 31, 2 (1997).

Owens, J.M.R., 'Christianity and the Maoris to 1840', *New Zealand Journal of History*, 2, 1 (1968).

Pawson, E. and Quigley, N.C., 'The Circulation of Information and Frontier Development: Canterbury 1850–90', *New Zealand Geographer*, 38, 2 (1982).

Perkin, H., 'Teaching the Nations how to Play: Sport and Society in the British Empire and Commonwealth', *International Journal of the History of Sport*, 6, 7 (1989).

Phillips, J.O.C., 'Rugby, War and the Mythology of the New Zealand Male', *New Zealand Journal of History*, 18, 2 (1984).

Richardson, L., 'Rugby, Race and Empire: The 1905 All Black Tour', *Historical News*, 47 (1983).

Richardson, L., 'The Invention of a National Game: The Struggle for Control', *History Now,* 1, 1 (1995).

Rosselli, J., 'The Self-Image of Effeteness: Physical Education and Nationalism in Nineteenth Century Bengal', *Past and Present,* 86 (1980).

Rubenstein, D., 'Sport and the Sociologist 1890–1914', *British Journal of Sports History*, 1, 1 (1984).

Ryan, G.J., 'Extravagance of Thought and Feeling: New Zealand Reactions to the 1932–33 Bodyline Controversy', *Sporting Traditions*, 13, 2 (1997).

Ryan, G.J., '"A Lack of Esprit de Corps": The 1908–09 Wallabies and the Legacy of the 1905 All Blacks', *Sporting Traditions*, 17, 1 (2000).

Ryan, G.J., 'Rural Myth and Urban Actuality: The Anatomy of All Black and New Zealand Rugby 1884–1938', *New Zealand Journal of History*, 35, 1 (2001).

Sandiford, K.A.P., 'The Victorians at Play: Problems in Historiographical Methodology', *Journal of Social History,* 15, 2 (1981).

Sandiford, K.A.P., 'English Cricket Crowds During the Victorian Age', *Journal of Sport History*, 9, 3 (1982).

Sandiford, K.A.P., 'Cricket and the Victorian Society', *Journal of Social History*, 17, 2 (1983).

Sandiford, K.A.P., 'Victorian Cricket Techniques and Industrial Technology', *British Journal of Sports History*, 1, 3 (1985).

Sandiford, K.A.P., 'The Professionalization of Modern Cricket', *British Journal of Sports History,* 2, 3 (1985).

Sandiford, K.A.P., 'Cricket and the Barbadian Society', *Canadian Journal of History*, 21, 3 (1986).

Sandiford, K.A.P. and Stoddart, B., 'The Elite Schools and Cricket in Barbados: a Study in Colonial Continuity', *International Journal of the History of Sport*, 4, 3 (1987).

Sandiford, K.A.P. and Vamplew, W., 'The Peculiar Economics of English Cricket Before 1914', *British Journal of Sports History*, 3, 3 (1986).

Scott, P., 'Cricket and the Religious World in the Victorian Period', *Church Quarterly*, 3 (1970).

Stewart, G.T., 'Tenzing's Two Wrist-Watches: The Conquest of Everest and Late Imperial Culture in Britain 1921–53', *Past and Present*, 149 (1995).

Stoddart, B., 'Sport, Cultural Imperialism and Colonial Responses in the British Empire', *Comparative Studies in Society and History*, 30, 4 (1988).

Thompson, E.P., 'Time, Work-Discipline and Industrial Capitalism', *Past and Present*, 38 (1967).

Toynbee, C., 'Class and Social Structure in Nineteenth Century New Zealand', *New Zealand Journal of History*, 13, 1 (1979).

Vamplew, W., 'Sports Crowd Disorder in Britain, 1870–1914: Causes and Controls', *Journal of Sport History*, 7, 1 (1980).

Vincent, G.T., '"A Tendency to Roughness": Anti-Heroic Representations of New Zealand Rugby 1890–1914', *Sporting Traditions*, 14, 1 (1997).

Vincent, G.T., 'Practical Imperialism: The Anglo-Welsh Rugby Tour of New Zealand, 1908', *International Journal of the History of Sport*, 15, 1 (1998).

Vincent, G.T. and Harfield, T., 'Repression and Reform: Responses Within New Zealand Rugby to the Arrival of the '"Northern Game", 1907–8', *New Zealand Journal of History*, 31, 2 (1997).

Walvin, J., 'Sport, Social History and the Historian', *British Journal of Sports History*, 1, 1 (1984).

Theses and Research Essays

Barclay, J., 'An Analysis of Trends in New Zealand Sport from 1840 to 1900' (BA Hons. research essay, Massey University, 1978).

Beckford, N., 'Working Class Participation in Wellington Club Cricket 1878–1940' (BA Hons. research essay, Victoria University of Wellington, 1981).

Branthwaite, J.S., 'American Cricket from its Beginnings, Through the Philadelphian "Golden Age" to its Death' (MA thesis, University of Canterbury, 1993).

Buchanan, T.N.W., 'Missionaries of Empire: 1905 All Black Tour' (research essay, University of Canterbury, 1981).

Crawford, S.A.G.M., 'A History of Recreation and Sport in Nineteenth Century Colonial Otago' (Ph.D. thesis, University of Queensland, 1984).

Crotty, M., 'Rowing in New Zealand to 1914: The Development of an old World Sport in a new World Setting' (BA Hons. research essay, University of Canterbury, 1993).

Elphick, J., 'Auckland 1870–74: A Social Portrait' (MA thesis, University of Auckland, 1974).

Gibson, C.J., 'A Demographic History of New Zealand' (Ph.D. thesis, University of California, Berkeley, 1971).

Hammer, M.A.E., 'Something Else in the World to Live For: Sport and the Physical Emancipation of Women in Auckland, 1880–1920' (MA thesis, University of Auckland, 1990).

Manley, A., 'Antidote to Depression: Rugby and New Zealand Society 1919–39' (Dip. Arts thesis, University of Otago, 1991).

McGeorge, C., 'Schools and Socialisation in New Zealand 1890–1914' (Ph.D. Thesis, University of Canterbury, 1985).

McLaren, I.A., 'Secondary Schools in the New Zealand Social Order 1840–1903' (Ph.D. thesis, Victoria University of Wellington, 1965).

Meuli, P.M., 'Occupational Change and Bourgeois Proliferation: A Study of New Middle Class Expansion in New Zealand 1896–1926' (MA thesis, Victoria University of Wellington, 1978).

Moore, K.E., 'The Concept of British Empire Games: An Analysis of its Origins and Evolution from 1891 to 1930' (Ph.D. thesis, University of Queensland, 1986).

Norman, E.J., 'The History of the Avonside Parish District' (MA thesis, Canterbury University College, 1951).

Norris, P.G., 'A Social Portrait of Canterbury in 1870' (MA thesis, University of Canterbury, 1963).

Phillips, J.R., 'A Social History of Auckland 1840–53' (MA thesis, University of Auckland, 1966).

Plumridge, E.W., 'Labour in Christchurch: Community and Consciousness 1914–1919' (MA thesis, University of Canterbury, 1979).

Richmond, D.M.J., 'Dunedin in the 1860s: Some Aspects of Settlement' (MA thesis, University of Otago, 1972).

Robilliard, D.F., 'Hagley Park: Some Aspects of its History and Landscape Since 1850' (MA thesis, University of Canterbury, 1971).

Ryan, G.J., 'The Originals: The 1888–89 New Zealand Native Football Team in Britain, Australia and New Zealand' (MA thesis, University of Canterbury, 1992).

Ryan, G.J., 'Where the Game was Played by Decent Chaps: The Making of New Zealand Cricket 1832–1914' (Ph.D. thesis, University of Canterbury, 1996).

Smith, C., 'Control of the Female Body: Physical Training at Three Secondary Schools, 1870–1920' (BA Hons. research essay, University of Otago, 1993).

Tait, G., 'The History of the Otago Cricket Association in the Nineteenth Century' (MA thesis, University of Otago, 1974).

Taylor, P. 'The Development of Sport and Physical Exercise in Single-Sex Girls' Secondary Schools in New Zealand Between 1877 and 1914', (Research Essay, University of Canterbury, no date).

Thompson, B.J.G., 'The Canterbury Farm Labourers' Dispute, 1907–8: a study of the first attempt by a union of farm labourers to come under the New Zealand arbitration system' (MA thesis, University of Canterbury, 1967).

Wood, D.A., 'Athleticism: A Study with Particular Reference to Christ's College' (research essay, University of Canterbury, 1985).

Index